BEST OF THE BEST
FROM
SOUTHERN COASTAL LADIES

OVER 1000 DELICIOUS RECIPES
FROM
THE BEST COOKS

EULA CRAIN

PublishAmerica
Baltimore

Hardcover 978-1-4512-3977-5
Softcover 978-1-4512-3976-8
PUBLISHED BY PUBLISHAMERICA, LLLP
www.publishamerica.com
Baltimore

Printed in the United States of America

ACKNOWLEDGMENTS

To my husband, Frank Crain, thank you for your endless love, patience, confidence and encouragement to write this book.

To my daughter, Kim Crain Phillips, thank you for helping me find, try and revise some of these old recipes.

Thanks to all my family and friends who donated their special recipes to me.

Thanks to PublishAmerica, and their staff for publishing my book

RECIPE DONORS

Frank Crain (my husband)
Kimberly Crain Phillips (our daughter)
Butch Phillips (our son-in-law)
Megan Phillips (our grand- daughter)
Matthew Phillips (our grand-son)
Alma Ford (sister)
Doris Simpson (sister)
Judy Crain Strange (sister-in-law)
Julia B Crain (mother-in-law and grand-mother) deceased
Granny Ewing (mother and grand-mother) deceased
Earle Flynn (friend)
Yvonne Andrews (friend)
Woodie Harlan (friend)
Other (family and friends) deceased

Contents

APPETIZERS

ASSORTED CHEESE BALLS

2 (8 oz) packages cream cheese, softened
1 cup parmesan cheese, grated

PINE NUT CHEESE BALL
2 tablespoons basil, minced
2 tablespoons, plus ½ cup pine nuts, toasted and divided

HORSERADISH - BACON CHEESE BALL
1 green pepper, chopped fine
2 tablespoons horseradish
½ cup bacon, cooked crisp and crumbled

SALSA CHEESE BALL
1 tablespoon onion, chopped fine
1 tablespoon jalapeno pepper, seeded and minced
2 tablespoons fresh cilantro, minced
2 tablespoons tomato paste
1/8 teaspoon salt
Assorted crackers

In a large bowl, beat the cream cheese, parmesan cheese and garlic until blended. Divide into 3 portions.

FOR PINE NUT

In a bowl, beat 1 portion of cream cheese mixture and basil until blended. Chop 2 tablespoons pine nuts; stir into cheese mixture. Shape into a ball; roll in remaining pine nuts. Wrap in plastic wrap; chill until firm

HORSERADISH

In a small bowl, beat 1 portion of cream cheese mixture and horseradish until blended. Stir in bacon and onion. Shape into a ball. Wrap in plastic wrap; chill until firm.

SALSA CHEESE BALL

In a small bowl, beat 1 portion of cream cheese mixture, tomato paste and salt until blended. Stir in the cilantro, onion and jalapeno. Shape into a ball. Wrap in plastic wrap; chill until firm. Serve with crackers.

QUICK AND EASY SAUSAGE BALLS

Mix 1 pound sausage with 1 cup cheddar cheese and ½ cup Bisquick; roll into small balls and bake at 350° for 15 minutes or until brown.

MAPLE GLAZED MEATBALLS

2 packages fully cooked frozen meatballs
1 cup maple syrup
1 tablespoon quick cooking tapioca
1 ½ teaspoon ground allspice
1 teaspoon dry mustard
1 (20 oz) can pineapple chunks, drained
1/3 cup soy sauce
1 ½ cups ketchup

Stir together the ketchup, syrup, tapioca, soy sauce, allspice and mustard in a slow cooker. Separate meatballs. Carefully stir meatballs and pineapple chunks into the ketchup mixture. Cover and cook on low heat for 4-6 hours. Stir before serving.

SWEET AND SOUR MEATBALLS

2 pounds lean ground beef
½ cup instant rice
1 egg
1 cup butter flavored cracker crumbs
2 tablespoons oil

SAUCE
1 ½ cups barbecue sauce
1 cup (12 oz) jar Smucker's pineapple topping
¼ cup brown sugar

Prepare rice according to package. Combine, ground beef, egg and cracker crumbs; mix well. Add cooked rice; mix thoroughly. Shape into 1 inch balls. Cook in oil over medium heat until browned, turning occasionally. Drain grease from skillet. Combine, all sauce ingredients; mix until brown sugar is dissolved. Pour over meatballs. Cover and simmer over low heat for 30-45 minutes or until meatballs are no longer pink in center. Serve with toothpicks.

HAM & SAUSAGE BALLS

1 pound ham, ground
1 ½ pound sausage, ground
2 cups bread crumbs
½ cup water
1 cup milk
1 eggs, beaten
1 ½ cups brown sugar
¼ cup vinegar
1 tablespoon dry mustard

Combine sausage, ham, egg, bread crumbs and milk. Shape into balls,.
Combine the brown sugar, mustard, water and vinegar; bring to a boil.
Pour sauce over ham balls and bake at 250° for 1 ½ hours.

PARTY MEATBALLS

4 pound frozen Italian-style meatballs
1 cup grape juice
1 cup apple jelly
1 cup ketchup
1 (8 oz) can tomato sauce

In a small saucepan, combine the jelly, ketchup and tomato sauce. Cook
and stir over medium heat until jelly is melted, remove from heat. Place
meatballs in a 5 quart slow cooker. Pour sauce over top and stir to coat.
Cover and cook on low for 4 hours or until heated through.

CAESAR POCKETS

4 pita breads, warmed, cut in half
4 cups romaine lettuce, torn
1 (6 oz) package shaved smoked turkey breast, cut into strips
3 tablespoons parmesan cheese, grated
¼ cup roasted red pepper strips, drained
¼ cup classic Caesar dressing

Toss all ingredients together, except the pita bread and spoon into the
pita bread.

HOLIDAY CHEESE BALL

1 8 oz) package cream cheese, softened
1 (8 oz) package cheddar cheese, shredded
2 green onions, chopped
1 (2 oz) jar pimentos, drained and diced
2 tablespoons butter or margarine, melted
2 teaspoons Worcestershire sauce
Assorted crackers

In a large bowl, beat cream cheese until fluffy. Beat the cheese, onions, pimentos, butter and Worcestershire sauce. Press into a small bowl; smooth top. Cover and refrigerate. Remove from the refrigerator 15 minutes before un-folding. Serve with you favorite crackers.

PARTY CHEESE BALL

1 (8 oz) can crushed pineapple, well drained
1 cup walnuts, chopped
2 (8 oz) packages cream cheese, softened
½ cup (about 14) maraschino cherries

Drain maraschino cherries on paper towel. Chop cherries and drain again. Beat cream cheese with electric mixer on medium speed 3-4 minutes, or until cream cheese is smooth. Stir in pineapple and cherries. Refrigerate until firm, about 1 hour. Shape cheese mixture into two (4 inch) balls. Roll cheese balls in walnuts, pressing nuts into surface to adhere. Refrigerate about 1 hour or until chilled. Serve as a spread with crackers.

SPINACH BALLS

2 (10 oz) boxes frozen spinach, cooked, drained and chopped
6 eggs, beaten
¾ cup butter, melted
½ cup parmesan cheese, grated
1 tablespoon garlic salt
½ teaspoon thyme
2 onions, chopped
2 cups herb bread stuffing mix

Mix all ingredients well. Form balls, using 1 teaspoon mixture for each ball and bake on a greased baking sheet at 350° for about 20 minutes.

CRAB BALLS

1 pound fresh crabmeat
½ teaspoon Worcestershire sauce
1 tablespoon mayonnaise
1 egg, beaten
1/3 cup heavy cream
1 teaspoon salt
½ teaspoon pepper
½ teaspoon garlic powder
2 cups bread crumbs
1 teaspoon fresh parsley
Vegetable oil for frying

Mix garlic powder, salt, pepper, parsley and bread crumbs. Mix Worcestershire sauce, mayonnaise and crabmeat together. Mix beaten egg with cream. Roll crabmeat mixture in ball size of a walnut. Dip in the egg mixture and roll in bread crumb mixture. Drop in hot oil in deep fryer and cook until brown. Drain on paper towels.

SPECIAL HAM BALLS

4-5 cups country ham, ground
1 cup bread crumbs
1 cup milk
½ pound sausage

Mix ingredients together and form into small balls. Place in a shallow pan and pour sauce over them and bake at 300° for 1 hour. Cover with foil the first 45 minutes. Turn once to absorb sauce.

SAUCE
½ cup vinegar
½ cup brown sugar
¼ cup water
½ teaspoon prepared mustard

Mix and cook until well mixed, pour over ham balls and bake.

SQUASH PATTIES

3 medium yellow squash, cut in cubes
1 medium onion, chopped
1 package Mexican cornbread mix
¾ cup whole kernel corn, drained
½ cup cheddar cheese, shredded
1 egg
½ teaspoon salt
½ teaspoon pepper

Cook squash and onion until tender and drain well. Add all other ingredients and mix well. Shape into a ball; roll in walnuts. Cover and refrigerate overnight. Serve with your favorite crackers.

CRAB BALLS

2 cups crabmeat
2 slices white bread, without crust
1/3 cup heavy cream
½ teaspoon each (salt and pepper)
1 teaspoon garlic powder
1 tablespoon mayonnaise
1 egg, beaten

Mix all ingredients together, add crabmeat and form into balls. Drop balls in deep fryer and fry until golden brown. Serve with tarter sauce if you like.

CARAMEL APPLE DIP

1 (8 oz) package cream cheese, softened
1 (8 oz) package frozen whipped topping, thawed
1 cup caramel ice cream topping
1 (8 oz) package toffee bits
Red delicious or granny smith apples, cored and sliced

In a large bowl, beat cream cheese at medium speed with an electric mixer until creamy. Add whipped topping and caramel, beating until smooth. Stir in toffee bits just before serving. Serve with apples slices.

FRUIT DIP

1 (7 oz) jar marshmallow crème
1 (8 oz) package cream cheese
¼ teaspoon nutmeg
¼ teaspoon cinnamon
½ teaspoon vanilla

Mix ingredients together and stir until smooth. Serve with all kinds of fruit, sliced bananas, apples, oranges, pineapple chunks, etc.

TOMATO BRUSSCHETTA

1 pound loaf French bread, cut into 1 inch slices
3 small tomatoes, chopped
1 tablespoon balsamic vinegar
¼ cup mozzarella cheese, shredded
½ cup olive oil, divided
½ teaspoon pepper
¼ cup fresh cilantro leaves, chopped coarse
¼ cup onion, chopped fine

Place bread on an un-greased baking sheet; brush with ¼ cup oil. Bake at 325° for 10-12 minutes or until golden brown. In a small bowl, whisk the vinegar and remaining oil together. Stir in the tomatoes, onion, salt, pepper and cilantro. Spoon about 1 tablespoon onto each slice of bread. Sprinkle with cheese. Serve immediately.

ASPARAGUS CRISPS

1 pound sharp cheddar cheese, grated
2 tablespoons mayonnaise
¼ teaspoon red pepper
1 loaf fresh bread
1 large bell pepper, minced
1 (10 oz) can asparagus tips
½ stick butter, melted
Horseradish and black pepper to taste

Blend the cheese, mayonnaise, red pepper and bell pepper together. Remove crust from bread and spread with a thin layer of cheese mixture. Sprinkle with pepper. Place asparagus on edge of bread and roll; fasten with toothpicks. Brush with melted butter before toasting. Place on broiler pan and toast until brown. Cut in half to serve with cocktails. Leave whole if you want to serve with salad.

PHYLLO ASPARAGUS WRAPS

1 bunch asparagus
6 sheets of phyllo dough
Parmesan cheese
Lettuce
Butter

Cut phyllo dough in long strips, brush with butter. Cut asparagus long wise down the center. Sprinkle with parmesan cheese. Roll asparagus (1-2) in each strip of phyllo dough. Sprinkle with more parmesan cheese and bake at 375° for 15 minutes. Serve on a bed of lettuce.

DEVILED DIP

1 ½ cups cottage cheese
1 tablespoon onion, chopped
1 teaspoon green pepper, chopped fine
1 (2 ¼ oz) can deviled ham
1/8 teaspoon black pepper

Blend all ingredients together and serve with chips or crackers.

HOT ARTICHOKE DIP

1 envelope Lipton onion soup mix
1 (14 oz) can artichoke hearts, drained and chopped
1 cup mayonnaise
1 (8 oz) container sour cream
1 cup shredded Swiss or mozzarella cheese

EASY ARTICHOKE DIP

1 (14 oz) can artichoke hearts, drained
1 cup mayonnaise
1 tablespoon lemon juice
1/8 teaspoon garlic salt
1 cup fresh parmesan cheese

Mash artichoke hearts and mix well with remaining ingredients. Bake at 350° for about 20 minutes or until warm through and cheese is melted. Serve with assorted crackers.

BAKED CRAB RAGOONS

1 (6 oz) can white crabmeat, drained and flaked
½ (8 oz) package cream cheese
¼ cup green onions, sliced thin
¼ cup mayonnaise
12 won ton wrappers

Mix crabmeat, cream cheese, onions and mayonnaise. Spray 12 medium cups with cooking spray. Place 1 won ton wrapper in each cup, allowing edges of wrappers to extend above sides of cups. Fill evenly with crabmeat mixture. Bake at 350° for 15-20 minutes or until edges are golden brown and filling is heated through. Garnish with chopped green onions.

WARM TURNIP GREEN DIP

5 slices bacon, cooked crisp, crumbled
½ sweet onion, chopped
2 garlic cloves, chopped
¼ cup dry wine
1 (16 oz) package frozen chopped turnip greens, thawed
2 (8 oz) packages cream cheese, cut into pieces
1 (8 oz) container sour cream
½ teaspoon dried crushed red pepper
¼ teaspoon salt
3/4 cup fresh grated parmesan

Cook bacon over medium heat for 5-6 minutes or until crisp; remove bacon and drain on paper towels, reserving 1 tablespoon of bacon drippings. Sauté onion and garlic in hot drippings 3-4 minutes. Add wine, and cook 1-2 minutes more, stirring to loosen particles from bottom of pan. Stir in turnip greens, next stir in rest ingredients, but only ½ cup of the parmesan cheese. Cook, stirring often, 6-8 minutes or until cream cheese is melted and mixture is thoroughly heated. Transfer to a lightly greased 1 ½ quart baking dish. Sprinkle evenly with remaining ¼ cup parmesan cheese. Broil 6 inches from heat, 4-5 minutes or until cheese is lightly browned. Sprinkle evenly with the crisp crumbled bacon.

FIVE - LAYERED MEXICAN DIP

½ cup sour cream
½ cup salsa
1 (16 oz) jar black bean dip (spicy or mild)
2 cups lettuce, shredded
½ cup tomato, chopped
¼ cup sharp cheddar cheese, shredded
1 large bag tortilla chips

Mix together, sour cream and salsa in a small bowl. Spread bean dip in shallow glass bowl. Top with sour cream- salsa mixture, spreading to cover bean dip. Just before serving, top with lettuce and tomato and cheese. Serve with tortilla chips.

CARAMELIZED ONION - BACON DIP

1 pound onions, halved and sliced thin
6 strips thick-sliced bacon, cooked crisp and crumbled
1 tablespoon olive oil
4 ounces cream cheese, softened
½ cup sour cream
2 teaspoons wine vinegar
½ teaspoon fresh thyme leaves, plus sprigs for garnish
¼ teaspoon salt
1/8 teaspoon ground pepper

In a large non-stick skillet, heat oil over medium heat. Add onion and cook, stirring frequently, until golden, about 15 minutes. Cover and reduce heat to low. Cook, stirring occasionally, until golden brown, 35-40 minutes. Cool slightly, then coarsely chop. In a medium bowl, stir together cream cheese and sour cream until smooth. Reserve 2 tablespoons bacon; stir remaining bacon, onion, vinegar, thyme, salt and pepper into the cream cheese mixture. Chill at least 30 minutes. Sprinkle with reserved bacon and garnish with thyme sprigs.

TWO CHEESE BACON DIP

1 (8 oz) package cream cheese, softened
2 (8 oz) cups cheddar cheese, shredded
1 pound bacon, cooked crisp and crumbled
1 (8 oz) cup sour cream
1 (16 oz) jar taco sauce
5 green onions, sliced thin
4 medium tomatoes, chopped
1 large green pepper, chopped
Tortilla chips

Beat cream cheese and sour cream. Spread in an un-greased 13 x 9 inch dish. Combine onions, tomatoes and green pepper; sprinkle over the cream cheese layer. Pour taco sauce over the vegetables. Sprinkle with cheddar cheese. Refrigerate. Just before ready to serve; sprinkle with bacon. Serve with tortilla chips.

CRAB DIP WITH ARTICHOKE DIPPERS

2 large artichokes
3 (6 oz) cans crabmeat, drained
1 teaspoon hot pepper sauce
2 teaspoons Worcestershire sauce
2 tablespoons prepared mustard
2/3 cup mayonnaise
2 tablespoons green onion, chopped

Place artichoke up-side down in a steamer. Place the basket in a saucepan over 1 inch of water. Bring to a boil; cover and steam for 25-35 minutes or until leaves near the center pulls out easily. Remove artichokes from the basket. Let artichokes drain for 10 minutes. Refrigerate until chilled. Combine the mayonnaise, mustard, Worcestershire sauce and onion together, stir in crab. Cover and chill for several hours. Just before serving, transfer crab dip in a serving bowl. Remove leaves from artichokes to use as dippers. Garnish with chopped green onion tops.

SEAFOOD DIP IN BREAD BOWL

1 round loaf sourdough bread
1 (8 oz) package cream cheese, softened
½ cup mayonnaise
½ cup green onions, chopped
2/3 cup Monterey jack cheese, shredded and divided
1 (6 oz) can small shrimp, rinsed and drained
1 (6 oz) crabmeat, drained
1 ½ teaspoons Dijon mustard
Assorted fresh vegetables, sliced

In a large bowl, beat the cream cheese, mayonnaise and mustard until smooth. Stir in the shrimp, crab, 1/3 cup Monterey jack cheese and onions. Cut the top ¼ off the loaf of bread; carefully hollow out bottom leaving a ½ inch shell. Set aside. Spoon seafood mixture into bread shell. Sprinkle with remaining cheese. Wrap tightly with heavy foil and place on baking sheet. Bake at 350° for 25 minutes. Un-wrap and cook 20-25 minutes longer or until cheese is melted and dip is heated through. Serve with vegetables and reserved bread cubes.

SPINACH DIP IN BREAD BOWL

2 (8 oz) packages cream cheese, softened
1 cup mayonnaise
1 (10 oz) package frozen spinach, thawed, drained and chopped
1 cup cheddar cheese, shredded
1 pound sliced bacon, cooked crisp and crumbled
¼ cup onion, chopped
1 tablespoon dill weed
1-2 garlic cloves, minced
1 round loaf sourdough bread, un-sliced
Assorted fresh vegetables

In a large mixing bowl, beat cream cheese and mayonnaise until blended. Stir in the spinach, cheese, bacon, dill weed and garlic; set aside. Cut a 1 ½ inch slice off top of bread; set aside. Carefully hallow out bottom, leaving a ½ inch shell. Cube and remove bread and place on a baking sheet. Broil 3-4 inches from the heat for 1-2 minutes or until golden brown; set aside. Fill bread shell with spinach dip; replace top. Place any dip that doesn't fit in shell in a greased baking dish. Wrap bread in a heavy-duty foil; place on baking sheet. Bake at 350° for 1 hour or until dip is heated through. Open foil carefully. Serve dip warm with vegetables and reserved bread cubes.

HOT SPINACH AND CHEESE DIP

2 (9 oz) packages Mexican cheese spread with jalapeno peppers, cut into ½ inch pieces
2 (9 oz) packages frozen spinach, thawed and drained
1 ½ cups milk
½ cup onion, chopped fine
2 tablespoons flour
¼ teaspoon pepper
1 teaspoon Worcestershire sauce

Put 1 ¼ cups of milk in a saucepan; place over medium heat. In a bowl, combine remaining ¼ milk and flour; blend with a whisk until smooth. Add to milk in saucepan. Cook 5 minutes, stirring constantly, until thickened. Add onion, pepper and Worcestershire sauce; mix well. Bring to a boil. Reduce heat; simmer 5 minutes or until onion is tender, stirring constantly. Stir in cheese until melted. Add spinach, mix well. Cook until thoroughly heated. Serve with French bread or vegetables.

AVOCADO TACO DIP

1 (16 oz) can refried beans
2/3 cup mayonnaise
1 envelope of taco seasoning
1 (4 oz) can green chilies, drained and chopped
4 medium ripe avocados, half, pitted and peeled
1 cup sour cream
2 teaspoons each (salt and garlic powder)
1 cup sharp cheddar cheese, shredded
½ cup green onion, sliced thin
½ cup fresh tomato, chopped
1 (2 ¼ oz) can sliced ripe olives, drained
Tortilla chips

Spread beans in shallow 2 ½ quart dish. In a bowl, combine the sour cream, mayonnaise and taco seasoning; spread over beans. Sprinkle with chilies. In a bowl, mash avocados with lime juice, salt and garlic powder. Spread over chilies. Sprinkle with cheese, onions, tomato and olives. Cover and refrigerate until ready to serve. Serve with tortilla chips.

TACO DIP

1 (8 oz) package cream cheese, softened
1 (16 oz) container sour cream
½ cup salsa, mild
1 packet taco seasoning mix
1 packet onion soup mix
4 big slices of lettuce, shredded
3 medium tomatoes, chopped
1 can French fried onions, coarsely crushed
3 cups Mexican style cheese, shredded

Combine cream cheese, sour cream, salsa, taco seasoning, and onion soup. Blend well with a mixer on low speed. Spoon into baking dish and smooth top. Sprinkle cheese and tomatoes over cream cheese mixture. Add French fried onions to the top before serving. Serve with tortilla chips.

GOOD HOT TACO DIP

1 pound ground beef
1 medium onion, chopped
1 (8 oz) jar taco sauce
½ teaspoon chili powder
¼ teaspoon salt
3 taco shells, crushed
2 cups lettuce, shredded
1 (4 oz) can green chilies, chopped
1 (4 oz) package cheddar cheese, shredded
1 teaspoon Worcestershire sauce
2 tomatoes, peeled and chopped
Corn chips

In a 3 quart saucepan, cook the beef and onion until browned; drain. Stir in taco sauce, Worcestershire sauce, chili powder and seasoned salt. Reduce heat and simmer for 8-10 minutes. Add crushed taco shells, lettuce, tomatoes, chilies and cheese. Stir gently to blend. Serve with corn chips.

SPECIAL SHRIMP DIP

2 (4 ½ oz) can shrimp
1 (8 oz) carton sour cream
1 (8 oz) package cream cheese, softened
½ cup onion, chopped
½ cup celery, chopped
Juice of 1 lemon
Salt and pepper to taste

Blend cream cheese and sour cream until smooth. Add onion and celery. Add salt, pepper and lemon juice. Mash shrimp with a fork and add to mixture. Refrigerate for several hours before serving. Serve with crackers of choice.

CREAMY SPINACH DIP

1 (10 oz) package frozen spinach, thawed, drained and chopped
1 cup mayonnaise
1 cup sour cream
½ cup green onion, sliced
½ cup parsley, chopped
1 teaspoon dill weed
½ tablespoon lemon pepper

Combine ingredients and mix well; chill. Serve with vegetables or crackers.

SPINACH DIP

1 box frozen spinach, thawed, drained and chopped
1 cup mayonnaise
1 cup Monterey jack cheese, grated
1 package ranch dressing mix
½ cup sour cream
1 cup water chestnuts, chopped

Combine all ingredients and heat in microwave until hot. Serve with tortilla chips.

ENCHILADA DIP

1 (8 oz) package cream cheese, softened
1 ½ cups Kraft Mexican cheese, shredded
1 (8 oz) chicken breast, chopped fine
1 (7 oz) can green chilies, un-drained and chopped
¼ teaspoon chili powder
1 teaspoon garlic powder

Beat cream cheese, 1 cup shredded cheese, chilies and seasonings in a small bowl with mixer on medium speed until well blended. Spread in a 9 inch pan or pie plate. Bake at 350° for 20 minutes. Sprinkle with remaining ½ cup cheese and let stand for about 10 minutes. Serve with wheat thins or chips.

AVOCADO SHRIMP DIP

1 cup avocado, mashed
1 (4 ½ oz) can shrimp, de-veined
2 teaspoons lime juice
½ cup mayonnaise
2 drops Tabasco sauce
½ teaspoon salt
1 teaspoon onion, grated

Combine all ingredients except shrimp. Fold in shrimp. Serve as a dip with chips.

GOOD SHRIMP DIP

1 (5 oz) can shrimp
1 (8 oz) package cream cheese
½ teaspoon Worcestershire sauce
¼ teaspoon red pepper
3 tablespoons chili sauce
2 teaspoons lemon juice

Soften cream cheese. Add all ingredients except shrimp, then add shrimp. Serve with chips

HOT ASPARAGUS DIP

1 ½ cups freshly grated parmesan cheese
2 (15 oz) cans cut asparagus spears, drained
1 ½ cups mayonnaise
1 clove garlic, crushed
1/8 teaspoon pepper

Grate or chop cheese in food processor. Add other ingredients and process until blended. Pour into baking dish and bake at 350° for 20-30 minutes or until slightly brown and bubbling. Serve hot with corn chips.

CHEDDAR - BEER DIP WITH SAUSAGE

2 tablespoons butter, un-salted
½ cup sweet onion, chopped fine
½ cup smoke sausage, cut into ½ inch pieces
2 tablespoons Dijon mustard
1 (8 oz) package cream cheese
1 (12 oz) dark beer
4 cups white cheddar cheese, shredded
6 drops hot pepper sauce

Lightly coat 1 quart baking dish with cooking spray. In a medium saucepan over medium heat, melt butter. Add onion and sauté for 2 minutes or until onion begins to soften. Add sausage and cook until cooked through, about 8-10 minutes. Drain and discard fat. Add mustard, cream cheese and beer, then stir until the cream cheese is melted. Remove the pan from the heat and stir in the cheddar cheese, handful at a time until it is all incorporated. Stir in the hot sauce, transfer to the baking dish; cool. Cover and refrigerate for a least 3 hours. When ready to serve, preheat oven to 350° and while the oven heats, let the dip sit at room temperature for about 30 minutes. Bake the dip for 20-25 minutes, or until bubbly. Serve warm with tortilla chips or crackers.

JUDY'S BRAUNSCHWEIGER BEER DIP

2 (8 oz) rolls braunschweiger, softened
1 (8 oz) package cream cheese, softened
½ cup sour cream
½ cup beer
1 tablespoon Worcestershire sauce
¼ teaspoon salt
¼ teaspoon garlic powder

Combine the braunschweiger, cream cheese and sour cream, beat until smooth. Add Worcestershire sauce, salt and garlic powder. Add the beer and mix well. Serve with rye bread or assorted crackers.

3 CHEESE ARTICHOKE DIP

1 can artichoke hearts, chopped
1 (8 oz) package cream cheese
1 cup each (mozzarella cheese and parmesan cheese)
2 cups mayonnaise
1 can water chestnuts
2 green onions
Dash Worcestershire sauce
Dash hot sauce

Mix all ingredients together and bake at 350° for 30 minutes.

GOOD PEPPERONI PIZZA DIP

1 (8 oz) package cream cheese
½ cup mozzarella cheese, shredded
¼ cup green pepper, chopped
½ cup sour cream
¼ cup green onion, sliced
1 teaspoon dried oregano
½ cup pizza sauce
1/8 teaspoon garlic powder
1/8 teaspoon red pepper, crushed
Pepperoni slices

Beat together cream cheese, sour cream, oregano, garlic powder and red pepper. Spread evenly in a 9 x 10 inch dish or pie plate. Spread pizza sauce over top. Sprinkle with pepperoni, green onions and green pepper. Bake at 350° for 10 minutes. Top with cheese; bake 5 minutes more or until cheese is melted and mixture is heated through.

WHITE PIZZA DIP

1 envelope herb with garlic soup mix
1 (16 oz) container sour cream
1 (8 oz) cup ricotta cheese
1 cup mozzarella cheese, shredded
½ cup pepperoni, chopped
1 loaf Italian or French bread, sliced

Mix soup, sour cream, ricotta cheese, ¾ cup mozzarella cheese and pepperoni. Sprinkle with ¼ cup mozzarella cheese. Bake at 350° for 30 minutes or until heated through.

7 LAYER TACO DIP

1 pound sausage, what ever you like, hot, or mild
1 (1.25 oz) package taco seasoning mix
1 (16 oz) can refried beans
2 (8 oz) cups Mexican cheese blend, shredded
1 (16 oz) container sour cream
1 (4.5 oz) can green chilies, chopped
1 large tomato, diced
1 (6 oz) can black olives, sliced
1 bunch green onions, chopped
1 (11 oz) jar salsa
Tortilla chips

In a large skillet, crumble and cook sausage over medium heat until browned. Stir in beans, chilies and taco seasoning mix. Spread sausage mix into 7 x 11 inch serving dish. Top with sour cream then salsa. Sprinkle olives, tomatoes and onion on top. Cover with cheese. Serve immediately with chips.

7 LAYER RANCH DIP

1 envelope Lipton ranch soup mix
1 (16 oz) container sour cream
1 cup lettuce, shredded
1 medium tomato, chopped (about 1 cup)
1 (2 ¼ oz) can ripe olives, pitted, drained and sliced
¼ cup red onion, chopped
1 (½ oz) can green chilies, drained
1 (4 oz) cup cheddar cheese, shredded

In a 2 quart shallow dish, combine soup mix and sour cream. Evenly layer remaining ingredients, ending with cheese; chill. Serve with tortilla chips.

EULA'S HOT SAUSAGE DIP

1 pound sausage, mild
1 can Ro-tel tomatoes
1 (8 oz) package cream cheese

Cook sausage in skillet until done; drain. Place cream cheese and tomatoes in a medium saucepan on low heat and melt until creamy. Add to sausage. Stir and mix well. Serve warm with scoops chips.

CREAMY LAYERED B L T DIP

1 (16 oz) container of sour cream
½ teaspoon onion powder
½ cup cheddar cheese, shredded
1 package ready to serve bacon
2 medium tomatoes, chopped, divided
1 cup lettuce, shredded

Mix sour cream and onion powder. Spoon onto bottom of shallow serving dish. Heat bacon as directed on package, cut into small pieces. Sprinkle over sour cream mixture. Top with cheese, ¾ cup of tomato and lettuce, sprinkle with remaining tomato. Serve with Ritz toasted chip.

SWEET AND SOUR DIP

3 tablespoons vinegar
4 tablespoons sugar
4 tablespoons ketchup
3 teaspoons cornstarch
1 teaspoon salt
¼ cup water

Combine cornstarch and water and blend until smooth, adding remaining ingredients. Mix together; heat until thicken. May be served hot or cold. Good on egg rolls.

GOOD RO - VISTA DEVILED EGGS

6 hard cooked eggs, chopped
2 slices of bacon, fried crisp, crumble
1 teaspoon onion, minced
½ teaspoon salt
Dash of pepper
¼ cup mayonnaise
Mild cheddar cheese, grated

Mix together and then form into small balls. Roll in grated cheese. Refrigerate for several hours.

MEXICAN DIP

1 (11 oz) can Mexican corn, drained
1 (4 oz) can green chilies, chopped
2 jalapeno peppers, chopped
5 green onions, chopped
1 tablespoon sugar
1 cup mayonnaise
1 cup sour cream
2 cups sharp cheddar cheese, shredded

Combine all ingredients in a mixing bowl; mix well. Refrigerate overnight. Serve with tortilla chips

WATER CHESTNUT DIP

1 (8 oz) can water chestnuts, drained and chopped
1 (8 oz) carton sour cream
1 cup mayonnaise
2 teaspoons Tabasco sauce
3 green onions, chopped
½ cup parsley, chopped
2 tablespoons soy sauce

Mix all ingredients together and serve with your favorite cracker.

BLACK - EYED PEA DIP

2 cans black-eyed peas
2 tablespoons sour cream
2 tablespoons salsa
Cheddar cheese, grated
Dash of hot sauce

Mix peas, sour cream and salsa. Place in baking dish. Top with cheddar cheese. Bake at 350° until cheese is melted. Serve with Fritos.

CREAMED CRABMEAT DIP

1 pound lump crabmeat
½ small onion, chopped
1 egg yolk, beaten
1 teaspoon lemon juice
1 ½ cups half and half
2 tablespoon flour
4 tablespoons butter
1 teaspoon Worcestershire sauce
½ teaspoon cayenne pepper
1 teaspoon parsley, chopped
¼ teaspoon celery salt
¼ teaspoon salt

Sauté onion in butter. Add flour and cream. Cook until thick. Stir in egg yolk and seasonings. Add crabmeat. Serve on sliced thin party bread squares.

HOT BROCCOLI DIP

2 packages frozen broccoli, chopped
1 large onion, chopped
1 cup butter
2 cans cream of mushroom soup
2-3 rolls of garlic cheese
1 (8 oz) can mushroom pieces
1 cup almonds, slivered

Cook broccoli by directions on package; drain. Add 2 cans cream of mushroom soup. Set aside. In a separate pan, sauté the onion in 1 cup of butter. Add the 3 rolls of garlic cheese. Heat and stir until cheese is melted. Pour into broccoli mixture. Add the mushroom pieces and almonds. Serve warm with corn chips.

EASY CRAB DIP

1 can crabmeat
1 (8 oz) package cream cheese
2 tablespoons each (chopped onion and catsup)
¼ teaspoon Worcestershire
2 tablespoons of each (cream and mayonnaise)

Combine all ingredients except crab; blend with mixer and fold in crab. Serve with crackers.

ARTICHOKE SQUARES

2 (6 oz) jars marinated artichoke hearts
2 medium onions, chopped
1 clove garlic, crushed
4 eggs, beaten
½ cup bread crumbs
¼ teaspoon salt
½ teaspoon pepper
½ teaspoon oregano
½ teaspoon Tabasco sauce
1 (8 oz) package sharp cheddar cheese, shredded
2 tablespoons parsley, chopped
Parmesan cheese
Paprika

Preheat oven to 325°. Drain marinade from 1 jar of artichokes into skillet. Discard marinade in second jar. Chop artichokes and set aside. Sauté onions and garlic marinade for 5 minutes. Combine beaten eggs, crumbs, seasonings, cheddar cheese and parsley with sautéed onions. Add artichokes. Pour into greased 8 x8 inch baking pan. Bake for 30 minutes or until set. Sprinkle with parmesan cheese and paprika during last 5 minutes of baking. Cut into small squares and serve.

GOOD VIDALIA ONION DIP

1 ½ Vidalia onion, chopped
2 cups mayonnaise
2 cups sharp cheddar cheese, shredded
Dash Tabasco sauce

Mix all ingredients together. Bake at 350° for about 30 minutes or until bubbly and brown around edges. Serve with tortilla chips.

HOT CRAB DIP

2 green onions and tops, chopped
1 small green pepper, chopped
4 ribs of celery, chopped
2 (6 ½ oz) cans of crabmeat, picked over well
1 (10 ¾ oz) cans cream of mushroom soup
½ cup parmesan cheese, grated
Dash Worcestershire sauce
Dash hot pepper sauce
Crackers for dipping

Combine all ingredients in a saucepan and simmer slowly for 15 minutes, stirring often.
Serve with crackers.

SPECIAL CRAB DIP

3 cans crabmeat or 1 ½ pounds fresh crabmeat
2 pounds Velveeta cheese
1 ½ cups mayonnaise
¾ cup chives, chopped
½ cup sour cream

Place the cheese, mayonnaise, sour cream and chives in a double boiler until it melts. Add crabmeat last. Serve with your favorite chips or crackers.

SIMPLE CRAB DIP

1 large container sour cream
1 large container crabmeat
Dash of each (sherry and Tabasco sauce)
Almonds

Mix together and bake at 350° for 20-30 minutes. Sprinkle with almonds on top. Serve with crackers.

STUFFED CUCUMBER RINGS

2 medium cucumbers
2 (3 oz) package cream cheese
½ teaspoon seasoned salt
1 tablespoon lemon juice, freshly squeezed
1 ½ teaspoons Worcestershire sauce
Paprika
Chopped parsley

Peel cucumbers and remove centers with an apple corer. Soften the cream cheese in a bowl; add remaining ingredients except paprika and parsley, and mix well. Stuff cavities of cucumbers with cream cheese mixture and chill until firm. Thinly slice and sprinkle with paprika and parsley.

CUCUMBER CANAPES

1 cup mayonnaise
1 (3 oz) package cream cheese, softened
1 tablespoon onion, grated
1 tablespoon chives, minced
½ teaspoon vinegar
½ teaspoon Worcestershire sauce
1 garlic clove, minced
¼ teaspoon paprika
1/8 teaspoon each (curry powder, oregano, thyme, basil, parsley flakes and dill weed)
1 loaf white or rye bread
2 medium cucumbers, scored and sliced thin
Pimentos diced and additional dill weed

Combine the mayonnaise, cream cheese, onion, chives, vinegar, Worcestershire sauce and seasonings. Cover and process in blender until well blended. Cover and refrigerate for 24 hours. Using a 2 ½ inch biscuit cutter, cut out circles from bread slices. Spread mayonnaise mixture over bread; top with cucumber slices. Garnish with pimentos and dill. Makes about 2 dozen.

ALMOND CHEDDAR APPETIZERS

1 cup mayonnaise
2 teaspoon Worcestershire sauce
1 cup (4 oz) sharp cheddar cheese, shredded
1 medium onion, chopped
6 bacon strips, cooked crisp and crumbled
½ cup almonds, sliced
1 loaf French bread

In a bowl, combine mayonnaise and Worcestershire sauce, stir in cheese, onion, almonds and bacon. Cut bread into ½ inch slices; spread with cheese mixture. Cut slices in half; place on a lightly greased baking sheet. Bake at 400° for 8-10 minutes or until bubbly.

PINEAPPLE - ALMOND CHEESE SPREAD

2 (8 oz) cans pineapple, crushed
1 (8 oz) package cream cheese, softened
4 cups (16 oz) sharp cheddar cheese, shredded
½ cup mayonnaise
1 tablespoon soy sauce
1 cup toasted almonds, chopped
½ cup green pepper, chopped fine
¼ cup green onions or chives, minced
Celery stalks or assorted breads

Drain pineapple. In a large bowl, beat cream cheese until smooth; beat in cheddar cheese, mayonnaise and soy sauce until smooth. Stir in pineapple, almonds, green pepper and onions. Refrigerate, covered. Use to stuff celery stalks or serve as a spread with assorted breads.

TURKEY TORTILLA ROLL - UPS

3 flour tortillas
3 tablespoons cream cheese with chive and onion
¾ cup lettuce, shredded
12 slices deli fresh shaved smoked turkey breast

Spread tortillas with cream cheese; top with remaining ingredients. Roll up. Cut each into 4 slices.

CUCUMBER SPREAD

1 (8 oz) package cream cheese, softened
1 cucumber, peeled and diced
2 tablespoons wine vinegar
1 tablespoon salad oil
2 dashes salt
3 garlic cloves, masked

Wrap cucumber in a paper towel until all liquid is out; set aside. Place the cream cheese, vinegar, oil, salt and garlic into mixing bowl; cream well. Add more oil and vinegar as needed for taste and consistency. Blend in the cucumber. Refrigerate. Serve with crackers, melba toast or toasted bread.

CUCUMBER SANDWICHES

1 medium cucumber, sliced
36 slices party rye bread
2 tablespoons Italian salad dressing
½ cup mayonnaise
1 (8 oz) package cream cheese, softened

Combine the cream cheese, mayonnaise and salad dressing until blended. Refrigerate for 1 hour. Just before serving, spread on rye bread; top with a cucumber slice.

PARTY CHEESE COOKIES

2 cups flour
1 ½ cups pecans, chopped
1 (16 oz) package cheddar cheese, shredded
2 sticks butter
1 teaspoon cayenne pepper
1 teaspoon salt

Cream cheese and butter together. Add flour, salt and pepper, then add pecans. The dough will be very stiff. Make small long rolls of dough and refrigerate for several hours or overnight. Slice thin and bake on an un-greased baking sheet at 275° for 45-50 minutes. Cool.

SEAFOOD CHEESECAKE APPETIZER

1 (8 oz) package cream cheese, softened
8 ounces crabmeat, fresh
4 green onions, chopped (separate the white and green part)
½ cup butter, melted
1 cup sour cream, divided
3 eggs
1/8 teaspoon black pepper
½ teaspoon salt
1 teaspoon lemon juice
1 sleeve Ritz crackers, crushed

Combine cracker crumbs and butter in a bowl; mix well. Press onto bottom of lightly coated 9 inch spring form pan. Bake at 350° for 10 minutes. Beat cream cheese and ¾ cup sour cream with a mixer until smooth. Add eggs, lemon juice, salt and pepper; beat until smooth. Stir in crabmeat and white part of the green onions. Spoon into crust. Bake on foil-lined baking pan for 50-60 minutes, until top is lightly browned and the center is set. Cover with foil during the last 10 minutes. Cool 20 minutes. Loosen sides of pan but do not remove until completely cooled. Transfer to a serving plate, cover and refrigerate until ready to serve. Remove from refrigerator, spreading remaining ¼ cup sour cream on top and garnish with the green part of the onions. Serve with crackers or bread.

BARBECUED CHICKEN WINGS

24 whole chicken wings
4 cups molasses
¼ cup lemon juice
1 (12 oz) bottle chili sauce
2 tablespoons Worcestershire sauce
2 teaspoons hot pepper sauce
1 teaspoon garlic salt
1 tablespoon salsa
1 tablespoon chili powder
6 garlic cloves, minced

Cut chicken wings into 3 sections; discard wing tips. Place the wings in a 5 quart slow cooker. In a bowl, combine the remaining ingredients; pour over chicken. Stir to coat. Cover and cook on low for 8 hours or until chicken is tender.

EASY PIMENTO CHEESE SLICES

1 (2 oz) package cream cheese, softened
½ cup each (cheddar cheese and pimentos, drained)
2 tablespoons pecans, chopped fine
½ teaspoon hot pepper sauce
24 French bread slices, about ½ inch thick, or party bread slices

Preheat broiler. Combine cream cheese and cheddar cheese in a small bowl; mix well. Stir in pimento, pecans and hot pepper sauce. Place bread slices on broiler pan or non-stick baking sheet. Broil 4 inches from heat, 1-2 minutes or until lightly toasted on both sides. Spread cheese mixture evenly onto bread slices. Broil 1-2 minutes or until cheese mixture is hot and bubbly. Transfer to serving plate.

HOT PEPPER JELLY APPETIZERS

2 cups cheddar cheese, shredded
¾ stick butter, chilled and chopped
1 cup flour
½ cup hot pepper jelly

Combine cheese, butter and flour in a food processor and process until mixture resembles coarse meal. Process for additional 1 minute or until mixture forms a ball. Chill. Wrap in plastic wrap for 30 minutes. Shape into 2 inch balls. Arrange 1 inch apart on an un-greased baking sheet. Bake at 400° for 5 minutes . Make small indention on the top of each ball. Spoon 1 teaspoon of the hot pepper jelly into each indention. Bake for 5 minutes or until golden brown. Cool on baking sheet.

FRIED CHEESE

4 slices Swiss cheese cut ¾ inch thick
½ cup flour
1 egg, beaten
2/3 cup bread crumbs
1 cup shortening
Salt and pepper

Sprinkle cheese with salt. Dip slices first in flour and bread crumbs, then in egg, fry quickly in hot shortening until golden brown.

CHEESE AND FIG SPREAD

¾ cup dried figs, snipped
¾ cup feta cheese, crumbled
½ cup sour cream
½ cup walnuts, toasted and chopped
3 tablespoon fresh basil
1 tablespoon fresh thyme
½ teaspoon each (salt and pepper)
2 tablespoons milk

In a small bowl, pour boiling water over figs, cover; let stand 15 minutes; drain well. In a medium bowl, stir together the cheese, sour cream, basil, milk and thyme. Season with salt and pepper. Stir in drained figs and half of the walnuts. Cover and chill in refrigerator up to 24 hours. Before serving, transfer spread to a serving bowl. Sprinkle with remaining walnuts and fresh thyme sprigs. Serve with toast points or crackers.

PARTY CHEESE STICKS

1 pound of pepper jack or mozzarella cheese
3 cups flour
3 cups cornflakes, crushed
3 eggs, beaten
Oil for frying
Salsa for dipping

Cut cheese into 2 ¾ x ½ inch sticks. Place the flour, eggs and cornflakes in separate bowl. Coat cheese sticks with flour; dip in egg, roll in cornflakes until well coated. Let stand for 5 minutes. In deep fryer, heat oil to 375o. Cook cheese sticks in batches for 30 seconds or until golden brown. Drain on paper towels. Let stand for 4-5 minutes.

CHEESY BACON DIP

2 (8 oz) packages cream cheese, softened
¼ cup green onion, chopped
1 cup mayonnaise
2 cups Swiss cheese, shredded
1 package Oscar Mayer bacon pieces (not bacon bits)
1 ½ cups almond slices

Mix everything together except almonds in a baking dish and bake at 350° for 20 minutes. Add almonds and bake an additional 10-15 minutes.

SWISS PUFFS

½ cup milk
½ cup water
¼ cup butter or margarine
¼ teaspoon salt
1/8 teaspoon nutmeg
1/8 teaspoon white pepper
1 cup all-purpose flour
4 eggs, room temperature
1 cup Swiss cheese, shredded and divided

Preheat oven to 400°. Heat milk, water, butter, salt, nutmeg and pepper in a 3 quart saucepan over medium heat until mixture boils. Remove pan from heat; add flour, mixing until smooth. Cook over medium-low heat, stirring constantly, until mixture leaves side of pan clean and forms a ball. Remove pan from heat. Add eggs, 1 at a time, beating until smooth. Continue beating until mixture looses its gloss. Stir in ¾ cup cheese. Drop teaspoonful of cheese batter, 1 inch apart onto 2 large greased baking sheets. Sprinkle with remaining ¼ cup cheese. Bake at 30-35 minutes or until puffs are golden brown. Cool completely, before filling. Cut tops of puffs; scoop out and discard moist dough in centers. Makes about 4 dozen.

PEPPER CHEESE COCKTAIL PUFFS

½ (17 ¼ oz) package frozen puff pastry, thawed
1 tablespoon Dijon mustard
½ cup cheddar cheese, shredded fine
1 teaspoon black pepper
1 egg
1 tablespoon water

Preheat oven to 400°. Grease baking sheet. Roll out 1 sheet of puff pastry dough on a well floured surface to 14 x 10 inch rectangle. Spread ½ dough (from 10 inch side) with mustard. Sprinkle with cheese and pepper. Fold dough over filling; roll gently to seal edges. Cut lengthwise into 3 strips; cut each strip diagonally into 1 ½ inch pieces. Place on baking sheet. Beat egg and water in a small bowl; brush on appetizers. Bake for 12-15 minutes or until puffed are deep golden brown. Remove from baking sheet to cool. Makes about 20 appetizers.

GOOD BLOOMING ONION

3 cups cornstarch
3 ½ cups all-purpose flour, divided
6 teaspoons paprika, divided
1 teaspoon salt
2 teaspoons garlic salt
2 teaspoons black pepper, divided
2 bottles beer
4-6 medium sweet onions
2 teaspoons garlic powder
¾ teaspoon cayenne pepper, divided
1 pint mayonnaise
1 pint sour cream
½ cup chili sauce

BATTER; Mix cornstarch, 1 ½ cups flour, 2 teaspoons paprika, garlic salt, salt and 1 teaspoon black pepper in a large bowl. Add beer; mix well. Set aside. Cut about ¾ inch off of each onion; peel onions. Being careful not to cut through bottom, cut onions into 12-16 wedges. Soak cut onions in ice water for 10-15 minutes. If onions do not bloom, cut petals slightly deeper. Prepare seasoned flour mixture. Combine remaining 2 cups flour, remaining 4 teaspoons paprika, garlic powder, remaining black pepper and ¼ teaspoon cayenne pepper in a large bowl; mix well. Dip cut onions into seasoned flour; remove excess by carefully shaking. Dip in batter; remove excess by shaking. Separate petals to coat thoroughly with batter. If batter begins to separate, mix thoroughly before using. Carefully place onions, 1 at a time in fryer basket and deep fry at 375° for 1 ½ minutes. Turn onion over and fry 1-1 ½ minutes or until golden brown. Drain on paper towels. Place onion upright in a shallow bowl and remove about 1 inch of petals from center of onion.
SAUCE; Combine mayonnaise, sour cream, chili sauce and remaining ½ teaspoon cayenne pepper in a bowl; mix well. Serve warm onions with the cream sauce.

SAUSAGE CHEESE PUFFS

1 pound rolled sausage
2 ½ cups sharp cheddar cheese, shredded
2 cups biscuit mix
½ cup water
1 teaspoon baking powder

Preheat oven 350°. Combine ingredients in bowl; mix until blended. Shape into 1 inch balls. Place on greased baking sheets and bake for 25 minutes or golden brown. Serve hot.

FESTIVE TACO CUPS

½ pound ground beef
1 tablespoon vegetable oil
½ cup onion, chopped
1 clove garlic, minced
½ teaspoon dried oregano leaves
½ teaspoon chili powder or taco seasoning
¼ teaspoon salt
1 ½ cups shredded taco-flavored cheese or Mexican cheese blend, divided
1 (11 ½ oz) can refrigerated cornbread dough
Chopped fresh tomato and sliced green onion for garnish.

Heat oil in large skillet over medium heat. Add onion and cook until tender. Add ground beef; cook until done. Stir in garlic, oregano, chili powder and salt. Remove from heat and stir in ½ cup cheese; set aside. Preheat oven to 375°. Lightly grease 36 mini muffin pan cups. Remove dough from container but do not un-roll dough. Separate dough into 8 pieces at perforations. Divide each piece into 3 pieces; roll or pat each piece into 3 inch circle. Press circles into prepared muffin pan cups. Fill each cup with 1 ½ -2 teaspoons ground beef mixture. Bake 10 minutes. Sprinkle tops of taco cups with remaining ¾ cup cheese; bake 2-3 minutes more or until cheese is melted. Garnish with tomato and green onions. Makes about 36 taco cups

BLACK BEAN QUESADILLAS

½ cup canned black beans, drained
½ cup sharp cheddar cheese, shredded
¼ cup canned green chilies, diced
2 flour tortillas
Canola or olive oil

Spread cheese, beans and chilies on 1 tortilla and top with the other. Preheat skillet, brush with oil. Place quesadilla in the skillet and cook until cheese starts to melt, about 5 minutes. Slide onto a dinner plate and turn it over, then slide back into skillet. Cook an additional 4-5 minutes. Remove from heat and cut into wedges.

PARTY CRAB PUFFS

2 (6 oz) cans crabmeat, drained
4 eggs
1 cup flour
3 green onions, chopped
½ cup sharp cheddar cheese, shredded
2 teaspoons Worcestershire sauce
1 teaspoon ground mustard
1 cup water
½ cup butter, cubed
¼ teaspoon salt

Combine the crab, onions, cheese, Worcestershire sauce and mustard; set aside. Ina large saucepan, bring water, butter and salt to a boil. Add flour and stir until a smooth ball forms. Remove from heat; let stand for 5 minutes. Add eggs, beating well. Continue beating until mixture is smooth. Stir in the crab mixture. Drop by tablespoonful, 2 inches apart onto an un-greased baking sheet. Bake at 400° for 20-25 minutes or until golden brown. Remove from heat. Serve warm.

EGG ROLLS

1 Pound hamburger or chicken
1 pound cabbage, chopped
1 carrot, grated
¼ cup onion, chopped
2 tablespoons soy sauce
½ teaspoon salt
1 teaspoon cornstarch, mixed with 2 tablespoons of water
Package egg roll wrappers

Brown hamburger with onion; drain. Add cabbage and carrot. Cook until tender. Add soy sauce, salt and cornstarch; simmer 4 minutes. Fill egg roll wrappers with 2-3 tablespoons of filling. Make paste of flour and water and spread on edge of egg roll wrapper to seal roll. Fry in 350° oil. Serve with sweet and sour sauce. (Buy at grocery store).

MARINATED ASPARAGUS

Microwave 1 pound of asparagus for 45 minutes; drain. Douse with soy sauce. Refrigerate. When cold rinse off excess soy sauce. Serve cold.

STUFFED TINY POTATOES

12 tiny red potatoes
1 cup smoked salmon, flaked
¼ cup sour cream
2 tablespoons green onion, chopped fine
1/8 teaspoon salt
1/8 teaspoon pepper
¼ teaspoon lemon juice
1 teaspoon fresh dill
Fresh dill sprigs
1 teaspoon hot pepper sauce
¼ cup mayonnaise

Cook potatoes in boiling water for 10-15 minutes or until tender, drain. Cut potatoes in half horizontally. Cut a thin slice from the bottom of each potato to level the potato. Scoop out the pulp with a teaspoon. Leaving a thick shell. Stir in the mayonnaise, sour cream, onion, dill, salt, pepper, hot sauce and lemon juice in a small bowl. Fold in salmon, garnish with dill sprigs

CHEESE AND SAUSAGE BUNDLES

1 pound hot Italian pork sausage
1 cup Monterey jack cheese, shredded
1 can green chilies, chopped
2 tablespoons green onion, chopped fine
40 wonton wrappers
1 quart vegetable oil for deep frying

Brown sausage in skillet for 6-8 minutes, stirring to separate meat, drain. Combine sausage, cheese, chilies and onion in a bowl. Spoon 1 round teaspoon sausage mixture near 1 corner of wonton wrapper. Brush opposite corner with water. Fold over corner; roll up jelly-roll style. Moisten ends of roll with water. Bring ends together to make a bundle overlapping ends slightly. Firmly press to seal. Repeat the remaining filling in wonton wrappers. Heat oil in heavy 3 quart saucepan over medium heat until deep-fat thermometer registers 365o. Fry bundles a few at a time, about 1 ½ minutes or until golden brown. Drain on paper towels. Serve with your favorite salsa.

PARTY BACON SQUARES

8 slices bacon, fried crisp and crumbled
1 cup mayonnaise
2 cups cheddar cheese, shredded
½ teaspoon each (salad seasoning and Worcestershire sauce)
¼ teaspoon paprika
1/3 cup peanuts, chopped
4 green onions, sliced (¼ cup)
14 slices white bread

Heat oven 400°. Mix mayonnaise, Worcestershire sauce, salad seasoning and paprika. Stir in cheese, bacon, peanuts and onions. Spread about 3 tablespoons of bacon mixture over each slice of bread. Bake on un-greased baking sheet for 10 minutes. Cut each slice into 4 pieces. Serve hot. Makes about 50 pieces

BACON WRAPPED SCALLOPS

2 ½ pounds scallops
2 ½ pounds bacon strips, cut in half
2 ½ tablespoons lemon juice
¾ cup butter, melted
½ teaspoon each (salt and pepper)

Cut bacon strips in half and cook until partially done. Drain. Rinse scallops. Drain and dry on paper towels. Combine butter and lemon juice; brush mixture over scallops. Sprinkle with salt and pepper. Wrap each scallop in ½ slice of bacon. Secure with toothpicks. Broil 5-6 inches from heat for 3 minutes. Turn scallops, broil 2-3 minutes more. Serve hot.

BACON ROLL - UPS

½ pound bacon, cooked crisp and crumbled
1 (8 oz) package crescent rolls, separated
½ cup sour cream
½ teaspoon onion salt

Mix all ingredients together, except the crescent rolls. Spread on rolls and roll up. Place on baking sheet and bake at 375° for 10-15 minutes.

BEER - BATTERED ONION RINGS

1 cup all-purpose flour
1 teaspoon each (seasoned salt and garlic powder)
2 teaspoons paprika
1 egg
½ (6 oz) can beer
2 cups corn Chex, crushed into powder
3 large onions, sliced into ½ inch rings
Freshly ground pepper

Heat oven to 375°. Line a baking sheet with foil. In a medium bowl, whisk flour, salt, paprika, garlic powder and pepper. In a small bowl, beat egg and beer. Put the Chex onto a plate. Working 1 ring at a time, dip into flour mixture, egg and crushed Chex. Lay onion rings in a single layer on the baking sheet. Mix the remaining egg mixture and Chex and pour over the rings. Bake 20 minutes or until golden brown. Makes 20.

DELICIOUS STUFFED GRAPES

1 pound grapes, seedless, rinsed and pat dry
1 (4 oz) package cream cheese, softened
½ teaspoon grated lemon peel and juice
3 tablespoons powder sugar

In a mixing bowl, beat cream cheese, powdered sugar, lemon juice and lemon peel until blended. Cover and refrigerate for 1 hour. Cut a deep X in the top of each grape to within ¼ inch of bottom. Carefully spread each grape apart.
Transfer cream cheese mixture to a heavy duty plastic bag; cut a small hole in a corner of bag. Pipe filling into grapes. Refrigerate until ready to serve. Makes about 3 dozens.

PICKLED ASPARAGUS

1 pound asparagus
Juice from 1 (24 oz) jar of Classic dill pickles

Snap off tough ends of asparagus. Place asparagus in a large pot and bring to a boil. Drain, and rinse under cold water. Cut spears to the height of the pickle jar. Place in juice. Cover with lid. Refrigerate at least 2 days before serving.

CRAB COCKTAIL

2 (8 oz) packages cream cheese, room temperature
2 (5 oz) boxes frozen crab meat, thawed, drained and shredded
1 small onion, minced
½ cup mayonnaise
1 tablespoon Worcestershire sauce
1 tablespoon lemon juice
¾ cup chili sauce
1 teaspoon garlic salt

Mix the cream cheese, onion, mayonnaise, lemon juice, Worcestershire and garlic salt and blend well. Place the cream cheese mixture onto a serving plate. Top with chili sauce. Cover all the top with crab meat. Serve with crackers.

OLIVE CRAB STUFFED EGGS

8 eggs, hard boiled
1/3 cup green olives, chopped
1/3 cup sweet pickle relish
¼ teaspoon mustard
½ cup celery, chopped fine
½ pound fresh crabmeat
¼ cup mayonnaise

Slice eggs lengthwise and remove yolks. Mix all together except egg whites. Stuff egg whites and chill.

WATER CHESTNUTS WITH BACON

1 pound bacon, sliced
2 (8 oz) cans whole water chestnuts, drained
½ cup each (chili sauce, mayonnaise and brown sugar)

Cut bacon strips in half. Cook bacon in skillet until almost crisp; drain. Wrap each bacon piece around a water chestnut and secure with a toothpick. Place in an un-greased 13 x 9 inch baking dish. In a small bowl, combine the brown sugar, mayonnaise and chili sauce; pour over water chestnuts. Bake un-covered at 350° for 30 minutes or until hot and bubbly.

SPINACH CHEESE BUNDLES

1 (6 ½ oz) container garlic and herb flavored spread able cheese
½ cup fresh spinach, chopped
¼ teaspoon pepper
1 (17 ¼ oz) package frozen puff pastry, thawed
Sweet and sour or your favorite dipping sauce

Preheat oven to 400°. Combine spread able cheese, spinach and pepper in a small bowl mix well. Roll out 1 sheet puff pastry dough on floured surface into 12 inch square.. Cut into 16 (3 inch) individual squares. Place about 1 teaspoonful cheese mixture in center of each square; brush edges of squares with water. Bring edges together up over filling and twist tightly to seal; fan out corners of puff pastry. Place bundles 2 inches apart on baking sheet. Bake about 13 minutes or until golden brown. Repeat with remaining sheet of puff pastry and cheese mixture. Serve warm with dipping sauce.

GRANNY'S STUFFED WANTONS

1 ½ bags greens, collard, kale, turnip or spinach
1 (8 oz) package cream cheese
4-5 slices bacon, fried crisp and crumbled
1 tablespoon hot sauce
1 package wantons
¼ teaspoon each (salt, pepper, garlic powder and Worcester sauce)
1 small - medium ham hock

Cook greens and ham hock in salted water until greens and ham hock is done. Drain; set aside; mix the cream cheese, Worcestershire sauce, pepper, garlic powder, meat from ham hock and crumbled crisp bacon. Mix well. Chop greens and add to the cream cheese mixture. Place 2 tablespoonful of greens mixture in each of the wanton wrappers and fold ends all together and bake at 350° until wrappers are lightly brown.

BACON - CHEDDAR DEVILED EGGS

12 eggs, hard boiled
½ cup mayonnaise
¼ teaspoon pepper
1 tablespoon honey mustard
2 tablespoons cheddar cheese, shredded
4-5 strips bacon, cooked crisp and crumbled

Slice eggs in half lengthwise; remove yolks. In a bowl mash yolks; stir in mayonnaise, bacon, cheese, mustard and pepper. Stuff into egg whites. Refrigerate.

CHEESY SPINACH TARTLETS

FILLING
4 cups fresh spinach, chopped
1 cup feta cheese, crumbled
1 teaspoon olive oil
½ cup ricotta cheese
½ teaspoon dill weed
1 egg
1/8 teaspoon of each (salt, pepper and nutmeg)
1 pie crust

Cook spinach in hot oil in skillet 2-3 minutes or until wilted and tender. Cool slightly. Combine feta cheese, ricotta cheese, dill, salt, nutmeg, pepper and egg in a bowl; mix well. Stir in spinach until well mixed. Place pie crust on cutting board. With 2 ½ inch round cutter, cut 12 rounds. Repeat with remaining pie crust and flour. Press rounds in bottom and up sides of 24 greased miniature muffin cups. Spoon 1 rounded tablespoon spinach mixture into each cup. Bake at 400° for 15-20 minutes or until filling is set and edges are light golden brown. Cool 5 minutes; remove from pan and serve.

SPINACH - ARTICHOKE PARTY CUPS

36 small wonton wrappers
1 (8 ½ oz) can artichoke hearts, drained and chopped
½ (10 oz) package frozen spinach, thawed, drained and chopped
1 cup Monterey jack cheese, shredded
½ cup mayonnaise
1 clove garlic, minced

Preheat oven to 300°. Spray mini muffin pan lightly with nonstick cooking spray. Press 1 wonton wrapper into each cup. Bake about 9 minutes or until light golden brown. Remove shells from muffin pan and set aside to cool. Repeat with remaining wonton wrappers. Combine artichoke hearts, spinach, cheese, mayonnaise and garlic in medium bowl; mix well. Fill wonton cups with spinach-artichoke mixture; about 1 ½ teaspoonful. Place filled cups on baking sheet. Bake about 7 minutes or until heated through. Serve immediately. Makes about 36 appetizers

BACON AND TOMATO CUPS

1 tomato, chopped fine
½ cup mayonnaise
1 (12 oz) can buttermilk biscuits, separated into 10 biscuits
½ cup Swiss cheese, shredded
½ cup real bacon bits
1 teaspoon dried basil
1 onion, chopped fine

Combine the tomato, bacon, mayonnaise, onion, cheese and basil; set aside. Split each biscuit into 3 layers; press each layer into an un-greased miniature muffin cups. Spoon tomato mixture into cups and bake at 450° for 8-10 minutes or until golden brown. Best served warm.

BACON AND ONION APPETIZERS

2 large onions, sweet
½ cup balsamic vinegar
½ cup brown sugar
12 strips bacon, hickory-smoked
2 tablespoons barbecue sauce
¼ cup molasses

Cut each onion into 12 wedges. Cut bacon strips in half widthwise; wrap a piece of bacon around each onion wedge and secure with toothpicks. Place in an un-greased 13 x 9 inch dish. Combine brown sugar, vinegar, molasses and barbecue sauce; pour ½ cup over onions. Cover and refrigerate for 1 hour, turning once. Cover and refrigerate remaining marinade for basting. Drain and discard marinade. Grill onions, cook over medium heat 10-15 minutes, turning and basting often with reserved marinade.

GREEN BEANS WRAPPED IN BACON

2 (16 oz) cans whole green beans
1 cup bean juice
¼ cup brown sugar
½ pound bacon, cut in half
½ teaspoon allspice

Wrap bacon around 10-12 beans and fasten with toothpicks; place in casserole dish. Combine allspice, bean juice and brown sugar, pour over beans and bake at 400° for 20-25 minutes. Turn once and baste.

ASPARAGUS - BEEF ROLL - UPS

35 fresh asparagus spears, trimmed
1 ½ cups water
1 (5 oz) package roast beef, sliced thin
3-4 tablespoons horseradish
1 (8 oz) carton spread able chive and onion cream cheese

Place asparagus in saucepan, cover and boil for 2 minutes or until crisp tender. Drain and immediately put asparagus in a bowl of ice water. Pat dry. In a small bowl, combine cream cheese and horseradish. Pat beef slices dry with paper towels. Spread each beef slice with a thin layer of cream cheese mixture; top with an asparagus spear. Roll up tight. Refrigerate until ready to serve.

HAM CUBES WITH HORSERADISH

10 square slices of deli ham
1 teaspoon Worcestershire sauce
½ teaspoon salt
1/8 teaspoon pepper
1 (8 oz) package cream cheese, softened
2 tablespoons horseradish

In a small bowl, beat the cream cheese, horseradish, Worcestershire, seasoned salt and pepper. Spread about 2 tablespoons on each ham slice. Make 2 stacks using 5 ham slices for each. Wrap each stack in plastic wrap; for 3 ½- 4 hours. Cut each stack into 1 inch cubes.

HAM ROLL - UPS

1 (3 oz) package cream cheese, softened
6 stuffed olives, chopped
2 tablespoons whipping cream
1 teaspoon horseradish
¼ teaspoon salt
¼ teaspoon paprika
6 slices boiled ham
Dash white pepper

Combine all ingredients, except ham; mix well. Spread cream cheese mixture on 1 side of each ham slice; roll up. Cover rolls and chill. Slice rolls into 1 inch pieces.

SHRIMP WRAPPED IN BACON

12 jumbo shrimp, un -cooked, peeled and de-veined
¼ cup Italian salad dressing
¼ cup orange juice
6 strips bacon, cut in half
1 ounce pepper jack or cheddar cheese, julienne

Cut a small slit on the back of each shrimp, not cutting all the way through. In a large plastic bag, combine the salad dressing and orange juice; add shrimp. Seal bag and turn to coat; refrigerate for 30 minutes. In a skillet cook bacon until cooked but not crisp. Drain on paper towels. Place a piece of cheese in the slit of each shrimp. Wrap bacon around shrimp; secure ends with toothpicks. Put in broiler for 3-4 minutes on each side or until shrimp turn pink and the bacon is crisp.

SALMON CANAPES

1 (8 oz) package cream cheese
1 teaspoon fresh dill or ¼ teaspoon dill weed
36 slices cocktail rye bread
12 ounces smoke salmon, sliced
1 medium red onion, sliced thin and separated into rings

In a mixing bowl, combine cream cheese and dill. Spread on rye bread.
Top with salmon and red onion. Garnish with dill sprigs

ALMA'S BACON CHEESE SPREAD

6-7 slices bacon, cook crisp and crumbled
¼ cup pecans, toasted and chopped
1 small onion, minced
2 tablespoons sweet red pepper, chopped fine
2 cups mayonnaise
4 cups sharp cheese, shredded

Cook bacon, drain. Mix with other ingredients. Serve with crackers.

PARTY PUFFS

2 cup water
1 cup butter, cubed
½ cup flour
½ cup rye flour
2 teaspoons dried parsley flakes
½ teaspoon garlic powder
¼ teaspoon salt
4 eggs
Caraway seeds

CORN BEEF FILLING

2 (8 oz) packages cream cheese, softened
2 (2 ½ oz) packages sliced corn beef, chopped
½ cup mayonnaise
¼ cup sour cream
2 tablespoons chives, minced
2 tablespoons onion, diced
1 teaspoon spicy brown or horseradish mustard
1/8 teaspoon garlic powder
10 small pimento stuffed olives, chopped

In a large saucepan over medium heat, bring water and butter to a boil. Add flour, parsley, garlic powder and salt all at once; stir until smooth balls forms. Remove from heat let stand for 5 minutes. Beat in eggs, 1 at a time. Beat until smooth. Drop batter by rounded teaspoonful 2 inches apart onto a greased baking sheet. Sprinkle with caraway seeds. Bake at 400° for 15-20 minutes or until golden brown. Remove from oven. Immediately cut a slit in each puff to allow steam to escape; cool. In a large mixing bowl, combine all ingredients together, stir olives in last. Split puffs; adding filling. Refrigerate. Makes about 4 ½ dozen.

RANCH HAM ROLL - UPS

2 (8 oz) packages of cream cheese, softened
1 envelope ranch salad dressing mix
3 green onions, chopped
11 flour tortillas (8 inches)
22 slices deli ham, sliced thin

Beat the cream cheese and salad dressing mix until smooth. Add onions, mix well. Spread about 3 tablespoons over each tortilla; top each with 2 ham slices. Roll up tightly and wrap in plastic wrap. Refrigerate until firm. Cut into ¾ inch slices.

MUSHROOM AND BROCCOLI CUPS

24 slices of bread
1 egg
1 egg white
1/3 cup milk
1 teaspoon dried parsley flakes
½ teaspoon salt
1/4 teaspoon dried thyme
Dash pepper
1/3 cup fresh broccoli, chopped fine
1/3 cup cheddar cheese, shredded
¼ cup fresh mushrooms, chopped fine
1 tablespoon onion, chopped fine

Roll bread flat; cut with a 2 ½ inch biscuit cutter. (discard bread scraps). Press bread rounds into miniature muffin cups coated with non stick cooking spray. Broil 6 inches from the heat until golden brown, about 2-3 minutes. Cool in pans. In a bowl, beat the egg, egg white, milk, parsley, salt, thyme and pepper. Stir in the broccoli, cheese, mushrooms and onions. Spoon about 1 teaspoon into each toast cup. Bake at 350° for 15-20 minutes or until set. Serve immediately.

SAUSAGE - STUFFED MUSHROOMS

12-15 large fresh mushrooms
2 tablespoons butter, divided
1 tablespoon onion, chopped
1 tablespoon lemon juice
4 ounces bulk Italian sausage
1 tablespoon dry bread crumbs
2 tablespoons parmesan cheese, grated
Salt and pepper to taste
1 tablespoon fresh parsley

Remove stems from the mushrooms. Chop stems finely; set mushroom caps aside. Place stems in paper towels and squeeze to remove any liquid. In a large skillet, heat 1 ½ tablespoons butter. Cook stems and onion until tender. Add the lemon juice, salt and pepper; cook until almost all the liquid has evaporated; cool. In a bowl, combine the mushroom mixture, sausage and parsley. Stuff reserved mushroom caps. Combine crumbs and cheese; sprinkle over top. Dot each with remaining butter. Place in a greased baking pan. Bake at 400° for 20 minutes or until sausage is no longer pink. Basting occasionally with pan juices. Serve hot.

STUFFED MUSHROOMS WITH CRABMEAT

1/3 cup lump crabmeat
½ cup bread crumbs
¼ cup fresh parmesan cheese
24 white mushrooms
1/3 cup green pepper, chopped
1/3 cup red pepper, chopped
¼ cup onion, minced
1 egg, beaten
½ cub butter, divided
1/8 teaspoon cayenne pepper
2 cloves garlic, minced

Sauté peppers, onion and garlic in a saucepan in ¼ cup of butter until soft. Remove from heat and add cheese, crabmeat, egg, cayenne pepper and bread crumbs. Remove stems from mushroom caps. Melt remaining butter and dip each mushrooms cap in melted butter. Stuff with crabmeat stuffing. Bake at 400° until lightly browned on the top.

GOOD FRIED MUSHROOMS

1 package whole mushrooms, washed and drained
½ cup flour
1 egg, beaten
2 teaspoon lemon juice
1 cup regular canned bread crumbs

Coat mushrooms in flour. Mix egg and lemon juice together. Dip mushrooms in egg and lemon juice and coat in bread crumbs. Deep fry until brown. Serve with horseradish dip.

HORSERADISH DIP

1 cup sour cream
2 teaspoons lemon juice
Horseradish to taste

Mix all ingredients together. Serve with hot fried mushrooms.

STUFFED MUSHROOMS

30 large mushrooms (about 1 pound)
½ pound pork sausage
1 cup dried tart cherries, chopped
1 (8 oz) package cream cheese, softened
2 green onions, sliced

Pull stems from mushrooms and discard. Wipe mushrooms with a damp paper towel. Set aside. Cook sausage in a large skillet, stirring to break up meat, 5 minutes or until sausage is done. Remove from heat. Add dried cherries, cream cheese and onions, mix well. Fill each mushroom cap with heaping teaspoonful of sausage mixture. Place filled mushrooms on a greased baking sheet. Bake at 425° for 6-8 minutes. Serve at once.

STUFFED MUSHROOMS

8 large mushrooms
1 box frozen spinach, drained
2 ounces cream cheese
4 ounces feta cheese
½ cup green onions, sliced
Parmesan cheese

Clean mushrooms with a damp paper towel and remove caps. Mix all ingredients together, except mushrooms and parmesan cheese. Stuff the mixture into the mushrooms. Sprinkle with parmesan cheese and bake at 350° for 15-20 minutes.

MUSHROOM CANAPAS

1 can mushrooms
½ cup mayonnaise
½ cup parmesan cheese
½ can fried onion rings
Party rye toasts
Fresh parsley

Mix all ingredients together, except parsley. Spread on toast squares, put under broiler until squares are hot and slightly brown. Sprinkle with parsley.

DEEP FRIED MUSHROOMS

1 pound fresh mushrooms, stems removed
1 cup bread crumbs
1 cup flour
½ teaspoon salt
½ teaspoon pepper
1 tablespoon water
3 eggs
Oil for deep frying

In a plastic bag, combine flour, salt and pepper. In a dish, beat eggs and water. Place the bread crumbs in another dish. Add mushrooms to the flour mixture; seal and shake to coat. Dip in egg mixture, coat with bread crumbs. In a saucepan or deep fryer heat oil to 375°. Fry mushrooms 6-8 at a time for 1-2 minutes or until golden brown, turning occasionally. Drain on paper towels.

POLISH SAUSAGE WITH HORSERADISH SAUCE

1 can beets, drained and pureed
2 ounces horseradish
1 tablespoon sugar
1 tablespoon white vinegar
Ring of polish sausage
Salt and pepper

Mix beets, horseradish, sugar, vinegar, salt and pepper together. Let stand several hours to blend flavors. At serving time, broil sausage until brown; turning once. Quickly slice sausage and arrange on platter with some of the sauce for dipping. Serve with toothpicks.

DEVILED HAM APPETIZERS

1 (4 ¼ oz) can deviled ham
½ teaspoon lemon juice
½ teaspoon Worcestershire sauce

Mix together and spread on crackers.

CRAB CAKES WITH SAUCE

SAUCE
½ cup mayonnaise
2 tablespoons Dijon mustard
1 tablespoon horseradish

CRAB CAKES

1 1/3 cups French fried onions, divided
3 (6 oz) cans jumbo lump crabmeat, drained
¼ cup dry bread crumbs, un-seasoned
¼ cup mayonnaise
1 egg, beaten
2 tablespoons pimentos, chopped
2 tablespoons parsley, chopped
1 tablespoon Dijon mustard
1 tablespoon horseradish
1 teaspoon garlic, minced

Combine horseradish, mustard in a small bowl; chill until ready to serve. Lightly crush 2/3 cup French fried onions. Place in a large bowl. Add remaining ingredients for crab cakes; mix until well combined. Shape mixture into cakes using about ¼ cup mixture for each; flatten slightly. Heat 2 tablespoons oil in a 12 inch nonstick skillet over medium heat. Cook crab cakes in batches; about 2-3 minutes per side or until golden; drain. Transfer crab cakes to serving platter. Serve each crab cake topped with horseradish-mustard sauce and remaining onions. Makes about 12 cakes.

CRAB MELTS

1 pound crabmeat
1 (12 oz) package sharp cheddar cheese, grated
1 cup butter
4 tablespoons mayonnaise
1 teaspoon salt

Mix all ingredients except crabmeat; mix well. Add crabmeat. Spread on top of ¼ piece of English muffins. Broil until browned. Serve warm.

CRAB RAMEKINS

1 pound crabmeat, cooked and flaked
6 slices bacon, fried crisp
1 ½ cups mayonnaise
½ cup chili sauce
1 teaspoon vinegar
1 teaspoon dry mustard
½ teaspoon Tabasco
Paprika and salt to taste

Divide cooked crabmeat into 6 lightly buttered ramekins (individual baking dishes). Cook in pre-heated oven at 400° for 5 minutes. Top each portion with 1 slice bacon. In a large bowl, combine mayonnaise, chili sauce, vinegar, dry mustard, Tabasco, paprika and salt to taste. Top crabmeat with this mixture. Put ramekins under a pre-heated broiler for 2-3 minutes, or until topping is bubbling.

CRAB AND BRIE APPETIZERS

½ pound fresh crabmeat
6 ounces brie cheese, rind removed and cut into small cubes
2 ½ cups ripe pears, chopped fine
½ cup green onions, sliced thin
¾ cup butter
½ cup ham, fully cooked and diced
1 garlic clove, minced
2 teaspoons lemon juice
14 sheets phyllo dough (14 and 9 inches)
1/8 teaspoon pepper

Combine the crabmeat, cheese, pears, green onions, ham, lemon juice, garlic and pepper; set aside. Place a piece of plastic wrap larger than a sheet of phyllo on a work surface. Place 1 phyllo sheet on plastic wrap; brush with butter. (keep remaining phyllo covered until ready to use). Repeat 6 times. Spread half of crab filling to within 1 inch of edges. Fold the 2 sides over the filling. Using the plastic wrap to lift 1 long side, roll up jelly-roll style. Transfer to a greased 15 x 10 inch baking dish or pan; discard plastic wrap. Brush top with butter. Score top lightly at 1 inch intervals. Repeat with remaining phyllo, butter and filling. Bake at 375° for 20-25 minutes or until golden brown. Let stand for 5 minutes. Cut into slices along scored lines. Makes about 2 dozens.

GOOD CRAB TASSIES

½ cup butter, softened
1 (3 oz) package cream cheese, softened
1 cup flour
¼ teaspoon salt
1 pound crabmeat
½ cup mayonnaise
1 tablespoon lemon juice
½ cup celery, chopped fine
2 small scallions, chopped fine
½ cup Swiss cheese, grated
½ teaspoon Worcestershire sauce
¼ teaspoon seasoned salt
Dash of Tabasco

Cream butter and cream cheese. Stir in flour and salt. Roll into 24 balls and chill for 1 hour. Press into mini muffin tins. Mix crab with remaining ingredients. Spoon into un-baked shells and bake at 350° for 30 minutes or until golden brown.

CRABMEAT APPETIZERS

1 (8 oz) package cream cheese
1 tablespoon milk
½ pound crabmeat
2 teaspoons horseradish
¼ teaspoon salt
Dash white pepper
Slivered almonds

Mix all ingredients together except almonds. Sprinkle almonds on top before baking at 375° for 20-25 minutes. Serve with your favorite crackers

CRAB AND CRACKERS

1 (8 oz) package cream cheese
1 carton pimento spread
1 bottle cocktail sauce, divided
2 tablespoons onion, minced
1 can crabmeat

Mix every thing but the crabmeat together. Spread on plate. Spread 3 tablespoons remaining cocktail sauce over mixture. Top with crabmeat and drizzle with sauce.

SMOKED SALMON CUCUMBERS

1 large English cucumber
1 (8 oz) carton spread able chive and onion cheese
1 (8 oz) package smoked salmon, chopped
Minced chives

With a fork, score cucumber, peel lengthwise; cut ¼ inch, slice. Pipe or spread cream cheese onto each slice; top with salmon. Sprinkle with chives. Refrigerate.

SALMON MOUSSE CUPS

1 (3 oz) package cream cheese, softened
½ cup butter, softened
1 cup all-purpose flour

FILLING

1 (8 oz) package cream cheese, softened
1 cup fully cooked salmon, chunks or 1 can salmon, drained, bones and skin removed
2 tablespoons chicken broth
2 tablespoons sour cream
1 tablespoon onion, chopped fine
1 teaspoon lemon juice
½ teaspoon salt
2 tablespoons fresh dill, minced

MOUSSE CUPS

In a mixing bowl, beat cream cheese and butter until smooth. Add flour; mix well. Shape into 24 balls; press onto the bottom and up sides of greased miniature muffin cups. Bake at 350° for 10-15 minutes or until brown. Cool 5 minutes before removing from pans. Then cool completely

FILLING;

In a mixing bowl, beat cream cheese until smooth. Add salmon, broth, sour cream, onion, lemon juice and salt; mix well. Spoon into the shells. Refrigerate for at least 2 hours.
Sprinkle with dill.

SMOKED SALMON CHEESECAKE

4 (8 oz) packages cream cheese, softened
3 tablespoons breadcrumbs
5 tablespoons parmesan cheese, grated and divided
½ cup onion, chopped
½ cup green pepper, chopped
3 tablespoons butter
½ cup heavy whipping cream
¼ teaspoon pepper
4 eggs
1 (5 oz) package smoked salmon ,diced
½ cup Swiss cheese, shredded
Assorted crackers

Grease the bottom and sides of a 9 inch spring form pan. Combine the bread crumbs and 2 tablespoons parmesan cheese; sprinkle into pan, coating bottom and side. In a skillet, sauté onion and green pepper in butter until tender; set aside. In mixing bowl, beat cream cheese until fluffy. Beat in the cream, pepper and remaining parmesan cheese. Add eggs, beat on low speed until combined. Fold in onion mixture, salmon and Swiss cheese Wrap a double thickness of heavy-duty foil around bottom of prepared pan. Pour salmon mixture in pan. Place in a large baking pan. Fill larger pan with hot water to a depth of 11/2 inch. Bake at 325° for 35-40 minutes or until center is almost set. Cool for 1 hour. Refrigerate overnight. Remove foil and sides of pan. Serve with crackers.

SMOKED SALMON APPETIZERS

1 (4 oz) package smoked salmon, sliced thin
¼ cup cream cheese, softened
1 tablespoon fresh dill
1/8 teaspoon ground red pepper
24 melba toast rounds or crackers

Combine cream cheese, dill and pepper in a small bowl; blend well.
Spread evenly over each slice of salmon. Roll up salmon slices jelly-
roll fashion. Place on plate; cover with plastic wrap. Chill 1-4 hours.
Cut salmon rolls crosswise into ¾ inch pieces. Place pieces, cut side
down on serving plate. Garnish each salmon with sprigs of dill.

COCONUT FRIED SHRIMP

1 pound large shrimp, un-cooked, peeled and de-veined
2 ½ cups flaked coconut
½ teaspoon vegetable oil
1 ½ cups cold water
4-5 teaspoons baking powder
1 ¼ cup honey
Additional oil for deep frying
2 tablespoons cornstarch
1 1/4 cups flour
1 cup orange marmalade
1/2 teaspoon salt

Combine the flour, cornstarch, baking powder and salt together. Stir
in water and oil until smooth. Dip shrimp into batter, then coat with
coconut. In deep fryer heat oil to 375°. Fry shrimp, a few at a time, for
3 minutes or until golden brown. Drain on paper towels. In a saucepan
heat the marmalade and honey; stir until blended. Serve as a dipping
sauce for the shrimp.

PARTY SHRIMP SQUARES

1 (8 oz) tube refrigerated crescent rolls
1 (8 oz) package cream cheese
¼ cup sour cream
½ teaspoon dill weed
1/8 teaspoon salt
½ cup seafood cocktail sauce
24 cooked medium shrimp, peeled and de-veined
½ cup green pepper, chopped
1/3 cup onion, chopped
1 (4 oz) cup Monterey jack cheese, shredded

In a greased 13 x 9 inch baking dish. Un-roll crescent dough into 1 long rectangle; seal the seams and perforations. Bake at 375° for 10-12 minutes or until golden brown. Cool completely. In a mixing bowl, beat cream cheese, sour cream, dill and salt until smooth. Spread over crust. Top with seafood sauce, shrimp, green pepper, onion and cheese. Cover and refrigerate for 1 hour. Cut into squares.

SHRIMP APPETIZER SPREAD

1 (8 oz) package cream cheese, softened
½ cup sour cream
¼ cup mayonnaise
3 (5 oz) packages frozen cooked salad shrimp, thawed
1 cup seafood sauce
2 (8 oz) cups mozzarella cheese, shredded
1 medium green pepper, chopped
1 small tomato, chopped
3 green onions with tops, sliced
Assorted crackers

In a mixing bowl, beat cream cheese until smooth. Add sour cream and mayonnaise, mix well. Spread mixture on a round 12 inch serving platter. Sprinkle with shrimp. Top with seafood sauce. Sprinkle with mozzarella cheese, green pepper, tomato and onions. Cover and refrigerate.

SHRIMP AND CRABMEAT SPREAD

1 (8 oz) package cream cheese, softened
1 tablespoon lemon juice
1 ½ tablespoons mayonnaise
1 ½ pounds shrimp, boiled, peeled and chopped
1 (6 ½ oz) can white crabmeat or ½ pound fresh crabmeat
½ cup green onion tops
Salt and pepper to taste
Worcestershire sauce
Tabasco sauce

Cream together the cream cheese, lemon juice and mayonnaise. Add the shrimp and crabmeat. Season with salt, pepper, Tabasco and Worcestershire sauce. Refrigerate for 8 hours before serving to allow seasonings to flavor the seafood.

RUEBEN DIP

1 (16 oz) jar or can sauerkraut
1 (8 oz) package swiss cheese, grated
1 cup thousand island salad dressing
1 (3 oz) package corned beef, chopped

Combine all ingredients in a baking dish and bake at 350° for 30 minutes.

PARTY SHRIMP SPREAD

1 (8 oz) package cream cheese softened
1 (4 ¼ oz) can small shrimp, rinsed and drained
2 tablespoons ketchup
1 tablespoon mayonnaise
2 teaspoon prepared mustard
2 teaspoons dried minced onion
1 teaspoon garlic salt
French bread baguette, sliced

Combine the cream cheese, ketchup, mayonnaise, garlic salt, onion and mustard. Stir in the shrimp. Cover and refrigerate for at least 2-3 hours. Serve on baguette slices.

DELICIOUS SHRIMP MOLD

1 (8 oz) package cream cheese, softened
1 pound shrimp, cooked cut into small pieces
1 can crab soup
2 small boxes un-flavored gelatin
1 cup mayonnaise
1 cup celery, chopped fine
1 tablespoon fresh lemon juice
4 green onions, chopped fine
1 teaspoon curry powder
1 small carton sour cream

Heat sour cream and cream cheese until creamy. Stir gelatin into soup-cheese mixture. Add rest ingredients and pour in a greased mold. (fish mold if you have one). Chill at least 4 hours. Un-mold and garnish with whole shrimp and parsley. Serve with crackers.

OYSTER BIENVILLE

1 quart oysters, raw
3 egg yolks
1 (2 oz) can mushrooms, drained and chopped
1 bunch of green onions or 2 white onions, chopped
1 pint fish stock
½ cup butter
½ cup flour
6 tablespoons white wine
½ teaspoon each (Tabasco sauce, cayenne pepper and salt)
¼ cup parmesan cheese
1/8 teaspoon paprika
Rock salt
1/4 cup bread crumbs
Oyster shells

Bake oysters in a baking dish at 375° for 10 minutes or until they curl around the edges. Remove pan and set aside. Reserve liquid. Cook onions in butter, stirring until golden. Do not brown. Add flour. Stir over low heat until mixture is smooth. Add fish stock which has been scalded not boiled. Add oysters and mushrooms. Simmer until sauce is smooth and begins to thicken. Set aside to cool. Beat egg yolks with the wine and cream. Pour the warm sauce into the egg mixture, beating constantly to keep mixture from curdling. Add reserved liquid from the pre-baked oysters to sauce and cook on low heat, stirring constantly for 10 minutes or until thickened good. Season with pepper, salt and Tabasco sauce. Place oysters in oyster shells. Spoon thick sauce over each oyster and sprinkle with the mixture of bread crumbs, cheese and paprika to form a thick cover. Place shells in oven and bake at 400° until tops begin to turn golden brown. Serve shells on a bed of rock salt. French bread and a tossed salad is also good.

PARTY OYSTER OR LOBSTER SHOOTERS

1-2 cartons of raw oysters
¼ cup lemon juice
¼ cup vodka
¼ cup shrimp sauce or hot sauce
¼ cup tomato juice
Several medium size shot glasses (1 for each guest)

Drop 1 teaspoon of the remaining ingredients in each glass on top of the oyster. Place lemon slice on side of glass. (you can use only 1 of the following, if you don't want to use all of them). Vodka, tomato juice, shrimp sauce, and hot sauce. Serve 1 at a time to your guest.

SOUPS & SANDWICHES

CREAM OF CRAB SOUP

1 pound crabmeat
1 vegetable bouillon cube
1 cup of water
¼ each (chopped onion and butter or margarine)
2 tablespoons flour
1 teaspoon celery salt
1/8 teaspoon pepper
1 quart milk
Parsley flakes for garnish
¼ teaspoon hot sauce

Remove cartilage from crabmeat. Dissolve bouillon in water. In a 4 quart saucepan, cook onions in margarine until tender. Blend in flour and seasonings. Add milk and bouillon gradually. Cook over medium heat; stir constantly until mixture thickens enough to coat spoon. Add crabmeat and hot sauce; do not boil. Garnish with parsley before serving.

FAVORITE TORTILLA SOUP

4 cups chicken, cooked, de-boned and cut up
2 cans kidney beans
5 tablespoons chicken broth
1 bag of corn, frozen
2 tablespoons cumin
2 (28 oz.) cans whole tomatoes, cut up
3 small cans green chilies
6 cups chicken broth
2 teaspoons garlic powder
2 medium onions
4 tablespoons butter or margarine
½ cup cheddar cheese, grated
1 small carton sour cream

Heat butter in skillet. Add garlic powder and onion. Cook until soft. Add onion mixture and all other ingredients (except corn) in a large pot. Bring to a boil, then add corn. Cook 45 minutes longer. Add cheese and sour cream before serving. Serve with tortilla chips.

CREAM OF SHRIMP SOUP

3 cans mushroom soup
3 cups milk
1 bunch green onions, chopped
5 stalks celery, chopped fine
1 (3 oz.) can of mushroom caps
½ teaspoon each (garlic powder and white pepper)
1 teaspoon salt
¼ teaspoon cayenne pepper
Dash of Tabasco sauce
1 tablespoon Worcestershire sauce
1 pound shrimp, cooked
¼ cup vermouth
2 tablespoons heavy cream

Combine soup and milk in saucepan over medium heat. Add onions, celery, mushroom caps and seasonings; simmer about 30 minutes. (Do not boil). Add shrimp and vermouth and cook until shrimp are well heated about 15 minutes. Add heavy cream during the last 5 minutes of cooking.

EASY CRAB SOUP

1 bunch green onions, chopped fine
1 stick butter
1 can tomato soup
2 cans cream of mushroom soup
1/3 sherry or wine
Half and Half
1 pound fresh crabmeat
Tabasco sauce to taste

Sauté onions in butter. Blend soups, add to onions. Add sherry. Fold in crab. Add cream to consistency desired, and season to taste with Tabasco sauce. Heat and serve.

CREAMY CABBAGE SOUP

2 cups ham, chopped
10 cups cabbage, coarsely chopped
1 ½ cups each (shredded carrots and chopped celery)
1 cups wild rice, cooked
¼ cup each (chopped onion and butter)
5 cups water
2 teaspoons instant chicken bouillon
½ teaspoon celery salt
1 (5 oz.) can evaporated milk
1/3 cup flour
¾ cup water
Salt and pepper to taste

Combine ham, cabbage, carrots, celery, onion, rice, 4 ½ cups of water, butter, chicken bouillon and celery salt in large saucepan; mix well. Cook for 10-15 minutes or until mixture comes to a boil; reduce heat. Simmer for 35-40 minutes or until vegetables are tender-crisp. Stir in evaporated milk and mixture of flour and ¾ cups of water. Cook for 10-15 minutes or until soup comes to a boil, stirring constantly. Cook for 1 minute longer. Season with salt and pepper to taste.

POTATO AND CABBAGE SOUP

6- 10 cups water
6-8 potatoes, peeled and diced
1 medium head cabbage, shredded
3 chicken bouillon cubes
1 medium onion
2 cups ham, diced
Pepper to taste

Put water in large pot; add the rest of the ingredients except ham. Cover to boil then turn to low heat for 25 minutes. Add ham in the last 5 minutes.

GOOD DIET SOUP

1 can each (tomato juice and French green beans)
3 celery stalks
½ head of cabbage
2-3 bouillon cubes (salt and pepper to taste)

Combine all ingredients together. Cook until all vegetables are done. Enjoy.

CREAMY PEANUT SOUP

1 medium onion, chopped
¼ cup each (chopped parsley and salted peanuts, chopped)
1 cup each (chopped celery, creamy peanut butter, half and half)
2 quarts chicken broth
½ cup butter
2 tablespoons flour

Sauté onion and celery in butter until tender. Stir in flour; blend. Add broth; strain. Blend in peanut butter, reduce heat and add half and half. Simmer for 5-10 minutes. Serve with parsley and chopped peanuts.

CREAM OF TOMATO SOUP

1 (#2 can) of tomatoes, chopped
2 slices onion
1 bay leaf
1 teaspoon pepper
1/8 teaspoon cloves
2 tablespoons each (flour, milk and butter)
¼ teaspoon cinnamon

Combine tomatoes, onions and seasonings; simmer 10 minutes. Make sauce of butter, flour and milk. Before serving, add hot tomatoes to sauce, stirring constantly.

WANTON SOUP

½ pound ground pork
1 egg
1 tablespoon onion, grated
4 tablespoons salt, separated in 2 tablespoons each
2 tablespoons soy sauce
6 cups chicken broth
Wanton skins

Brown pork. Combine egg, onion, salt and 1 tablespoon soy sauce. Wrap small amount of mixture in wanton skins; fold in triangle and wet edges with water to stick together. Combine chicken broth, 1 tablespoon soy sauce and 2 teaspoons salt. Add filled wantons and simmer until heated through.

DELICIOUS TURNIP SOUP

2 cups turnips, grated
1 medium onion, minced
1 quart half and half
2 tablespoons each (butter, flour, chopped parsley)
1 teaspoon salt

Heat half and half and onion in double boiler. Mix flour and melted butter into paste. Add slowly to milk and onion. Add grated turnips and salt. Cook until turnips are soft. Approximately 10-12 minutes. Sprinkle parsley over soup just before serving. Serves 6.

OLD FASHION TURNIP SOUP

2 pounds turnip greens and roots (frozen or fresh)
2 cans great northern beans, drained and rinsed
1 box Knorr vegetable soup mix
3 cups chicken broth
1 pound smoked sausage, cut into small pieces

Combine all ingredients in a large pot. Cook until sausage and turnips are thoroughly cooked. I like mine with cornbread, you may also serve it with your favorite crackers.

CREAMY CORN SOUP

1 cup each (boiling water and corn)
2 cups milk, hot
3 tablespoons each (flour and margarine)
½ tablespoon onion, minced
1 tablespoon celery leaves, chopped
Salt and pepper to taste

Cook onion and celery until browned. Add flour. Mix until smooth. Add milk, stirring constantly. Add water. Cook over hot water until thickened. Add corn, season to taste. Heat thoroughly. Add celery leaves. Makes about 5-6 servings.

BEER CHEESE SOUP

¾ cup carrots, chopped fine
½ cup celery, chopped fine
¼ cup onion, chopped fine
½ cup butter or margarine
1 cup Bisquick
½ teaspoon paprika
1/8 teaspoon each (black pepper and red pepper)
3 (10 oz) cans chicken broth
2 cups each (sharp cheddar cheese, shredded and half and half)
4- 8 ounce cans of beer

In a skillet, cook the chopped vegetables in butter until soft. Stir in the Bisquick, paprika, black pepper and red pepper. Stir in the chicken broth. Heat to boiling over medium heat, stirring constantly. Boil and stir 1 minute; reduce heat and gradually stir in the half and half, cheese and beer. Cook and stir until cheese is melted.

QUICK ONION SOUP

½ stick of butter
3 large onions, thinly sliced
3 (10 oz.) cans of beef broth
¼ cup red wine
1 cup Swiss or Parmesan cheese, grated
1 cup croutons

Melt butter and sauté onions until clear. Add broth and wine. Pour into casserole dish; sprinkle with cheese, and bake in a pre-heated oven at 350° for 30 minutes. To brown the cheese, boil for a minute after cooking. Serve with croutons.

CREAM OF POTATO SOUP

6 cups hash brown potatoes, frozen
½ cup carrots, sliced
6 slices bacon
1 cup celery, chopped
1 onion, chopped
1 teaspoon of each (salt and pepper)
2 cups each (light cream, half and half and milk)
Parsley sprigs
Cheddar cheese, shredded fine

Cook potatoes and carrots in water until tender; drain. Cook bacon until crisp; drain and crumble. Sauté onion and celery in 2 tablespoons bacon fat. Combine all remaining ingredients, except cheese and parsley, and simmer for 30 minutes. Don't boil. Garnish with the cheese and parsley.

POTATO AND HAM SOUP

3 pounds baking potatoes, cut in 1 inch cubes
1 thick slice of cooked ham, cut into small pieces
1 stick butter
1 cup half and half
½ cup sour cream

Place potatoes in a large pot, add water to cover potatoes. Cover and bring to a boil, then un-cover and cook over medium heat for 20 minutes. Reduce the heat and add the ham and butter. Season with salt and pepper to taste. Over low heat, add the half and half and sour cream; keep warm until serving.

CREAMY BROCCOLI SOUP

¼ cup onion, chopped
1 tablespoons butter or margarine
2 cups milk (I use half and half)
1 (8 oz.) package cream cheese, cubed
Dash of pepper
¾ pound of Velveeta cheese spread, cubed
1 (10 oz.) package frozen broccoli, drained and chopped
¼ teaspoon ground nutmeg

In a 3 quart saucepan, sauté onions in butter until tender. Add milk and cream cheese; stir over medium heat until cream cheese is melted. Add remaining ingredients; heat thoroughly, until all cheese is melted, stirring occasionally. Add additional milk if soup is too thick. Makes about 5 cups.

FRENCH ONION SOUP

2 large onions
1 tablespoon butter
1 teaspoon cornstarch
2 (10 ½ oz. each) cans beef broth
Salt and Pepper to taste
½ cup light cream
1 egg yolk, beaten
Worcestershire sauce
Swiss cheese, about 12 slices
French Bread, toasted

Peel and slice onions into rings. Sauté onions in butter until soft and golden. Stir in cornstarch. Add beef broth. Simmer about 10 minutes. Add cream and beaten yolk, stirring constantly. Add several shakes of Worcestershire sauce. Put a piece on bottom of serving bowl; ladle soup on top. Top with a piece of bread and a piece of cheese. Brown under broiler. Makes 6 servings.

TACO SOUP

In 2 tablespoons of oil, brown 1 pound of ground round beef until meat is done. Crumble with a fork in a saucepan. Put a 10 ounce can of French onion soup through the blender to puree and pour over beef. Add 1 tablespoon chili powder, 2 teaspoons cumin, a dash of Tabasco and black pepper, 21 ounces of red kidney beans, un-drained, 6 ounces of tomato paste, and 8 ounces of tomato sauce. Heat and stir until heated through.

SOUTHERN LIMA BEAN SOUP

2 (1 pound) bags lima beans, frozen
1 onion, chopped
1 carrot, chopped
½ cup heavy cream
1 medium potato, peeled and diced
2 teaspoons garlic, minced
½ cup country ham, baked and chopped
8 cups chicken broth
½ teaspoon each (salt and black pepper)
1 tablespoon fresh thyme

Combine all ingredients, except the cream, in a large stockpot. Cook over medium heat until vegetables are tender. Add cream, but don't boil. Add seasonings and serve.

JUDY'S CHICKEN NOODLE SOUP

1 (3-5 pounds) chicken, cooked, skin and fat removed
3 ½ quarts water
3 medium onion, sliced
3-4 celery stalks, cut into halves
2 teaspoons garlic, minced
2-3 bay leaves
1 ½ teaspoon salt
1/8 teaspoon pepper
Fresh parsley
5-8 ounce bag of egg noodles

Put the chicken in large pot with water over medium heat, next add the vegetables, parsley, bay leaves, garlic, salt and pepper. Bring to a boil; now reduce heat and simmer, half way covered for 1 ½ to 2 hours. Remove chicken and remove the meat from the bones, cut into bite size pieces. Remove the bay leaves. Remove the rest of the liquid from the pot and transfer them to a blender. Puree the liquid or stock, adding some of the liquid from the pot if it is too thick. Set aside. Bring remaining liquid or stock to a boil; now add the noodles and cook until tender. Reduce heat, add in the pureed vegetables and chicken. Now soup is ready to serve.

POTATO SHRIMP SOUP

1 pound shrimp
1 stick butter
2 carrot, diced
1 onion, diced
1 potato, diced
2 cups chicken broth
1 cup half and half
¼ cheddar cheese, shredded
4 slices bacon, fried crisp, crumbled
¼ cup flour
4 cups milk
½ teaspoon each (salt and pepper)

Cook carrots and onions. Add flower, milk, chicken broth, shrimp, half and half, salt and pepper. Cook until thick. Sprinkle cheese and bacon crumbs on top when ready to serve.

BROCCOLI AND CHEESE SOUP

2 ½ pounds broccoli, cut into 1 inch florets
1 cup green onion, chopped
4 tablespoons each (butter and flour)
4 cups chicken broth
1 cup each (light cream and Swiss cheese, shredded)
1/8 tablespoon nutmeg
Salt and pepper to taste

Cut enough florets to measure 2 cups. Cut the rest of the broccoli into 1 inch pieces. Cook florets and broccoli pieces separately in lightly salted water until tender (florets will be done first). Immediately rinse in cold water, drain. Set florets aside until serving time. In a large saucepan, sauté onion in butter until tender, usually about 4 minutes. Sprinkle in the flour and cook 1 more minute, stirring with a whisk. Remove from the heat and stir in broth and puree in blender in batches, until smooth. Just before serving, blend in cream and Swiss cheese. Simmer until cheese melts. Add nutmeg, salt and pepper. Add reserved florets and heat through.

LIME SOUP

3-3 ½ pounds of chicken
10 cups water
6 peppercorns
½ teaspoon each (coriander and thyme)
1 stalk celery
1 medium onion, quartered
2 teaspoons each (salt and pepper)
2 tablespoons vegetable oil
1 medium onion, chopped
1 medium green pepper, chopped
3 large tomatoes, chopped
Juice of 3-4 limes
3 tablespoons fresh parsley

Simmer chicken in an un-covered dutch oven in water, peppercorns, parsley, celery, onion, salt, pepper and thyme until chicken is tender; about 1 ½ hours. Remove chicken. Strain broth, cool chicken, remove from bones and cut into bite size pieces. Sauté chopped onion and green pepper in oil until tender, 3-4 minutes. Add tomatoes; cook 5 minutes. Add strained broth and lime juice. Simmer 20 minutes longer. Add chicken and heat thoroughly. Garnish with lime slices.

ITALIAN WEDDING SOUP

2 tablespoons olive oil
2-3 cloves fresh garlic
6-8 ounce cups of chicken broth
1 box frozen spinach or fresh, broken in 2 inch pieces
About 6 ounces cheese tortellini (frozen or fresh)
About 1 ¼ cups cooked chicken breast, sliced
2 teaspoons parsley, chopped
Parmesan cheese, grated
Salt and pepper to taste

Heat olive oil and garlic until lightly brown. Add chicken broth and garlic and bring to a boil; strain. Add spinach and cook for 10 minutes. Add tortellini and cook about 10-12 minutes. Add sliced chicken and heat thoroughly. Add parsley, salt and pepper in the last 2 minutes of cooking. Serve with Parmesan cheese.

CREAMY ASPARAGUS SOUP

1 small onion, chopped
1 tablespoon butter
2 stalks celery, chopped fine
1 cup asparagus spears, chopped (tips reserved)
1 green onion, white part only, chopped fine
2 cups chicken broth, divided
1 cup half and half
1 ½ teaspoons cornstarch
1 tablespoon water
¼ teaspoon each (salt and white pepper)

Melt butter in saucepan over low heat. Add onions, celery, green onion and asparagus. Cook 5 minutes, or until softened. Add 1 cup chicken broth; cover and simmer until asparagus is tender, about 10 minutes. Place vegetables and broth in a blender, working in batches, if necessary. Process until smooth. Return to saucepan. Add remaining broth and half and half. Cook over low heat. Dissolve cornstarch in water and whisk into soup. Continue stirring until soup thickens and comes to a boil. Add salt and white pepper. Reduce heat; add asparagus tips and cook 3 minutes.

GOOD CAULIFLOWER SOUP

1 medium cauliflower
2 chicken bouillon cubes
2 tablespoons each (butter and flour)
2/3 cup onion, chopped
2 cups half and half
½ teaspoon Worcestershire sauce
¾ teaspoon salt
1 cup each (cheddar cheese, grated and chicken broth)
Parsley, chopped

Chop cauliflower into small pieces and cook in 3 cups of boiling water about 15 minutes. Remove from heat and add bouillon cubes. Set aside. In a 3 quart saucepan, melt butter and add onion. Cook until soft. Blend in flour; add cauliflower and broth gradually, stirring constantly until mixture comes to a boil. Stir in half and half, Worcestershire sauce and salt. Heat to a boil and stir in cheese until melted. Garnish with parsley and serve.

CRAB AND CORN BISQUE

½ cup each (celery, onions, chopped and butter)
¼ cup green pepper, chopped
1 (10 ½ oz.) can cream of potato soup
1 (17 oz.) can cream-style corn
1 ½ cups each (milk and half and half)
2 bay leaves
1 teaspoon each (thyme, garlic powder and white pepper)
Dash of hot sauce
¼ teaspoon Old Bay seasoning
1 pound crabmeat
Parsley, chopped

Sauté celery, green onions and green pepper in butter, in dutch oven. Add soup, corn, half and half, milk, bay leaves, thyme, garlic powder, white pepper, hot sauce and seasoning; cook until thoroughly heated. Stir in crabmeat and heat thoroughly. Discard bay leaves and garnish with parsley.

LOBSTER BISQUE

1 (10 ¾ oz.) can tomato soup
1 (10 ¾ oz.) can green pea soup
2 tablespoons butter
1 cup lobster tail meat, cooked and diced
1/3 cup sherry or wine
1 soup can of hot milk
1 soup can of hot light cream
¼ teaspoon curry powder
½ teaspoon paprika
1 teaspoon accent

Pour sherry over lobster meat and let stand 1 hour in refrigerator. Drain off sherry and reserve. Sauté lobster meat and curry powder in butter. Blend soups with warmed milk, cream, paprika and accent; add lobster. Heat thoroughly. Just before serving add sherry, salt and pepper to taste.

FRANK'S SEAFOOD GUMBO

1 cup each (flour, bacon grease or margarine, onions and celery chopped)
½ green pepper, chopped fine
3 cups hot water
1 large can tomatoes, mashed
2 tablespoons catsup
3 bay leaves
3 tablespoons parsley, chopped
4 tablespoons Worcestershire sauce
8-10 drops Tabasco sauce
Salt and pepper to taste
2 cups okra, sliced or 1 box, frozen
3 pounds shrimp, raw and cleaned
1 pound dark crabmeat, claw
1 pint oysters

116

2 teaspoons gumbo file
Rice, cooked

First, make a dark roux by browning flour in bacon grease. Add the chopped vegetables and cook slowly for a few minutes. Then add water, tomatoes, catsup and seasoning. Cook slowly for about 1 hour. Add okra and cook until soft. Add the seafood and cook until the shrimp is done. At the last, add the gumbo file, and season to taste; 1 or more teaspoons of kitchen bouquet seasoning can be added to give it color. Don't cook after these are added. Serve over cooked rice in a large bowl.

ALL AMERICAN CLAM CHOWDER

7 ounces clams, canned
1 cup each (cream of celery soup and potatoes, cubed)
1 ½ cups milk
3 slices bacon, fried crisp
½ cup onion, chopped fine
1 can creamed corn
Salt and pepper to taste

Fry bacon until crisp, remove from heat and crumble. Brown onion in bacon grease. Add liquid from potatoes and clams. Cook over low heat until potatoes are done. Add bacon, clams and the remaining ingredients. Heat (don't boil). You can use some crumbles bacon for garnish if you like.

FAVORITE CORN CHOWDER

3 cups each (fresh or frozen white or yellow corn and chicken broth)
2 ½ cups half and half
2/3 cup flour, self-rising
2 sticks of butter or margarine
½ cup onion, chopped
½ cup carrots, chopped
1 celery stalk, chopped
1 teaspoon garlic, minced
½ teaspoon ground nutmeg
½ teaspoon each (salt and pepper)

Melt ½ of the butter in a skillet. Add onion, carrot, celery and garlic. Sauté for 2-3 minutes. Add flour and stir to make a roux. Cook until roux is browned. Set aside to cool at room temperature. Combine the corn and chicken broth in a saucepan and bring to a boil. Simmer for 10-12 minutes. Pour stock with corn into the skillet with the roux, whisk to prevent any lumps. Return skillet to heat and bring to a boil. This should be thick. In another saucepan, heat the half and half; stir it into the corn mixture. Add nutmeg, salt and pepper to taste. When ready to serve, cut the remaining stick of butter into large pieces. Add it to the soup, stirring it until the butter melts.

SIMPLE SEAFOOD CHOWDER

6 tablespoons each (flour and butter)
1 ½ cups milk
½ teaspoon pepper
7-8 drops of Worcestershire sauce
½ cup green onions, chopped
1 cup fresh mushrooms, sliced
3 to 3 ½ cups seafood, cooked (shrimp, scallops, crab and clams)
2/3 cup white wine

Melt butter in saucepan. Add flour and milk. Stir often to keep lumps from forming. Cook until liquid boils and becomes thickened. Add wine, Worcestershire sauce and pepper; simmer for 2-3 minutes. In another pan, sauté onions and mushrooms. Add to the liquid. Cook seafood until heated through.

OYSTER BISQUE

1 quart oysters
4 tablespoons each (flour, butter, onion and celery, chopped)
Oyster liquor
3 ½ cups warm milk
1 ½ cups warm chicken broth
2 ½ tablespoons parsley, chopped
1 teaspoon each (salt, pepper, accent and Worcestershire sauce)

Drain oysters. Keep liquor. Heat oysters in pot for 2 minutes or until edged curl. Remove oysters and liquor. Heat butter in pot. Sauté onion and celery until tender. Then add flour and cook 5 minutes, stirring constantly. Stir in stock, milk and oyster liquor. Cook on simmer for 10 minutes, stirring often. Add oysters and seasonings. Keep hot in top of double boiler for at least 1 hour before serving. Add parsley when ready to serve.

SOUTHERN CRAB BISQUE

1 can of cream of asparagus soup
1 can of cream of mushroom soup
½ cup half and half
¼ cup white wine
¾ pound crabmeat, remove shells if any

Combine all ingredients in a saucepan and bring to a boil. Reduce heat and simmer for about 5-7 minutes.

FRANK'S CLAM CHOWDER

1 can clams
1 quart half and half
2 ½ onions, small and chopped
2 celery stalks, chopped
5 bacon slices, fried crisp and crumbled
4-5 potatoes
1 ½ teaspoon each (salt, pepper, thyme and Old Bay seasoning)
Worcestershire sauce
White wine

Fry bacon and set aside. Sauté onions and celery in bacon drippings. Add potatoes and enough wine to cook potatoes until tender. About 10-12 minutes before ready to serve, add half and half and clams. Garnish with crumbled bacon.

EASY CHILI

2 pounds ground beef
1 large onion, chopped
1 medium can hot chili beans
1 medium can mild chili beans
1 medium can tomatoes, diced
1 large can tomato puree
1 large can chili mix with beans
¼ teaspoon chili powder
1 small handful spaghetti, broken up

Cook spaghetti in a large pan until tender; drain. Cook beef and onion in skillet until beef is done; drain. Add all ingredients together and cook on low heat for about 20 minutes. Stir if needed.

ONE POT BEEF STEW

2 pounds stew meat
Flour
2-3 tablespoons oil
2 medium onions, chopped
6-7 potatoes, chopped
4 carrots, chopped
2 (8 oz.) cans beef broth

Coat meat with flour. Brown meat in pot. Add onions and cook until tender. Add potatoes, carrots and beef broth. Cook over medium heat until meat is tender.

FRANK'S SEAFOOD CHOWDER

1 pound medium sized shrimp, peeled and de-veined
1 (8 oz.) package fresh lump crabmeat
1 (32 oz.) box chicken broth
¼ cup self-rising flour
6 slices of bacon, cut in small pieces
1 large onion, chopped
2 ½ cups milk or half and half
½ cup celery, chopped
2 large potatoes, peeled and diced
1 teaspoon dried thyme and fresh thyme leaves
½ teaspoon each (salt and pepper)

Cook bacon until crisp. Remove from pan, leaving grease in pan. Add onion and celery; cook 5-6 minutes or until tender. Add potatoes; cook 5 minutes, stirring frequently. Stir in flour, cook about 2 minutes, stirring constantly. Stir in broth, thyme, milk, salt and pepper; simmer and cook for 15 minutes or until potatoes are tender. Add shrimp and crab; cook 3-5 minutes. Use thyme leaves for garnish.

NO FAIL OYSTER STEW

2 cups each (milk and cream)
24 small oysters
4 tablespoons butter
Paprika
White pepper
Celery salt
Salt

Combine and scald milk and cream, but don't boil. Drain off almost all of the juice from the oysters, leaving about 2 tablespoons on oysters. Heat the drained-off oyster juice to the boiling point only in a separate pan. Add the butter to oysters (a few drops of Worcestershire sauce) and place over high heat just long enough for the oysters to fatten up and the edges begin to curl. Take oysters off stove, add both liquids, and stir in salt, celery, salt and pepper to taste. Serve immediately with oyster crackers.

IRISH STEW

2 pounds lamb shoulder, cubed
½ cup Wesson oil
3 tablespoons flour
3-4 cups chicken stock
2 tablespoons Worcestershire sauce
Salt and pepper to taste
1 cup each (chopped onions, sliced thick carrots, coarsely diced turnip roots)
1 cup each (diced raw potatoes, frozen English peas)
1 tablespoon parsley, chopped

Season lamb cubes with salt and pepper. Dredge lamb in flour. Sauté in Wesson oil until brown. Add chopped onions and sauté stirring until onions are tender. Add 3 cups of hot stock and Worcestershire. Cover and cook until meat is almost tender. Add carrots, turnip roots and potatoes. When vegetables are half cooked, add peas. Season to taste. Continue until vegetables are done.

GOOD SOUTHERN CRAB STEW

4 tablespoons flour
1 teaspoon salt
¼ teaspoon white pepper
1 quart milk
1 tablespoon each (butter, Worcestershire sauce, and lemon juice)
¼ cup of sherry
½ pound crabmeat
Dash of Tabasco sauce

Combine flour, salt and pepper. Add mixture to milk in saucepan. Add butter and stir until smooth. Cook over low heat until slightly thickened. Add remaining ingredients and serve at once.

LOUISIANA JAMBALAYA

½ pound fully cooked smoked sausage, halved and sliced
1 green pepper, chopped
1 large onion, chopped
2 celery ribs, chopped
¼ cup vegetable oil
2 cups ham, cooked and cubed
5-6 green onions, sliced thin
2 cloves of garlic, minced
1 (14 ½ oz.) can of tomatoes, diced and un-drained
½ teaspoon pepper
1 teaspoon each (dried thyme and salt)
2 pounds shrimp, cooked peeled and de-veined
4 ½ teaspoons Worcestershire sauce
2 (14 ½ oz.) cans chicken broth
1 cup long grain rice, un-cooked
1/3 cup water
¼ teaspoon cayenne pepper

Sauté sausage and ham in oil until slightly browned. Remove and keep warm. In the drippings, sauté the celery, onion, green pepper, green onions; cook 5 minutes longer. Stir in broth, rice, water and Worcestershire sauce. Bring to a boil. Reduce heat; cover and simmer for 20 minutes or until rice is tender. Stir in sausage mixture and shrimp; heat through. Serve immediately. Makes about 10-12 servings.

NEW ENGLAND CLAM CHOWDER

1 medium onion, chopped
¼ cup bacon, cooked crisp and cut up
2 (8 oz.) cans clams, minced and drained (reserve liquid)
1 cup of potato, chopped fine
½ teaspoon each (salt and pepper)
2 cups milk

Cook onion and bacon in saucepan until onion is tender and bacon is crisp. Add enough water to reserve liquid to make 1 cup. Stir clams, liquid, potato, salt and pepper into onion mixture. Bring to a boil; reduce heat; cover and simmer until potato is tender; stir in milk; heat thoroughly, stirring occasionally.

KENTUCKY STYLE BURGOO

3 pounds of round steak, cut into cubes
All-purpose flour
Salt and pepper
½ cup salad oil
1 large onion, chopped
2 cups water
1 (29 oz.) can tomato juice
1 large fryer chicken, cooked and cut into 1-inch pieces

Dredge steak in seasoned flower and brown in hot oil. Add onion and brown slightly. Add water and tomatoes; simmer mixture for 1 hour, covered. Add chicken pieces and the following ingredients:

1 bay leaf
2 tablespoons Worcestershire sauce
2 tablespoons vinegar
1 tablespoon hot pepper sauce
¼ teaspoon cayenne pepper
½ teaspoon black pepper
5 teaspoons seasoned salt
1 (29 oz.) can tomatoes and juice

Combine ingredients; simmer with chicken and steak mixture for 1 hour, stirring occasionally. Then add the following:

2 pounds potatoes, peeled and cut into pieces
6 carrots, scraped and cut into pieces
¼ head cabbage
12 small onions, diced
1 cup fresh corn

Simmer entire mixture for 1 hour longer and serve. Makes about 12 servings.

CHILI LIKE WENDY'S

Brown 1-2 pound of ground round beef in 2 tablespoons oil. Cool until done. Put 10-ounce can of French onion soup through the blender to puree and pour over beef. Stir in consistency of rice. Add 1 tablespoon chili powder, 2 teaspoons cumin, dash of Tabasco, dash of black pepper, 21- ounce can of red kidney beans, un-drained, 6-ounce can of tomato paste, 8-ounce can tomato sauce. Heat and stir until heated through.

LOUISVILLE HOT BROWN

8 slices toast, trimmed
8 slices of chicken or turkey breast, cooked
¼ cup Parmesan cheese
Bacon, fried crisp and crumbled
Mushrooms, sliced and sautéed
4 tablespoons butter
1 small onion, chopped
3 tablespoons flour
2 cups milk
½ teaspoon salt
¼ teaspoon white pepper
¼ cup cheddar cheese, shredded

Sauté onion in butter until transparent, add flour and combine. Add milk, salt and pepper and whisk until smooth. Cook on medium heat until sauce thickens, stirring occasionally. Add cheese and continue heating until they blend. Remove from heat. Put 1 slice of toast and turkey in each of 4 oven-proof individual serving dishes. Cut remaining toast slices diagonally and place on sides of sandwiches. Ladle cheese sauce over sandwiches. Place sandwiches under broiler until sauce begins to bubble. Garnish with crumbled bacon and sautéed mushroom slices and serve immediately.

SHRIMP TOSTADAS

8 corn tostada shells
1 (8 oz.) can tomato sauce
1 pound shrimp, frozen, thawed, cooked and tails removed
½ (1 ¼ oz.) package taco seasoning mix
Toppings of choice (listed below)

Heat tostada shells until crisp; set aside. Heat tomato sauce in large skillet, add cooked shrimp and taco seasoning mix. Bring to a boil; reduce heat. Simmer un-covered for 2-3 minutes or until shrimp are heated through, stirring occasionally. When ready to serve; spoon shrimp mixture unto warm tostada shells and top with shredded lettuce, shredded cheese, sour cream and sliced green onions, chopped tomato, avocado and or salsa, if desired.

CHICKEN – APPLE – SALAD WRAP

1 ½ cups rotisserie chicken
1 large tart apple, cored and chopped
1/3 cup drained cranberries
1 stalk celery, chopped
1 green pepper, sliced
1/3 cup each (mayonnaise and sour cream)
1 tablespoon lemon juice
1/8 teaspoon each (cinnamon, salt and pepper)
4 multi-grain tortillas or whole wheat pita bread rounds

Place chicken in bowl, add cranberries, apple, celery and green onion; set aside. In a small bowl stir together the mayonnaise, sour cream, lemon juice, salt, cinnamon and pepper. Add to chicken mixture, stir to coat. Spoon chicken mixture onto tortillas or pita bread rounds and roll or fold up.

HOT POCKETS

1 pound hamburger
1 small onion, chopped
2 packages Hungry Jack refrigerated biscuits
Franks hot sauce
Sharp cheddar cheese, shredded
Salt and pepper to taste

Preheat oven to 350°. In a frying pan, brown hamburger and onions. Drain grease. Add salt and pepper. Sprinkle mixture with hot sauce to taste. Open biscuits using 2 for each sandwich. Flatten 1 biscuit and spoon the hamburger mixture on it. Add cheese. Take the other biscuit and flatten for the top. Seal the edges and set on an un-greased cookie sheet. Repeat for the rest of the biscuits. Bake for 15-20 minutes. Remove when brown.

EGG AND AVOCADO SANDWICH

1 egg for each person, break the yolk and cook done
2-3 strips bacon for each sandwich, fried crisp
1 teaspoon green onion, chopped
4 ounces cream cheese, softened
1 teaspoon each (fresh parsley, salt and pepper)
Fresh tomatoes
2-3 avocados
Bread for sandwiches, toasted
Butter for bread

Mix cream cheese, onion, parsley, salt and pepper together. Butter toast on 1 side, but toast on both sides. Spread cream cheese mixture on both sides of toast. Next, layer the tomato, sliced avocado, 2 strips of bacon and fried egg.

A B C SANDWICH

½ granny smith apple, cored and sliced
5 slices bacon, fried crisp
½ cup cheddar cheese, shredded
1 tablespoon mustard
2 slices multi-grained bread

In a medium skillet, cook the bacon until crisp, drain on paper towels. Spread the bread with mustard, and then cover 1 slice with cheddar cheese and bacon. Top with the apple slices and the other bread slice. Spread diagonally.

SOUTHERN FRIED BEAN SANDWICH

2 cups dried beans (pinto or navy beans) cooked with ham
1 sweet onion
Cooking oil for frying
Flour
Bread for sandwiches, your choice
Mayonnaise

Mash cooked beans with some ham, add enough to bind together. Make small patties and fry in skillet until brown on both sides. Spread mayo on slices of bread, add slice of onion. Enjoy.

CRAB SALAD SANDWICH

2 hot dog rolls
1 (8 oz.) carton lump crabmeat, picked clean
2 tablespoons mayonnaise
2 stalks celery, chopped fine
½ red bell pepper, chopped fine
1 teaspoon celery seed
2 tablespoons dried minced onion
Seasoning salt and pepper to taste
1 tomato, sliced
4 tablespoons butter

Butter the rolls and fry butter side down. Remove from heat when golden. In a small bowl, use a fork to mix the crabmeat, melted butter, mayo, celery, pepper, celery seed, onion, salt and pepper. Line the hot dog rolls with tomato slices, then spoon crab salad over top. Good served with onion rings.

SHRIMP SALAD SANDWICH

1 pound shrimp, cooked, peeled, de-veined
3 eggs, hard boiled, chopped
1 teaspoon onion powder
1 ½ ribs celery, chopped
1 teaspoon each (salt and pepper)
Mayonnaise enough to spread on the bread, lettuce and tomato

Place shrimp in the food processor, chop coarsely. Put in bowl. Add eggs, celery, shrimp, onion powder, salt and pepper and enough mayonnaise to get the right consistency for spreading. Place on white toast with lettuce and tomato. Enjoy.

TUNA PATTY MELT

1 (6 oz.) can tuna, drained
1 egg, hard boiled, chopped
1 teaspoon each (vegetable oil and prepared mustard)
¼ cup bread crumbs
2 sandwich rolls, split
½ small onion, sliced

In a bowl, combine all ingredients except rolls and oil. Shape into 4 patties (mixture will be soft). In skillet over medium heat, fry patties in hot oil, on both sides, until lightly browned. Place 2 patties on each roll.

BENEDICTINE SANDWICH

1 (8 oz.) package cream cheese
¼ cup (cucumber, onion, chopped and mayonnaise)
¼ teaspoon salt
Few drops of green food coloring
Bread of choice

Soften cream cheese with cucumber and onion. Fold in mayonnaise, salt and a few drops of food coloring (gives a nice green shade to cheese). Spread on thin slices of bread.

GRILLED TOMATO AND CHEESE SANDWICH

8 slices of bread
4 slices of cheddar cheese
8 slices of tomato
Salt and pepper
Butter or margarine

Place a slice of cheese and 2 slices of tomato on 4 slices of bread. Dust lightly with salt and pepper, top with another piece of bread and spread both sides with butter. Grill on griddle or frying pan until both sides are light brown and the cheese is melted.

FRIED BANANA AND PEANUT BUTTER SANDWICH

3 tablespoons honey or maple syrup
1 banana
Crunchy peanut butter
White bread

Mix peanut butter with honey. Spread on both slices of bread. Slice banana lengthwise. Put butter on top of both sides of bread and grill in skillet. Brown on both sides. Cut sandwich diagonally and serve.

PARTY SANDWICH

1 red onion, grated
1 green pepper, chopped fine
1 ½ pounds of bacon, fried crispy and crumbles
½ cup mayonnaise

Combine all ingredients thoroughly. Serve on bread rounds or party rye slices.

SMOKED B L T SANDWICH

6-7 slices bacon, fried crisp
¼ cup mayonnaise
Juice of ½ a lemon
1 tablespoon lemon zest
2 tomatoes, sliced thin
2 slices smoked salmon, sliced thin
Fresh dill (optional)
Sandwich bread of choice (we like the dark wheat bread)
Leaf of lettuce

Cook bacon crisp, drain and set aside. Mix the mayonnaise, lemon zest and lemon juice and dill together; mix well. Spread mixture on both sides of the bread. Add slice of smoked salmon, 2 slices of tomato cut in half, 2-3 slices of bacon and lettuce. Cut sandwich in half and serve.

HAM AND CHEESE SANDWICH

2 packages tea rolls
8 slices of ham
1 package of Swiss cheese, shredded
1 stick butter
1 ½ teaspoon poppy seed
1 ½ teaspoon prepared mustard
½ teaspoon Worcestershire sauce
1 tablespoon onion flakes

Don't break tolls apart. Slice lengthwise through the center. Layer ham and cheese between layers. Mix remaining ingredients and pour over rolls, leave un-covered until butter melts. Cover and bake at 350o for 15 minutes.

MONTE CRISTO SANDWICH

8 slices of bread
12 slices of Swiss cheese
Sliced chicken or turkey
Sliced ham
3 eggs, beaten
1/3 cup milk
Salt and pepper to taste

Place ham, chicken or turkey slices of cheese onto bread. Top with second piece of bread and press lightly. Cut into halves, diagonally, and secure with a toothpick. In a bowl, combine eggs and milk, add salt and pepper. Dip sandwich halves into the egg mixture. In a well-seasoned cast-iron skillet or griddle, heat about 1 tablespoon of butter. Spread on both sides of sandwich halves, adding more butter if necessary. Remove toothpicks before serving.

REUBEN SANDWICH

1 (1 pound) loaf of pumpernickel bread
8 slices corned beef
8 slices of Swiss cheese
8 slices turkey breast
1 cup sauerkraut, drained
1 (8 oz.) bottle thousand island dressing

Butter both sides of the bread, place buttered side down in skillet, layer the corned beef, sauerkraut, cheese, turkey and drizzle thousand island dressing on top of the turkey. Place second slice of buttered bread on top, butter side out. Toast and brown on both sides.

EGG SALAD AND BACON SANDWICH

6 eggs, hard boiled
¼ cup mayonnaise
6 slices of bacon, fried crisp and crumbled
2 green onions and tops, chopped
Lettuce, shredded
Tomatoes, sliced
Wheat bread

Mix eggs with mayonnaise, salt, bacon and onion. Refrigerate for several hours; serve on wheat bread with lettuce and tomato.

TURKEY AND BACON CLUB

4 slices of bread, whole wheat
12 slices of Deli fresh roasted turkey breast
6 slices of center cut bacon, cooked crisp
2 lettuce leaves
2 tablespoons olive oil or mayonnaise
2 large tomatoes, sliced
¼ cup cucumbers, sliced

Toast bread with olive oil or mayonnaise; fill with remaining ingredients.

CHICKEN OR PORK CHOP PACKET

1 small chicken breasts, skinless, boneless, halved or 1 pork chop
1 pineapple ring
1 green pepper ring
1 tablespoon barbecue sauce or steak sauce
1 pat butter

Place chicken or pork chop in center of a large sheet of heavy-duty foil; top with remaining ingredients as listed. Bring foil sides up. Double fold top and ends to seal packet, leaving room for air to circulate inside. Place on grill to medium heat for 15 minutes or until chicken or chop is done. Cut slits to release steam before opening.

GOOD MOZZARELLA SANDWICH

½ pound mozzarella cheese, sliced
2 medium tomatoes, sliced
4 slices of sweet onion, sliced thin
8 fresh basil leaves
8 slices sourdough bread, toasted
¼ cup mayonnaise

Spread toasted bread with mayonnaise on all 4 slices. Layer the cheese, tomato, onion and basil; top with remaining toast.

SALADS

BROCCOLI SLAW

1 package broccoli slaw
1 package cole slaw
½ cup each (sunflower seeds and sliced almonds)
3 green onions, chopped
1 cup oil
4 tablespoons sugar
1 tablespoon black pepper
1 tablespoon salt
6 tablespoons rice vinegar
2 packages Ramen noodles, broken into pieces

Mix cole slaw, broccoli slaw and green peppers in a large bowl.
Combine oil, sugar, vinegar, salt and pepper in a large jar or container.
Shake until blended and pour over slaw. Mix Ramen noodles, sliced
almonds and sunflower seeds together with slaw mixture and chill.

GOOD CRACKER SLAW

1 medium head of cabbage, grated
1 medium onion, chopped fine
1 cup sharp cheddar cheese, grated
4 tablespoons mustard
2 cups mayonnaise
2 tablespoons pickle relish
2/3 cup celery, chopped
2/3 cup bell pepper, chopped
2 packages Ritz crackers, crushed
Salt and pepper to taste

Chop cabbage, onion, celery and bell pepper. Crush crackers. Mix all
ingredients together except the cheese. Place grated cheese on top of
slaw.

TROPICAL SLAW

1 (20 oz.) can pineapple tidbits
1 (8 oz.) carton pineapple yogurt
1 (11 oz.) can mandarin oranges, drained
3 cups cabbage, shredded
1 tablespoon lemon juice
1 medium banana, sliced
1 cup miniature marshmallows
1 cup raisins
1 cup walnuts, chopped
1 cup flaked coconut
¼ teaspoon salt

Drain the pineapple, keep 2 tablespoons of the juice; set aside. Stir lemon juice and banana into reserved juice. In a large salad bowl, combine the cabbage, oranges, marshmallows, coconut, walnuts, raisins, salt, pineapple and banana mixture. Add yogurt; toss to coat. Cover and refrigerate until serving.

ORIENTAL SLAW

2 packages Ramen noodles (oriental-flavored)
1 cup almonds, sliced and toasted
1 cup dry-roasted sunflower seeds
1 bunch green onions, sliced
1 package broccoli slaw
¾ cup vegetable oil
½ cup sugar
1/3 cup apple cider vinegar

Crumble noodles in bowl and keep the flavor packets for the dressing. Add almonds and sunflower seeds, onions, broccoli slaw. In a jar, combine the flavor packets, oil, sugar and vinegar. Whisk until everything is dissolved then pour over salad mixture before serving.

FRANK'S FAVORITE COLE SLAW

1 package slaw mix
1 green pepper, chopped
1 medium onion, chopped
½ cup seedless raisins
½ teaspoon salt

DRESSING:
¼ cup red wine vinegar
¼ cup sugar
½ cup milk
½ cup mayonnaise

Mix all slaw ingredients together. Mix the dressing ingredients and pour over slaw. Stir until thoroughly mixed. It's better if it sets for several hours (overnight) before serving. You might have to drain some of the liquid off before serving.

SWEET AND SOUR SLAW

1 large head of cabbage, shredded or 1 large bag shredded
3 stalks celery, chopped
1 bell pepper, chopped
1 (4 oz.) jar pimentos, chopped
1 large red onion, chopped
½ cup each (red wine vinegar and white vinegar)
¾ cup sugar
1 ½ teaspoons salt
Ground black pepper
¾ cup vegetable oil

Layer cabbage, celery, bell pepper, pimento and onion in a bowl. Boil vinegar, sugar and salt for 2 minutes. Remove from heat; add vegetable oil and black pepper, bring to a boil. Pour over vegetables while hot. Cover tightly. Refrigerate before serving.

YVONNE'S DELICIOUS SHRIMP SALAD

1/4 cup of olive oil
Juice of 4 limes
Juice of 1 lemon
1/4 cup onion, chopped, soaked in ice water for a little while in the
refrigerator
2 mangos, sliced
6 avocados, sliced
2 jalapeno peppers, seeded
2/3 bunch cilantro
2 teaspoons kosher salt
1 teaspoon ground pepper
1 pound shrimp, boiled and peeled
1/2 red onion julienne

Place sliced avocado in bowl. Put 1/2 of the lime juice over avocado. Fold together carefully, keeping the avocado together. Add soaked and drained onion. Add mangos, peppers, olive oil, kosher salt, cilantro, jalapeno peppers and shrimp. Mix carefully. Add a little more olive oil, add a little more kosher salt. Salad is better at room temperature. Serve over a bed of lettuce with some good crispy bread.

MANGO AND SHRIMP SALAD

2 firm ripe mangoes, pitted, peeled and diced
16 jumbo shrimp, shelled and de-veined
2 tablespoons salad oil
1 tablespoon jalapeno chilies, minced
2 teaspoon cumin
1/2 teaspoon salt
2 tablespoons dark brown sugar
2 tablespoons fresh lime juice
1/8 teaspoon red chili powder
4-5 green onions, sliced thin
1/4 cup fresh cilantro
2 tablespoons fresh mint, chopped
Lime wedges

Cook shrimp for about 3-4 minutes. Add all other ingredients together, add shrimp and toss.

GOOD CRAB SALAD

1 pound lump crabmeat
1/4 cup sour cream
1/4 cup mayonnaise
4 cups lettuce, shredded
2 eggs, hard boiled, chopped
1/2 cup celery, minced
1/4 cup green onion, minced
1/2 teaspoon dry mustard
1 teaspoon Worcestershire sauce
2 tomatoes, cut into wedges
1 small jar pimentos, diced
1 teaspoon fresh parsley, chopped
1 teaspoon fresh chives, chopped
2 tablespoons old Bay Seasoning
1/2 teaspoon salt

Set crabmeat aside. Soak lettuce in cold water; set aside. Add celery, green onions and eggs to crabmeat; set side. In a small bowl, mix mayonnaise, sour cream, dry mustard, Worcestershire sauce, pimento, parsley, chives, salt and old Bay Seasoning until well mixed. Drain lettuce. Mix mayonnaise mixture and crab mixture together. Chill crab salad and lettuce (separately) for 1 hour. When ready to serve, place lettuce on 4 plates and top with 1/4 of crab salad. Place tomato wedges around plate.

CRAB LOUIES

1 1/2 pound crabmeat
1/3 cup heavy cream
1 cup mayonnaise
1 avocado, sliced
4 tomatoes, cut into wedges
6 eggs, hard boiled
4 tablespoons chili sauce
1 teaspoon Worcestershire sauce
1 teaspoon parsley, chopped
1 small onion, chopped
3 stuffed olives, chopped
1 green pepper, chopped
1/2 teaspoon each (salt and pepper)

Place and arrange crab, tomato wedges, avocado slices and egg slices in a bed of lettuce. Mix remaining ingredients; pour over salad and serve cold.

SOUTHERN SEAFOOD SALAD

1 pound medium shrimp, cooked, peeled and de-veined
3 cups crabmeat, cooked or canned, drained and cartilage removed
1 small onion, chopped
1 rib celery, sliced thin
1/2 cup mayonnaise
1/8 teaspoon each (salt and pepper)
1/2 teaspoon seafood seasoning
1 teaspoon lemon juice
1 egg, hard boiled and sliced
Leaf lettuce

Combine shrimp, crab, onion and celery together. In another bowl; combine mayonnaise, seafood seasoning, lemon juice, salt and pepper; add to shrimp mixture and mix gently. Cover and refrigerate for at least 1 hour. Serve in a lettuce lined bowl and garnish with the egg.

AVOCADO CRAB SALAD

1 head of lettuce
2 avocados
2 apples
1/2 teaspoon lemon juice
1 teaspoon catsup
1/3 cup mayonnaise
1/2 pound crabmeat
Dash paprika

Separate the leaves of the lettuce; wash and drain. Peel avocado and cut into small chunks. Cut the crabmeat into chunks. Peel and dice apples. Mix mayonnaise, catsup, paprika and lemon juice. Add dressing to salad. Place on lettuce leaves and serve.

STUFFED TOMATOES WITH CRAB

1 pound crabmeat
1/2 cup celery, chopped
4 tomatoes (can use avocado halves in place of tomatoes)
2 tablespoons basil, chopped
1/2 cup mayonnaise
2 tablespoons onion, chopped
Juice of 1/2 lemon
Lettuce
Lemon slices for garnish

Combine all ingredients, except tomatoes, lettuce and lemon. Core out tomatoes. Spoon the crabmeat mixture into each tomato. Serve on lettuce leaf. Garnish with lemon slices.

APPLE AND TUNA SALAD

1 medium to large apple, peeled and cubed
1 (3 1/2 oz) can tuna, washed and drained
1/4 cup dry roasted peanuts
2 medium stalks celery, sliced
1 tablespoon mayonnaise

Mix all ingredients well and serve cold on lettuce leaves.

CRAB AND AVOCADO SALAD

1/2 pound lump crab
1 teaspoon Dijon mustard
1 avocado, diced
2 tablespoons lemon juice
2 tablespoons chives
Salt and pepper to taste

Mix salad ingredients together, except crab and chives. Take an empty tin can or any fancy glass and fill it with avocado mixture. Place crab on top, chives on top of crab. Chill. The can or glass makes the mold.

PEACH TOSS SALAD

8 cups fresh spinach, torn into pieces
8 cups Bib or Boston lettuce, torn into pieces
4 medium fresh peaches
4 bacon strips, cooked crisp and crumbled
1/2 - 3/4 cup vegetable oil
1/4 teaspoon pepper
1/2 teaspoon salt
2 tablespoons cider vinegar
2 tablespoons yogurt, plain
1/4 cup orange juice
1 tablespoon grated orange peel
2 teaspoons sugar
1/2 teaspoon garlic powder

In a blender, combine the orange juice, vinegar, yogurt, grated orange, sugar, garlic, salt and pepper. While processing, add oil. Process until sugar is dissolved. In a salad bowl, combine the spinach, lettuce, peaches and bacon. Drizzle with dressing; toss to coat.

FRUIT SALAD WITH DRESSING

2 grapefruits, peeled and sectioned
1 envelope gelatin
20 marshmallows, chopped
2 oranges, peeled and sectioned
1/2 pound almonds, blanched

DRESSING

4 egg yolks
4 teaspoon sugar
1 teaspoon mustard
2 tablespoon vinegar
2 tablespoons water
1 pint whipping cream
Juice of 1 lemon

Mix the fruit all together in a bowl. Mix all the dressing and pour over fruit.

ORANGE AND PRETZEL SALAD

2 cups pretzels, crushed
1 (8 oz) package cream cheese, softened
1 (11 oz) can mandarin oranges, drained
2 cups boiling water
2 (8 oz) cans crushed pineapple, drained
1/4 cup butter, melted
3/4 cup sugar, plus 3 teaspoons, divided
2 cups whipped topping
2 (3 oz) boxes orange jell-o
Some additional whipped topping

Combine pretzels and 3 teaspoons sugar; stir in butter. Press into an un-greased 13 x 9 inch baking dish. Bake at 350° for 10 minutes; cool. In a large bowl, dissolve jell-o in boiling water. Add pineapple and oranges. Chill until slightly set. In a small bowl, beat cream cheese and remaining sugar until smooth. Fold in whipped topping. Spread over crust. Spoon jell-o mixture over cream cheese layer. Refrigerate for 2-4 hours or until firm. Cut into squares. Garnish with additional whipped topping.

EASY LIME SALAD

2 (3 oz) packages of lime jell-o
1 cup hot water
1 cup marshmallows
1 cup cottage cheese
1 cup whipping cream
1 cup pecans
1 cup pineapple, crushed
1/8 cup sugar
Pinch of salt
Juice of 1 lemon

Dissolve jell-o in hot water. Add marshmallows, lemon juice, salt and sugar and set in refrigerator until it begins to jell. After mixture has jelled enough to hold the other ingredients, add the pineapple, cottage cheese and pecans. Whip the cream and fold into the mixture. Place in refrigerator to finish setting.

DORIS'S FRUIT SALAD

1 large can peaches, drained and sliced
1 cup miniature marshmallows
1 tablespoon lemon juice
1/3 cup whipping cream, whipped
1/2 cup pecans, chopped
1/2 cup maraschino cherries, halved
1 large banana, sliced
1/3 cup mayonnaise

Mix fruit and nuts. Make a dressing of whipped cream, mayonnaise and lemon juice. Fold gently into fruit and chill.

APRICOT SALAD

1 (13 oz) can evaporated milk, chilled
1/2 cup sugar
1 # 2 can pineapple, crushed
1 cup nuts, chopped
1 cup celery, diced
2 (3 oz) boxes apricot gelatin
1 large package cream cheese, crumbled

Combine pineapple and sugar in saucepan; bring to a boil. Add gelatin, mixing well; cool and congeal slightly. Add cream cheese; beat with electric mixer until well blended. Add celery and nuts. Whip milk; fold into gelatin mixture. Pour into a 13 x 9 inch baking dish; refrigerate.

PARTY CHAMPAGNE SALAD

1 (10 oz) package strawberries, frozen
2 bananas, mashed
1 cup nuts, chopped
1 large container cool whip
3/4 cup sugar
1 (8 oz) package cream cheese
1 large can pineapple; crushed and drained

Cream sugar and cream cheese together. Mix the rest of the ingredients together and freeze.

24 HOUR SALAD

1 can fruit cocktail
1 can mandarin oranges
1 can coconut, grated
1/4 cup orange juice
1 carton sour cream
2 cups miniature marshmallows
3 teaspoons sugar
1 can pineapple, chunks

Drain all fruit. Mix and fold in sour cream. Refrigerate for 24 hours.

MARSHMALLOW AND CREAM CHEESE SALAD

1 (8 oz) package cream cheese, softened
1 (3 oz) package orange jell-o gelatin
1 1/2 cups miniature colored marshmallows, divided
1 (15 oz) can mandarin oranges, drained
1 cup whipping cream, whipped
Maraschino cherries

Beat cream cheese and gelatin powder. Stir in water until gelatin is dissolved. Refrigerate for 1 hour or until thickened, stirring often. Set aside 10-12 orange slices for garnish. Fold whipped cream, 3/4 cup marshmallows and remaining oranges into gelatin mixture. Transfer to a 2 1/2 quart serving bowl or dish. Sprinkle with the remaining marshmallows. Chill until firm. Garnish with reserved orange slices and a maraschino cherry.

SUNSHINE GELATIN MOLD

1 (3 oz) box lemon jell-o gelatin
1 (11 oz) can mandarin oranges, drained
1 cup boiling water
1 quart vanilla ice cream, softened
1 (8 oz) can un-sweetened crushed pineapple, drained

Dissolve gelatin in boiling water. Whisk in ice cream until melted. Stir in oranges and pineapple. Pour into a 6 cup ring mold coated with cooking spray. Refrigerate for 2 hours or until completely firm. Un-mold onto a serving plate.

HOLIDAY APPLE SALAD

1 (20 oz) can crushed pineapple, drained
1/2 cup halved maraschino cherries
1 cup nuts, chopped
1/2 stick butter
1 cup heavy cream
1/3 cup flour
3/4 cup sugar
3-4 large red apples, diced

Stir together the sugar and flour. Whisk in the cream. Pour the cream mixture into a heavy saucepan. Continue mixing, add the pineapple, and cook over medium heat; stirring constantly, until mixture thickens. Add butter; remove pan from heat and let the mixture cool. When cooled, add apples, nuts and cherries and mix well. Refrigerate.

GOOD APPLE SALAD

4 granny smith apples, cut into bite sizes
6 snicker candy bars, cut into bite sizes
1 cup milk
1 small package vanilla pudding mix
1 (12 oz) container of whipped topping

Mix together; milk and pudding mix in a bowl and beat until thickened. Fold in whipped topping, snickers and apples. Refrigerate until time to serve.

LIME AND PEAR SALAD

1 large package lime gelatin
1 cup each (pear juice, cold water, and heavy cream)
1 large package cream cheese
1 medium can pears

Heat cold water and pear juice with gelatin; cook and partially congeal. Whip cream; fold in cream cheese. Mash pears; add to cooled mixture. Fold all ingredients together.

STRAWBERRY AND BANANA SALAD

1 (6 oz) box strawberry jell-o gelatin
1 cup boiling water
1 (10 oz) packages frozen sweetened strawberries, sliced and partially thawed
1/2 - 3/4 cup walnuts, chopped
1 (16 oz) carton sour cream
2 teaspoon sugar
1/2 teaspoon vanilla extract
1 (20 oz) can crushed pineapple, un-drained
3 medium bananas, mashed

Dissolve gelatin in water. Stir strawberries, pineapple, bananas and nuts. Pour half of the mixture into a 13 x 9 inch dish. Refrigerate for approximately 1 hour or until set good. Put the remaining gelatin mixture aside. Combine the sour cream, sugar and vanilla; mix well. Spread over chilled gelatin. Spoon remaining gelatin mixture over the top. Chill at least overnight.

STRAWBERRY AND CRANBERRY SALAD

1 large box strawberry jell-o gelatin
1 can cranberry sauce
1 small can crushed pineapple
1 (8 oz) carton cool whip
1 (8 oz) package cream cheese
1 1/2 cups boiling water
Pecans

Mix together strawberry jell-o and 1 1/2 cups boiling water. Mix jell-o, cranberry sauce and crushed pineapple; chill. Mix the cool whip and cream cheese for topping, add pecans on top.

SIMPLE BUT GOOD ORANGE SALAD

1 can mandarin oranges
1 large can pineapple, drained
1 (8 oz) carton sour cream
3 ounces orange gelatin
1 package miniature marshmallows

Combine all ingredients together and chill. Enjoy.

DELICIOUS GRAPE SALAD

1 3/4 pounds white grapes, seedless, cut in half
1 3/4 pounds red grapes, seedless, cut in half
1 (8 oz) package cream cheese, softened
1 (8 oz) carton sour cream
1/2 cup white sugar
1 teaspoon vanilla extract

TOPPING

1/2 cup brown sugar
1/2 cup pecans, chopped
1 (8 oz) package Heath English Toffee bits

For the GRAPES; beat together with an electric mixer the cream cheese, sour cream, sugar and vanilla. Lightly fold in the grapes and pour into a 2 quart bowl. TOPPING; combine the brown sugar, pecans, and heath bits in another bowl. Sprinkle the mixture thickly over the top of the grape mixture. Refrigerate until completely chilled before serving.

EASY GRAPE SALAD

1 (8 oz) package cream cheese, softened
1 (8 oz) carton sour cream
1/3 cup sugar
3 tablespoons pecans, chopped
3 tablespoons brown sugar
2 teaspoons vanilla extract
1 3/4 pounds green grapes, seedless, cut in half
1 3/4 pounds red grapes, seedless, cut in half

In a mixing bowl, beat the cream cheese, sour cream, sugar and vanilla until blended. Add grapes and toss to coat. Transfer to a serving bowl. Cover and refrigerate until ready to serve. Sprinkle with brown sugar and pecans just before serving.

DELICIOUS APPLE SALAD

2 1/2 tablespoons wine vinegar
3-4 bunches of endive lettuce, cored and leaves separated
1 bag spinach
1 tart cooking apple, sliced
4-5 ounces of feta cheese
1/2 teaspoon Dijon mustard
1 teaspoon each (salt and pepper)
1/3 - 1/2 cup olive oil
1 1/2 tablespoons parsley, chopped
1/4 cups, chopped (walnuts, pecans or sliced almonds)

Combine vinegar, garlic, salt, pepper and mustard, blend well. Then add the parsley and oil. Place endive leaves on plates; placing the spinach in the center. Cut cheese into 4-5 slices and top each apple with a slice of cheese. Place apple slices and cheese on top of the lettuce. Broil in broiler for 3-5 minutes or until golden brown. Drizzle the dressing over salads then sprinkle with nuts. Now it's ready to serve.

WALDORF SALAD

3 medium apples
1 cup celery
1/2 cup walnuts, chopped
1/2 cup mayonnaise
1 tablespoon each (sugar and lemon juice)
1/8 teaspoon salt

Combine mayonnaise, lemon juice, sugar and salt in a bowl; mix well. Add apples, celery and walnuts, mix well. Cover and chill until ready to serve.

PINEAPPLE AND CHEESE SALAD

1 (3 oz) box strawberry gelatin
1 (16 oz) carton cottage cheese
1 (8 oz) can crushed pineapple, un-drained
1 cup each (whipped cream and chopped nuts)

Boil pineapple and gelatin until gelatin is dissolved good. Add cottage cheese, nuts and whipped cream. Chill until firm.

COMPANY APPLE SALAD

8 cups tart apples, chopped
2 cups green grapes
2 teaspoons poppy seeds
3/4 cup pecans, toasted and chopped
1 cup mayonnaise
2 tablespoons cold water
2 tablespoons cornstarch
1 tablespoon lemon juice
1 (20 oz) can un-sweetened pineapple chunks
1/4 cup sugar
1 cup butter or margarine

Drain pineapple, reserve juice; set aside. Place juice in a saucepan; add butter, sugar and lemon juice, bring to a boil. Combine cornstarch and cold water until smooth; add to the saucepan, stirring constantly. Return to a boil, cook and stir for 2 minutes; chill. Sir in mayonnaise. In a large bowl, combine pineapple, apples, grapes, poppy seeds and cooked dressing. Fold in the pecans just before ready to serve.

TAFFY APPLE SALAD

2-3 un-peeled apples, coarsely chopped (red or yellow)
1 cup Spanish peanuts, chopped
1 (8 oz) carton whipping cream
1 1/2 tablespoons white vinegar
4 cups miniature marshmallows
1 egg, beaten
1 tablespoon flour
1 (16 oz) can pineapple, crushed
1/2 cup sugar

Drain pineapple, save juice. Combine pineapple and marshmallows in a bowl; set aside. Combine the reserved juice with the flour, sugar, egg and vinegar in a saucepan; mix well. Cook until thickened, stirring constantly. Cool to room temperature. Fold in whipped cream, marshmallow mixture, apples and peanuts. Chill for several hours before serving.

PEAR SALAD

1 (29 oz) can pear halves, drained
1 (29 oz) can sliced peaches, drained
1 (14 oz) can pineapple chunks, drained
1/3 cup raisins
1/3 cup dried cranberries
3/4 cup sugar, divided
12 maraschino cherries
6 tablespoons butter or margarine
1/2 teaspoon cinnamon
2 tablespoons cornstarch
1/2 cup water

Spread pineapple chunks and sliced peaches in bottom of an 8 x 8 inch casserole dish. Sprinkle raisins and dried cranberries over fruit. Sprinkle 1/2 cup sugar over mixture. Sprinkle with cinnamon and dot with 4 tablespoons butter. Arrange pear halves in a nice pattern, putting a cherry in each half and remaining cherries over fruit mixture. Sprinkle with remaining sugar, a little cinnamon and dot with remaining butter. Bake at 400° for 30 minutes. Remove from oven. Stir cornstarch into water. Pour carefully around pears, stir gently and put back in oven for 15 minutes longer. Remove from oven and cool to warm before serving.

JUDY'S VEGETABLE SALAD

1 cup sugar
3/4 cup vinegar
1/2 cup vegetable oil
1 medium onion, chopped
1 (7 oz) jar pimentos, un-drained
1 can French style green beans
1 (11 oz) can shoepeg corn
1/2 teaspoon salt
1/4 teaspoon pepper
1 medium green pepper, chopped
1 small can peas, drained

Bring the sugar, vinegar and oil to a boil. Boil for 5 minutes. Cool for 30 minutes. Mix all other ingredients together and pour the vinegar mixture over the vegetables. Serve the salad with a slotted spoon.

SPINACH SALAD

2 (10 oz) bags fresh spinach, torn into pieces
2 ripe avocados, peeled and sliced
1 pint cherry tomatoes, halved
1 (5 oz) package frozen cooked salad shrimp, thawed
3/4 pounds fresh mushrooms, sliced
3 eggs, hard boiled and chopped
1/2 cup sesame seeds, toasted
1/4 cup parmesan cheese, shredded

CREAMY DRESSING

2 (16 oz) cartons sour cream
1 cup mayonnaise
1/4 cup onion, chopped fine
1/2 teaspoon garlic powder
1 teaspoon salt
2 tablespoons sugar
2 tablespoons white vinegar

In a large bowl, toss the spinach, avocados, shrimp, tomatoes, mushrooms, eggs and sesame seeds together. Sprinkle with parmesan cheese. In a small bowl combine, the dressing ingredients; mix well. Serve with salad.

MANDARIN ORANGE AND SPINACH SALAD

1 large can mandarin oranges, drained
1 pound fresh spinach
1 large avocado, sliced
1/4 pound bacon, fried crisp and crumbled
1/4 - 1/2 medium red onion, sliced
1 tablespoon poppy seeds
2/3 cup vegetable oil
2 teaspoons lemon juice
1/3 - 1/2 cup white vinegar
4 teaspoons sugar
2/3 teaspoon salt
2/3 teaspoon mustard

Combine vinegar, salt, lemon juice, sugar, vegetable oil and poppy seeds, in a food processor. Combine remaining ingredients and pour dressing over salad. It's ready to eat.

BANANA SALAD

2 bananas, sliced
1 (20 oz) can crushed pineapple, drained
2 (15 oz) cans mandarin oranges, drained
2 (16 oz) jars maraschino cherries, drained
2 (30 oz) can fruit cocktail, drained
1 (16 oz) container whipped topping, thawed
2 (3 oz) boxes vanilla instant pudding mix
2 cups buttermilk

Combine the pudding mix and the buttermilk and beat for 1 minute with an electric mixer. Add the fruit cocktail, oranges, cherries pineapple and bananas, stir to combine. Chill until time t serve.

ORANGE SHERBET SALAD

2 packages orange jell-o gelatin
1 cup boiling water
1 pint orange sherbet
1 small can crushed pineapple, drained
1 can mandarin orange slices
1 cup mini marshmallows
1 pint cool whip

Dissolve jell-o in water, add sherbet, stir until dissolved. Add orange slices, pineapple and marshmallows. Fold in cool whip. Refrigerate.

5 CUP SALAD

1 cup pineapple tidbits, drained
1 cup mandarin oranges, drained
1 cup sour cream
1 cup coconut
1 cup miniature marshmallows

Combine all ingredients together. Chill until ready to serve.

CHICKEN SALAD PANINI

2 1/2 cups chicken breast, cooked and chopped
4 slices cheddar cheese
1 tomato, sliced thin
8 slices multi-grain bread
2 tablespoons ranch dressing
1 green onion, sliced thin
2 tablespoons real bacon bits
1/4 cup mayonnaise

Mix chicken, mayonnaise, bacon bits, onion and ranch dressing together. Spread onto 4 slices of bread and top with tomato and cheese and remaining bread. In a grill pan or skillet sprayed with cooking spray; cook 3 minutes on each side or until golden brown on both sides.

EULA'S CHICKEN SALAD

3 chicken breasts, cooked
2 small cans mandarin oranges, drained
1 cup celery, chopped
1 cup seedless red grapes, cut in half
1 teaspoon salt
1 cup almonds, sliced
Mayonnaise
Croissants

Crumble cooked chicken breasts in small pieces. Add celery, salt, almonds and enough mayonnaise to spread good. Fold in the grapes and oranges, mix well. Refrigerate until ready to serve. When ready to serve, brush croissants lightly with honey and place in oven on 250° until warmed. Fill croissants with salad and enjoy.

GOOD HOT HAM SALAD

3 cups ham, fully cooked and cut into cubes
1 (11 oz) can mandarin oranges, drained
1/2 cup slivered almonds
1 cup mayonnaise
1 (8 oz) can pineapple tidbits, drained
1/4 cup each (sweet red pepper, green pepper, chopped and mozzarella
cheese)

Combine the ham, pineapple, green pepper, red pepper, mayonnaise, and mozzarella cheese. Fold in oranges. Sprinkle almonds on top and bake at 350° for 30 minutes.

SUMMER TURKEY AND GRAPE SALAD

SALAD
4 cups turkey, cooked and cut into about 2 inch pieces
1 cup green grapes, seedless
1 cup red grapes, seedless
8 lettuce leaves
Cluster of seedless green and red grapes

DRESSING
1 cup vegetable oil
1 tablespoon Dijon mustard
1/4 cup lemon juice
1/3 cup parmesan cheese, grated
2 egg yolks
1 teaspoon basil leaves
1/4 teaspoon each (salt and pepper)

In a bowl, stir together all salad ingredients except lettuce. In a blender, combine all dressing ingredients except oil, lemon juice and parmesan cheese. Blend thoroughly until combined. With blender still running add 1/2 cup oil, lemon juice, and remaining 1/2 cup oil. Blend until thickened. By hand stir in parmesan cheese. Stir 1/2 cup dressing into the salad. On platter or individual salad plates, place lettuce leaves. Spoon turkey salad on lettuce. Place cluster of grapes around the salad. Serve with remaining dressing.

CANTALOUPE AND TURKEY SALAD

SALAD
2 cantaloupes, cut into quarters (reserve 2 quarters)
2 cups turkey, cooked and cubed
1/2 cup celery, chopped
2 tablespoons green onion, chopped
1/2 cup pecans, chopped---Lettuce leaves

DRESSING
3 ounces cream cheese, softened
1/4 teaspoon nutmeg
1 tablespoon milk

Peel and cube reserved cantaloupe quarters (2). In a big bowl stir together cubed cantaloupe and all salad ingredients, except lettuce; set aside. In a blender, combine dressing ingredients. Blend until smooth. Add turkey mixture and refrigerate for 2 hours. Place lettuce on plate and spoon salad into cantaloupe quarters on lettuce.

ENGLISH PEA SALAD

1 can green peas
2 tablespoons lemon juice
3 eggs, hard boiled
5-6 strips bacon, fried crisp and crumbled
3 tablespoons mayonnaise

Mix all ingredients together except the bacon. Sprinkle bacon on the salad just before serving.

GOOD CHICKEN SALAD

2 cups chicken, cooked and chopped
1 1/2 tablespoons purple onion, chopped
1/2 red bell pepper, chopped
1 can whole kernel corn

DRESSING
1/4 cup lemon juice
1/4 cup olive oil
2 tablespoons parsley, chopped
1 tablespoon Dijon mustard
Mayonnaise

Mix chicken mixture together; set aside. Mix the dressing ingredients together and pour over the chicken mixture; mix well. Keep refrigerated.

FETA CHEESE AND TOMATO SALAD

6 medium tomatoes, cut into wedges
1 1/2 cups feta cheese, crumbled
1/4 - 1/2 cup green onion, chopped
3 tablespoons olive oil
2 garlic cloves, minced
1 teaspoon each (salt, pepper and garlic powder)
Lettuce leaves

Combine tomatoes, cheese, onions, oil and garlic. Refrigerate for 2-3 hours. At serving time, add garlic powder, salt and pepper to taste. Spoon the salad onto a bed of lettuce leaves.

HOT WEATHER PEA SALAD

1 (15 oz) can peas
1 (16 oz) can white corn
1 cup onion, chopped
1 cup celery, chopped
1/2 cup red bell pepper, chopped
1/2 cup green pepper, chopped
1/2 teaspoon celery seed
1/2 cup sugar
1/2 cup vinegar
1/2 cup cooking oil
1/2 teaspoon pepper
1 teaspoon salt

Drain corn and peas, combine with other ingredients. Chill thoroughly.
Serve.

EASY MUSHROOM SALAD

1/4 pound of fresh mushrooms
1 head lettuce, shredded
1 large tomato, cut into wedges
1 cup red onion, sliced
1/2 teaspoon Tabasco sauce
1/4 teaspoon tarragon, crumbled
1/2 teaspoon salt
2 tablespoons vinegar
1/2 cup vegetable oil
1/3 cup clam juice

Clean mushrooms with wet paper towel; cut off dry tips of stems, slice
mushrooms lengthwise. Combine clam juice, oil, vinegar, tarragon,
salt and Tabasco sauce; shake well to mix. Add mushrooms and onion;
shake to coat; chill. Combine tomato and lettuce; add mushroom
dressing. Toss lightly to mix.

BLACK - EYED PEA SALAD

3 cups black-eyed peas, cooked
1 red bell pepper, diced
1/2 cup green onion, with tops, chopped
1 large tomato, diced
1/4 cup sugar
3/4 cup vegetable or olive oil
1/4 cup balsamic vinegar
1 hot green pepper, diced
1 tablespoon thyme (fresh or dried)
4 tablespoons oregano (fresh or dried)
1 large banana pepper, mild, diced

Combine oil, vinegar and sugar together and pour over the rest of the ingredients. Mix well and chill. Use slotted spoon to serve.

CRISPY GREEN PEA SALAD

1 (10 oz) bag frozen peas
1 cup celery, sliced
1 cup cauliflower, flowerets
1/4 cup pimentos, sliced
1/4 cup green pepper, diced
1 cup cashews, roasted
1/4 teaspoon Dijon mustard
1/4 cup bacon, fried crisp and crumbled
1 cup ranch dressing
1 cup sour cream
1 clove garlic, minced

Rinse frozen peas; combine peas with vegetables, cashews, bacon and sour cream. Mix together the dressing, mustard and garlic. Pour over salad and toss.

MARINATED ASPARAGUS SALAD

2 bunches of asparagus, trim off hard tops and cooked (or canned
asparagus spears)
1 teaspoon each (tarragon, garlic salt and pepper
1 (7 oz) bottle Italian dressing
1/2 cup each (wine vinegar and mayonnaise
Some lettuce leaves

Wash and drain asparagus and layer in dish. Sprinkle each layer with
tarragon, garlic, salt and pepper. Pour wine vinegar and Italian dressing
over asparagus, cover and let stand for 8-10 hours at room temperature.
Chill. Serve asparagus on lettuce bed topped with 1 tablespoon of
mayonnaise.

ASPARAGUS AND TOMATO SALAD

2 (15 oz) cans asparagus spears, drained
1 cup water chestnuts, chopped
2 medium plum tomatoes, diced
1/2 cup mayonnaise
Dash of hot pepper sauce
1 teaspoon vinegar
1 tablespoon Dijon mustard
1 bunch of bibb lettuce
4 eggs, hard boiled and chopped

DRESSING
Mix together the mustard, vinegar, mayonnaise and hot pepper sauce.
Cover and chill for several hours or up to (24 hours). Place lettuce leaves
on 4 salad plates or bowls. Top each with asparagus, eggs, tomatoes
and water chestnuts. Serve with dressing.

CRACKER SALAD

1 sleeve crackers (saltine)
1/2 cup mayonnaise
1 egg, hard boiled, chopped
1 large tomato, chopped
3 green onions, chopped
Leaf lettuce, optional

Crush crackers. Mix all ingredients together and serve immediately.

STUFFED CUCUMBER SALAD

2 large cucumbers
4 eggs, hard boiled
1 cup mayonnaise
1 cup romaine lettuce, chopped
1 medium onion, chopped
1 medium size tomato, chopped
6 green olives, stuffed with pimentos
4 leaves of iceberg lettuce
3-4 black olives
1/4 teaspoon cayenne pepper

Cut cucumbers in half, lengthwise. Scoop out seeds and discard them. Scoop out meat of the cucumbers and cut into small cubes. Next, cut romaine into small pieces. Chop eggs into small cubes. Chop onion into cubes, chop tomato into cubes, chop green olives, chop 2 black olives. Mix cucumber, eggs, romaine, onion, olives with mayonnaise. Put cucumber shells on lettuce cups. Fill shells with vegetable mix, put a dot of mayonnaise on top. Garnish with olives and cayenne pepper.

CUCUMBER AND TOMATO SALAD

2 large cucumbers, peeled and diced
2 large tomatoes, diced
1 (8 oz) bottle Italian salad dressing
1 medium onion, diced
1 medium green pepper, diced
2 teaspoons sugar

Combine the cucumbers, tomatoes, green pepper and onion together. Combine salad dressing and sugar; pour over vegetables. Refrigerate for at least 1 hour before serving.

SIMPLE CUCUMBER SALAD

6 medium cucumbers, peeled and sliced thin
1 onion, sliced thin
2 tablespoons mayonnaise
1 tablespoon each (salt and vinegar)

Add cucumbers and salt in bowl. Mix and place saucer down over slices to weight it down. Place in refrigerator for 4 hours. Drain off brine and discard it. Add onions, vinegar, sugar and mayonnaise. Blend well.

BROCCOLI AND CAULIFLOWER SALAD

1/2 pound bacon, cooked crisp and crumbled
1 head cauliflower, broken into small pieces
1 bunch broccoli, broken into small pieces
1/2 cup raisins
1 cup sunflower seeds
1 cup mayonnaise
1/2 cup sugar
2 tablespoons vinegar

Mix broccoli, cauliflower, raisins, bacon and sunflower seeds together. Mix mayonnaise with sugar and vinegar. Pour over broccoli mixture. Keep refrigerated.

BROCCOLI SALAD

2 bunches broccoli, chopped
1/3 cup sugar
1 onion, chopped
1/2 cup mayonnaise
1 cup raisins
1/2 cup bacon bits
1/3 cup oil
1/4 cup vinegar
1 can water chestnuts, drained and chopped

Combine broccoli, raisins, onion and water chestnuts in a serving bowl, combine mayonnaise, vinegar, sugar and oil, blend well. Pour over salad mixture, toss to blend. Cover and refrigerate several hours or overnight. Sprinkle with bacon bits before serving.

SIMPLE BROCCOLI SALAD

1 bunch broccoli, cut into bite size pieces
1 small onion
1/4 pound bacon, cooked crisp and crumbled
1/4 cup sunflower seeds
2 tablespoons cider vinegar
1/4 cup sugar
1/2 cup mayonnaise

Combine mayonnaise, sugar and vinegar, add broccoli. Stir in mayonnaise mixture. Add sunflower seeds, bacon and onion. Mix thoroughly. Chill until ready to serve.

EASY SPINACH SALAD

2 bags baby spinach, remove stems
10 slices bacon, fried crisp and crumbled
1/4 pound fresh mushrooms, sliced
1 small can water chestnuts, drained and chopped

Toss all ingredients together with salad dressing before serving.

DRESSING
1 cup vegetable oil
1/2 cup sugar
2 tablespoons onion, chopped
1/4 teaspoon ketchup
2 teaspoons Worcestershire sauce
Mix oil into rest of the ingredients and pour over salad when ready to serve.

YVONNE'S SALAD

1 bag spinach
1 medium size tomato, cut fine
1 small reed onion, cut into small strips
3 tablespoons olive oil
1/3 cup wine
Salt and pepper to taste

Combine all ingredients together except spinach. Put in skillet and sauté; pour over or across salad when ready to serve.

OLD FASHION CUCUMBER SALAD

2 medium cucumbers
2 medium onions
1/2 cup sugar
1 cup vinegar
1 teaspoon salt

Slice cucumbers and onions thin. Boil together the remaining ingredients; pour over the onions and cucumbers. Let stand for 1 1/2 hours. Toss together and refrigerate.

SOUTHERN COBB SALAD

2 chicken breasts, cooked and diced
1 avocado, chopped
6 slices of bacon, cooked crisp and crumbled
1/2 head of iceberg lettuce
2 ounces blue cheese, crumbled
2 tablespoons fresh chives
3 eggs, hard boiled and chopped
1/4 teaspoon each (olive oil, lemon juice, salt and pepper)
2 tomatoes, sliced thin

Mix together the chicken, lemon juice, olive oil, salt and pepper, cover and chill. Place egg in a bowl and season with salt and pepper; add chives and blue cheese and toss. Tear lettuce into a large bowl; place chicken in a row down the center of the bowl; top with bacon. Place half of tomato on each side of chicken. Place half of egg mixture on each side of tomato. Place half of the avocado on each side of egg mixture. Chill salad until ready to serve. Place dressing on the side (Blue cheese dressing in your grocery store).

LAYERED CORNBREAD SALAD

1 (8 1/2 oz) package cornbread or muffin mix
1/2 cup cheddar cheese, shredded
6 green onions, chopped
2 medium tomatoes, chopped
1 medium green pepper, chopped
3/4 cup sour cream
1 (15 1/4 oz) can whole kernel corn, drained
3/4 cup mayonnaise
1 (15 oz) can pinto beans, drained and rinsed

Bake cornbread as directions on package, cool. Crumble cornbread into a glass serving bowl. Layer with onions, green pepper, corn and beans. In smaller bowl, combine mayonnaise and sour cream; spread over vegetables. Sprinkle with the tomatoes and cheese. Refrigerate until chilled.

MOZZARELLA AND TOMATO SALAD

3 medium tomatoes, sliced
1 (8 oz) package mozzarella cheese, sliced thin
1/4 cup vegetable or olive oil
2 tablespoons basil, minced
1/4 teaspoon each (salt and pepper)

Layer and alternate cheese slices and tomato on serving platter. Drizzle with the oil; sprinkle with basil, salt and pepper.

MY FAVORITE WEST INDIES SALAD

1 pound lump crabmeat
1 medium to large onion, chopped
6 ice cubes
4 ounces ice water
3 ounces cider vinegar
4 ounces vegetable oil
Salt and pepper to taste

Put 1/2 of the onion in bottom of a bowl. Add 1/2 of the crabmeat and the remaining onion. Top with the remaining crabmeat. Salt and pepper to taste. Pour over the vinegar, oil and ice water. Put the ice cubes on top. Cover and let set overnight. Toss salad before serving. Serve with your favorite crackers.

ASPIC SALAD

2 envelopes un-flavored gelatin
3 1/4 cups tomato juice
1/4 cup lemon juice
1/2 teaspoon salt
1/4 teaspoon Tabasco sauce
1 teaspoon each (sugar and Worcestershire sauce)

Sprinkle gelatin over 1 cup tomato juice in saucepan to soften. Heat on medium heat for 3 minutes or until gelatin is dissolved. Stirring constantly.
Remove from heat; stir in remaining ingredients. Pour into mold; chill until firm; un-mold. Fill the center of the mold with another one of your favorite salads; like coleslaw or potato salad or leave plain.

ASIAN SALAD

1 cup fresh cauliflower florets
1/2 cup fresh snow peas
1 cup fresh broccoli florets
1 cup cherry tomatoes
2 green onions, sliced thin
1/2 cup water chestnuts, drained and sliced
1/2 teaspoon vegetable or olive oil
3/4 cup sugar
1/2 teaspoon sesame seeds, toasted
1 tablespoon cider vinegar
1 1/2 teaspoons soy sauce
1 tablespoon sesame oil
Dash pepper

In a bowl, combine the broccoli, cauliflower, tomatoes, peas and onions. Stir in the water chestnuts. In another bowl, whisk the say sauce, sesame oil, sugar, vinegar, sesame seeds, oil and pepper. Pour over vegetables and stir until coated. Refrigerate and chill.

RAMEN NOODLE SALAD

1 pound bag of broccoli coleslaw
2 bunches of green onions, chopped
1 cup sunflower seeds
1 cup almonds, sliced
2 packages Ramen noodle soup mix

DRESSING
3/4 cup vegetable or olive oil
2/3 cup sugar
1/3 cup white vinegar
2 seasoning packs from the soup mix

Mix together the broccoli, onion and almonds. Mix dressing ingredients and pour over vegetable mixture. Refrigerate several hours or overnight. Crunch noodles and add to salad 1/2 hour before serving.

CHINESE SALAD

2 heads Napa cabbage or bok choy cabbage, sliced thin
1/2 cup sunflower seeds
10 slices bacon, fried crisp and crumbled
1/2 cup slivered almonds
6-8 green onions, sliced thin

Combine all ingredients into a large bowl and top with noodles and dressing.

DRESSING

1/2 cup red wine vinegar
1 cup sugar
1 cup vegetable oil
2 seasoning packets from Ramen chicken flavored noodles
2 packs Ramen noodles
1 tablespoon sesame oil, more if needed

Mix dressing and refrigerate.(best if made several hours ahead of time). Shake and mix often. Bread up noodles in the 2 packages of Ramen noodles and brown in 1/4 cup butter.

ORIENTAL SALAD

1 large head of cabbage
5-7 green onions and tops
3 packages Ramen noodles
1/2 cup salted sunflower seeds
1 package slivered almonds
2 tablespoons sesame seeds
1/2 cup butter
1/2 cup vegetable oil
1/2 cup sugar
2 tablespoons soy sauce

Chop cabbage, green onions and tops. Combine in a large bowl and set aside. Break up Ramen noodles and combine with sunflower seeds, almonds, sesame seeds and butter in frying pan. Brown; drain on paper towels. Combine oil, vinegar, sugar and soy sauce in saucepan. Bring to a boil; boil for 1 minute, then cool. Combine all ingredients in a large bowl and serve.

TACO SALAD

1/2 head lettuce
1 large tomato
1 1/2 pounds ground beef
1 regular size onion, sliced
1 bottle of taco sauce
1 package cheddar cheese
1 package taco shells
1 package taco seasoning
Sour cream
Black olives

Brown beef and onion together. Drain and mix in taco sauce and seasoning. Simmer for a few minutes on low heat. Add olives. In separate bowl, combine lettuce, tomatoes, beef and cheese. Break up taco shells and add to mixture. Top with sour cream.

KIM'S TACO SALAD

1 pound ground beef
3 tomatoes
1 head lettuce
1 package taco seasoning mix
1 can kidney beans, drained
1 large onion, chopped
1 package cheddar cheese, shredded
1 package Doritos, broken up
Catalina salad dressing

Brown beef and drain. In a large bowl, mix the lettuce, beans, tomatoes and onions; sprinkle with dry taco seasoning mix. Add cheese and chips. Add enough salad dressing to moisten good. Toss and serve.

GOOD DORITO SALAD

1 head lettuce
1 package of each (Doritos and mozzarella cheese, grated)
1 can chili beans
1 bottle of French dressing

Break up lettuce. Drain beans. Add beans, cheese and salad dressing to lettuce. Crush Doritos and add to salad.

4 BEAN SALAD

1 pound can each (kidney beans, wax beans, green beans and lima beans, drained)
2 tablespoons parsley, crushed
1 medium green pepper, diced
1 medium onion, sliced thin
1/2 cup each (sugar, vinegar and salad oil)
1/2 teaspoon each (basil leaves, tarragon leaves, both crushed and dry mustard)

Place beans, green pepper and onion in a large bowl. Combine remaining ingredients; drizzle over vegetables; cover and marinate for several hours, stirring once or twice. Stir again before serving, stir and drain. Flavors improve the longer it stands.

GREEN BEAN SALAD

1 can French cut green beans, drained
1-2 cans pimentos, chopped
1/4 cup each (oil and chopped onion)
2 tablespoons water
1/2 cup each (vinegar and sugar)
1 green pepper, chopped
1 1/2 cup celery, chopped
1 can green peas
Salt and pepper to taste

Mix beans, peas, pimentos, celery, green pepper and onions together. Combine remaining ingredients; pour over vegetables. Let sand overnight.

RED BEAN SALAD

1 (15 oz) can red kidney beans, drained
1/2 cup sweet pickle relish
2 gees, hard boiled and chopped
Salt and pepper to taste
Mayonnaise, enough to mix well

Combine beans, eggs, relish and mayonnaise. Refrigerate until ready
to serve, then add salt and pepper.

POTATO SALAD FOR COMPANY

4 cups water
4 cups small new potatoes washed, skin left on and quartered
1/3 cup sour cream
1/2 teaspoon dill weed
1/4 teaspoon each salt and pepper
1 tablespoon Dijon mustard
2 tablespoons fresh parsley, chopped
1/2 teaspoon fresh garlic, minced
4 slices bacon, cooked crisp and crumbled
2 tablespoons green onion, sliced
1/3 cup mayonnaise

In a saucepan, bring water and salt to a full boil; add potatoes. Cook until
potatoes are tender. Rinse under cold water and drain. In a large bowl
combine together the remaining ingredients except bacon and green
onion. Add potatoes; toss to coat. Sprinkle with bacon and green onion.

SWEET POTATO SALAD

2 pounds sweet potatoes
1 1/2 cup mayonnaise
2 teaspoons Dijon mustard
8 green onions, sliced fine
4 eggs, hard boiled and chopped
1/4 teaspoon salt
1/2 cup celery, chopped

Place sweet potatoes in a large saucepan and cover with water. Boil until potatoes can easily be pierced with the tip of a knife, about 30-40 minutes. Drain. When cool, peel and dice potatoes. In a large bowl, combine mayonnaises, mustard and salt. Stir in eggs, celery and onion. Add potatoes; stir gently to mix. Cover and refrigerate for 2-4 hours.

CARROT AND RAISIN SALAD

4 cups carrots, shredded
3/4 - 1 1/2 cups raisins
1/4 cup mayonnaise
2 tablespoons each (milk and sugar)

Place carrots and raisins in a bowl. In a small bowl whisk the mayonnaise and sugar and enough milk to be creamy. Pour over carrot mixture and mix.

MACARONI SALAD WITH BACON

2 cups elbow macaroni, un-cooked
1 pound sliced bacon, cooked crisp, crumbled
5-6 green onions, chopped fine
1 large tomato, chopped
1 1/4 cups celery, diced
1 1/4 cups mayonnaise
5 teaspoons white vinegar
1/4 teaspoon pepper
1/4 teaspoon salt

Cook macaroni according to package directions; drain and rinse. In a large bowl, combine the macaroni, green onions, tomato and celery. In a small bowl, combine the mayonnaise, vinegar, salt and pepper. Pour over macaroni mixture and toss to coat. Refrigerate 2 hours before serving.

LINGUINE SALAD

1 box linguine, cooked until tender
2 cucumbers
3 tomatoes
2 onions
1 (16 oz) bottle of Zesty Italian dressing

Cook noodles 12-15 minutes. Drain and rinse. Place in a large bowl. Pour about 1/2 bottle of the dressing over noodles to keep them from sticking; toss. Add remaining ingredients. Toss immediately. Place in refrigerator and chill.

SAUERKRAUT SALAD

1 large can sauerkraut
1/3 cup vinegar
1/3 cup vegetable oil
1 cup each (celery, onion, green pepper, all chopped)
1 cup sugar

Bring oil, vinegar and sugar to a boil; cool. Pour over remaining ingredients. Refrigerate for 24 hours.

ORZO SALAD WITH BLUE CHEESE

3/4 cup orzo pasta, un-cooked
1/2 cup walnuts, toasted and chopped
1/4 cup green onions, sliced
3 cups fresh argula, torn in pieces
3/4 cup blue cheese, crumbled
5-6 strips bacon, fried crisp and crumbled
Vinaigrette dressing

VINEGARETTE DRESSING
1/2 teaspoon brown sugar
1/2 teaspoon salt
1/4 cup walnuts, toasted and chopped
1/4 cup vegetable or olive oil
1 teaspoon mustard
2 tablespoons wine vinegar

Cook orzo pasta according to the package directions; drain and place in a large bowl. Add the argula, bacon, blue cheese, onions and walnuts. In blender, combine the wine vinegar, garlic clove, mustard salt, brown sugar and walnuts. Cover and process until smooth until smooth. Gradually add oil. Drizzle over salad; toss to coat salad.

COLORED PASTA SALAD

1 (12 oz) bag colored pasta
6 ripe tomatoes, seeded and chopped
1 cup green olives, sliced
1 cup cucumber, seeded and chopped
2 tablespoons wine vinegar
3/4 cup vegetable oil
1 tablespoon dried cilantro
1 tablespoon garlic powder
1 1/2 tablespoon salt
Cayenne pepper to taste

Place pasta in boiling water, stirring often. Cook 4-5 minutes. Do not over cook; drain. Combine pasta with remaining ingredients; mix well. Cover and chill. Serve cool not cold.

PICKLED ONION AND BEETS

2 (16 oz) can sliced beets
1 medium onion, sliced
1/4 cup salad oil
1/4 cup vinegar
2 tablespoons sugar
Salt and pepper to taste

Mix vinegar, sugar, salad oil, salt and pepper. Place sliced onion and beets in a bowl; add vinegar mixture. Refrigerate for 8-10 hours or overnight. Serve on lettuce leaf.

PICKLED BEETS AND EGG SALAD

1 (15 oz) can whole beets, drained, juice reserved
2/3 cup sugar
1/2 cup vinegar
1/2 teaspoon cloves
1 teaspoon salt
6 hard boiled eggs, peeled

Combine the reserved beet juice, sugar, vinegar, cloves and salt in a saucepan and heat until sugar has dissolved. Place the eggs in a large bowl; add the beets. Pour in the juice, cover and refrigerate overnight.

BEET AND CELERY SALAD

1 can beets, drained and sliced
2 stalks celery, chopped, cut on the bias (save tips)
2 tablespoons orange juice
1 bottle Italian dressing

Mix all ingredients together, garnish with the celery tips. Pour dressing over salad just before serving.

AVOCADO SHRIMP SALAD

2 ripe avocados, peeled and halved
1 pound raw shrimp, peeled
1 (8 oz) can crushed pineapple, drained
1/2 teaspoon lemon juice
1/2 cup bell pepper, chopped
1/2 cup celery, chopped
2/3 cup sour cream
1 cup swiss cheese, shredded
1 teaspoon onion salt
Red tip lettuce for garnish

Soak avocado halves in lemon juice and chill. Cook shrimp in boiling water (salted) for 3 minutes. Drain and cool in refrigerator. Combine pineapple, bell pepper, celery, sour cream, onion, salt and shrimp. Refrigerate for 30-40 minutes. Scoop and hollow out avocado to allow room for mixture. Stack mixture on halves and cover with shredded cheese. Refrigerate. Serve on bed of lettuce.

SHRIMP SALAD BOATS

2 pounds fresh or frozen shrimp
1/2 cup mayonnaise
2 cups celery
24 poppy seed rolls
Butter or margarine
Chives, chopped
Salt and pepper to taste

Shell, de-veined and cook shrimp about 3 minutes; drain and chill. Cut 12 shrimp in half lengthwise and chop remaining shrimp. Mix with celery, mayonnaise, salt and pepper then chill. Slice the rolls almost through, leaving a hinge; spread with butter and sprinkle with chives. Fill each roll with a heaping tablespoon of shrimp salad; garnish with a shrimp half. Wrap and chill until serving.

KENTUCKY 7 LAYER SALAD

1 head lettuce, torn into small pieces
4 ribs celery, chopped
1 bunch green onions, chopped
2 boxes frozen green peas, un-cooked
8 slices bacon, fried crisp and crumbled
1/2 cup parmesan cheese
1/3 cup sugar
1 1/2 cup mayonnaise
1 1/2 cups sour cream

Arrange lettuce pieces in bottom of a clear salad bowl. Sprinkle celery over lettuce, then the green onions, then peas. Making a dressing by, combining the sour cream, mayonnaise and sugar. Pour over peas. Sprinkle parmesan cheese over dressing. crumble bacon and sprinkle on top.

CRUNCHY LETTUCE SALAD

1 large head of lettuce, sliced
3/4 cup chow mien noodles
4 green onions, sliced
1/4 cup sesame seed
1/2 cup salad oil
1/3 cup slivered almonds
6 strips bacon, fried crisp and crumbled
1/4 cup sugar
2 tablespoons vinegar
1 teaspoon salt
1/4 teaspoon pepper

In a jar, combine oil, vinegar, sugar, salt and pepper. Shake well. Chill for 1 hour. Combine the lettuce, bacon, almonds, sesame seeds and onion in a large bowl; add dressing and toss; top with chow mien noodles.

CESAR SALAD

1/2 head Romaine lettuce
1/2 bunch curly endive
1 cup croutons
2-3 tomatoes, diced
1 garlic clove, minced
1/2 cup salad oil
1 egg, beaten
1 tablespoon Worcestershire sauce
1/4 cup lemon juice
1/2 teaspoon each (salt, pepper, parmesan cheese)

Add garlic and salad oil. Mix eggs, Worcestershire sauce, lemon juice, salt, pepper and cheese in a jar and shake well. Just before serving break the lettuce and endive into a bowl, strain oil over this, add tomatoes and croutons to lettuce. Pour above mixture over all and toss well.

BACON - LETTUCE - AND - TOMATO - SALAD

12 strips bacon, cooked crisp, crumbled
1 pound fresh mushrooms
4 large ripe tomatoes, peeled
Red leaf, Boston and Bibb lettuce
4 green onions, with tops sliced thin
6 tablespoons vegetable oil
2 tablespoons red wine vinegar
1 1/2 teaspoons salt
1/8 teaspoon each (black pepper and garlic salt)
Swiss or mozzarella cheese, grated

Cut 18 slices of tomatoes. Lightly salt and arrange the tomatoes in 6 lettuce lined salad bowls. Coarsely chop remaining tomatoes and toss with the mushrooms, bacon, onion, oil, vinegar, salt, pepper and garlic salt. Spoon over sliced tomatoes in lettuce lined salad bowls. Sprinkle grated cheese on top and serve. You may also use a platter with lettuce and all of the ingredients. Also, you may add boiled shrimp or lump crabmeat, making this dish a special meal.

ROMAINE SALAD - AVOCADO DRESSING

1 medium ripe avocado, peeled and cubed
1 (2 1/4 oz) can ripe olives, drained and sliced
2 green onions, chopped
1/2 cup mayonnaise
1/4 cup vegetable oil
3 tablespoons lemon juice
1 (4 oz) cheddar cheese, shredded
3 medium tomatoes, cut into wedges
1/4 teaspoon hot pepper sauce
1/2 teaspoon salt
2 garlic cloves, peeled
1 bunch each (romaine and leaf lettuce, torn into pieces)
Corn chips

DRESSING;

Place the avocado, mayonnaise, oil, lemon juice, garlic, salt and hot pepper sauce in a blender; cover and process until blended. In a large bowl, combine the romaine, tomatoes, cheese, olives and onions. Drizzle the dressing and toss to coat well. Sprinkle with corn chips.

TOSS SALAD WITH ARTICHOKES

1 (6 1/2 oz) jar marinated artichoke hearts, drained and sliced
1 bunch each (romaine and leaf lettuce, torn into pieces)
1 pound sliced bacon, cooked crisp and diced
1 (4 oz) package blue cheese, crumbled
1 medium sweet yellow pepper, sliced
1 medium sweet red pepper, sliced
1 cup celery, sliced
6 tablespoons cider vinegar
1/4 onion, sliced
4 teaspoons brown sugar
4 teaspoons brown mustard
1/4 cup vegetable oil
1/2 teaspoon pepper
1 teaspoon salt

In a bowl; mix both of the lettuce, bacon, artichoke, blue cheese, celery, red and yellow peppers; cover and refrigerate. In a blender, mix vinegar, onion, brown sugar, mustard, salt and pepper; cover and process until smooth. Add oil, blend until thick. Drizzle over salad. Toss and serve.

HEARTS OF PALM SALAD

1 can hearts of palm, drained and chopped
1 1/2 pounds spinach, washed and torn into pieces
3 cups strawberries, stemmed and sliced
1 cup walnuts, chopped
1/3 cup vinegar
1 teaspoon dry mustard
1 1/2 tablespoons poppy seeds
1/2 small red onion, grated
1 cup vegetable oil
3/4 cup sugar
1 teaspoon salt
1/2 teaspoon paprika
2 tablespoons lemon juice

DRESSING

Combine the vinegar, sugar, lemon juice and salt in a saucepan and heat until sugar dissolves, stirring often. Cool to room temperature. Whisk in the oil, onion, poppy seeds, dry mustard and paprika; set aside. Combine the spinach, hearts of palm, strawberries and walnuts in a salad bowl. Add a little of the dressing at serving time; toss. Serve the remaining dressing along side the salad.

GREEN HOT PEPPER SALAD

1 (3 oz) box lemon jell-o
1 small jar pimentos, chopped
1 (10 oz) jar green pepper jelly (hot)
1 (3 oz) package cream cheese, softened
1 cup boiling water
1 small can pineapple, crushed
2 tablespoons half and half cream
1/4 cup pecans, chopped
Dash of Tabasco sauce
Mayonnaise (enough to mix good)

Dissolve jell-o in boiling water. Also, dissolve hot pepper jelly in hot jell-o. Add pineapple with its juice and pimentos. Mix cream cheese and half and half, a dash of Tabasco sauce, mayonnaise to taste, add pecans. Grease muffin pans with oil. Add small amount of jell-o. Put in tablespoonful of cream cheese mixture. Fill muffin cups with remaining jell-o mix. Refrigerate.

GRANDMA'S FAVORITE CORN SALAD

2 small cans shoepeg corn, white and drained
1 small onion, chopped fine
1 large tomato, chopped coarse
1 cup green pepper chopped
Mayonnaise

Mix all ingredients together and sir in mayonnaise until well blended.

EASY SQUASH SALAD

2 small zucchini, ends trimmed
2 small yellow squash, ends trimmed
1 large bunch arugula salad greens
1 large ripe tomato, cored
2 tablespoons red wine vinegar
1 tablespoon Dijon mustard
2 tablespoons extra virgin olive oil
Salt and pepper to taste
Parsley

Cut zucchini and squash in thin slices on the diagonal, place in a bowl. Prepare the dressing. Whisk the vinegar, mustard, together in a bowl. Slowly add the oil, whisking constantly until thickened. Toss with squash. Let stand 10 minutes. Place the arugula in a salad bowl. Cut tomato in half lengthwise; cut very thin into wedges; spread over greens. Be ready to serve; spoon the squash and dressing over arugula. Sprinkle parsley and season with salt and pepper. Serve immediately.

AVOCADO SALAD

2 cans shoepeg corn
6 cherry tomatoes, split in half
Juice of 1 lemon
4 avocados
Olive oil
1/4 cup purple onion, diced
2 tablespoons fresh parsley
Black pepper to taste

Mix the corn, tomatoes, lemon juice, onion and pepper together. Set aside. DRESSING; Mix olive oil, parsley and black pepper. Slice the avocado last and place on salad. Can be put in avocado or taco shells, or eat it like it is.

VEGETABLES & SIDES

EULA'S SWEET POTATOES IN RAISIN SAUCE

2 cans (or fresh) sweet potatoes. Peel, slice and cook potatoes in salted water until tender. Put into baking dish. Pour raisin sauce over potatoes and bake at 350° for 30 minutes or until thick and bubbly.

RAISIN SAUCE
½ cup raisins
2/3 cup brown sugar
2 tablespoons butter
2 tablespoons flour
¼ teaspoon salt
1 cup water

Cook raisins in small amount of water until soft. Add remaining water, brown sugar, flour and salt. Cook until thick, stirring constantly to avoid lumps forming. Remove from heat and add the butter. Stir until butter melts, then pour over sweet potatoes.

SWEET POTATO PUDDING

2 cups sweet potatoes, grated fine
3 eggs, beaten
½ stick butter or margarine
1 cup milk
1/3 cup plus 1 tablespoon sugar
½ teaspoon (vanilla, nutmeg and salt)

Mix all ingredients and pour in a well greased baking pan. Bake at 375° for 30 minutes. Remove from oven and stir. Return to oven and cook 40 minutes longer.

GRANDMA'S STEWED TOMATOES

2 cups canned tomatoes, chopped
2/3 cup onion, chopped fine
2 tablespoons each (vinegar, butter and sugar)
1 tablespoon Worcestershire sauce
½ teaspoon each (salt and pepper)
Croutons

Combine all ingredients and cover. Simmer for about 1 hour or until onions are tender. Boil slowly until liquid is reduced. Stirring constantly. Top with croutons.

SWEET POTATOES AND PEARS

9 cups sweet potatoes, peeled and cubed
4 cups water
1/3 cup brown sugar
¼ cup butter, softened
1 (15 oz) can pear halves, drained
¼ teaspoon cinnamon

Put sweet potatoes in a microwave dish; add water. Cover and microwave on high for 10-15 minutes or until tender. Drain, and place in a large mixing bowl. Add the remaining ingredients; stir until well mixed.

YAM BAKE WITH MARSHMALLOWS

1 large can yams
¼ cup miniature marshmallows
2 cups apples, sliced
1/3 cup pecans, chopped
½ cup brown sugar
½ teaspoon cinnamon
Butter or margarine

Combine apples, brown sugar, cinnamon and nuts. Alternate layers of yams and apple mixture in a 1 ½ quart casserole dish. Dot with butter. Cover and bake at 350° for 35-40 minutes. Cover with marshmallows and put back in oven to brown.

WONDERFUL YAMS

2 cups yams, or sweet potatoes, whipped
1 egg, separated
1 teaspoon cinnamon
½ teaspoon salt
2 tablespoons each (sugar and butter)

Mix yams and egg yolk, beat until smooth; blend in butter, sugar, salt and cinnamon. Place in a greased pie pan. Bake at 350° for 25-30 minutes. Top with meringue of beaten egg whites and sugar, put back in oven to brown.

SWEET POTATO COBBLER

4 medium sweet potatoes
2 cups sugar
1 stick butter
1 teaspoon cloves
½ teaspoon each (allspice, cinnamon and salt)
2 pie crusts, un-baked

In a large pan, slice 2 sweet potatoes and place in bottom of pan. Add 1 cup sugar and salt. Slice half of the butter over sugar, add ¼ teaspoon allspice, cloves and cinnamon to crust. Repeat layers. Top with remaining crust and bake at 350° for 1 hour.

TWICE BAKED SWEET POTATOES

6 medium sweet potatoes
6 strips bacon, cooked crisp, crumbled
2 cups cheddar cheese, shredded
¼ cup butter, cubed
1/8 teaspoon pepper
½ teaspoon salt

Bake potatoes at 375° for 1 ¼ hours or until tender. When cooled enough to handle, cut a thin slice off the top of each one and discard. Scoop out the pulp, leaving a thin shell. In a large bowl, mash the pulp with butter. Stir in the cheese, bacon, salt and pepper. Spoon into potato shells. Place on baking sheet and bake for 20-30 minutes or until heated through.

ORANGE SWEET POTATOES

6 large sweet potatoes
1 bag miniature marshmallows
1 cup pecans, chopped
¾ cup orange juice
½ pound butter
1 ½ cups sugar 6 oranges

Peel and slice potatoes. Cook until tender and drain. Whip until fluffy. Add other ingredients, reserving a few marshmallows for topping. Put in casserole dish and top with marshmallows. Bake at 350° until bubbly and marshmallows are browned. Scoop out orange shells and fill with mixture.

DELICIOUS SWEET POTATO SOUFFLE

2 cups sweet potatoes, cooked and mashed
1 cup half and half cream
½ stick butter or margarine
2 eggs
1 ½ cups white sugar
1 teaspoons each (nutmeg and cinnamon)

TOPPING
¾ cup cornflakes, crushed
¾ stick butter
½ cup each (brown sugar and chopped pecans)

Mix all of the ingredients to the soufflé together, except the sweet potatoes. Add those last. Place in a baking dish at 400° for about 20-30 minutes. For topping; Melt butter and add all other topping ingredients, stir well. Cover sweet potato mixture with the topping and bake for 10 more minutes.

KENTUCKY BOURBON SWEET POTATOES

3 (18 oz) cans sweet potatoes, un-drained
1/3 cup Kentucky bourbon
½ cup each (brown sugar, white sugar and butter)
½ teaspoon vanilla
2 cups miniature marshmallows

Cut sweet potatoes into bite-size pieces. Place potatoes, with the juice, into a large saucepan. Cook over medium heat, stirring often, until heated through. In a 2 quart baking dish, add all sugars, bourbon, butter and vanilla; blend until well blended. Stir in sweet potatoes, coating well with sauce. Sprinkle marshmallows over the top and bake un-covered at 350° for 30 minutes or until marshmallows are golden brown.

FRIED SWEET POTATOES

3 large sweet potatoes, peeled and sliced
¾ cup milk
1 cup vegetable oil
4 teaspoons brown sugar

Fry potatoes in hot oil in skillet until brown on both sides. Sprinkle with brown sugar. Add milk, simmer on low heat until tender. Serve hot.

STUFFED EGG AND MUSHROOM BAKE

12 eggs, hard boiled
3 (4 oz) jars button mushrooms, drained and divided
¾ pound sharp cheddar cheese, grated and divided
½ pound bacon, fried crisp, divided
¼ teaspoon Tabasco sauce
1 tablespoon Worcestershire sauce
½ teaspoon red pepper
Salt and pepper to taste

Slice eggs lengthwise; remove yolks and mash. Mince 2 jars mushrooms in warm butter. Add to the yolks. Season mixture with salt, pepper, Worcestershire sauce and Tabasco sauce. Mix well and stuff back into egg whites. Press 2 halves together. Arrange in lightly greased baking dish. Sprinkle remaining 2 jars of mushrooms over eggs. Sprinkle half of the crumbled bacon and half of the cheese over eggs. Reserve remainder for the sauce. SAUCE; Melt remaining cheese, add bacon and pour over all.

MUSHROOMS IN SOUR CREAM

2 pounds fresh mushrooms
1 bunch green onions, chopped
1 (8 oz) carton sour cream
½ cup butter
3 tablespoons white wine
2 teaspoon salt
½ teaspoon each (white pepper and nutmeg)
Few sprigs of parsley
3 English muffins, split
Juice of ½ lemon

Clean mushrooms with a damp paper towel. Sauté onions in butter until wilted. Add mushrooms and sauté for 5 minutes. Add lemon juice, salt, pepper and nutmeg. Fold in sour cream. Add wine, heat until warm. Serve on buttered toasted English muffin halves. Garnish with a sprig of parsley.

BAKED MUSHROOMS

1 pound fresh mushrooms, sliced thin
1 cup whipping cream
1/3 cup butter, softened
1 tablespoon parsley, chopped

1 tablespoon Dijon mustard
1 teaspoon salt
1/8 teaspoon ground nutmeg
1/8 teaspoon cayenne pepper
1 ½ tablespoons flour
1 tablespoon onion, grated

Blend butter with parsley, onion, mustard, salt and pepper. Place a layer of mushrooms in the bottom of a 1 ½ quart casserole dish; dot with half the butter. Add another layer of mushrooms and top with remaining butter. Pour the cream over all and bake at 375° for 40-45 minutes.

COMPANY MUSHROOMS WITH NOODLES

½ pound fresh mushrooms, sliced
½ cup butter
¼ cup onion, chopped
1 clove garlic, minced
1 (10 ½ oz) can beef stock
1 tablespoon lemon juice
1 (4 oz) package medium size noodles
¼ cup almonds, sliced

Melt the butter, add mushrooms, garlic and almonds. Cook for 10 minutes over medium heat. Add remaining ingredients and cook until noodles are tender, about 10 minutes. Good served with any beef dishes.

FRESH MUSHROOM BAKE

¾ pound of fresh mushrooms, sliced thin
1 cup heavy cream
2 eggs, beaten
2 tablespoons parmesan cheese

2 tablespoons bread crumbs
1 tablespoon each (minced onion, lemon juice and flour)
4 tablespoons butter or margarine
¼ teaspoon salt
1 teaspoon pepper

Sprinkle mushrooms with lemon juice in saucepan. Cover and simmer lightly. Add 3 tablespoons of butter, salt, pepper, flour, onion and cheese. Simmer 3 minutes. Place in a buttered 1 ½ quart baking dish. Beat together cream and eggs; pour over mushrooms. Sprinkle bread crumbs on top. Dot with butter and bake at 375° for 15 minutes.

MUSHROOMS WITH CREAM

½ pound mushrooms
1 cup sour cream
1 tablespoon each (salt and pepper)
English muffins or toast points
2 tablespoons butter
Paprika

Slice mushrooms through cap and stem. Melt butter in skillet, add mushrooms and cook stirring occasionally, about 8 minutes or until slightly browned. Leave liquid in skillet, add cream and seasonings. Cook on low heat until heated through, sprinkle with paprika.

GREEN PEAS AND MUSHROOMS

1 (10 oz) package frozen English peas
1 (4 oz) can mushrooms, drained and sliced
1 teaspoon each (onion flakes, salt and pepper)
1 tablespoon butter

Cook peas until done; drain. Add mushrooms and remaining ingredients, cover and let stand about 5 minutes. Mix well.

EULA'S BEST PEAR CASSEROLE

6 whole fresh pars or 2-3 cans of pears, drained (save juice)
1 cup sugar
¾ stick butter
3 tablespoons flour
1 ½ cups cheddar cheese, grated
Ritz crackers, crumbled

Cut pears in chunks. Make sauce of flour, sugar, ½ stick of butter and 1 cup of juice. Cook over medium heat until sauce thickens. Place cut pears in a greased casserole dish. Pour sauce over pears. Add cheese and cover with crumbled Ritz cracker crumbs soaked in butter. Bake at 350° until cheese is melted and sauce is bubbling

MY FAVORITE BAKED BANANAS

5 bananas (medium ripe)
¼ cup butter or margarine, melted
2-3 cups cornflakes, crushed (or any cereal)
1 ½ teaspoons each (cinnamon, and curry powder)

Peel and halve bananas lengthwise, next crosswise. Combine melted butter, curry powder and cinnamon. Dip bananas in batter, coating well. Roll bananas in cereal coating completely. Next, place in a greased baking dish and bake at 350° for 10-15 minutes or until lightly brown.

GOOD APPLE CASSEROLE

4-5 tart apples
1 cup each (sugar and flour)
¼ cup butter or margarine
2 tablespoons each (cinnamon, lemon juice and water)
1 ½ cups sharp cheddar cheese, grated

Mix cinnamon, flour and sugar; cut butter fine into mixture. Add grated cheese and fold into mixture. Peel apples and place in a 2 quart baking dish. Adding 2 tablespoons water and lemon juice, and pour over apples. Spread above mixture over the top of apples and bake at 350° for 30 minutes.

DELICIOUS APPLE AND CHEESE CASSEROLE

5-6 apples
1 (12 oz) box Velveeta cheese, shredded
1 stick butter
1 cup milk
2 cups flour, self-rising
1 ½ cups sugar

Peel and slice apples, place in skillet sprayed with non-stick spray. Sprinkle an additional ½ cup sugar over apples and let sit for 30-35 minutes, then sauté; cook until slightly tender. Melt butter in mixing bowl, add sugar, flour and milk. Mix well. Add cheese and apples. Pour into a 13 x 9 inch baking dish and bake at 325° for 40-45 minutes or until lightly brown.

EASY APPLE AND CHEESE CASSEROLE

2 cans of apple pie filling
1 stick butter
1 (8 oz) box velveeta cheese
¾ cup flour
1 cup sugar
1 teaspoon cinnamon

Place apples in a butter 13 x 9 inch baking dish. Sprinkle with cinnamon. Mix cheese, flour and sugar. Spread over apples and bake at 350° for 30-40 minutes.

GOOD PINEAPPLE CASSEROLE

2 large cans of pineapple chunks, drained (save the juice)
2 cups sharp cheddar cheese, grated
7 tablespoons flour self-rising
1 stick butter, melted
1 sleeve Ritz cracker crumbs

Combine sugar and flour. Add cheese. Add pineapple and stir well. Pour mixture into a greased baking dish. Mix cracker crumbs, butter and about 5-7 tablespoons of pineapple juice and spread on top of pineapple mixture. Bake at 350° for 30-40 minutes or until golden brown.

SOUTHERN EGGPLANT CREOLE

1 large eggplant, peeled and chopped
1 onion, chopped
1 green pepper, chopped
½ cup butter
1 cup sharp cheddar cheese, grated
½ cup rice, raw
¼ teaspoon each (basil and oregano)
2 teaspoons Tabasco sauce
1 cup beef broth
½ teaspoon each (salt and pepper)

Sauté green pepper and onion in butter. Add the rice and sauté until golden. Add all other ingredients except cheese. Bake in a greased 2 quart casserole dish at 350° for 30 minutes. Sprinkle cheese on top and cook 15 minutes longer. Serve hot.

GOOD STUFFED EGGPLANT

2 large eggplants
2 eggs
¾ cup bread crumbs
1 cup ground ham
2 cloves garlic, chopped
¾ cup onion, chopped
½ cup each (celery, pepper and parsley, all chopped)
¼ teaspoon salt, pepper, sugar and paprika)

Toast bread crumbs; sauté the onion, garlic, pepper, and celery in butter. Scoop out center of eggplant and boil in salted water. Drain and add to ingredients, (leaving a very little water). Add bread crumbs, eggs and ham. Season with salt, pepper and sugar. Scald eggplant shells. Place mixture into scalded shells. Mix melted butter and paprika with bread crumbs and sprinkle over top and bake at 375° for 15 minutes.

218

FRIED EGGPLANT

1 of each (medium eggplant and egg, beaten)
Flour
¼ teaspoon salt

Peel top stem and lower blossom from eggplant. Slice widthwise thin. Put slices in cold water until ready to fry. Dip eggplant in egg, roll in flour, fry in hot oil until browned. Drain on paper towels.

COMPANY SPECIAL EGGPLANT

1 large eggplant, peeled and sliced thin
1 ½ cups cracker crumbs
2 eggs, beaten
2 (8 oz) can tomato sauce
1 (8 oz) package American cheese slices
1 teaspoon oregano
½ teaspoon Worcestershire sauce
Vegetable oil for cooking

Dip eggplant slices in egg, roll in crackers crumbs. Brown in skillet in hot oil, drain. Mix tomato sauce, Worcestershire sauce and oregano together. Place ¼ of eggplant slices in a greased 2 quart baking dish, top with ¼ of the cheese. Spoon ¼ of sauce mixture over cheese. Repeat layers until all ingredients are used, ending with the sauce. Cover and bake at 350° for 55-60 minutes.

FRIED EGGPLANT STICKS

1 pound eggplant
¾ cup bread crumbs
6 tablespoons parmesan cheese, grated
2 tablespoons milk
2 eggs, beaten
¼ teaspoon ground black pepper
1 ½ teaspoon salt
Celery salt

Peel and cut eggplant into crosswise slices one half inch thick. Cut each slice into one half inch strips, soak in water for 15 minutes. Combine bread crumbs, cheese, salt and pepper. Beat eggs with milk. Dip eggplant sticks into egg mixture, then into the bread crumbs. Fry sticks in deep fryer or oil at 360°. Sprinkle with celery salt. Drain on paper towels.

BROCCOLI FRITTERS

2 broccoli stems, peeled (not tops)
4 tablespoons flour
2 tablespoons each (butter and milk)
½ cup onion, chopped
1 teaspoon baking powder
1 egg
½ teaspoon salt
1/8 teaspoon pepper
Oil for frying

Peel broccoli stems and chop fine (makes about ½ cup). Sauté broccoli and onion in butter until soft and beginning to brown. Remove from heat and cool. Combine remaining ingredients in a bowl and mix with a wire whisk. With a spoon, stir sautéed vegetables into batter mixture.

Adjust consistency with extra milk or a little flour, if needed. Spoon dollops of batter and drop in hot oil, a few at a time in about 1 inch of heated oil until golden brown. Makes 5-6 fritters.

GOOD BROCCOLI CASSEROLE

2 (10 oz) packages frozen broccoli spears, cooked and drained
½ cup swiss cheese, shredded
1 (10 oz) can cream of celery soup
3 eggs, hard boiled, sliced
2/3 cup milk
2 cups French fried onion rings

Put broccoli in a 2 quart baking dish. Layer the eggs, 1 cup of the onion rings, then the cheese over the broccoli. Combine the soup and milk, mix well. Pour over the cheese and bake at 350° for 25 minutes. Top with the remaining onion rings and bake for 5 more minutes.

CRUSTY TOPPED CAULIFLOWER

1 large head of cauliflower
¾ cup cheddar cheese, shredded
½ cup mayonnaise
2 tablespoons Dijon mustard

Cook whole cauliflower in small amount of salted water for 20 minutes. Place in a flat baking pan. Mix the mayonnaise and Dijon mustard together. Pour over cauliflower. Sprinkle with the cheese and bake at 350° for 10 minutes or until cheese melts.

BROCCOLI AND CAULIFLOWER CASSEROLE

1 (20 oz) package cauliflower, frozen
1 (10 oz) package broccoli, frozen
1 can each (celery and mushroom soup)
1 (9 oz) jar of cheese whiz
French fried onion rings

Cook broccoli and cauliflower until tender, drain. Combine cheese whiz and soups together and add vegetables. Bake un-covered at 350° for 20-25 minutes. Place 1 can of fried onion rings on top and bake for 5 minutes more.

BROCCOLI CASSEROLE

1 (10 oz) package broccoli, frozen and chopped
½ cup each (cream of mushroom soup and Ritz crackers, crushed)
¼ cup mayonnaise
1 small onion, chopped
½ stick butter
½ teaspoon garlic powder
¼ teaspoon each (salt and pepper)

Cook broccoli until limp. Remove from heat, drain. Sauté onion with butter add to broccoli. Add all remaining ingredients, mix well. Put into a casserole dish. Add topping by taking ½ cup crushed Ritz crackers and 1 tablespoon of melted butter.

CAULIFLOWER AND POTATO BAKE

1 cup potatoes, cooked and mashed
1 cup sharp cheddar cheese, grated
2 heads of cauliflower, cooked and drained
½ cup mayonnaise
1 clove garlic, minced
1/8 teaspoon pepper
Bacon, fried crisp and crumbled
Milk as needed

Mash cauliflower like you would potatoes. Add mashed potatoes, cheddar cheese, pepper, mayonnaise and garlic. Stir until cheese melts. Stir until you get the consistency of mashed potatoes. Add warm milk, if needed. Stir bacon in or put onto serving dish and sprinkle with bacon on top.

GOOD CAULIFLOWER CASSEROLE

2 packages frozen cauliflower or (1 head fresh)
¾ pound Velveeta cheese
½ pint sour cream
1 large can green peas
4 tablespoons butter
¾ cup Ritz crackers, crumbled

Cook cauliflower and drain; drain peas. Mix cauliflower, peas, cheese and sour cream. Pour into a buttered casserole dish. Cover top with buttered Ritz cracker crumbs. Bake at 350° for 15-20 minutes or until brown on top and bubbling.

CAULIFLOWER AND MUSHROOMS

½ large head of cauliflower
2 cups mushrooms
1 ½ tablespoons butter
Salt and pepper to taste
Corn meal

Melt butter in skillet; Sauté cauliflower and mushrooms; cool. Shape into patties. Roll in cornmeal; fry until done.

SPRING GREENS WITH BEETS

1 (5 oz) package spring salad greens
1 (14 ½ oz) can beets, drained and sliced
1 cup goat cheese, crumbled
2/3 cup pecan halves
3 tablespoons balsamic vinegar, divided
1 tablespoon water
1 tablespoon sugar
¼ cup olive oil
1 teaspoon mustard
¼ teaspoon salt
3 tablespoons maple syrup

Cook pecans in skillet with 1 tablespoon vinegar and water over medium heat until nuts are toasted, about 3-4 minutes. Sprinkle with sugar. Cook and stir for 2-4 minutes or until sugar is melted. Spread on paper towels to cool. In another bowl, combine the oil, syrup, mustard, salt and remaining vinegar. Refrigerate until ready to serve. In a large bowl, combine salad greens and dressing; toss to coat. Divide among 8 plates. Top with beets, goat cheese and glazed pecans.

BEETS IN ORANGE SAUCE

8-9 whole beets
¼ cup sugar
1 cup orange juice
1 medium orange, sliced and halved
2 teaspoons grated orange peel
1/8 teaspoon pepper

Place beets in a large pan of water, bring to a boil. Reduce heat; cover and cook for 20-30 minutes or until done. Drain and cool. Peel and slice; place in a serving bowl. Keep warm. Mix remaining ingredients and cook until thick and pour over beets.

JUDY'S HOLIDAY ASPARAGUS

2 (10 oz) packages frozen asparagus, chopped
1 (10 ¾ oz) can cream of mushroom soup
2 tablespoon milk
1 (8 oz) can water chestnuts, drained and sliced
1 (2 oz) jar pimentos, drained and sliced
1 (4 oz) can mushrooms, drained and sliced
1 egg, hard boiled, sliced
1 (2.8 oz) can fried onion rings
1 teaspoon Worcestershire sauce
¼ teaspoon each (salt and pepper)

Thaw and drain asparagus, set aside. Combine the soup, milk, Worcestershire sauce, salt and pepper, mix well. Set aside. Layer each of the asparagus, chestnuts, mushrooms, pimentos, egg and soup mixture in an 8 inch baking dish. Bake at 350° for 20-30 minutes.

GOOD ASPARAGUS CASSEROLE

1 large can of asparagus tips
1 can cream of mushroom soup
½ pound sharp cheddar cheese, grated
2 eggs, boiled hard and sliced
½ cup each (butter and sliced almonds)
2 cups Ritz crackers, crumbled

Mix cheese and crumbs, add asparagus liquid to soup. Butter casserole dish. Layer ingredients in this order.1 /3 crumb and cheese mixture, ½ of asparagus, ½ of soup mixture, ½ of melted butter and 1 egg, sliced. Repeat layers once more. Finish with the remaining 1/3 crumbs and cheese mixture, now add sliced almonds and bake at 350° for 30 minutes.

FRIED ASPARAGUS

Wash fresh asparagus and cut off the tough ends. Cut diagonally into 1 inch pieces. Drop in hot oil and fry 3-4 minutes. Salt lightly and serve.

ASPARAGUS SOUFFLE

1 (15 ½ oz) can asparagus spears, drained
1 cup cheddar cheese, shredded
1 cup mayonnaise
1 (10 ½ oz) can cream of mushroom soup
2 eggs

Beat eggs; add remaining ingredients and blend. Pour into greased soufflé dish. Place soufflé dish in a second pan and add 2 inches of water and bake at 350° for 1 hour.

ASPARAGUS AND SQUASH SAUTE

½ pound yellow squash, sliced
1 pound asparagus, trimmed
½ red onion, peeled and sliced
1 tablespoon olive oil
1/3 cup orange juice
½ teaspoon salt

Cook squash, asparagus and onion in olive oil for 5 minutes. Add orange juice and salt, cook 5 minutes longer

BEETS WITH SOUR CREAM

2 cups cooked hot beets, drained and cubed
½ cup sour cream
½ cup green onion, minced
¼ cup French dressing

Combine beets and the dressing and heat, add sour cream and pour into serving dish. Sprinkle with the minced onion.

CREAMED CELERY WITH WATER CHESTNUTS

4 cups celery, sliced
½ cup water chestnuts, sliced
½ cup canned mushrooms, drained and sliced
¼ cup almonds, slivered
½ teaspoon salt
5 tablespoons butter or margarine, divided
½ cup milk
½ cup Ritz crackers, crushed
½ cup parmesan cheese, grated
1 cup chicken broth
3 tablespoons flour

Cook celery with salt in boiling water for 5 minutes; drain. Mix celery with almonds, water chestnuts and mushrooms in a bowl. Stir flour into 3 tablespoons melted butter and cook until well blended. Add milk and chicken broth and stir until thickened. Combine cream sauce with celery mixture. Place mixture in a buttered casserole dish. Cover with parmesan cheese. Melt remaining butter and add cracker crumbs, sprinkle over cheese and bake at 350° for 30 minutes or until bubbly.

GRANNY'S CELERY AND POTATOES

2 cups celery roots, diced up
2 ½ cups potatoes, peeled and diced up
1 cup heavy whipping cream
¼ cup sour cream
4 tablespoons butter
!/2 teaspoon each (salt and pepper)

Peel and dice celery roots, place in pan of boiling water, boil until done. Peel and dice potatoes and cook in boiling water until done. Add 2 tablespoons of butter and ½ cup of the cream to the celery root. Put in food processor and process until all is mixed well; set aside. Mash the potatoes and add ½ of the cream, 2 tablespoons of the butter and the sour cream to the mashed potatoes. Stir well. Add salt and pepper. Best served hot.

SOUTHERN GRITS PIE

1 stick butter or margarine
¼ cup each (grits and buttermilk)
3 eggs, beaten
¾ cup sugar
2 tablespoons flour
1 teaspoon vanilla
Whipping cream
1 pie crust, un-baked

Cook grits, add butter and stir constantly. Set aside. Mix sugar and flour and stir. Add eggs, vanilla and buttermilk. Add this to the grits mixture. Pour all into an un-baked pie crust and bake at 325° for 40 minutes. Serve with whipped cream.

GOOD CHEESE GRITS

1 cup grits
4 ½ cups half and half
½ stick butter or margarine
2 eggs
1 roll each (garlic cheese and cheddar cheese)
1 teaspoon salt
Cornflakes

Cook grits with half and half and salt in a double boiler. Add butter, garlic cheese and eggs. Cut cheddar cheese into small pieces and add to hot grits. Stir until cheese is melted. Pour into a baking dish, cover and top with crushed cornflakes and bake at 350° for 1 hour.

SPECIAL GRITS SOUFFLE

½ cup grits
2 cups water
½ stick butter
3 eggs, separated
¼ cup sharp cheddar cheese, grated
1 teaspoon salt

Boil grits in salted water until done. Add butter, cheese and egg yolks; cool. Fold in stiffly beaten egg whites. Pour into soufflé dish and bake at 375° until puffed and golden brown 30-40 minutes.

VEGETABLE CASSEROLE

3 cups zucchini, grated
2 medium tomatoes, sliced thin
3-4 tablespoons dried bread crumbs
½ teaspoon each (salt, basil, minced garlic and oregano)
1/8 teaspoon pepper
1 tablespoon lemon juice
3 tablespoons each (flour and butter)
4 large eggs
½ cup each (mozzarella and parmesan cheese, grated and onion diced)
1 cup swiss cheese, grated
3 (8 oz) package cream cheese, softened
1 medium carrot, grated

Salt zucchini lightly; let stand 25 minutes, drain excess water thoroughly. Sauté the zucchini, onion, garlic, carrot and salt in a large skillet, until onion is translucent. Remove from heat and set aside. In a mixing bowl, beat softened cream cheese until smooth. Add mozzarella and parmesan cheese. Add eggs; beat 1 minute. Add remaining ingredients except bread crumbs and tomatoes. Add sautéed vegetables. Butter a 9 inch spring form pan and dust with bread crumbs. Pour cheese and vegetable mixture into a prepared pan. Bake at 375° for 30 minutes. Arrange thinly sliced tomatoes on top and bake for 30 minutes.

MULTI - VEGGIE COINS

3 medium carrots, sliced thin
1 small head cauliflower, broken into florets
2 medium yellow squash, sliced
2 medium zucchini, sliced
2 garlic cloves, minced
4 tablespoons butter or margarine, divided
1 cup chicken broth
1 teaspoon white pepper
1 teaspoon salt

Place carrots, squash and cauliflower in a 3 quart baking dish. In a small saucepan, sauté garlic in 2 tablespoons of butter for 2-3 minutes. Stir in the broth, salt and pepper. Pour over vegetables; dot with remaining butter. Cover and bake at 350° for 50 minutes or until vegetables are tender.

BRUSSELS SPROUTS

2 pounds fresh Brussels sprouts
1 cup chicken broth
1 medium onion, chopped
2 bacon strips, diced
1 teaspoon caraway seeds
¼ teaspoon each (salt and pepper)

Trim Brussels sprouts and cut an X in the core of each one. In a large saucepan, put 1 inch of water and bring Brussels sprouts to a boil. Reduce heat; and cook for 8-10 minutes or until crisp-tender. In a large skillet cook bacon until crisp, drain on paper towels. Reserve bacon drippings. In the same skillet, sauté onion in the drippings until tender. Stir in broth, caraway seeds, salt and pepper. Bring to a boil. Reduce heat; simmer, un-covered until liquid is almost evaporated. Drain sprouts, add sprouts and bacon to onion mixture. Toss to coat.

BRUSSELS SPROUTS WITH CHESTNUTS

3 pounds fresh Brussels sprouts
1 ½ cups water chestnuts, sliced
¾ cup chicken broth
2 tablespoon butter
2 teaspoons flour
¼ teaspoon each (basil, salt and pepper)

Cook Brussels sprouts in salted water until tender. For the cream sauce; melt butter in skillet, add flour, salt, pepper and basil. Then add the chicken broth stirring constantly until thickened. Pour cream sauce over Brussels spouts and chestnuts.

SWEET AND SOUR BRUSSELS SPROUTS

4 (16 oz) packages frozen Brussels sprouts, thawed
1 medium onion , chopped fine
1/3 cup cider vinegar
½ pound sliced bacon, fried crisp and diced
3 tablespoons sugar
1/8 teaspoon pepper
1 teaspoon each (ground mustard and salt)

Cook bacon until crisp. Drain on paper towels. In the drippings, sauté Brussels sprouts and onion until crisp-tender. Add sugar, vinegar, salt, mustard and pepper. Bring to a boil. Reduce heat, cover and simmer for 4-5 minutes or until tender. Stir in the bacon.

ZUCCHINI BOATS

1 large zucchini
1 pound sausage
1 can stewed tomatoes
1 egg
2 cloves garlic, minced
Parmesan cheese
Tomato sauce
Parsley or sage or both
Bread crumbs

Wash zucchini, cut in half lengthwise. Microwave until crisp-tender 5-8 minutes. Scoop out the insides of the zucchini, leaving about ½ inch thickness remaining. Place cooked zucchini in a large bowl and set aside. Sauté sausage and garlic over medium heat until cooked done, drain. Combine sausage in bowl with zucchini, add egg, parmesan cheese, bead crumbs, stewed tomatoes, salt, pepper, parsley and sage. Mix by hand. Stuff zucchini shells with sausage mixture. Pour tomato sauce over stuffed zucchini and bake at 350° for 20 minutes or until thoroughly heated.

EASY ZUCCHINI CASSEROLE

6 cups zucchini, sliced thin
3 strips bacon, cut in small pieces
1 cup fresh or canned tomatoes
1 cup cheddar cheese, shredded
1 teaspoon salt
1/8 teaspoon pepper
1 tablespoon flour

Fry bacon, add zucchini; cover and simmer 5 minutes. Add all other ingredients and pour into a 1 ½ quart casserole dish. Bake at 375° for 30-35 minutes.

ZUCCHINI AND YELLOW SQUASH

2 small yellow squash
2 small zucchini
2 tablespoons butter
1 red or green pepper, cut into strips
½ teaspoon each (basil, salt and pepper)

Combine vegetables and put in skillet with melted butter, sprinkle with basil. Cover and cook until tender. Season with salt and pepper.

STUFFED SQUASH

½ cup each (chopped green pepper and shredded cheddar cheese)
1 medium tomato, chopped
2 tablespoons onion, chopped
2 slices bacon, fried crisp and crumbled
Dash of Worcestershire sauce
½ teaspoon each (salt and pepper)
Butter
Ritz cracker crumbs

Cook squash until barley tender. Drain. Cool slightly and cut a slice from each.
Remove seeds. Combine remaining ingredients except butter and cracker crumbs. Mix well. Spoon into shells. Top each with cracker crumbs and butter. Bake at 400° for approximately 20 minutes.

FRANK'S FAVORITE SQUASH CASSEROLE

3 cups of squash, cooked and drained
1 large onion, chopped
½ stick butter
1 cup cheddar cheese, grated
½ cup sour cream
1 cup Ritz crackers, crushed (extra for topping)
1 teaspoon garlic powder
½ teaspoon each (salt and pepper)

Sauté onion in butter for 45 minutes. Remove from pan and combine the rest of the ingredients together. Pour into a buttered casserole dish and top with cracker crumbs, soaked in butter. Bake at 350° for 30 minutes.

GOOD SQUASH CASSEROLE

4-6 squash, partially cooked and sliced
1 can cream of mushroom soup
1 cup American cheese, grated
1 cup potato chips, ranch flavored, crushed

Grease casserole dish, layer squash, soup and potato chips. Repeat layer and top with grated cheese. Bake at 350° for 30 minutes or until bubbly.

FRIED SQUASH FRITTERS

4 cups yellow squash, cooked and mashed
½ cup each (flour, meal and vegetable oil)
2 eggs, beaten
1 small onion, chopped
½ teaspoon each (salt and pepper)

Combine squash, eggs, meal, flour, onion, salt and pepper in bowl; mix well. Shape into patties. Fry patties in hot oil in skillet until brown on both sides. Serve hot with butter.

SOUTHERN FRIED SQUASH

3 medium size squash, sliced
½ cup water
1 tablespoon sugar
¼ cup heavy cream
2 tablespoons each (bacon drippings and onion, diced)

Remove stem and bottom ends of squash. Cut squash into ½ inch rounds. Place squash and bacon drippings and 1 teaspoon salt in a skillet. Add water, cover and cook until squash is tender and water has absorbed. Mash with fork, add sugar and onion. Cook slowly until flavors develop.

SQUASH WITH ALMONDS

8-10 yellow squash, sliced
1 large onion, sliced thin
1 cup whipping cream
¼ cup almonds, slivered and toasted
½ cup bread crumbs
2 teaspoon salt
¼ teaspoon pepper

Cook squash in water with onion, salt and pepper. Drain well. Mix with cream; stir in almonds. Spoon in baking dish. Spread bread crumbs on top and bake at 325° for 35 minutes or until set.

HOT CABBAGE CREOLE

1 bag of cabbage slaw, plain and chopped
2 slices of bacon
1 large green pepper, chopped
1 (28 oz) can whole tomatoes, chopped (save juice)
1 large onion, chopped
1/3 cup vinegar
2 teaspoons salt
¼ teaspoon black pepper
¼ teaspoon cayenne pepper

Cut bacon in pieces and fry in large skillet. Add onion and green pepper and sauté with bacon. Add tomatoes and juice. Stir, add cabbage, salt and pepper. Sprinkle with cayenne pepper. Add vinegar, bring to a boil and cover. Simmer for about 45 minutes.

SWEET AND SOUR CABBAGE

1 medium head of red cabbage
¼ cup brown sugar
½ cup vinegar
2 cups tart apples, peeled and sliced thin
½ cup water
6 slices bacon
1 medium onion, chopped
1 teaspoon salt
1/8 teaspoon pepper

Strip off outer leaves of the cabbage; cut into quarters and remove hard core. Shred fine. Cook bacon until crisp. Remove bacon from drippings. Cook onion 2-3 minutes in drippings. Add cabbage, apples, salt, pepper and water. Cover and cook 10-15 minutes longer or until apples are tender and liquid is absorbed. Crumble bacon on top of cabbage.

FRIED CABBAGE

8 strips bacon, fried crisp and crumbled
½ head cabbage, cut into 1 inch pieces
1 medium green bell pepper, diced
½ medium onion, diced
½ teaspoon caraway seed
2 tablespoons sugar
1 tablespoon vinegar
¼ teaspoon Tabasco sauce
1 teaspoon salt
¼ teaspoon pepper

Fry bacon crisp and set aside, reserve drippings. Place reserved drippings in dutch oven over medium heat. Add onions, bell pepper, cabbage, salt, pepper, Tabasco sauce, caraway seed, vinegar and sugar. Mix together to coat cabbage. Cook 3 minutes. Crumble bacon on top when ready to serve.

CABBAGE ROLLS

1 large head of cabbage
1 pound hamburger
2 cans tomato soup
½ cup water
1 ½ cups rice, un-cooked
1 green pepper, chopped
1 large onion, chopped
1/ teaspoon salt
½ teaspoon pepper

Cook cabbage in boiling water until tender. Separate the leaves. Mix hamburger, onion, rice, green pepper, salt and pepper and 1 can of the soup together. Fill each cabbage leaf with the mixture; wrap securely. Line baking dish with the un-used cabbage leaves; place rolls on leaves. Place extra cabbage leaves on top of rolls. Pour remaining soup and water over top. Simmer for 2-3 hours or until cabbage is tender and done.

CREAMY CABBAGE WITH BACON

4 cups cabbage, shredded
4 strips bacon, cooked crisp and crumbled
1 cup bread crumbs
1 cup half and half
1 tablespoon flour
¼ teaspoon paprika
½ teaspoon salt
1/8 teaspoon pepper

In a large saucepan, bring 1 inch of water and cabbage to a boil. Reduce heat, cover and simmer for 3-5 minutes or until crisp-tender. Cook bacon until crisp. Drain on paper towels; keep 1 tablespoon of drippings. Stir the flour, paprika, salt and pepper into the drippings until smooth; gradually add the half and half. Bring to a boil; cook and sir for 2 minutes or until thickened. Place cabbage in an un-greased 1 quart baking dish. Top with sauce. Sprinkle bread crumbs and bacon over the top and bake at 400° for about 15 minutes or until heated through.

CRUNCHY CABBAGE

1 large head of green cabbage, shredded
2 packages Ramen noodles (chicken)
6 green onions, chopped
½ cup almonds, slivered
6 tablespoons sesame seeds

DRESSING
1 cup peanut oil
¼ cup red wine vinegar
1 teaspoon soy sauce
2 packages chicken seasoning (in Ramen noodle packages)
4 tablespoons sugar

Combine sesame seeds, almonds and Ramen noodles in a pan and toast. Toss together with cabbage and onions. Combine all of the dressing ingredients and drizzle over cabbage.

CABBAGE CASSEROLE

1 small head of cabbage, shredded
1 cup cheddar cheese, grated
2 eggs
½ cup mayonnaise
1 cup milk
1 can cream of celery soup
1 stick butter
1 ¾ cup Ritz cracker crumbs

Steam cabbage. Melt butter in a 13 x 9 inch baking dish and sprinkle enough cracker crumbs to cover bottom of dish. Reserve some for the top. Mix together soup, milk, mayonnaise and eggs. Put cabbage in dish over butter; pour soup mixture over cabbage. Top with cheese and remaining crumbs and bake at 350° for 30 minutes.

GOOD CREAMED CABBAGE

1 medium head cabbage
½ stick butter
2 tablespoons flour
Salt and pepper to taste
Some cheddar cheese, grated
Milk
Ritz crackers

Cut cabbage coarsely and drop in boiling water. Cook until transparent, (don't over cook) drain cabbage; add butter, sprinkle flour over all and toss lightly. Add enough milk to moisten good. Add salt and pepper to taste. Sprinkle heavy with grated cheese. Crumble 8-10 Ritz crackers on top and bake at 350° for about 30 minutes.

CABBAGE WITH SOUR CREAM

1 medium head of green cabbage
1 cup sour cream
3 tablespoons drippings or vegetable oil
½ teaspoon each (salt and pepper)

Slice cabbage thin. Sauté in bacon drippings for 8 minutes. Stir in sour cream and warm thoroughly. Season with salt and pepper. Serve hot.

FAVORITE POTATOES

2 large red potatoes
10 slices bacon, cooked crisp and crumbled
4 large slices swiss cheese
2 small onions, sliced thin
1 ½ teaspoons each (seasoning salt and pepper)
1 cup tomatoes, diced

With skin left on, slice potatoes into rounds. Season with pepper and seasoning salt; brown lightly in oil. While potatoes are still hot, cover with onion slices. Remove from heat. Layer on a platter; potatoes, onions, crumbled bacon and swiss cheese. Microwave for 1 minute or until cheese melts. Top with diced tomatoes and serve.

CROSS CUT POTATOES

4 large baking potatoes
1/8 teaspoon paprika
2 tablespoons butter or margarine, melted and divided
1 tablespoon fresh parsley, minced
1/8 teaspoon pepper
¼ teaspoon salt

Cut potatoes in half lengthwise. Slice each half widthwise 6 times, but not all the way through; fan potatoes slightly in a shallow baking dish. Brush potatoes with 1 tablespoon butter. Sprinkle with paprika, parsley, salt and pepper. Bake un-covered at 350° for 50 minutes or until tender. Drizzle with remaining butter.

BAKED NEW POTATOES

8 small new potatoes
½ cup butter, melted
Cornflakes, crushed

Boil and cook potatoes until done; peel. Dip potatoes in melted butter and roll in crushed cornflakes, Bake at 400° until cornflakes are brown.

HASH BROWN POTATO BAKE

2 pounds hash browns, frozen and thawed
2 cans cream of chicken soup
1 pint of sour cream
2 cups cornflakes, crushed
¼ cup onion, chopped
2 cups cheddar cheese, shredded
¼ cup butter, melted
1 teaspoon salt
¼ teaspoon pepper

Combine all ingredients in a greased 13 x 9 inch casserole dish. Sprinkle a few more cornflakes on top. Pour extra ¼ cup butter on top and bake at 350° for 1 hour.

OVEN FRIED POTATOES

3 large baking potatoes
2 cups cornbread dressing mix
½ cup mayonnaise
½ teaspoon hot pepper sauce
¼ teaspoon onion salt
¼ teaspoon garlic powder
1/8 teaspoon black pepper

Wash potatoes and cut into wedges. Mix mayonnaise with hot sauce, onion, salt, garlic powder and black pepper. Coat potato wedges with the mayonnaise mixture and roll in dressing mix. Place in a greased baking dish and bake at 375° for 50-60 minutes or until potatoes are tender.

GRILLED POTATOES IN FOIL

3 large baking potatoes, pared
4-5 slices bacon, fried crisp
1 large onion, sliced
8 ounces sharp American cheese, cubed
½ cup butter or margarine
Salt and ground black pepper

Slice potatoes on to a big piece of heavy foil and sprinkle with salt and pepper. Crumble bacon over the potatoes. Add onion and cheese. Slice the butter over all. Mix on the foil; bring the edges of foil up, leaving space for steam to escape and seal with double fold. Place the package on a grill and cook over coals for 1 hour.

GOOD POTATOES AU GRATIN

6 medium potatoes
1/3 cup onion, chopped
2 cups cheddar cheese, shredded
6 tablespoons butter, divided
2 cups sour cream
1 teaspoon salt
¼ teaspoon pepper

Boil potatoes with skins left on. Chill peel and shred. Stir in cheese, add 4 tablespoons melted butter. Fold in sour cream, onion, salt and pepper. Place in a greased casserole dish and dot with remaining butter and bake at 350° for 30 minutes.

NEW POTATOES WITH PEAS

1 pound small new potatoes
1 cup frozen green peas, cooked
1 ½ cups cream sauce

Peel potatoes and drop in boiling salted water. Drain potatoes, when done and combine cream sauce and cooked peas. Season to taste with salt and pepper. Make sauce with oil, flour and milk.

NOT YOUR NORM MASHED POTATOES

5-6 potatoes, cooked and drained
½ cup swiss cheese, shredded
½ pound bacon, fried crisp and crumbled
1 (12 oz) carton sour cream
Salt and pepper to taste

Mash cooked potatoes, add all of the ingredients, whip until smooth. Enjoy

CHEESY MASHED POTATOES

6 large potatoes, peeled and quartered
1 (8 oz) package cream cheese, softened
1 cup cheddar cheese, shredded
½ cup sour cream
1/3 cup onion, chopped
1 egg
2 teaspoons each (salt and pepper)
Additional cheddar cheese, shredded

Cook potatoes, drain and mash. In a mixing bowl, combine mashed potatoes, cream cheese, cheddar cheese, sour cream, egg, onion, salt and pepper; beat until fluffy. Transfer to a greased 2 quart baking dish. Cover and bake at 350° for 30-40 minutes or until heated through. Sprinkle with additional cheese.

MASHED POTATO CASSEROLE

1 cup mashed potatoes (leftovers are fine)
1 medium red pepper, cut in strips
½ onion, diced
1 stick butter or margarine
3 cooked potatoes with skins on, sliced
1 cup cheddar cheese, shredded
1 carton sour cream
5-6 slices bacon, fried crisp, crumbled

Sauté pepper and onion in butter. Layer, mashed potatoes, red pepper, onion, cooked sliced potatoes, sour cream and cheddar cheese. Sprinkle with bacon and bake at 350° until hot and bubbly.

EASY SCALLOPED POTATOES

3 medium potatoes
1 cup cheddar cheese, grated
1 cup milk, scalded
1 large onion, diced
Salt and pepper to taste

Peel and shred potatoes. Spread in greased casserole. Add onion. Season to taste. Add milk and 2/3 of the cheese mix. Bake at 350° for 1 hour. The last 15 minutes, spread remaining cheese over top and finish baking.

JUDY'S POTATO BAKE

4-5 cups frozen hash brown potatoes
5 ¼ cups water
1 ½ cups cheddar cheese, grated
1 cup sour cream
9 tablespoons butter, softened
½ of (8 oz) package of cream cheese
2 ¼ cups French fried onion rings
½ teaspoon each (salt, pepper and garlic powder)
¾ teaspoon salt

Cook hash browns in boiling water for 8 minutes; drain. Combine butter and cream cheese together. Mix together the hash browns, butter, cream cheese, cheddar cheese, sour cream, garlic powder, salt and pepper in a large bowl. Next, place in a 2 quart greased casserole pan or dish. Bake at 350° for 25-35 minutes or until golden brown. Spread onion rings over top of casserole and bake 5-10 minutes longer, or until onions are golden brown.

SPECIAL POTATOES

8 medium potatoes, boiled with skins
½ cup green onions and tops, chopped
1 ½ cups sour cream
11 tablespoons butter, divided
2 cups cheddar cheese, grated
2 tablespoons butter
1 cup potato chips, crushed
1 teaspoon salt
1/8 teaspoon pepper

Peel and cut potatoes in large cubes. Combine cheese and 9 tablespoons of butter in a large pan. Cook until melted. Remove from heat and stir in the sour cream, onions, salt and pepper. Add in potatoes, put in greased 2 quart baking dish. Dot with remaining butter. Melt 2 tablespoons butter, cheese and potatoes. Place on top of casserole and bake at 350° for approximately 25-30 minutes or until heated through.

EULA'S TURNIP SOUFFLE

3-4 medium turnips, peeled and diced
2 eggs, beaten
¼ cup half and half
¼ cup Ritz crackers, crushed, soaked in butter
½ teaspoon nutmeg
3 tablespoons butter or margarine
1 teaspoon salt

Cook turnips until tender. Drain and mash. Add cream, nutmeg, salt and eggs. Combine with the mashed turnips. Place in casserole dish, top with butter soaked cracker crumbs. Bake at 350° for 30-40 minutes or until browned.

EGG CASSEROLE

8 eggs, hard boiled
1 can mushrooms
¾ cup cheddar cheese, grated
2 tablespoons flour
2 tablespoon butter
2 cups half and half
Bread crumbs

Make the sauce, using milk, flour and mushroom liquid. Melt cheese in hot sauce. Place a layer of sliced eggs in bottom of a greased casserole dish; add layers of sauce and mushrooms. Repeat layers. Sprinkle with buttered bread crumbs. Bake at 350° for 40 minutes.

CREAMED TURNIP GREENS

1 (16 oz) bag frozen turnip greens, thawed
½ onion, chopped
2 garlic cloves, minced
1 cup milk
½ cup chicken broth
1 tablespoon butter
2 tablespoons flour
½ teaspoon red pepper
1 (5 oz) package cream cheese, cut into pieces
½ teaspoon salt
¼ teaspoon pepper
Parmesan cheese

Combine onion and garlic, sauté over medium heat for 3 minutes or until tender. Stir in the greens, chicken broth and red pepper, cook 4-5 minutes or until all liquid is evaporated. Sprinkle turnip green mixture with flour and sauté for 2 minutes longer. Gradually stir in milk and cook stirring occasionally, about 3 minutes. Add cream cheese, stirring until melted. Add salt and pepper and serve.

TURNIP GREEN CASSEROLE

1 (15 oz) can turnip greens, chopped
½ (10 ½ oz) can cream of mushrooms soup
½ cup mayonnaise
2 tablespoons wine vinegar
1 teaspoon horseradish
2 egg, beaten
Cheddar cheese, grated
Bread crumbs
1 teaspoon sugar
Salt and pepper to taste

Blend all ingredients together except the crumbs and cheese. Spoon into a casserole dish, cover top with bead crumbs and cheese and bake at 350° for 1 hour.

COLLARD GREENS AND DUMPLINGS

COLLARDS
1 large bunch of collard greens
½ stick butter
2 quarts of chicken broth
1 teaspoon each (Tabasco sauce, salt and pepper)
½ teaspoon garlic powder
1 ham hock

DUMPLINGS
½ cup flour
1 ½ cups white cornmeal
1 teaspoon baking powder
½ cup milk
2 eggs
½ teaspoon salt

Combine the ham hock, Tabasco sauce, garlic powder, salt and chicken broth together in a large pot and simmer for about 40-50 minutes. Add the greens and cook, stirring often until tender, about 30 minutes longer. Stir in the butter. Remove ham hock from pot. Place the greens in individual serving dishes, cover with foil to keep hot. Keep cooking liquid in pot.

DUMPLINGS
Combine the flour, cornmeal, baking powder and salt in a bowl. Whisk the eggs and milk in another bowl. Add the wet mixture to the dry mixture to make the batter. Bring the broth to a boil and drop the dumplings into it, 1 at a time. Cook through 10-15 minutes. Place the dumplings on the bowl of greens. Spoon broth over the greens and dumplings. Serve hot.

OLD FASHION TURNIP CASSEROLE

3 cups turnips, peeled, cooked and mashed
3 eggs, beaten
1 ¼ cups bread crumbs
3 tablespoons butter
4 teaspoons sugar
1 teaspoon each (salt and pepper)
Extra butter

Mix turnips, 3 tablespoons butter, sugar, salt, pepper and ¾ cup bread crumbs. Add egg to turnip mixture. Place in a buttered casserole, topped with remaining bread crumbs, drizzle with butter and bake at 350° for 30-45 minutes.

PICNIC SWEET PEA CASSEROLE

2 (16 oz) packages frozen green peas, thawed and drained
1 (16 oz) can French-fried onion rings
1 cup parmesan cheese
2 cups cheddar cheese, grated
¼ cup butter
1 (8 oz) package baby bella mushrooms, sliced
1 cup onion , chopped
2 cloves garlic, minced
2 tablespoons flour
1 cup milk
¼ teaspoon each (nutmeg and black pepper)
1 teaspoon sugar
¾ teaspoon salt
1 cup heavy whipping cream

In a dutch oven melt the butter. Add mushrooms, garlic and onions. Cook 5-6 minutes or until tender. Stir in sugar, flour, nutmeg, salt and pepper; cook stirring constantly for 2 minutes. Add milk and cream; cook, stirring constantly for 6-8 minutes, or until slightly thickened. Add the cheese, stirring until melted and smooth. Add peas, mix well. Spoon mixture into a 13 x 9 inch baking dish; bake at 350° for 30 minutes. Top evenly with French fried onion rings and bake 5 minutes longer. Serve at once.

CREAMED PEAS

1 (10 oz) package frozen green peas
½ cup half and half
1 tablespoon flour
1 tablespoon butter
1 tablespoon sugar
1/8 teaspoon pepper
¼ teaspoon salt

Cook peas according to directions on package. In a small saucepan, melt butter, stir in flour, salt and pepper until blended; add the milk and sugar. Bring to a boil; cook and stir for 1-2 minutes longer or until thickened. Drain peas; stir into the sauce and heat through.

PEAS AND MUSHROOMS

2 pounds fresh English peas
2 tablespoons bacon grease
½ pound mushrooms, sliced
1 cup pearl onions, peeled
Salt and pepper

Shell and wash peas. Cover the peas and onions with water and bring to a boil. Reduce heat and simmer for 10-12 minutes or until peas are tender. Sauté mushrooms in bacon grease in a large skillet until tender. Stir in the peas, onions, salt and pepper. Cook, stirring constantly until heated through.

NEW PEAS AND POTATOES

3 cups fresh peas
12 small new potatoes
1 ½ cups milk or half and half
2 tablespoons butter
1 ½ teaspoons each (flour, salt and sugar)

Cook potatoes in salted water. Cook peas separately in salt water; drain. Combine potatoes and peas in same pan, add 1 cup milk. Mix remaining ½ cup milk with flour and sugar. Add to potatoes and peas. Cook until thickened. Add butter.

NOODLE BAKE

2 cups noodle, broken
2 eggs, beaten
½ cup American cheese, diced
1 cup cottage cheese
1 can cream of mushroom soup
1 pound ground beef
1 small onion, chopped
1 teaspoon salt

Cook noodles; drain. Brown meat and onion. Mix all ingredients in a casserole dish and bake at 350° for 30 minutes.

BLACK - EYED PEA CASSEROLE

1 cup blank-eyed peas, cooked
1 cup white cornmeal
½ cup flour
1 cup onion chopped
¾ cup creamed corn
1 pound hamburger meat, browned
½ pound cheddar cheese, grated
½ cup oil
1 teaspoon each (salt and soda)

Mix all ingredients together except cheese. Pour into a greased casserole dish. Add cheese last, by pressing down into top of casserole and bake at 350° for 45 minutes.

GOOD BLACK - EYED PEAS

2 (15.8 oz) cans black-eyed peas, drained
1 medium onion, chopped
1 (4 ½ oz) can hot stewed tomatoes, un-drained and chopped
1 medium green pepper, seeded and chopped
4 slices bacon, cooked crisp
½ teaspoon each (salt and pepper)

Cook bacon until crisp, keep drippings in skillet. Crumble bacon, set aside. Cook pepper and onions in drippings until tender. Add peas, tomatoes, salt and pepper to skillet. Cook until thoroughly heated, stirring often. Sprinkle crumbled bacon on top.

GRANDMOTHER'S FRIED BLACK- EYED PEAS

1 can black-eyed peas
3-4 strips bacon, fried crisp and crumbled
1/3 cup red peppers, roasted
½ cup onion, shopped
½ teaspoon hot sauce
A little flour
Oil for frying

Mash peas with fork, (peas mash better if warm). Add remaining ingredients except flour. Mix well. Add a little flour to the mixture, so patties will stick together. Shape into patties and fry in skillet of hot oil until browned on both sides.

FRIED GREEN TOMATOES

6 large green tomatoes, cut into ¼ inch slices
1 cup corn meal
Vegetable oil
Salt and pepper to taste

Slice tomatoes ¼ inch thick. Dredge tomatoes in corn meal. Season with salt and pepper. Fry in hot oil until brown on both sides.

OKRA - CORN - TOMATOES

10 pods small okra
3 cups corn, cooked
3 cups tomatoes, cooked
1 small green pepper
1 medium onion

Slice okra and onions in rings, dice pepper and add to corn and tomatoes. Add salt and pepper. Cook slowly about ½ hour.

BAKED TOMATOES

1 quart of canned tomatoes
1 can biscuits, cut into 1/3 and buttered
1 ½ cups sugar

In a large baking dish, put enough tomatoes to cover the bottom. Sprinkle heavy with sugar. Put layer of biscuits to cover bottom of dish. Top with tomatoes, add 1/3 of sugar. Repeat layering until all is used up and bake at 375o for 45 minutes or until browned.

CHERRY TOMATOES IN CREAM

1 quart of cherry tomatoes
1 pint of whipping cream
3 tablespoons each (butter and brown sugar)
½ teaspoon salt

In skillet, melt butter, salt and sugar. Add tomatoes; when tomatoes begin to split open, add the cream. Serve hot in individual dishes.

FRIED OKRA PATTIES

4 cups fresh or frozen okra, cut in slices
1 ½ cups flour
6 cups vegetable oil (for deep frying)
1/3 cup buttermilk
¼ teaspoon each (salt and garlic powder)
1/8 teaspoon pepper

Mix flour, garlic powder, salt and pepper together. Toss okra in buttermilk to coat. Place okra in the flour mixture and shake off excess flour. Heat oil in dutch oven or deep fryer to 350°. Make patties and fry until golden brown, usually 5-10 minutes.

OKRA AND TOMATOES

1 pound okra, sliced
2 pounds tomatoes, peeled
½ cup onion, chopped
2 tablespoons butter or margarine
1 teaspoon each (curry powdered and seasoned salt)

Sauté onion in butter in a large skillet until transparent. Add okra slices and sauté 5 minutes more. Add remaining ingredients and simmer, covered for 20 minutes longer.

SIMPLE RUTABAGAS

1 large or 2 medium rutabagas, peeled and cut in cubes
4-5 slices of bacon, cut in 1-2 inch squares
2 tablespoons butter
Pinch of sugar
Salt and pepper to taste

In a medium size pot, combine bacon and butter, cook until bacon is crisp. Add the rutabagas, sugar, salt and pepper. Add enough water so the rutabagas won't stick. Cook until done. Drain off most all liquid. Mash rutabagas with potato masher, add a little cream if too thick.

BEST TOMATO QUICHE

¾ cup flour
4-5 tablespoons cold water
½ cup cornmeal
1/3 cup vegetables oil
½ teaspoon salt
1/8 teaspoon pepper

FILLING
2 cups plum tomatoes, chopped
½ teaspoon dried basil
1/8 teaspoon pepper
½ cup each (chopped green onions, cheddar and swiss cheese, grated)
2 tablespoons flour
1 cup evaporated milk
2 eggs

In a bowl, combine flour, cornmeal, salt and pepper. Add vegetable oil until crumbly. Add water, tossing with a fork until dough forms a ball. Refrigerate for 30 minutes. On a lightly floured surface, roll out dough to fit a 9 inch pie plate; transfer pastry to plate. Trim to ½ inch beyond edge of plate; flute edges. Bake at 375° for 10 minutes. Cool completely. Place tomatoes in the crust; sprinkle with salt, basil, pepper, onions and cheese. In a bowl, whisk flour, milk and eggs until smooth. Pour over filling and bake at 375° for 40-50 minutes or until a knife inserted in the center comes out clean. Let stand for 10 minutes before cutting.

DELICIOUS TOMATOES WITH SHRIMP

4 large tomatoes
1 tablespoon butter or margarine
2 tablespoons each (chopped green pepper and cheddar cheese, grated)
1/3 cup each (celery and onion, chopped)
½ pound small shrimp, cooked
¼ teaspoon each (dill weed, salt, pepper and Worcestershire sauce)
¼ cup bread crumbs

Remove pulp from tomatoes, don't break skin. Put the shells in a quart baking dish; set aside. Melt butter in skillet, add onion, celery and green pepper, sauté over low heat 5 minutes. Cut up shrimp. Mix tomato pulp, shrimp and chopped vegetables, add bread crumbs, Worcestershire sauce, salt, pepper and dill weed. Fill each shell with ¼ of mixture. Sprinkle with ½ tablespoon of cheese. Bake at 375° for 20 minutes.

FRESH GARDEN TOMATOES

4 large tomatoes
¼ cup flour
1 cup Japanese bread crumbs
1 egg
1 tablespoon milk
3 tablespoons each (olive oil and butter)
1 (8 oz) package cream cheese, softened
¼ cup fresh parsley, minced
1 ½ teaspoons fresh basil, minced
1 garlic clove, minced
¼ teaspoon salt

Cut each tomato into 4 thick slices; place on paper towel to drain. In a small bowl, beat the cream cheese, parsley, basil, garlic and salt until blended. Spread cream cheese mixture over 8 tomato slices; top with remaining tomato slices. Place flour and bread crumbs in separate bowls. In another bowl, whisk egg and milk. Coat the top and bottom of each sandwich with flour, dip into egg mixture, then coat in crumbs. Heat butter and oil over medium heat. Fry tomato sandwiches in batches for 3-4 minutes on each side or until golden brown. Drain on paper towels. Serve immediately.

SOUTHERN TOMATO PIE

4 tomatoes, peeled and sliced
2 cups each (mozzarella and cheddar cheese, grated)
1 cup mayonnaise
1 9 inch pre-baked deep dish pie shell
1/3 cup green onions, chopped
8-10 fresh basil leaves, chopped
Salt and pepper to taste

Layer tomato slices, basil and onion in pie shell. Add salt and pepper to taste. Mix together the cheese and mayonnaise. Spread on top tomatoes and bake at 350° for 30 minutes or until lightly browned.

SOUTHERN CORN FRITTERS

2 cups corn
1 egg, beaten
1/3 cup milk
1 teaspoon baking powder
¼ teaspoon salt
1/3 cup flour
1 ½ teaspoons sugar
Vegetable oil

Mix flour, baking powder and salt in a bowl. Combine milk and egg and stir into the flour mixture. Add the corn and stir until the mixture is moist. Add ½ inch of oil to a large skillet over medium heat. Drop tablespoonful of the mixture into the hot oil and fry for 3-4 minutes or until golden brown.

DELICIOUS CORN PUDDING

1 cup each (cream style and whole kernel corn)
2 cups half and half
2 eggs, beaten
4 tablespoons flour
1 tablespoon butter, melted
2 teaspoons sugar
1 teaspoon salt

Mix corn, flour, sugar and salt together. Stir in eggs, melted butter and half and half. Mix with the corn mixture. Pour into a greased baking dish and bake at 350° for 1 hour. For the first ½ hour, stir from the bottom 2-3 times.

EULA'S FAVORITE CORN CASSEROLE

10 strips bacon, fried crisp
1 medium onion, chopped
12 ounces fresh corn (may use canned corn, cream style and whole kernel mixed)
1 (8 oz) carton sour cream

Fry bacon crisp; set aside. Sauté onions in bacon grease. Combine 8 strips of crumbled bacon, corn, sour cream and onions. Bake at 350° for 20 minutes or until bubbly. Top with remaining bacon.

GARDEN FRESH CORN PUDDING

2 cups fresh corn (or frozen)
1 cup whipping cream
½ cup each (sugar, half-half and butter)
3 eggs, beaten
2 tablespoons flour
¼ teaspoon nutmeg
½ teaspoon salt

Combine sugar and flour together; beaten eggs, corn and half and half. Pour into a greased casserole dish and bake at 350°. Stir after baking 30 minutes. Top with butter and nutmeg and bake 30 minutes longer.

EASY CORN PUDDING

1 can each (cream style and whole kernel corn)
1 ½ cups Ritz cracker crumbs
2 eggs
½ cup butter
Salt and pepper to taste

Beat eggs until foamy. Add corn, seasonings and crackers. Melt butter and pour into center of pudding. Stir lightly. Bake at 350° for 45 minutes to an hour.

SHOE PEG CORN BAKE

1 (12 oz) can shoe peg, whole kernel white corn, drained
2 tablespoons butter
½ pint whipping cream
¼ teaspoon salt
2 tablespoons flour
¼ teaspoon pepper

Melt the butter and add in flour. Stir in the cream, corn, salt and pepper.
Bake at 350° for 30 minutes or until consistency is very creamy and
thick. Stir often. Serve immediately.

FRANK'S VIDALIA ONION CASSEROLE

3-4 Vidalia onions, medium size and quartered
1 ½ cups cheddar cheese, grated
1 (5 oz) can evaporated milk
½ cup butter, melted, divided
4 eggs
1 ½ tubes of Ritz crackers, crushed
½ teaspoon each (salt and pepper)

Cook onions in water until tender; drain. Sauté the onions in skillet
with ½ of the butter. Beat eggs, add milk together. Add onions, ½ of
the cracker crumbs, the cheese, salt and pepper. Bake in a buttered
casserole dish at 350° for 35 minutes. Take the remaining melted butter
and stir in the remaining cracker crumbs. Place on top of casserole and
bake for 15 minutes longer.

GOOD ONION CASSEROLE

4 large onions, sliced
1 loaf of French bread, cut in ½ inch slices
1 pound swiss cheese, sliced
1 (10 ¾ oz) can cream of mushroom soup
5 tablespoons butter
1 soup can of milk

Sauté onion in butter until clear. Butter a 9 x 13 inch casserole dish, place a layer of French bread; cover with ½ onion and ½ cheese. Repeat layers. Combine soup and milk; pour over casserole. Refrigerate overnight. Bake at 350° for 30 minutes.

FRIED ONION RINGS

2 large onions, Bermuda or yellow
1 cup beer
1 cup flour
Vegetable oil for frying

Mix beer and flour, make sure you let stand for 3-4 hours. Cut onion into rings, at desired width. Dip rings in batter and fry in 375o oil in deep fryer until golden brown. Drain on paper towels.

CREAMED PEARL ONIONS

45-50 pearl onions
½ cup butter
1 cup each (chicken broth and half and half)
¼ cup each (flour and chopped parsley)
3 tablespoons parmesan cheese
½ teaspoon salt
1/8 teaspoon pepper

Place 6 cups of water in a large kettle and bring to a boil. Add onions; boil for 10-12 minutes or until tender; drain, rinse in cold water; peel and set aside. In a saucepan, melt butter and stir in flour, salt and pepper until smooth. Stir in broth and cream. Bring to a boil, cook stirring constantly or 2 minutes or until thickened. Add the cheese, onions and parsley. Pour into an un-greased 1 quart baking dish. Cover and refrigerate over night. Remove from refrigerator about ½ hour before baking. Cover and bake at 350° for 15 minutes; stir.

BAKED STUFFED ONIONS

6 medium white onions
1 (4 oz) can mushrooms, chopped (keep stems and pieces)
3 tablespoon butter
1 tablespoon pecans, chopped fine
1 cup beef broth
Cheddar cheese, grated
½ teaspoon each (salt and pepper)
Paprika

Peel and core onions, leaving shells about ½ inch thick. Reserve pulp. Cook onions in boiling water until slightly tender. Chop raw onion pulp, sauté chopped onion, mushrooms and pecans in butter for 10 minutes. Add salt and pepper.
Stuff onions with mushroom mixture. Arrange onions close together in a baking dish. Pour broth around them and bake at 300° for 30 minutes.

CREAMED SPINACH

4 pounds fresh spinach, steamed
2 cups heavy cream
1 ½ tablespoons flour
¼ cup butter
1 (9 oz) package swiss cheese
1 (8 oz) package cream cheese, softened
½ teaspoon ground red pepper
1 teaspoon salt

Wash, drain and squeeze out excess water in the spinach and place in a large bowl and set aside. In a large skillet, melt butter, add flour; cook stirring constantly for 2 minutes. Stir in cream; bring to a boil, reduce heat and simmer for 4 minutes, stirring constantly or until thickened. Add cheese, salt and red pepper. Stir until cheeses are melted and smooth. Pour cheese mixture over spinach, stirring to mix good.

GOURMET SPINACH

3 packages frozen spinach, chopped, cooked and drained
1 small can sliced mushrooms, chopped
1 envelope Lipton onion soup mix
1 small can water chestnuts, chopped
½ pint sour cream
Parmesan cheese

Mix all ingredients together and put in a baking dish. Sprinkle with parmesan cheese. Bake at 350° for about 25 minutes.

CREAMED SPINACH WITH BACON

2 bags or boxes baby spinach, frozen
3-4 slices bacon, fried crisp
1/3 cup onion, chopped
¼ - ½ cup heavy cream
½ teaspoon each (salt and pepper)

Cook bacon crisp, drain. Save 1 tablespoon of the drippings in skillet, add onion and cool, stirring until softened. Add spinach, stir until wilted. Add cream, salt and pepper. Cook until bubbly and until the cream is thickened. Crumble bacon over spinach.

SPINACH AND ARTICHOKE CASSEROLE

1 can artichoke hearts, cut in half
2 packages frozen spinach, cooked, drained and chopped
1 large can mushrooms, drained
½ cup mayonnaise
1 can cream of mushroom soup
1 teaspoon lemon juice
½ cup sour cream
¼ teaspoon garlic salt
Parmesan cheese

Combine all ingredients together, mix well. Put in baking dish and sprinkle with parmesan cheese. Bake at 350° for about 25 minutes.

GOOD SPINACH CASSEROLE

1 (10 oz) package frozen spinach, chopped
4 slices bacon, fried crisp
¾ cup cheddar cheese, grated
1 egg
½ cup milk
1/3 cup bread crumbs
½ teaspoon salt
1 teaspoon onion, minced
Paprika

Cook bacon until crisp; drain. Cook spinach, drain. Beat egg with milk and salt. Add spinach, bacon, bread crumbs, onion and ½ cup cheese. Pour into a greased casserole dish; sprinkle with additional cheese and paprika. Bake at 350° for approximately 25 minutes.

SPINACH WITH SOUR CREAM

2 packages frozen spinach, chopped
1 (14 oz) can artichoke hearts, quartered
1 medium onion, chopped
½ stick butter
1 (1 ½ oz) can parmesan cheese
1 pint sour cream

Cook and drain spinach. Sauté onion in butter. Add sour cream, parmesan cheese and onion to spinach. Put in a buttered casserole dish. Arrange quartered artichoke hearts on top and bake at 325° for 30 minutes.

STUFFED PEPPERS WITH SPINACH

1 (12 oz) package frozen spinach soufflé, thawed
1 small sweet red pepper, seeded and cut in half lengthwise
¼ cup bread crumbs (Italian seasoned)

Combine spinach and bread crumbs together; spoon into pepper halves. Place in a baking dish and sprinkle with parmesan cheese. Cover and bake at 350° for 35 minutes.

GRITS AND CHEESE CASSEROLE

1 cup grits
1 stick butter or margarine
4 ½ cups water
1 teaspoon salt
2 eggs, beaten
½ cup cheddar cheese, grated
¼ cup milk
Cornflakes

Boil grits slowly in salted water; about 20 minutes, stirring often. Remove from heat. Add the cheese and butter; cool. Beat eggs and milk until fluffy. Stir into grits mixture. Pour into a buttered casserole dish. Top with cornflake crumbs and bake at 350° for approximately 45 minutes or until set.

GREEN BEANS & CABBAGE

1 large can green beans, French-style, drained
3 cups cabbage, shredded
5 slices bacon, cooked crisp and crumbled
½ cup vinegar
3 tablespoons onion, chopped
¼ cup sugar
½ teaspoon each (salt and pepper)

Cook bacon crisp, reserve the drippings. Add vinegar, sugar, onion, cabbage, green beans, salt and pepper to remaining drippings in skillet. Simmer for 5 minutes more. Crumble bacon on top and serve.

GREEN BEAN CASSEROLE WITH MUSHROOMS

1 (16 oz) package frozen green beans, French style, thawed and drained
1 (8 oz) can water chestnuts, drained and sliced
1 pound of fresh, mushrooms, sliced
1 large sweet onion, chopped
½ teaspoon each (hot pepper sauce and black pepper)
2 tablespoons soy sauce
1 (16 oz) jar cheese whiz or cheese sauce
½ cup butter or margarine
¼ cup flour, self-rising
1 cup half and half
Slivered almonds

Sauté onions and mushrooms in butter. Add in flour until blended. Add in cream. Bring to a boil; cook and stir for 2 minutes. Add in cheese sauce, soy sauce, pepper and hot pepper sauce until cheese is melted. Remove from heat; add in water chestnuts. Place beans in an un-greased 3 quart baking dish. Pour the cheese mixture over top. Sprinkle with almonds and bake un-covered at 375° for 25-30 minutes or until bubbly.

GRANNY'S FRIED BEANS

2-3 cups beans, great northern or pintos, cooked and mashed
½ cup onion, diced
Dash hot sauce
Butter Ritz cracker crumbs and some flour

Mix beans, onion and hot sauce together. Add enough cracker crumbs and flour to hold balls or patties together. Drop in hot grease in skillet and brown on all sides.

DELICIOUS BAKED BEANS

2 (28 oz) cans baked beans, country style
8 ounces ground beef
8 ounces pork sausage
5 strips bacon
½ cup each (chopped onion, ketchup and mustard)
¼ cup each (maple syrup and dark brown sugar)

Cook beef and sausage in a large skillet until brown; drain. In the same skillet cook bacon for 2-3 minutes or until nearly done (not crisp). Drain on paper towels. In a baking dish combine beef, sausage, baked beans, onion, ketchup, mustard, brown sugar and maple syrup. Top with bacon strips. Bake un-covered for 45-50 minutes or until bacon is done and mixture is bubbly. Let stand 10 minutes before serving.

BOURBON BAKED BEANS

1 (32 oz) can pork and beans
6 slices bacon
1 cup each (diced onion and ketchup)
1 teaspoon each (dry mustard and Worcestershire sauce)
1 tablespoon molasses
1 cup green pepper, chopped fine

Cook bacon until done (not crisp). Remove from pan, dice and set aside. In the same skillet, add onions and green pepper. Sauté until soft. Combine all ingredients and pour into 1 quart casserole dish. Top with bacon and bake at 350° for 40 minutes.

BEST BAKED BEANS

1 (6 oz) can fried onion rings
1 cup each (brown sugar and molasses)
5 strips bacon, fried crisp
2 tablespoons mustard
1 (20 oz) can pineapple, crushed and drained
1 (15 oz) cans pork and beans
1 can dark beer

Combine all ingredients together using ½ of the onion rings. Place in a baking dish; add the remaining onion rings and crisp bacon on top. Bake at 350° for 1 hour.

LIMA BEANS IN SOUR CREAM

2 (10 oz) packages frozen lima beans
1 (8 oz) carton sour cream
1 (2 oz) jar pimento, drained and diced
2 tablespoons butter or margarine
½ teaspoon salt
¼ teaspoon pepper
2 tablespoons onion, chopped

Cook butter and onion in saucepan until tender, stirring constantly; set aside. Cook beans according to directions on package; drain. Add to onion mixture in saucepan. Stir in sour cream, salt and pepper. Add pimento. Cook over low heat until thoroughly heated. Serve at once.

EASY LIMA BEAN CASSEROLE

1 bag or box of lima beans, frozen
1 small can pimento, chopped
½ can mushroom soup
2/3 cup cheddar cheese, grated
1 tablespoon butter
1 teaspoon sugar
Salt and pepper to taste
Ritz crackers

Cook beans until tender, drain. Combine rest of all ingredients. Crumble Ritz crackers on top and bake at 350° for 30 minutes.

CARROT BUNDLES

4 large carrots
8 chives, blanched
3 tablespoons each (butter and brown sugar)
¼ cup white wine

Julienne carrots into 3 inch by ¼ inch strips. Cook carrots until tender; drain. Stack carrots into 8 bundles, tie with a blanched chive. In a saucepan melt the butter; stir in sugar until dissolved. Stir in wine; and simmer 2 minutes. Add carrot bundles to sauce, and cook 3 minutes or until coated good with sauce.

GREEN BEAN CASSEROLE

2 cups green beans, cooked and drained
½ cup fresh mushrooms
1 (10 ¾ oz) can cream of mushroom soup
½ cup onion, diced
1 (2.8 oz) can French fried onion rings
1 cup cheddar cheese, grated
3 tablespoons butter
½ teaspoon each (garlic powder, salt and pepper)

Melt butter in large skillet. Sauté onion and mushrooms in butter. Add green beans, mushroom soup, onion rings, garlic powder, salt and pepper. Stir well. Pour into a greased 1 ½ quart baking dish. Bake at 350° for 20 minutes, then top casserole with cheddar cheese and bake for 10 more minutes or until casserole is hot and cheese is melted.

NOT YOUR ORDINARY GREEN BEANS

2 (15 oz) cans Italian green beans, drained
6 slices bacon
½ onion, diced
½ (28 oz) package small potatoes, frozen and quartered
½ teaspoon each (salt and pepper)

Cook bacon in skillet until crisp, crumble and set aside; save the drippings from bacon. Add onion and potatoes to the drippings. Cook until potatoes are nearly done. Add green beans and seasonings, mix well. Cook additional 10-12 minutes, stirring frequently. Add crumbled bacon, stir lightly.

GREEN BEANS IN A BUNDLE

3 (14 ½ oz) cans whole green beans, drained
1 bottle Catalina salad dressing
6 slices bacon, cut in thirds
¼ cup butter

Put 6-7 beans in a stack and wrap a piece of bacon around the middle of the bean bundle. Secure with a toothpick. Place bundles in a baking dish and put a little butter over each bundle, along with the salad dressing. Bake at 350° for about 20 minutes.

GREEN BEANS WITH ALMONDS

3 (16 oz) packages frozen green beans, thawed, drained (canned is ok)
1 medium onion, sliced
2 (4 oz) cans mushrooms, sliced
½ cup butter
¼ teaspoon flour
½ teaspoon salt
1 ½ cups milk
¾ pound sharp cheddar cheese
½ teaspoon hot sauce
2 teaspoons soy sauce
½ teaspoon pepper
Sliced almonds

Sauté mushrooms and onion in butter until onion is transparent. Add flour, stirring until blended. Add milk and cook until smooth. Add cheese, salt, soy sauce, hot sauce and pepper. Cook until cheese is melted. In a separate saucepan, cook beans and drain well. Add to sauce mixture and pour into a large casserole dish. Sprinkle with sliced almonds and bake at 350° for 20 minutes.

GREEN BEANS AND ONION CASSEROLE

2 pounds fresh green beans, trimmed ends
2 green onion, minced
2 tablespoons each (cider vinegar and Dijon mustard)
1 (2.8 oz) can French fried onion rings
½ cup olive oil
¼ teaspoon each (salt and pepper)

Bake onions on a baking sheet until crisp; 7-10 minutes. Turn off oven, leave onions in oven to keep warm. Mix together; mustard and vinegar in a saucepan. Mix in green onions and slowly add the olive oil. Season to taste with salt and pepper. Bring the mixture to a boil, stirring constantly and cook for 2 minutes. Keep warm on low heat. Cook beans in a large pot of boiling water until crisp tender (5-10) minutes. Drain and transfer to mixing bowl. Mix with warm dressing and mix in onion rings. Best to serve immediately.

MEATS

SWEET AND SOUR MEAT BALLS

1 pound ground beef
6 ginger snaps cookies, crumbled
4 tablespoons each (milk, catsup and butter)
4 tablespoons each (chopped onion and bread crumbs)
1 teaspoon salt
½ teaspoon each (dried basil leaves and pepper)
2 tablespoons each (dark corn syrup and butter)
2 teaspoons vinegar
1 cup water

Combine beef, milk, onion, bread crumbs, salt and pepper together. Shape into balls; brown in butter on all sides. Mix vinegar, catsup, syrup, basil, water and salt; pour over met balls. Add ginger snaps; cover and cook for 20-25 minutes.

HOT BEEF AND RO-TEL TOMATOES CASSEROLE

2 pounds ground beef
1 (16 oz) package cheddar cheese, shredded
6 tortillas
1 (15 oz) can chili beans
1 teaspoon salt
2 teaspoons cumin
2 tablespoons chili powder
1 large onion, chopped
1 (10 oz) can Ro-tel tomatoes

Cook beef and onion until done; drain drippings. Add chili powder, salt, cumin and tomatoes; stir well. Cook over low heat for 10 minutes. Place tortillas in casserole. Spoon meat mixture onto tortillas and refrigerate overnight; bake un-covered at 350° for 45 minutes. Sprinkle with cheese and cook 15 minutes longer, or until cheese melts.

MEAT LOAF WITH POTATO CRUST

1 ½ pounds ground beef
¾ cup bead crumbs, soft
2 eggs
2 green onions sliced thin
1 ½ teaspoons thyme
¾ cup vegetable broth
½ teaspoon each (allspice, curry powder, salt and pepper)
1 clove garlic, minced
1 medium onion, chopped fine

POTATO TOPPING

1 ½ pounds red potatoes, peeled and cubed
¼ teaspoon pepper
1 teaspoon salt

Sauté onion and garlic in oil in skillet until tender. Stir in the seasonings. Add broth, bring to a boil. Reduce heat; simmer, un-covered for 5 minutes. Stir in green onions and thyme. Transfer to a large bowl, cool to room temperature. Whisk in the eggs, stir in bead crumbs. Crumble beef over mixture and mix well. Shape into a loaf and place in an un-greased 13 x 9 inch baking dish. Bake un-covered at 350° for 30 minutes. Place potatoes in a large saucepan and cover with water; add salt. Bring to a boil. Reduce heat. Simmer un-covered for 15-20 minutes or until tender; drain, reserving ¼ cup liquid. Mash potatoes with the broth, pepper and reserved liquid. Spoon or pipe mashed potatoes on to the meat loaf. Bake 45 minutes longer or until meat is done.

CHILI BURGERS

1 pound ground beef
4 hamburger buns, split and toasted
1 ½ teaspoons chili powder
1 (15 oz) can chili with beans
½ cup cheddar cheese, shredded
1 small can French fried onions

Mix beef and chili powder, make 4 patties. Fry patties in hot oil in skillet. Bring chili to a boil. Cook 5 minutes. Put burgers on buns and top with chili; cheese and onions.

MEAT AND POTATO CASSEROLE

1 pound ground beef
6 slices bacon
4 cups potatoes, cooked, hot, mashed
½ cup cheddar cheese, shredded
1 egg, beaten
1 teaspoon salt
1/3 cup onion, chopped
1 cup dry bead cubes
¼ cup ketchup
1 teaspoon chili powder
½ teaspoon pepper

Fry bacon until crisp. Drain on paper towel. Add beef and onion to the bacon drippings in skillet. Cook until beef is brown and crumbly. Add bread cubes, ketchup, chili powder and pepper; mix well. Mash potatoes with cheese, egg and salt in a bowl. Spread ½ of the potato mixture in a greased baking dish. Add beef mixture; top with remaining potato mixture and bake at 350° for 30 minutes. Crumble bacon on top.

GROUND BEEF CASSEROLE

1 pound ground beef
1 (6 oz) package cream cheese, softened
1 bunch green onions, chopped
2 cups cheddar cheese, shredded and divided
1 clove garlic, minced
1 (15 oz) can tomato sauce
1 cup sour cream
1 (5 oz) package egg noodles
1 teaspoon sugar
Salt and pepper to taste

Brown beef in skillet until crumbly. Stir in garlic, tomato sauce, sugar, salt and pepper. Simmer for 15 minutes. Combine sour cream, cream cheese, 1 ½ cups cheddar cheese and green onions; mix well. Cook noodles, drain. Alternate layers of noodles, beef mixture, ending with cheese mixture. Sprinkle remaining ½ cup cheddar cheese over top and bake at 350° for 30 minutes.

BEST MEAT LOAF

1 ½ pounds ground beef
1 soup can of boiling water
1 ½ cups milk, scalded
1 egg, beaten
1 can tomato soup
1 small onion, chopped
¼ cup green bell pepper, chopped
1 ½ cups Ritz cracker crumbs
1 teaspoon seasoned salt
¼ teaspoon each (baking powder and parsley)

Combine ground beef, cracker crumbs, milk, egg, salt, baking powder, onion and pepper together. Place into a greased loaf pan. Bake at 350° for 10 minutes. Combine soup and bring to a boil in saucepan; pour over meat loaf. Cover and bake for 1 ½ hours. Garnish with parsley. The tomato sauce makes the gravy for the meat loaf.

MEAT LOAF SUPREME

2 pounds ground beef
2 eggs
¾ cup catsup
¼ cup evaporated milk
1 teaspoon salt
2 tablespoons horseradish sauce
¼ cup green pepper, chopped fine
¾ cup onion, chopped fine
¼ cup mustard
2 cups bead crumbs

In a large bowl, beat eggs. Mix in beef, then crumbs, onion and pepper. Add horseradish sauce, salt, mustard, milk and ¼ cup catsup; mix well. Form into a loaf and place in a 9 x 13 inch baking pan. Spread remaining catsup on top and bake at 350o for 1 ½ hours.

ENCHILADA CASSEROLE

1 pound ground beef
1 (8 oz) can tomato sauce
¼ cup each (sour cream and chopped onion)
½ cup each (water and tomatoes)
1 cup cheddar cheese, shredded
4 corn tortillas
2 teaspoons chili powder

Cook meat and onions in skillet until done; drain. Stir in tomato sauce, water and chili powder. Cook 10 minutes longer or until slightly thickened. Place tortilla in dish; top with layers of ¼ each meat sauce and cheese. Repeat layers 3 times. Bake at 350° for 10-15 minutes or until heated through. Let stand 5 minutes and top with tomatoes and sour cream.

TEX - MEX TACO DINNER

1 pound ground beef
1 tablespoon chili powder
1 large tomato, chopped
2 cups lettuce, shredded
2 cups instant white rice, un-cooked
1 cup each (water and chicken broth)
½ cup each (Cheez Whiz and sour cream)

Brown meat in skillet, add chili powder, broth and water, stir. Bring to a boil. Stir in rice and Cheez Whiz; cover and simmer on low heat for 5 minutes, stirring occasionally. Serve topped with lettuce and tomato. Top with sour cream.

GROUND BEEF CASSEROLE

1 ½ pounds ground beef
1 can cream style corn
3 large potatoes, sliced thin
2 medium onions, diced
1 teaspoon each (salt and pepper)

Add salt and pepper to ground beef. Line bottom of baking dish with beef. Placing onions on top of meat. Spread potatoes on top of onions. Sprinkle remaining salt over potatoes. Pour cream style corn over top of potatoes and bake at 350° for about 1 hour.

PRIZE BEEF STROGANOFF

2 pounds sirloin steak, cut ¼ - ½ inch cubes
1 cup sour cream
1 (6 oz) can mushrooms
½ cup water
1 garlic clove, chopped
1 can each (mushroom soup and cream of chicken soup)
½ cup each (minced onion and butter)
½ teaspoon pepper
5 tablespoons flour
1 teaspoon salt

Combine flour, salt and pepper. Rub both sides of meat with garlic; rub flour into meat. Brown meat and onion in butter in large skillet, stirring often to dissolve brown particles in bottom of skillet. Add water and soups. Cook un-covered on low heat for 1 hour, stir often. Approximately 10 minutes before ready to serve add mushrooms and sour cream; heat, but don't boil. Serve over noodles, mash potatoes or rice. Sprinkle parsley over top.

BEEF ENCHILADA CASSEROLE

2 ½ pounds ground beef
3 tablespoons chili powder
2 (16 oz) jar salsa
½ stick butter or margarine
20-24 tortillas
1 (4 oz) can sliced olives
4 cups cheddar cheese, shredded
1 cup water

In a large skillet, brown the beef, then drain. Cover all meat with a layer of chili powder, then pour salsa over meat. Mix well and set aside. In a 9 x 13 inch pan, spread a thin layer of meat mixture on bottom. Butter one side of corn tortillas, and place over meat mixture with butter side up. Add more meat mixture on top of tortillas, then continue layering in the following order 3 times; olives, tortillas, meat, cheese, etc. You should have 6 buttered tortilla on each layer. Pour 1 cup water around sides of casserole, then cover with foil. Bake at 350° for 30 minutes. Remove foil and continue baking for 15 minutes more, until cheese is bubbly.

HAM CASSEROLE

1 ½ cups ham, cut in chunks
1 (8 oz) can artichoke hearts, halved
2 tablespoons each (butter and flour)
1 cup milk
¼ cup each (grated parmesan cheese, sour cream and ripe olives, sliced)
½ clove garlic, grated
½ cup bread crumbs, buttered

Place ham and artichoke hearts in a greased casserole dish. Make a cream sauce with the butter, flour and milk. When the sauce has thickened, add sour cream, garlic and olives. Pour sauce over the ham and artichoke hearts. Top with bread crumbs and cheese. Bake at 400° for 20 minutes.

HAM WITH WINE AND GRAPES

1 cup seedless green grapes
2 slices of ham, 1 inch thick
1 tablespoon cornstarch
¾ cup burgundy (wine)
¼ cup cold water
2 tablespoons each (butter and sugar)

Melt butter in skillet, add sugar and ham; brown on both sides. Remove ham. Add wine and bring to a boil stirring constantly. Combine cornstarch and water, add wine mixture. Cook and stir until thick and boiling. Lower heat, add ham, cover and simmer for 15 minutes. Add grapes and cook 2 minutes longer. Serve sauce over ham.

CHERRY GLAZED HAM

1 (5-6 pound) ham
1 cup orange marmalade
¼ cup each (pineapple or orange juice and white wine)
1 (21 oz) can cherry pie filling

Strain pie filling, keep syrup; set cherries aside. Stir together cherry syrup and rest of the ingredients; set aside. Bake ham as directed on package. Remove from oven 30 minutes before done. Pour mixture on ham and bake 30 minutes longer or until ham is done and glaze is lightly brown. Baste often with glaze. Garnish ham with remainder of the cherries.

TANGY BAR - B - Q - RIBS

3 pounds of ribs, pork or beef (we prefer pork)
1 (12 oz) bottle of chili sauce
1 large onion, chopped fine
2 cloves garlic, chopped fine
2 tablespoons cooking oil
½ cup lemon juice
4 cups molasses
¼ cup dark rum
1 tablespoon Worcestershire sauce
3 tablespoons Dijon mustard

Cut ribs into serving size pieces, placing in a large dutch oven. Cook ribs with water and simmer for 4 minutes. Drain ribs, and place in baking dish. Set ribs aside. Sauté onion and garlic in saucepan until onion is tender. Stir in remaining ingredients; reduce heat and cook for 25 minutes. Pour Bar-B-Q sauce over ribs. Cover and marinate in refrigerator overnight. Place ribs, bone side down on grill. Grill 20 minutes, turn and cook 15 minutes longer. Brush ribs with sauce, cook 5-10 minutes longer on each side.

HAM AND BROCCOLI CASSEROLE

Enough baked ham slices to cover a 13 x 9 inch dish
4 packages frozen broccoli spears, cooked and drained
4 tablespoons butter
¼ teaspoon nutmeg
¼ teaspoon salt
1/8 teaspoon pepper
½ pound mozzarella cheese slices, divided
3 cups hot milk
2 tablespoons flour
Buttered bread crumbs
Toasted almonds

Place ham slices in buttered casserole dish. Cover ham with broccoli. Make a white sauce by melting butter, adding flour and cooking 2 minutes; stirring constantly. Add milk, stir until bubbly. Remove from heat and add seasonings and 1/3 of the cheese. Pour sauce over broccoli. Top with remaining 2/3 of the cheese slices, bread crumbs and almonds. Bake at 350° for 40-45 minutes.

SPECIAL HAM CASSEROLE

2 pounds ham, cooked and cut up in pieces
1 (10 oz) package noodles, cooked
1 package frozen peas, un-cooked
½ cup catsup
2 ½ cups milk or half and half
3 tablespoons flour
1 stick butter
Potato chips, crushed
1 cup cheddar cheese, shredded

Melt butter; add flour, milk, catsup and cheese; cook until thick. Add noodles and peas to ham; mix well. Spread top with crushed potato chips and bake at 350o for 45 minutes.

BAKED BEANS WITH HAM AND PINEAPPLE

1 pound ham, fully cooked and chopped
4 (16 oz) cans baked beans
1 (20 oz) can crushed pineapple in it's own juice
½ cup each (dark corn syrup, ketchup and green pepper, chopped)
¾ cup onion, chopped
1 cup brown sugar

Mix all ingredients together; place mixture in a baking dish and bake at 350° for 1 ½ hours until hot and bubbly.

HAM AND NOODLE CASSEROLE

2 pounds ground ham
1 (12 oz) package wide noodles
1 quart milk
1 tablespoon mustard
1 pound cheddar cheese, grated
½ cup each (margarine and flour)
1 can cream of celery soup

Cook noodles, drain. Combine cheese, margarine, flour, soup and milk. Heat until cheese melts. Place noodles in a 9 x 13 inch pan, top with ham. Pour sauce over top and bake at 350° for 1 ½ hours.

CORNED BEEF AND MACARONI BAKE

1 (12 oz) can corned beef, cut up
½ cup each (American cheese, cubed and chopped onion)
¾ cup cracker crumbs, buttered
1 (6-8 oz) package macaroni, cooked
1 ¼ cups milk
1 can cream of chicken soup
½ teaspoon each (salt and pepper)

Combine all ingredients except macaroni and cracker crumbs. Place half of macaroni in a buttered baking dish; top with half of meat mixture. Repeat layers. Top with cracker crumbs and bake at 350° for 30-35 minutes.

PEPPERED STEAKS

4 boneless rib-eye steaks
1/8 teaspoon each (dried oregano, cayenne pepper and ground cumin)
¼ teaspoon each (garlic powder and lemon pepper)
½ teaspoon each) paprika, salt and black pepper)
2 tablespoons vegetable oil

Combine oil and seasonings; brush on steaks. Broil or grill over medium heat for 5 minutes on each side or until meat reaches desired doneness. (for rare, a meat thermometer should read (140°) (medium 160°) (well done 170°). Brush and baste occasionally with seasoning mixture.

EASY SALISBURY STEAK

1 pound lean ground beef
1/3 cup bread crumbs
1 egg, beaten
¼ cup onion, minced
1 (7 oz) can mushrooms, sliced
1 can cream of mushroom soup, divided
1 package egg noodles

Beat egg, add ¼ cup soup, onion, crumbs and meat. Mix well and shape into 6 oval patties. Cook patties in hot oil until browned on both sides, drain. Remove from skillet. Stir in remaining soup and mushrooms, return patties to skillet. Simmer 20 minutes or until done. (Add water to sauce and serve over egg noodles or mashed potatoes).

CORNED BEEF WITH SAUCE

3-4 pounds of corned beef (round or brisket)
2 ribs of celery
1 small onion, quartered
1 clove garlic
2 bay leaves

SAUCE
½ cup brown sugar
3 tablespoons orange juice
2 teaspoons red wine
1 teaspoon each (soy sauce, Dijon mustard and horseradish)

Cook corned beef in water with onion, celery, garlic and bay leaves for about 2-2 ½ hours at 350°. Corned beef is most tender when a little under-cooked. SAUCE; Bring all ingredients to a boil. Pour over the corned beef and bake at 350° for about 15 minutes longer.

CORNED BEEF AND CABBAGE CASSEROLE

1 (1 2 oz) can corned beef
1 (10 ¾ oz) can cream of mushroom soup
1 ½ cups milk
3 large potatoes, sliced
1 large onion, sliced
½ head green cabbage, chopped
½ stick margarine
½ teaspoon each (salt and pepper)
1 cup cheddar cheese, shredded

Peel and slice potatoes. Arrange in a layer over bottom of a greased baking dish. Peel and slice onion; arrange in layer over potatoes. Dot with margarine. Sprinkle with salt and pepper. Arrange cabbage over layers. Spread corn beef over cabbage. Spread soup and milk over corned beef. Sprinkle with cheese on top. Cover with foil and bake at 375° for about 1 hour.

COUNTRY FRIED STEAK

1 pound ground beef
4 tablespoons flour
2 tablespoons each (dry milk and Worcestershire sauce)
Salt and pepper t taste
Oil for frying

Combine all ingredients, make into patties, roll in additional flour. Brown on both sides. Place in casserole dish. Make gravy with drippings. Pour gravy over steak and bake at 350° for 30 minutes.

ROAST BEEF WITH GRAVY

1 (2-3 pounds) beef roast
1 cup water
1 envelope Lipton onion soup mix
1 (10 ¾) can cream of mushroom soup

Place roast in pan. Spread the mixture of mushroom soup and water over roast. Sprinkle onion soup over soup mixture. Cover with foil and bake at 350° for 2 hours or until done.

SAUSAGE AND RICE CASSEROLE

1 pound sausage
2 (14 oz) cans chicken broth
½ cup onion, chopped
½ cup celery, chopped
1 ½ cups rice, raw
½ cup slivered almonds, toasted
1 tablespoon soy sauce

Cooke sausage, celery and onion until done. Drain and pour into a 3 quart covered casserole dish. Add rice, chicken broth, almonds and soy sauce. Bake at 350° for 45-60 minutes. Serve hot.

COMPANY SWISS STEAK

2 pounds round steak, cut into serving size pieces
¼ cup flour
½ teaspoon each (salt and pepper)
2 tablespoons Worcestershire sauce
2 cup water
1 medium onion, sliced thin
2 tablespoons vegetable oil
1 (4.5 oz) can tomatoes, diced

GRAVY
¼ cup flour
1/8 teaspoon pepper
¼ teaspoon salt
1 ¼ cups beef broth
Hot cooked noodles or mashed potatoes

Combine flour, salt and pepper. Pound steak with a mallet to tenderize.
Dredge in flour mixture, a few pieces at a time. In a dutch oven, brown
steak in oil on both sides. Arrange onion slices between the layers of
meat. Add water, Worcestershire sauce and tomatoes. Cover and bake
at 325° for 2-2 ½ hours or until meat is good and tender. Remove to a
serving platter and keep warm. In a small bowl, combine flour, broth,
salt and pepper until smooth; stir into pan juices. Bring to a boil over
medium heat; cook and stir for 2 minutes. Serve gravy over steak and
noodles or mashed potatoes.

GRANNY'S SOUTHERN STEAK AND PRESERVES

4 (6-8 oz) filet or sirloin steaks
2 tablespoons each (vegetable oil and butter)
½ cup green onions, chopped fine
½ cup red wine
1 cup beef broth
3 tablespoons , blackberry, raspberry, or blueberry preserves or jam
½ teaspoon each (salt and pepper)
Berries for garnish (optional)

Season steaks with salt and pepper on both sides. Cook on grill; 3-5 minutes on each side (depending on how thick the steaks are). Place steak on serving plate, cover with foil and let stand. Sauté the onions in oil for 1-2 minutes; add wine and boil until liquid is reduced by half. Add broth and berry preserves; return to boil and reduce liquid down by ½. Whisk in butter and a little more salt and pepper. Pour a little of the sauce over steak. Scatter a few whole berries around the steak on the plate if you desire.

CHURCHILL DOWNS PRIME RIB

1 (8 pound) boneless prime rib roast, trim off tail fat
2 tablespoons each (ground black pepper and coarse salt)
1 cup cajun seasoning
½ cup fresh garlic, chopped

Rub seasonings into meat. Place rack in the bottom of the roasting pan that you will be cooking the prime rib in. Place the rib on top of the rack. Cook at 325° for about 2 hours or until meat thermometer inserted in thickest part of the roast reads 130°. This is for medium rare. Remove the prim rib from the pan and allow it to sit on top of stove for 30 minutes to let the meat rest. This will allow the natural juices in the meat to relax and return to the entire roast, giving the roast a juicer more flavorful prime rib.

COMPANY POT ROAST

1 2-4 pounds roast
1 can cream of mushroom soup
½ teaspoon pepper
1 teaspoon each (seasoning salt and garlic powder)
Olive oil
2 garlic cloves
¼ cup onion, chopped
¾ cup water
1 cup red wine
1 tablespoon Worcestershire sauce

Combine pepper, garlic powder and seasoning salt, rub into roast on both sides. Place roast in skillet with olive oil and sear on both sides. In another skillet with olive oil; sauté the onion and garlic. Place roast in roasting pan and add the rest of the ingredients and bake at 350o for 2 ½- 3 hours. The liquid will make the gravy for the roast. Dip gravy over roast when serving.

EULA'S LASAGNA

1 pound ground round beef
2 pounds pork sausage
3 (15 oz) cans tomato sauce
1 box lasagna noodles
2 teaspoons minced garlic
Salt to taste
1 (32 oz) package mozzarella cheese, sliced thin
1 cup parmesan cheese, grated
3 tablespoons fresh parsley

In skillet cook beef and sausage over medium heat until done; drain. Add the tomato sauce, garlic, parsley and salt. Simmer un-covered for 1 hour. Stirring often. Next, cook noodles in boiling water until done; set aside. Spray (2) 13 x 9 inch baking pan or dish with cooking spray. Layer; noodles, beef and sausage mixture, sliced mozzarella cheese and sprinkle with parmesan cheese. Repeat layers, ending with parmesan cheese. Bake at 350° for 25-20 minutes or until cheese melts and bubbly.

BEEF TENDERLOIN STROGANOFF

1 ½ pounds beef tenderloin, cut into thin strips
2 tablespoons each (all-purpose flour, butter or margarine and olive
or vegetable oil)
1 ½ cups beef broth
¼ cup sour cream
2 tablespoons tomato paste
½ teaspoon paprika
Salt to taste
Hot cooked noodles

In a bowl or sealable plastic bag, toss beef in flour. In a large skillet, brown beef in butter and oil. Gradually stir in broth. In a bowl, combine the sour cream, tomato paste, paprika and salt. Bring beef mixture to a boil. Reduce heat; slowly stir in sour cream mixture (do not boil). Cook un-covered over low heat for 15-20 minutes, stirring frequently. Serve over noodles.

BEST POT ROAST

1 (3-4 pounds) chuck roast
1 large onion, chopped coarsely
4-5 potatoes, cut into halves
5 carrots, cut into 1 inch pieces
2 envelopes, onion and mushroom soup mix
¾ cup coffee, brewed
1 ½ cups cooking wine (red)
4 garlic cloves
2 tablespoons olive oil
1 teaspoon each (salt and pepper)
Flour for coating

Cut 4 slits in sides of roast and insert garlic cloves. Sprinkle with salt and pepper. Coat lightly with flour. Brown roast in hot oil in a dutch oven. Combine wine, coffee and soup mix in a bowl; mix well. Pour over roast and bake at 350° for 1 hour. Add carrots and onion. Bake for 1 more hour. Add potatoes and bake addition hour. Place vegetables in a separate bowl. Serve roast and pour gravy over top.

ONE DISH STEAK AND POTATO DINNER

4 cubed steaks
¾ cup flour
2 tablespoons cooking oil
2-3 cups frozen crinkle steak fries
1 medium onion, sliced thin
1 (10 ¾ oz) can cream of mushroom soup
½ cup milk
Salt and pepper to taste

Sprinkle steaks with salt and pepper. Coat with flour. Brown steaks on both sides in skillet in hot oil. Place potatoes and onion in baking dish; top with steaks. In a bowl, stir soup and milk together. Pour over steaks and vegetables. Cover with foil and bake at 350° for 1 hour or until steaks and onions are tender.

PORK CHOPS AND APPLES

4 (¼ inch) loin chops
¼ cup oil
1 cup apple juice
1 granny smith apple, cored and cut into 12 slices
Brown sugar
Salt and pepper to taste

In a large skillet with tight fitting lid, add the salted and peppered pork chops. Brown in oil and drain on paper towels. Remove chops from skillet. Add apple juice and scrape bottom to de-glaze. Put chops back in skillet and place 3 slices of apple on each pork chop. Sprinkle brown sugar over apples and pork chops. Cover and reduce heat to simmer. Cook for 30 minutes. Remove chops to platter. Stir sauce in skillet and pour over chops. Ready to serve.

PORK CHOPS WITH APPLE STUFFING

4-6 thick cup pork chops, sliced in half, but not all the way through (make a pocket) set aside.

APPLE STUFFING
½ cup apple , diced
1 cup bread crumbs
1 ½ tablespoons butter, melted
3 tablespoons each (minced onion and chopped raisins)
½ teaspoon each (salt, pepper, sugar and sage)

Combine all stuffing ingredients together; mix well. Stuff pork chops. Place in baking dish and bake at 350° for 1 ½ 2 hours.

GOOD AND CREAMY PORK CHOPS

4 pork chops
1/3 cup water
1 can cream of celery soup

Brown chops in skillet; drain. Stir in soup and water. Cover and bake at 350° for about one hour or until chops are tender.

SWEET AND SOUR PORK

1 ½ pounds lean pork, cut into 2 inch strips
1 medium can pineapple chunks
¼ cup each (onion, sliced fine, brown sugar and water)
¾ cup green pepper, cut into thin strips
1 tablespoon soy sauce
½ teaspoon salt
2 tablespoons each (cornstarch and cooking oil)
1 cup pineapple juice
1/3 cup vinegar

Brown pork in skillet with oil. Add water; cover and simmer for 1 hour. Combine cornstarch, salt, brown sugar, vinegar, pineapple juice and soy sauce; cook, stirring constantly, until slightly thickened. Pour sauce over hot pork; let stand for 10 minutes. Add green peppers, onion and pineapple chunks. Cook for 5 minutes.

ORANGE PORK CHOPS

4 pork chops, center cut
1 medium green pepper
1 (11 oz) can mandarin oranges, drained
½ cup orange juice
¼ cup water
3 tablespoons brown sugar
2 tablespoons lemon juice
1 tablespoon each (vegetable oil and cornstarch)

Brown pork chops on both sides in skillet with hot oil. Remove from skillet and set aside. Add water, brown sugar, lemon juice, orange juice and cornstarch to skillet. Cook until thickened, stirring constantly. Add pork chops, cover and simmer for 20 minutes or until chops are tender and cooked through. Add oranges and green pepper. Cook until heated through.

PORK CHOP CASSEROLE

4 pork chops
4 potatoes, sliced
1 cup each (cheddar cheese, grated and milk)
1 can each (green peas, drained and cream of chicken soup)
1 small onion, chopped
Salt and pepper to taste

Brown shops in skillet, salt and pepper to taste; set aside. Layer ingredients in casserole dish in the following order. Sliced raw potatoes, chopped onion, peas, grated cheese and pork chops. Pour chicken soup over casserole. Cover with foil and bake at 350° for 1 ½ hours.

GOOD PORK CHOPS

8 center cut pork chops, trimmed
2 cups cracker crumbs
1 egg
2 tablespoons milk
¾ cup flour
½ teaspoon salt
Cooking oil

Salt chops on both sides. Beat egg with milk. Coat chops with flour; dip in egg mixture and cracker crumbs. Cook chops in cooking oil until brown on both sides and done.

KENTUCKY PORK LOIN

2-3 pounds pork loin
¼ cup dark maple syrup
2 tablespoons of Kentucky Whiskey
1 teaspoon dry mustard
Salt and pepper to taste

Rub loin with salt and pepper and place in baking pan. In a bowl; whisk together the whiskey, mustard and syrup. Brush the pork loin with ½ of the glaze. Bake at 350° for 2 ½ hours. Brush the remaining glaze on the last 45 minutes of cooking. Let rest 10-15 minutes before serving.

SMOTHERED PORK CHOPS

6-8 pork chops, boneless, cut ¾ inch thick
1 medium onion, cut into chunks
1/3 cup flour
¼ cup molasses
1 cup raisins, golden
2 tablespoons vinegar
3 medium cooking apples, sliced
1 package savory herb roasted potatoes
¾ teaspoon each (salt and pepper)
¼ teaspoon sage
5 tablespoons olive oil
4 cups water

Rub chops on both sides with salt, pepper and sage. In large skillet cook chops in hot oil over medium heat until brown. Transfer chops to a greased baking dish. Cook onion in drippings in skillet until onions begins to brown. Remove onion from skillet. Set aside. Stir flour into drippings in skillet. Stir in 4 cups water and molasses. Cook and stir over medium heat until mixture comes to a boil. Cook and stir for 1 minute longer. Remove onions on both sides of baking dish. Pour molasses mixture over all. Bake at 350° un-covered for 45 minutes. Add potatoes and bake 30 minutes more or until potatoes are tender.

PORK CHOPS WITH DRESSING

4-5 pork chops
½ cup each (melted butter and chicken broth)
2 tablespoons onion, chopped
4 cups bread crumbs
1 (12 oz) carton sour cream
1 can cream of mushroom soup
Flour
Salt and pepper to taste

Coat chops in flour salt and pepper; brown in skillet of hot oil. Mix bead crumbs, onion, butter and chicken broth. Place in bottom of baking dish. Place browned chops on top. Mix together sour cream and mushroom soup. Spread over chops and dressing. Cover with foil and bake at 350° for 1 hour or until chops are tender.

PORK CHOP CASSEROLE

4 pork chops
4 cups potatoes, sliced thin
1 cup half and half
1 can cream of celery soup
2 onions, chopped
½ teaspoon salt
1 teaspoon pepper
American cheese, grated

Season and brown chops on both sides in skillet. Arrange sliced potatoes in a 2 quart casserole dish. Mix remaining ingredients except cheese; pour over potatoes. Place chops over potatoes. Sprinkle with grated cheese. Bake at 350° for 1 ½ hours.

COUNTRY STYLE PORK RIBS

4 pounds boneless country-style pork ribs
1 medium onion, chopped
½ cup water
¼ cup lemon juice
2 tablespoons each (vegetable oil and white vinegar)
2 tablespoons each (brown sugar and ketchup)
1 cup chili sauce
1 tablespoon Worcestershire sauce
¼ teaspoon each (salt and pepper)
Hot cooked rice

Place ribs in roasting pan. Cover and bake at 350° for 30 minutes. In a skillet, sauté onion in oil until tender. Add the chili sauce, water, lemon juice, brown sugar, ketchup, vinegar, Worcestershire sauce, salt and pepper. Add ribs. Reduce heat; 325°. Cook un-covered for 1 ½ - 2 hours, brushing occasionally with sauce. Serve with rice.

PORK CHOPS WITH GRAVY

6 (1 inch) pork chops, center cut
¼ teaspoon pepper
1 teaspoon salt
½ cup pancake mix, dry
3 onions, sliced
Vegetable oil

GRAVY
1 teaspoon salt
¼ teaspoon pepper
1 tablespoon sugar
2-3 tablespoons flour
2 cups boiling water

Season chops with salt and pepper, coat with pancake mix. Brown in oil and place in small covered baking pan. Sauté onions with salt, pepper and sugar until lightly brown. Stir in flour. Cook and stir for 1 minute then add boiling water. Pour over pork chops. Cover and bake at 350° for 1 ½ hours.

PORK CHOP CASSEROLE

4 pork chops
1 large onion
1 cup tomatoes, cooked
2 teaspoon salt
1/8 teaspoon pepper
1 green pepper
½ cup rice, un-cooked
2 cups hot water

Place chops in bottom of baking dish; place rice over chops. Slice onion and green pepper over rice and pour in hot water and tomatoes. Add salt and pepper. Cover and bake at 350° for 1 hour or until rice is cooked and chops are tender.

SMOKED PORK CHOPS AND DRESSING

2 smoked pork rib chops (¾ inch thick)
¼ cup each (celery, sliced thin and walnuts, coarsely chopped)
1 ½ teaspoons vegetable oil
2 tablespoons each (fresh parsley minced, onion chopped fine and chicken broth)
3 tablespoons butter or margarine
¼ teaspoon pepper
1 cup seasoned croutons
1 navel orange
1 teaspoon orange peel

313

Set aside 1 teaspoon orange peel. Peel and section the orange. Set 4 segments aside; coarsely chop remaining segments and set aside. In a skillet, brown chops on both sides in oil. Place chops in an un-greased 9 inch baking dish; set aside. In the same skillet, sauté the celery, onion and parsley in butter until tender. Add croutons, walnuts and pepper. Cook for 1-2 minutes. Stir in broth and reserve chopped orange peel. Cook 1 minute longer.

PORK TENDERLOIN WITH SAUCE

1 pound pork tenderloin
1 green pepper
¾ cup whiskey
1 tablespoon each (oil and butter)
½ teaspoon salt
¼ teaspoon pepper
1 small onion, chopped

Chop onion. Cut pork diagonally into 8 slices and sprinkle with salt and pepper. Heat butter and oil In a large frying pan. Add pork and cook until browned, 3-5 minutes on each side. Remove pork and keep warm. Reduce heat to medium. Add green pepper to pan. Stir and cook 1 minute. Add whiskey, ½ teaspoon salt and ¼ teaspoon pepper. Bring to a boil and cook about 2 minutes; stirring to scrape all the brown bits from bottom of pan, until liquid is reduced to about 1/3 cup. Serve pork with the whiskey sauce.

POULTRY AND GAME

FAVORITE MEXICAN CHICKEN

3-4 cups chicken, cooked and chopped
3 ½ cups cheddar cheese, grated
1 (6-7 oz) bag of tortilla chips
1 (16 oz) jar salsa
1 ¼ teaspoon salt
½ teaspoon red pepper
½ cup chicken broth

Place the salsa, broth, salt and pepper in blender and blend until smooth. Place 2 cups of salsa mixture with the tortilla chips. In another bowl, place the chicken with the remaining cheese and chips. In another bowl, place the chicken with the remaining cheese and chips. Cover with foil and bake at 375° for 30 minutes or until cheese is melted.

CHICKEN AND CHIPPED BEEF

6 chicken breasts, de-boned and halved
1 small jar chopped beef
1 can cream of mushroom soup
1 can cream of chicken soup
1 (8 oz) carton sour cream
6 slices of bacon

Roll each chicken breast in a strip of bacon. Lay on chipped beef in a 13 x 9 inch casserole dish. Blend sour cream and soups well. Spoon mixture over chicken; no salt. Cook un-covered at 300° for 2 hours.

GOOD QUESADILLAS

Plain burrito flour tortillas. Stuff with chopped onion, fried crisp bacon crumbled, chopped tomatoes and shredded cheese. Fold tortilla in half and cook in skillet with no grease or oils until cheese is melted. When ready to serve top with taco sauce and sour cream.

PINEAPPLE CHICKEN

6 chicken breasts halved, de-boned and skinned
1 (8 oz) can un-sweetened, crushed pineapple, un-drained
2 tablespoons each (cider vinegar and soy sauce)
1 clove garlic, minced
1/8 teaspoon pepper

In a plastic bag, combine the pineapple, vinegar, soy sauce, garlic and pepper together. Add chicken. Seal bag and turn to coat. Refrigerate for 30 minutes. Place the chicken and marinade in a 11 x 7 inch baking dish coated with cooking spray. Cover and bake at 350° for 25 minutes or until chicken juices run clear.

CHICKEN CORDON BLUE

8 pieces boneless chicken breast
8 pieces boiled ham, sliced thin
1 egg, beaten
8 slices mozzarella cheese`
1 cup sliced mushrooms
¼ stick butter
¼ cup white wine
Bread crumbs

Dip chicken in beaten egg, then bread crumbs. Fry in oil until evenly brown. Place chicken in a baking dish. Layer each piece of chicken with a slice of ham folded over evenly covering the chicken breast. Top with mozzarella cheese. Sauté mushrooms in butter or margarine and place on top of chicken. Melt remaining butter and add the wine. Pour over chicken. Bake at 325° for 40-50 minutes.

GOOD CHICKEN POT PIE

4-6 chicken breasts, skinned, cooked and cut in pieces
1 stick butter
1 can each (cream of chicken soup and chicken broth)
1 can mix vegetables, drained
1 ½ cups of each (Bisquick and milk)

Mix all ingredients together in a casserole dish except the **B**isquick and milk. Mix the Bisquick and milk. Spread over mixture and bake at 350o until golden brown.

ALMOND CRUSTED CHICKEN

4 chicken breasts, boneless, and halved
1 egg, beaten
1 teaspoon each (peanut oil and salt)
1 shallot, chopped
8 cups fresh spinach leaves
¼ teaspoon ground black pepper
2 teaspoons rosemary
½ cup bread crumbs, chopped fine (Japanese-style)
2 tablespoons buttermilk
½ cup almonds, chopped fine

Place chicken breasts on plastic wrap and pound with a meat mallet until the breasts is ¼-½ inch thickness. In a bowl whisk together the egg and buttermilk. In another bowl, combine the bread crumbs, almonds, rosemary and ¼ teaspoon salt. Dip chicken breasts, 1 at a time, in egg mixture, turning to coat. Next, dip chicken pieces in almond mixture, turning to coat. In non-stick skillet cook chicken in hot oil over medium heat for 4-6 minutes, turning once half way through cooking. Remove chicken from skillet. Keep warm. In same skillet cook shallots in drippings 3-5 minutes or until tender. Add spinach and ¼ teaspoon salt. Cook and toss for about 1 minute or until spinach is wilted. Serve chicken with spinach. Sprinkle with pepper.

CRISPY CHICKEN CASSEROLE

2 cups chicken, cooked and diced
1 (10 ¾ oz) can cream of mushroom soup
¾ cup mayonnaise
3 tablespoons butter, melted
1 cup cornflakes, crumble
½ cup almonds, toasted and sliced
1 (3 ½ oz) can mushrooms, drained and sliced
1 teaspoon onion, grated
1 cup rice, cooked in chicken broth
1 cup celery, diced
1 tablespoon lemon juice

Mix all ingredients together in a greased 2 quart casserole dish, except cornflakes and butter. Spread cornflakes and butter on top and bake at 350° for 30 minutes.

STUFFED CHICKEN BREASTS

4 large chicken breasts, halved, skinned and de-boned
2/3 cup water
1 ½ cups herb stuffing mix
1 small clove garlic, minced
5 tablespoons green pepper, chopped
½ cup onion, chopped
¼ teaspoon each (salt and pepper)
4 tablespoons butter or margarine, melted
1 can cream of chicken soup
3 tablespoons dry white wine
4-5 tablespoons of the stuffing

Flatten chicken breasts to ¼ inch thickness, using a meat mallet. Set aside. Sauté onion, green pepper and garlic in 3 tablespoons butter. Stir in 1 ½ cups of stuffing, water, salt and pepper. Spread stuffing mixture on each chicken breast, leaving a ½ inch margin on all sides. Fold short ends of chicken over stuffing. Roll up and secure with toothpicks. Brown chicken in 2 tablespoons butter. Place in a 9 x 13 inch dish. Combine soup and wine; pour over chicken. Sprinkle with 4-5 tablespoons dressing. Cover with foil and bake at 325° for 50-60 minutes.

CHICKEN BREASTS WITH MUSHROOMS

8 chicken breasts, halved and boneless
1 (8 oz) carton sour cream
1 (10 ¾ oz) can cream of mushroom soup
8 slices dried beef
8 half strips of bacon

Arrange beef slices on bottom of a 9 x 13 inch baking dish. Place 1 chicken breast on each slice of beef and top with 1 strip of bacon. Bake at 325° for 45 minutes. Remove from oven. Mix together sour cream and soup. About 15 minutes before serving, pour mixture over meat.

Return to oven and bake at 400o for about 15-20 minutes longer or until golden brown and bubbly. Serve with wild rice and a green salad.

PUFF PASTRY CHICKEN BUNDLES

8 chicken breasts, halved, skinless and boneless
40 spinach leaves
2 (8 oz) chive and onion cream cheese, softened
½ cup walnuts, toasted and chopped
2 sheets frozen pastry, thawed
1 teaspoon salt
½ teaspoon each (pepper and cold water)
1 egg

Cut a lengthwise slit in each chicken breast to within ½ inch of the other side; open meat so it lies flat. Cover with plastic wrap; and pound to flatten to 1/8 inch thickness. Remove plastic wrap. Sprinkle salt and pepper over chicken. In a saucepan, bring 1 inch of water to a boil; add spinach. Cover and cook for 1-2 minutes or until spinach is wilted; drain. Place 5 spinach leaves on each chicken breast. Spoon 2 tablespoons of cream cheese down the center of each chicken breast; sprinkle with walnuts. Roll up chicken and tuck in ends. Un-roll puff pastry; cut into 8 portions. Roll each into 9 x 7 inch rectangle. Combine egg and cold water; brush over edges of pastry. Place chicken on the short end; roll up tightly, tucking in ends. Place on a greased 15 x 10 inch baking sheet. Bake at 350° for 30-45 minutes or until golden brown.

CHICKEN WITH BOURBON

6 chicken breasts, floured
1 cup mushroom caps, sautéed
1 cup heavy cream
¼ cup each (butter, bourbon and green onion chopped)
1 tablespoon olive oil
1 teaspoon each (salt and pepper)
Rice

Flour, salt and pepper chicken breasts in skillet. Sauté onions in oil and butter; add chicken and brown lightly on both sides. Remove chicken from heat. Mix cream and bourbon and stir until smooth. Place chicken in gravy and cover with sautéed mushrooms. Cover and cook for about 30-45 minutes or until done. Serve over rice.

APRICOT CHICKEN

4 chicken breasts fillet
1 medium onion, chopped
½ cup each (chopped green pepper and dried apricots, chopped fine)
2 tablespoons butter
¼ teaspoon each (white pepper and lemon rind, grated)
1 tablespoon each (paprika and flour)
2 cups chicken broth
2 cups egg noodles, cooked and hot
1 cup sour cream

Rinse chicken fillet and dry. Sauté chicken in butter in skillet until brown. Arrange chicken in a baking dish. Add onion and green pepper in pan drippings. Cook until vegetables are tender, stirring constantly. Add flour, paprika, salt and white pepper, mix well. Stir in chicken broth. Cook until thickened, stirring constantly. Remove from heat. Stir in sour cream, lemon rind and apricot. Pour sauce over chicken and bake at 350° for 20-30 minutes or until chicken is tender. Place noodles on serving platter. Place chicken over noodles; top with sauce.

GOOD PINEAPPLE CHICKEN

4 cups of chicken, cut up (6 breasts)
1 large onion, sliced
2 bell peppers, sliced in thin strips
1 cup raisins
1 can water chestnuts, sliced
1 large can pineapple, crushed
½ cup brown sugar
Curry powder
Salt and pepper

Sprinkle salt, pepper and curry powder on chicken breasts. Brown in a small amount of oil. Place breasts in casserole dish. To thicken drippings; add onions, peppers, pineapple, sugar, water chestnuts and raisins. Cook on low heat for 15 minutes and pour over chicken. Bake at 350° for 1 hour.

GOOD CHICKEN CASSEROLE

3 - 3 1/3 pounds of chicken, cut up
4-5 slices bacon, fried crisp and crumbled
4 tablespoons butter
1 ½ teaspoons curry powder
1 - 1 ½ cups water
3 tablespoons raisins
¼ teaspoon thyme
1 onion, chopped
1 clove garlic, chopped
6 fresh tomatoes, peeled
1 green pepper, chopped
1 teaspoon parsley
½ cup almonds, sautéed in butter until golden brown
Flour

Flour cut up chicken (about 9-10 pieces). Heat butter and brown the chicken pieces. When browned, place chicken in a casserole dish. In same frying pan, sauté green pepper, garlic and onion for 5 minutes, stirring constantly. Add water mixed with curry powder, tomatoes, parsley and thyme. Pour over chicken in casserole. Cover and bake at 350° until chicken is very tender (about 2 hours). Add sautéed almonds and raisins. Place chicken pieces on serving dish and pour the gravy over it. Garnish with chopped bacon.

CHICKEN AND RICE CASSEROLE

2 cups chicken, cooked and cut up into pieces
2 cups rice, cooked
4 eggs, hard boiled
¾ cup celery, chopped
1 package frozen peas, cooked
1 cup mayonnaise
2 small onions, chopped
1 can each (cream of celery soup and cream of mushroom soup)
½ cup almonds, slivered
1 teaspoon salt
2 teaspoons lemon juice
Potato chips, crushed

Combine all ingredients except the potato chips. Place in 1 quart casserole dish and refrigerate overnight. Sprinkle with potato chips on top. Bake at 375° for 1 hour. Let stand for about 15-20 minutes.

CHINESE CHICKEN

4 chicken breasts, de-boned
2 eggs, beaten
¼ cup cornstarch
Garlic powder, salt and pepper to taste

Cut chicken into bite size pieces. Sprinkle with garlic powder, salt and pepper. Place in refrigerator for a least 1 hour. Coat pieces with egg, then cornstarch. Deep fry until lightly browned. Drain chicken and line 1 layer in a greased shallow pan.

SAUCE

1 cup sugar
¼ cup water
½ cup vinegar
4 tablespoons catsup
1 tablespoon soy sauce
¼ teaspoon salt

Heat all ingredients until smooth, (do not boil). Spoon half of mixture over chicken. Bake at 350° for 10 minutes. Add remaining sauce and bake additional 10 minutes.

CHICKEN AND SPAGHETTI CASSEROLE

1 ½ cups chicken, cut up
¼ cup pimento
1 ¼ cups spaghetti, cooked
¼ green pepper, chopped
½ pound sharp cheddar cheese, grated
1 can mushroom soup
½ teaspoon each (salt and pepper)
¼ cup onion, chopped
½ cup chicken broth

Place spaghetti in a casserole dish; add chicken, green pepper, pimento, onion, salt and pepper. Cover with soup; add broth and cheese. (keep back ½ cup cheese). Mix lightly and bake at 350° for 55-60 minutes. Add remaining cheese.

CHICKEN CHOW MEIN CASSEROLE

2 whole chicken breasts, cooked and de-boned
2 medium onions, chopped
1 cup celery, chopped
1 small can pimento, chopped
2 cans chicken with rice soup
2 cans cream of mushroom soup
1 ½ cans chicken broth
1 can mushrooms
1 cup rice, un-cooked or instant
Toasted almonds, slivered
Butter or margarine

Sauté celery and onion in butter until onions are transparent but not brown. Combine all ingredients except almonds. Put in a greased 9 x 13 inch baking dish and bake at 350° for 25-30 minutes. Serve almonds on top.

GOOD CHICKEN TACOS

1 (10 oz) can white chicken, drained
½ cup cheddar cheese, shredded
1 small tomato, chopped
1 cup iceberg lettuce, shredded
1/3 cup salsa
¼ cup sour cream
1 rib celery, chopped
1 teaspoon cumin
8 taco shells

Combine chicken, sour cream, celery, salsa and cumin in a bowl; mix well. Spoon chicken mixture into taco shells. Top each taco with lettuce, tomato and cheese.

ITALIAN CHICKEN

2 chickens, cut up
1 stick butter
1 (8 oz) bottle Italian dressing
1/8 teaspoon each (salt and pepper

Pour dressing over chicken in casserole dish; dot with butter, salt and pepper and bake at 350° for 1 ½ hours.

CRAB - STUFFED CHICKEN BREASTS

¼ cup all-purpose flour
4 tablespoons butter or margarine, divided
1 cup chicken broth
¼ cup onion, chopped
¾ cup milk
1 (6 oz) can crabmeat, drained, flaked and cartilage removed
1 (4 oz) can mushrooms stems and pieces, drained
2 tablespoons fresh parsley, minced
1/3 cup saltine crackers, crushed (about 10-12 crackers)
½ teaspoon salt
1/8 teaspoon pepper
1 cup Swiss cheese, shredded
½ teaspoon paprika
4 chicken breasts halved, boneless and skinless
 Hot cooked rice, optional

In a saucepan, melt 3 tablespoons butter. Stir in flour until smooth. Gradually stir in broth and milk. Bring to a boil; boil and stir for 2 minutes. Remove from heat; set aside. In a skillet, sauté onion in remaining butter until tender. Add crab, mushrooms, cracker crumbs, parsley, salt, pepper and 2 tablespoons of the white sauce; heat through. Flatten chicken to ¼ inch thickness. Spoon about ½ cup of the crab mixture on each chicken breast. Roll up and secure with a toothpick. Place in a greased 9 inch square baking dish. Top with remaining white sauce. Cover and bake at 350° for 45 minutes or until chicken juices run clear. Sprinkle with cheese and paprika. Bake un-covered, 5 more minutes or until cheese is melted. Remove toothpicks. Serve with rice if desire. Makes 4 servings.

WOODY'S CHICKEN

1 fresh roaster chicken
Lemon and pepper, garlic salt, jalapeno peppers, Italian dressing,
lemon juice, hot sauce, and heavy duty aluminum foil.

Clean and rinse chicken, season with liberal amount of lemon and
pepper and garlic salt. Place chicken in heavy duty foil and cook at
275° un-covered until fully cooked and brown. Place peppers in cavity,
pour lemon juice and dressing over chicken. Wrap tightly and cook in
oven for another 1-2 hours at 225°. Delicious.

ALMOND CRUSTED CHICKEN

4 chicken breasts, halved and de-boned
1 egg, beaten
1 teaspoon each (peanut oil and salt)
1 shallot, chopped
8 cups fresh spinach leaves
½ teaspoon ground black pepper
2 teaspoons rosemary
½ cup bread crumbs, chopped fine (Japanese-style)
2 tablespoons buttermilk
½ cup almonds, chopped fine

Place chicken breasts on plastic wrap and pound with a meat mallet
until the breast is ¼ inch thick. In a bowl, combine the bread crumbs,
almonds, rosemary and ¼ teaspoon salt. Dip chicken breasts, 1 at time,
in egg mixture, turning to coat. Next, dip chicken pieces in almond
mixture, turning to coat. In a non-stick skillet, cook chicken in hot
oil over medium heat for 4-6 minutes, turning once half way through
cooking. Remove chicken from skillet. Keep warm. In same skillet
cook shallots in drippings 3-5 minutes or until tender. Add spinach and
¼ teaspoon salt. Cook and toss for about 1 minute or until spinach is
wilted. Serve chicken with spinach. Sprinkle with pepper.

CRISPY CHICKEN CASSEROLE

2 cups chicken, cooked and diced
1 (10 ¾ oz) can cream of mushroom soup
¾ cup mayonnaise
3 tablespoons butter, melted
½ cup almonds, toasted and sliced
1 (3 ½ oz) can mushrooms, drained and sliced
1 teaspoon onion, grated
1 cup rice, cooked in chicken broth
1 cup celery, diced
1 tablespoon lemon juice
Cornflakes, crushed

Mix all ingredients together in a greased 2 quart casserole dish, except cornflakes and butter. Sprinkle cornflakes and butter on top and bake at 350° for 30 minutes.

SPECIAL CHICKEN CASSEROLE

6 chicken breasts
1 can each (cream of mushroom and cream of chicken soup)
1 can water chestnuts, drained and sliced
1 sleeve of soda crackers, crushed
1 (8 oz) carton sour cream
1 stick butter
¼ teaspoon pepper

Cook chicken until tender, cut into bite size pieces. Place ½ of the crushed crackers on the bottom of baking dish. Mix the chopped chicken, sliced chestnuts, soups, sour cream and pepper. Pour over the cracker lined baking dish. Sprinkle remaining crackers with melted butter over the top of the mixture and bake at 350° for 25-30 minutes.

GOOD PECAN CHICKEN

2 ½ cups chicken, cooked
3 tablespoons onion, minced
1 cup celery, minced
½ cup pecans, toasted and chopped
3 tablespoons lemon juice
¾ cup mayonnaise
1 small can mushrooms, drained and sliced
1 can cream of mushroom soup
1 cup potato chips, crushed
½ teaspoon salt
¼ teaspoon pepper

Mix all ingredients except soup and chips. Place in a 2 quart baking dish or pan and pour the soup over top and layer with the crushed potato chips. Bake at 300° for 30 minutes.

CHICKEN AND DRESSING CASSEROLE

1 whole chicken, boiled or baked
½ (13 oz) can evaporated milk or whole milk
½ stick butter
½ (10 ¾ oz) can cream of chicken soup
1 box corn bread stuffing mix
½ (10 ¾ oz) can cream of celery soup
1 ½ cups chicken broth

De-bone chicken and place in a 2 quart casserole dish. Melt butter and add soups and milk. Pour over chicken in casserole. Mix stuffing with broth and spoon over mixture in casserole dish. Bake at 425° for 25 minutes or until brown and bubbly.

PRIZE CHICKEN CASSEROLE

3 cups chicken, cooked and diced
2 (10 ¾ oz) cans mushroom soup
1 (3 oz) package almonds, slivered
4 eggs, hard boiled and chopped
2 cups rice, cooked
1 cup each (bread crumbs and mayonnaise)
2 tablespoons margarine melted
1 teaspoon salt
1 ½ cups celery, chopped
1 small onion, chopped

Combine all ingredients except bead crumbs and margarine, mix well. Pour into a 3 quart casserole dish. Combine melted margarine and bread crumbs and sprinkle over top and bake at 350° for 40 minutes or until hot and bubbly.

CHICKEN CASSEROLE

3-4 chicken breasts, boiled
1 can each (cream of chicken and cream of celery soup)
1 (8 oz) carton sour cream
2-3 sticks butter
1 box Ritz crackers

Boil chicken breasts for about 30 minutes. Crush 2-3 packages of Ritz crackers. Melt butter. In a bowl, mix crackers and butter. Firmly press down crackers in bottom of 9 x 13 inch baking dish. Cut up chicken breasts in cubes. In a medium bowl, mix chicken, sour cream and soups, mix well. Spread in dish. Sprinkle with remaining cracker crumbs. Bake at 350° for 45-60 minutes or until bubbly on the sides.

MY FAVORITE CHICKEN

4 cups chicken, cooked, de-boned and sliced
6 eggs, hard boiled
2 cans cream of chicken soup
1 cup each (evaporated milk, sliced almonds, Velveeta cheese, shredded)
¼ cup cooking sherry or wine
2-4 ounce cans mushrooms, sliced
2 tablespoons onion, chopped
Ritz crackers, crushed

Layer the chicken, eggs, mushrooms almonds and onion in a 9 x 13 inch casserole dish. Make a sauce from the soup milk, cheese and sherry and pour over the chicken. Top with Ritz crackers and bake at 350° for 30 minutes.

SIMPLE CHICKEN CASSEROLE

2-3 pounds of chicken pieces
1 cup rice, un-cooked
1 package dry onion soup mix
1 can cream of celery soup

Place rice in a greased dish with chicken on top. Sprinkle the onion coup mix, celery soup and 2 cans of water; pour over all. Bake at 325° for 2 hours.

BEST CHICKEN DIVAN

4 chicken breasts, cooked
2 (10 oz) packages of frozen broccoli
1 cup sherry or wine
½ cup cheese, Romano or Parmesan
3 tablespoons butter

Cook broccoli and drain. Place broccoli in bottom of a greased baking dish. Sprinkle with butter, 3 tablespoons cheese and ¾ cup sherry. Add layer of chicken. Sprinkle with half of remaining cheese and remaining sherry. Add cream sauce. Sprinkle with reminder of cheese. Bake at 300° for 15 minutes until bubbly.

CREAM SAUCE
3 tablespoons each (butter and flour)
3 cups milk
4 tablespoons whipping cream
4 egg yolks, beaten

Melt butter in saucepan. Remove from heat and add flour and blend well. Stir in milk and cook until thick. Add egg yolks and whipping cream.

CHICKEN AND HAM

4 chicken breasts, de-boned
1 rib celery, chopped
4 green onions, chopped
1 cup butter
4 small slices ham (to fit inside of chicken breasts)
1 can cream of chicken soup
½ pint sour cream
Bread crumbs
Mozzarella cheese

Sauté onion and celery in butter. Stuff chicken breast with celery, onions, butter and ham slices. Roll chicken breasts in bread crumbs. Mix sour cream and chicken soup and pour over chicken. Put bread crumbs on top and bake at 350° for 30 minutes covered and 25 minutes un-covered for a total of 55 minutes. You'll have gravy for rice, if you use rice. A small amount of cheese can be used with rest of the ingredients inside each chicken breast.

CHICKEN AND DUMPLING CASSEROLE

4 cups chicken, cooked and chopped
2 cups baking mix flour
2/3 cup milk
4 cups chicken broth
1 (10 oz) package green peas, frozen
½ cup each (celery and onion, chopped)
½ stick butter or margarine
2 cloves garlic, minced
½ cup flour
2 teaspoons sugar
½ teaspoon pepper
3 teaspoons basil, divided
1 teaspoon salt

Sauté celery, onion, garlic in butter in saucepan until vegetables are tender. Stir in sugar, 1 teaspoon basil, salt and pepper. Add broth, stirring until mixed well. Bring to a boil. Boil for 1 minute, stirring constantly; reduce heat. Add peas, cook 5 minutes, stirring constantly. Add chicken; mix well. Place into a greased baking dish. Combine baking mix flour and 2 teaspoons basil in a bowl; mix well. Add milk, stirring constantly until moistened. Drop dough by tablespoonful over chicken mixture. (Makes about 12 dumplings). Bake at 350° for 30 minutes; cover and bake 10 minutes more or until dumplings are done.

CRISP BAKED CHICKEN

2 ½- 3 pound chicken
1 package herb stuffing
½ teaspoon salt
Dash pepper
½ pint sour cream
2 teaspoons lemon juice
2 tablespoons Worcestershire sauce
1 teaspoon each (paprika and celery salt)
3 tablespoons butter

Mix sour cream, lemon juice, Worcestershire sauce, celery salt and paprika together. Place chicken pieces in baking dish. Pour sour cream mixture over chicken. Dip chicken in herb stuffing and brush with melted butter. Bake un-covered at 350° for 1 hour or until chicken is tender and crust is brown.

GOOD ALMOND CHICKEN

4 cups chicken, cooked, de-boned and sliced
2 cans cream of chicken soup
1 cup evaporated milk
1 cup Velveeta cheese, shredded
¼ cup white wine
6 eggs, hard boiled, sliced
1 cup almonds, sliced
2-4 ounce cans mushrooms, sliced
2 tablespoons onion, chopped
Ritz crackers, crushed

Layer the chicken, eggs, mushrooms, almonds and onion in a 9 x 13 inch casserole dish. Make a sauce with the soup, milk, wine and cheese; pour over chicken. Top with Ritz crackers and bake at 350° for 30 minutes.

ALMA'S SPECIAL CHICKEN

4-6 chicken breasts
1 ¾ cup rice, raw
1 can each (cream of mushroom, cream of celery, cream of chicken soup)
1 package Lipton dry onion soup mix
1 cup white wine

Place un-cooked rice in bottom of a large baking pan, sprayed with cooking spray. Place chicken breasts on top of rice. Mix soups and wine together and pour over chicken. Sprinkle dry onion soup mix over all. Cover securely with foil and bake at 350o for 2 hours.

SOUTHERN FRIED CHICKEN

1 fryer chicken, cut in serving pieces
1 cup flour
½ cup each (corn meal and cream)
1 egg
1 teaspoon each (salt and pepper)
Oil for frying

Mix meal and flour; set aside. Beat egg until creamy; add cream, salt and pepper. Dip chicken pieces in egg mixture, then in flour mixture; fry slowly in skillet of hot oil until golden brown. Drain on paper towels.

A LOT LIKE KENTUCKY FRIED CHICKEN

3 pounds chicken, cut up
½ cup Italian salad dressing
¼ cup lemon juice
1 ½ cups baking mix
3 tablespoons flour
½ teaspoon each (sage and black pepper)
2 teaspoons salt
1 cup milk
2 tablespoons butter, melted
1 teaspoon paprika
Oil for frying

Combine chicken and lemon juice in a bowl. Toss to coat well. Marinate in refrigerator for 50-60 minutes; drain. Combine baking mix, flour, salad dressing, paprika, sage, salt and pepper in a separate dish. Mix well. Whisk milk and butter until blended. Dip chicken in milk mixture and coat with flour mixture. Fry chicken in hot oil in skillet until brown on both sides; drain. Transfer to a baking pan and bake at 350° until cooked through and good and crispy.

CRISPY FRIED CHICKEN

2 pounds chicken, cut up
40 saltine crackers
1 cup flour
2 teaspoons pepper
2 tablespoons each (seasoned salt and paprika)
½ cup milk
1 teaspoon salt
2 eggs
Oil for frying

Rinse chicken in cold water, pat dry, set aside. Crush crackers into crumbs in a bag. Add flour and pepper, shake until well blended. Whisk together the milk, eggs, paprika and salt. Dip chicken pieces into egg mixture. Next, place chicken pieces 1 at a time in a plastic bag and shake until well coated. Deep fry chicken at 325° for 10-20 minutes or until golden brown.

KIM'S CHICKEN ENCHILADAS

2 cups chicken, cooked and chopped
1 cup green pepper, chopped
1 (8 oz) package cream cheese
1 jar salsa
¾ cup Velveeta cheese, cut up
1 ¼ cups milk
8 flour tortillas

Stir chicken, pepper, cream cheese and ½ salsa in saucepan on low heat; until cheese melts. Spoon 1/3 cup chicken mixture into each tortilla and roll up. Place seam side down in lightly greased 12 x 8 inch baking dish. Stir Velveeta and milk in saucepan on low heat until smooth. Pour sauce over tortillas. Cover and bake at 350° for 20 minutes. Pour remaining salsa on top and serve.

CHICKEN WITH MUSHROOMS AND ASPARAGUS

4 chicken breasts, de-boned, skinned and cut into bite size pieces
1 can each (cream of mushroom soup, cream of chicken soup and milk)
¼ stick butter, cut into pieces (reserve 1 tablespoon)
3 tablespoons olive oil (reserve 1 tablespoon)
1 (6.5 oz) jar mushrooms, sliced
1 can asparagus spears, cut into pieces
1 small onion, sliced
½ cup cheddar cheese, shredded
Salt and pepper to taste

Mix 3 tablespoons butter and 2 tablespoons olive oil on medium heat in sauté pan. Brown chicken pieces. When chicken is browned, remove from pan and set aside. Add remaining butter and olive oil and cook the sliced onions until soft. When onions are done; add 2 cans of soup and milk. Cook until warmed and add the chicken back into the mixture. Add mushrooms and asparagus. Simmer covered for 5 minutes or until warmed through. Add the cheese just before serving. Serve over rice or pasta.

CHICKEN AND BROCCOLI CASSEROLE

2 chicken breasts, cooked and diced
2 (10 oz) packages broccoli, cooked and chopped
1 stick butter, melted
1 package Pepperidge farm herb dressing
2 (10 ¾ oz) cans cream of chicken soup
1 cup mayonnaise
1 tablespoon lemon juice
1 teaspoon curry powder

Place chicken in casserole dish. Top with broccoli. Mix soup, lemon juice, curry power and mayonnaise. Pour over chicken and broccoli. Sprinkle herb dressing over top. Pour butter over all. Cover with foil to keep topping from burning and bake a t 350° for 30 minutes.

BROCCOLI CHICKEN AND RICE CASSEROLE

2 chicken breasts, cooked and diced
1 (10 oz) package broccoli, cooked, drained and chopped
1 cup white rice
1 (8 oz) jar cheese whiz
1 can cream of mushroom soup
1 cup water chestnuts, sliced
1 medium onion, chopped
Cornflakes, crushed for topping

Cook broccoli and drain; cook rice. Sauté onions until tender; mix all ingredients together, except chicken and cornflakes. Coat a 3 quart casserole with cooking spray. Place chicken in casserole dish. Add the broccoli mixture. Sprinkle heavy with crushed cornflakes on top or any topping of choice. Bake un-covered at 325° for 30 minutes.

PRETZEL CHICKEN

1 ½ pounds chicken breasts
4 slices bread, toasted
Mayonnaise and Pretzels

Place crushed pretzels and bread in food processor. Dip chicken in mayonnaise, then in crumb mixture. Bake at 375° for 1 hour or until tender.

SWEET AND SOUR CHICKEN

6 chicken breasts, halved and cut into chunks
1 green pepper, cut in ½ inch strips
1 chicken bouillon cube
1 tablespoon soy sauce
¾ cup vinegar
½ cup each (flour and sugar)
1/3 cup salad oil
1 (13 ½ oz) can pineapple chunks, reserved juice
2 tablespoons cornstarch
1 teaspoon each (ginger, salt and pepper)

Roll chicken in flour and brown in skillet. Remove to a baking dish and sprinkle with salt and pepper. Drain pineapple, pour juice into a 2 cup container. Add water to make about 1 ¼ cups. In a saucepan, combine sugar pineapple juice, vinegar, soy sauce, ginger, bouillon cube and cornstarch. Bring to a boil, stirring constantly. Boil 2 minutes; then pour over chicken. Bake un-covered for 30 minutes, baste often. Add pineapple and green pepper. Bake 30 minutes longer, or until chicken is tender and done. Place chicken on a serving platter or a bed of rice and pour pan juices and pieces of pineapple and green pepper over chicken. Serve immediately.

ORIENTAL CHICKEN CASSEROLE

2 cups chicken, cooked and diced
1 cup Chinese noodles
1/3 cup cashew nuts
1 cup celery, chopped fine
1 tablespoon butter
1 can mushroom soup
1/3 cup chicken broth
1 tablespoon soy sauce
1 cup onion, chopped fine
2 tablespoons Tabasco sauce

Sauté celery and onion in butter. Add mushroom soup, chicken broth and seasonings; add chicken. Put into a casserole dish. Top with noodles; sprinkle with nuts and bake at 350° for 35 minutes.

ORANGE CHICKEN RICE BOWL

1 pound chicken breasts, boneless, skinless, cut up into strips
¼ cup each (planters peanuts and orange juice)
¼ cup Asian roasted sesame dressing
3 cups frozen stir fry vegetables
3 cups long grain rice, cooked

In a large skillet, on medium heat, add chicken; cook 15-20 minutes. Add vegetables, orange juice and sesame dressing and cook 5-7 minutes more. Serve over hot cooked rice. Sprinkle with nuts.

CHICKEN WITH CASHEWS

5 ½ cups chicken, boiled and diced (2 chickens)
2 tablespoons soy sauce
4 teaspoons Tabasco sauce
1 1/3 cups cashew nuts
2/3 cup onion, chopped
2/3 cup celery, sliced
3 tablespoon butter
3 cans mushroom soup
1 cup chicken broth
1/8 teaspoon black pepper
½ cup Chinese noodles

Sauté onions and celery in butter. Add soup and broth, making certain it is not too soupy. Simmer the mixture until blended. Stir in the chicken, soy sauce, Tabasco sauce and pepper to taste. Pour into a 3 quart casserole dish and sprinkle noodles and nuts on top. Bake at 350° until hot and bubbly.

BEER BUT CHICKEN

1 whole chicken
1 (12 oz) can beer
1 teaspoon each (salt, pepper, garlic powder and dry mustard)

Rub outside surface of chicken with all of the seasonings. Place chicken upright on an open can of beer. Cook chicken in a smoker or out door grill. Be careful taking chicken from the smoker or grill. Be sure and use a spatula under the can of beer to help remove the chicken.

BAKED CORNISH HENS

4 Cornish hens
1 cup vodka
8 slices lemon, sliced thin
½ cup sour cream
2 tablespoons whipping cream
8 slices butter, sliced thin
2 teaspoons each (crushed tarragon, lemon rind, white pepper and salt)
3 tablespoons lemon juice
1 ½ cups chicken broth

Rub hens with vodka inside and out; let rest 15-20 minutes. Loosen skin over breast with fingers, making a pocket. Place 2 slices of lemon and 2 slices of butter in the skin pockets of each hen. Season inside and out with a mixture of white pepper, salt and tarragon. Place chicken and broth in bottom of a baking pan. Bake at 450° for 15 minutes; baste. Reduce heat to 375° and cook for 30-45 minutes or until done. Remove hens from pan. Reduce pan liquids to ½ cup, adding whipping cream and sour cream. Simmer to thicken. Serve over hens.

CORNISH HENS WITH PEACHES

2 Cornish hens
1 onion, chopped
2 tablespoons oil
6-8 peaches
½ cup each (chicken broth and wine vinegar)
Salt and pepper

Peel and slice peaches. In a large frying pan, sprinkle hens with salt and pepper, brown in hot oil and remove. Put peaches in the pan and cook until softened, about 3 minutes. Remove; put vinegar, onion, 1 teaspoon salt and ¼ teaspoon pepper in the pan. Cook stirring constantly and scraping any brown bits, until vinegar is reduced to about ¼ cup. Reduce heat to low and add broth and the hens. Cover and cook until hens are done, 25-30 minutes. Remove hens and keep warm. Bring pan juices to a boil and cook to thicken. Add peaches and cook until heated through. Pour over the hens and serve.

LEMON HERB CORNISH HENS

4 (1 ½ pound) Cornish hens, thawed
2 tablespoons butter, softened
1 lemon, sliced thin
2 teaspoons dried crushed rosemary
1 teaspoon each (salt and pepper)

Line a roasting pan with heavy duty foil. Lightly grease rack from roasting pan, and place over foil. Remove and discard giblets from hens. Rinse hens and pat dry with paper towel. Loosen skin from neck end, insert 2 lemon slices between skin and meat of breast. Place remaining lemon slices in neck cavity, rub softened butter over hens. Sprinkle each evenly with rosemary, salt and pepper. Place hens on prepared roasting pan and bake at 350° for 1 hour or until done.

SPECIAL BAKED DOVE

16-18 Doves
¼ cup each (white wine and water)
4 strips bacon
2 tablespoons each (butter and cooking oil)
Juice and grate rind of ½ lemon
1/8 teaspoon garlic salt
1 tablespoon Worcestershire sauce
2 tablespoon s liquid smoke
Salt and pepper

Brown doves in oil and butter. Salt and pepper while browning. Remove doves to a large baking dish. Sprinkle with garlic salt, lemon juice, rind, liquid smoke, Worcestershire sauce and more salt and pepper. Cover the doves with bacon. De-glaze the skillet the doves were cooked in with the wine and water. Pour over doves. Cover and bake at 325° for 1 ½ hours.

SMOTHERED DOVE

12 Doves
2 cups chicken broth
½ cup white wine
6 tablespoons butter
3 tablespoons flour
Salt and pepper to taste

Brown doves in heavy skillet in melted butter. Place doves in a large baking dish, breast down. Add flour to skillet and stir well. Slowly add chicken broth, wine, salt and pepper; blend well and pour over doves. Cover baking dish and bake at 350° for 1 hour or more. Serve over cooked rice.

QUAIL IN WINE

6-8 Quail
2 cups fresh mushrooms, sliced
1 cup each (white wine and chicken broth)
6 tablespoons butter
1 rib celery, quartered
6-8 lemon slices
2 tablespoons fresh parsley, chopped
Flour
Salt and pepper to taste

Lightly salt, pepper and flour each quail. Brown quail in melted butter. Remove quail to a baking dish. Sauté mushrooms in remaining butter; add wine and chicken broth and bring to a boil. Pour over quail. Add celery and lemon slices; sprinkle with parsley. Cover and bake at 350° for 1 hour or until tender. When done, remove lemon slices and celery from sauce. Serve with wild rice and topped with sauce.

SMOTHERED QUAIL

6-8 Quail, cleaned
½ cup butter
Milk
Flour
½ teaspoon each (salt and pepper)

Salt, pepper and roll quail in flour, brown in skillet. Remove from skillet, add a little more flour and enough milk to make a gravy. Return quail to skillet with gravy. Simmer on low for 45 minutes, basting often. Serve the gravy on rice and or biscuits.

DUCK IN ORANGE SAUCE

3-4 wild ducks
Bacon
Celery
Onion
Salt and pepper
Apple slices
Worcestershire sauce

Wash and dry the ducks. Stuff each duck with equal amounts of celery, onion and apple. Salt and pepper all over and place bacon strips over top. Place in a baking pan. Add about ½ inch water in the bottom of the pan and sprinkle Worcestershire sauce to slightly color the water. Cook ducks at 325° for about 2 hours. When done remove stuffing and discard. Reserve bacon and place around duck for serving. Serve with orange sauce.

ORANGE SAUCE

2/3 cup each (brown sugar and white sugar)
2 cups orange juice
2 tablespoons flour
1 teaspoon orange peel, grated
¼ teaspoon salt

Combine all ingredients and simmer until thickened. Spoon over duck slices.

DUCK STUFFED WITH WALNUTS

1 (4-5 pound) duck
¼ cup butter, melted
1 ¾ cups celery, sliced
½ cup each (chopped walnuts and hot water)
3 ½ cups bread cubes
1 egg, beaten
Pulp of 1 large orange
2 tablespoons orange peel
½ teaspoon each (poultry seasoning, salt and pepper)

Toast walnuts and bread cubes in 300° oven 7-8 minutes; pour hot water over bread; let stand. Beat egg with ½ teaspoon salt, pepper and seasoning; add walnuts, bread, orange pulp, celery and orange peel. Pour batter over all. Rub inside of duck with salt; spoon in stuffing and bake at 325° for 2-2 ½ hours. Garnish with orange slices.

BAR - B - Q DUCK BREASTS

4-5 wild ducks
8 slices bacon
1 (10 ½ oz) can onion soup
2 cloves garlic, chopped fine
1 medium green pepper, chopped fine
¼ teaspoon each (salt and pepper)
¼ cup margarine
2 teaspoons Tabasco sauce
½ cup ketchup

Combine the onion soup, ketchup, margarine, Tabasco sauce, salt, garlic, pepper and green pepper in a sauce pan. Bring to a boil and simmer about 10 minutes, stirring often. Remove from heat and allow to cool while preparing breasts. Remove each breast half from duck, remove skin if preferred. Wrap each breast side with a slice of bacon and secure with toothpicks. Cover breasts with sauce and marinate 3 hours in refrigerator. Grill over hot coals 3-4 minutes on each side for rare to medium. When duck is pink its more tender and juicy. Heat remaining marinade for gravy. You may also warm a glass of currant jelly with about ½ as much as port wine, and serve over duck breasts.

WILD DUCK

1 wild duck
½ medium apple, cut in half and seeded
4 strips of bacon
½ medium onion

Place onion and apple in cavity of duck. Place bacon slices over duck breast. Wrap in foil; place in baking pan and bake at 325° for 3-4 hours or until tender.

PHEASANT WITH WHISKEY

1 pheasant, cleaned and cut in quarters
½ cup each (chicken broth and whiskey or wine)
4 tablespoons butter
¼ teaspoon each (salt and pepper)

Salt and pepper pheasant, in skillet of melted butter; sauté until golden brown. Transfer to baking pan, add enough water to cover the meat half way; add chicken broth. Cover pan and bake at 350° for 3 hours. Add whiskey 30 minutes before done. The liquid makes a good gravy to spoon over meat. Serve with wild rice.

BEST PHEASANT

4 cups pheasant cooked and chopped
3 cups Ritz cracker crumbs
1 can each (green asparagus and pimento, chopped)
¾ cup butter
½ cup each (milk and flour)
½ teaspoon each (salt and pepper)
4 eggs, hard boiled and chopped
1 cup cheddar cheese, grated

SAUCE; Melt ½ cup butter, blend in flour. Add milk and seasoning, stirring constantly; cook until thickened. Add cheese and pimento. Place 1 cup Ritz cracker crumbs in a buttered 2 quart casserole and a layer of sauce; pour ¼ cup melted butter over top and bake at 350° for 30 minutes or until top is browned.

PHEASANT IN WINE

1 pheasant
4 ounces red wine
8 ounces chicken broth
4 ounces cream or sour cream
2 tablespoons butter
1 apple, sliced
Oil
Flour
Salt and pepper

Salt and pepper pheasant. Roll in flour and brown in heavy skillet in 2 tablespoons of butter and a little vegetable oil. Transfer to baking pan and place a few apple slices along sides of pan. Add the wine to skillet and simmer, scraping brown bits from the bottom and sides. Add the chicken broth and cook 5 minutes. Add this to the pheasant in the baking pan. Cover and cook at 375° for 30 minutes. Reduce heat to 350° and cook 1 hour longer or until done. Remove the pheasant to a platter. Let stand 10 minutes before serving. Now, add the cream or sour cream to juices and simmer until cooked together, pour over pheasant and serve.

COMPANY LEG OF LAMB

1 (5 pound) leg of lamb
1 (12 oz) can tomatoes
1 clove of garlic, crushed
1 medium green pepper, chopped
4 medium onions, chopped
2 teaspoons salt
1 teaspoon ground black pepper
1 teaspoon oregano, crushed

Sprinkle lamb with salt, pepper and oregano; place in roasting pan. Bake at 325° for 1 ½ hours; drain off drippings. Combine onions, garlic, peppers and tomatoes. Baste lamb with some of tomato mixture; bake for 1 hour, basting occasionally. Add water to sauce if needed during the part of cooking. Serve with sauce.

GRILLED LAMB CHOPS

2 pounds lamb chops
2 teaspoons garlic, chopped
1 tablespoon rosemary, chopped
2 tablespoons olive oil
½ teaspoon salt
¼ teaspoon black pepper

Rub the chops with salt and pepper. Stir together the rosemary, oil and garlic. Add the chops, turning to coat. Cover and place in the refrigerator for several hours (2-24 hours). Heat the grill and grill the chops until done, turn chops so they will brown on both sides.

VENISON STROGANOFF

2 pounds venison steak
3 cloves garlic, minced
2 tablespoons tomato paste
1 teaspoon salt
5 tablespoons flour, divided
4 tablespoons butter, divided
2 cups each (beef stock, sour cream and mushrooms, sliced)
3 tablespoons red wine
1 cup onion, chopped

Cut venison into ¼ inch strips; salt and dust with 2 tablespoons of flour. In a heavy skillet add 2 tablespoons of butter and place steak strips in skillet, browning on all sides. Add mushrooms, garlic and onion. Cook 3-4 minutes until onion is tender. Remove meat and add remaining butter to the pan drippings. Blend in remaining flour, tomato paste and beef stock. Stir mixture constantly until it thickens. Return meat to skillet. Stir in sour cream and wine and heat briefly. Serve over rice or noodles.

FRIED VENISON STEAK

6-8 venison steaks, cubed
1 ½ cups flour
½ teaspoon black pepper
1 ½ teaspoons salt
¾ cup cooking oil
4 cups water, hot
1 small bunch green onions, sliced

Combine 1 ½ cups flour and ¼ teaspoon pepper. Dredge the steaks in the flour mixture. Heat ½ cup oil in a large skillet over medium heat, add the steaks and fry until nice and brown on both sides. When all steaks are cooked, make gravy, by adding 2 tablespoons of flour to the pan drippings; stir in ¼ teaspoon pepper and salt. Stir until the flour is browned and the mixture is bubbly. Add water, stirring constantly. Return the steaks back in the skillet and bring to a boil; reduce heat, put onions on top of steak, cover and low simmer for about 30 minutes.

VENISON CHILI

Sauté 1 cup each, green pepper and green onion, minced in a little oil. Add 2 pounds ground venison and brown; add 1 can tomato sauce, 2 cups water, 1 large can chili beans and 1 package of chili mix. Cook 1 hour on low heat.

STUFFED VENISON CHOPS

4 venison loin chops (1 ¼ inch thick)
2 tablespoons vegetable oil

APPLE STUFFING
1 cup tart apple, peeled and chopped
2 cups day old bread, cubed
¼ cup each (chopped onion, sugar, raisins, hot water and butter, melted)

In skillet, brown chops in oil on both sides. Transfer to a greased 11 x 7 inch baking dish; add enough broth to reach top of chops In a bowl, combine stuffing ingredients; mix well. Spoon over chops. Cover and bake at 350° for 30 minutes. Un-cover; bake 20-30 minutes longer or until meat is done.

SMOKED VENISON

Venison, of any cut
Sour cream
Hot pepper jelly
Red wine
½ cup cooking oil
¼ cup lemon juice
1 teaspoon black pepper

Marinate venison in wine for at least 24 hours. Prepare and light fire in covered grill. Place meat on spit and cook, basting with sauce made with the oil, lemon juice and black pepper. When the meat gets warm, add wet hickory chips to the fire (add more briquettes if necessary to keep an even heat). Smoke venison for 3 hours and continue basting. Remove meat from spit and baste with wine. Wrap in foil and allow meat to cool to room temperature. Re-heat, when ready to serve in foil at 250° for 20 minutes. Place a dab of sour cream and a teaspoon of hot pepper jelly on each piece of meat.

VENISON MEAT LOAF

2 ½ pounds ground venison
¾ cup each (bread crumbs and milk)
½ teaspoon each (salt and pepper)
2 eggs, beaten

Mix all ingredients together. Place into a loaf pan and bake at 350° for 2 ½ hours.

SEAFOOD

GOOD BAKED SALMON

2 pounds salmon fillets
1 each (green and red pepper, chopped)
1 onion, sliced
1 can mandarin oranges
1 pint fresh strawberries
2 green onions, chopped
½ cup honey, syrup or molasses
4 teaspoon minced garlic
2 lemons, juiced
1 teaspoon salt
½ teaspoon each (garlic powder and black pepper)
Box of your favorite pasta
½ cup water

Place salmon fillets in baking dish, pour lemon juice over salmon and dot with butter. Cook pasta according to package instructions; set aside. Sauté peppers and onion. Mix green onions, garlic, ½ cup water, strawberries, oranges and honey; pour strawberry mixture over salmon. Cover with foil and bake at 350° for 30-35 minutes. Remove from oven and place salmon and all ingredients over the pasta and serve.

EASY SALMON BAKE

4 (½ pound) salmon fillets
1 (10 oz) package frozen spinach, thawed and drained
1 egg, beaten
1 onion, chopped
1 (8 oz) container cream cheese, with chives, softened
¼ cup parmesan cheese, grated
¾ cup herb stuffing mix
2 tablespoons each (white wine and milk)
¼ teaspoon garlic, chopped fine

Rinse salmon and pat dry with paper towel. Place in baking dish. Drain spinach. Combine egg, ½ the cream cheese and parmesan cheese. Stir in drained spinach and stuffing mix. Spoon ¼ over each fillet. Bake at 350° for 20-25 minutes. Combine remaining cream cheese, milk, wine and garlic in saucepan, cook over low heat until smooth and creamy. Serve over fillets.

EULA'S BAKED SALMON

4 (4-5 oz) salmon fillets
¼ cup each (chopped pecans, bread crumbs and melted butter)
1 ½ tablespoons honey
3 tablespoons Dijon mustard
4 tablespoons parsley
½ teaspoon each (salt and pepper)
1 lemon, cut into wedges

Combine the mustard, butter and honey together. Set aside. Mix chopped pecans, bread crumbs and parsley in another bowl. Brush each salmon fillet with honey mustard mixture. Sprinkle bread crumb mixture on top of fillets. Bake salmon at 400° for about 10-15 minutes or until salmon flakes easily with a fork.

WHISKEY SOUSED SALMON

4 (4 oz) salmon steaks
4 slices onion
2 bay leaves
1 cup white wine
3 carrots, sliced
½ cup mayonnaise
2 tablespoons each (lemon juice and whiskey)

Put carrots, onion, wine and bay leaves in a saucepan and bring to a boil. Boil for 5 minutes. Rinse the salmon and place in a large pan. Completely cover the salmon with the liquid. Bring to a simmer and slowly cook for 5 minutes. The salmon will be opaque. Remove to individual dishes. Whisk the mayonnaise, lemon juice and whiskey together in a small bowl and spoon over salmon.

SALMON AND CORN LOAF

1 can each (salmon and corn)
1 cup each (milk and cracker or bread crumbs)
1 tablespoon butter
3 eggs, beaten
½ teaspoon each (salt and pepper)

Combine all ingredients; place into a buttered casserole. Bake at 350° for about 40-45 minutes.

EULA'S ORIGINAL KING PATTIES

1 pound fresh king or Spanish mackerel, cleaned, cooked and cut into
small pieces
2 eggs, beaten
1 large onion, chopped (more if needed)
2 tablespoons horseradish sauce
2 tablespoons Worcestershire sauce
1 tablespoon red pepper
¼ cup mayonnaise
Flour
Oil for frying
Salt and pepper to taste

Combine and mash mackerel. Mix all the rest of the ingredients together
with mackerel, except flour and oil. Mix well. Sprinkle enough flour to
hold patties together. Make patties about 2-3 inches around. Fry in hot
oil in skillet until brown on both sides. Drain on paper towel. These
patties are good hot, warm or cold.

DELICIOUS SMOKE SALMON

1 (5 oz) package smoked salmon
2 cucumbers
4 tablespoon each (cream cheese and butter, both softened)
1 tablespoon horseradish
Rye bread, sliced thin

Mix cream cheese, butter and horseradish until smooth. Score
cucumbers with a fork. Cut into thin slices. Cut salmon into pieces.
Cut each slice of bread into 4 triangles. Arrange on platter. Makes
about 3 dozen.

EULA'S SALMON CAKES

1 (16 oz) can salmon, drained
1 egg beaten
1 small onion, chopped
20-25 soda crackers, crumbled
Oil for frying

Drain salmon, add egg, onion and cracker crumbs to salmon. Shape into patties and fry in hot oil in skillet until brown on both sides.

SALMON BAKE

1 can red salmon
2 eggs, hard boiled
2 slices of bread, diced
¼ cup each (chopped pimento and butter)
1/3 cup almonds, slivered
2 cups milk
4 tablespoons flour
1 teaspoon salt

Make cream sauce using milk flour, butter and salt. Add remaining ingredients to cream sauce. Pour into a greased 8 x 12 inch baking dish and bake at 350° for 25 minutes.

RED SNAPPER WITH TOMATO GRAVY

1 large red snapper
1 clove garlic, sliced
2 cans tomatoes
Fresh parsley, chopped
2 large onions, chopped
1 bell pepper, chopped
2 tablespoons each (flour, bacon fat or salad oil)
2 bay leaves
Lemon juice
Salt and pepper

Wash fish and put in baking pan. Squeeze fresh lemon juice over fish and dot freely with butter, salt and pepper. To make the gravy, make a roux using the drippings and flour. Get the roux as dark as possible without burning. Add tomatoes and some hot water if needed. After this simmers for a few minutes, add other ingredients and let simmer again for 1 minute. Pour hot gravy over fish and bake at 325° for 1 hour. The gravy is good over creamed potatoes or rice also.

RED SNAPPER WITH SAUCE

4 pounds red snapper or red fish fillets, cut in medium size pieces
1 pint oysters, drained
1 (4 oz) can mushrooms, drained and sliced
¼ cup white wine
1 lemon, sliced thin
2 tablespoons parsley, chopped
2 pounds shrimp, raw, peeled
Creole sauce (in grocery store)

Place fish fillets in a large baking dish. Place oysters, shrimp and mushrooms over fish. Cover with Creole sauce. Sprinkle with wine, lemon slices and parsley. Bake at 350° for 25-30 minutes. Serve over rice.

SPECIAL SNAPPER FILLETS

2 pounds fresh snapper fish fillets
½ cup mayonnaise
1 medium each (tomato and onion, sliced thin)
1 small green pepper, sliced in thin rings
2 tablespoons lemon juice
3 tablespoons butter or margarine
½ teaspoon each (salt and pepper)
Paprika

Grease baking dish. Salt and pepper both sides of fillets and place in baking dish. Spread mayonnaise on tops of each fillets. Layer each fillet with slices of onion, tomato and green pepper. Sprinkle fillets with lemon juice and paprika; dot with butter and bake at 350° for 20-30 minutes.

EASY RED SNAPPER

4 red snapper fillets, ½ inch thick
1 cup each (chopped onion and parmesan cheese, grated)
1 stick butter
1 green bell pepper, chopped
1 teaspoon each (Worcestershire sauce, salt and pepper)

Spread Worcestershire, salt and pepper on fish. Spread onion and green pepper in 13 x 9 inch baking pan, place fish on top. Dot with butter and bake at 350° for 8 minutes, then baste with juices in pan. Bake for 8 minutes longer. Cover fish with parmesan and place under broiler until cheese browns. Spoon vegetables over fish when ready to serve.

STUFFED FLOUNDER WITH CRABMEAT

1 egg
1 cup crabmeat
¾ cup bread crumbs
1 medium onion, chopped
2 cloves garlic, crushed
2 tablespoons each (bacon drippings, green pepper and celery, chopped)
1 teaspoon each (thyme, salt and pepper)

STUFFING; Sauté vegetables in bacon drippings. Mix with remaining ingredients.

1 (3-4 pound) flounder
1 stick butter
1 teaspoon each (salt and pepper)

Clean fish, cut large pockets in fish. Salt and pepper. Put large amount of stuffing in each pocket. Pour melted butter in a baking dish and place fish, dark side down. Cover and bake at 375° for about 30 minutes. Un-cover for the last 5-10 minutes.

CRAB AU-GRATIN

1 pound fresh crabmeat
8 ounce package sharp cheddar cheese, grated
¼ teaspoon each (salt and pepper)
1 cup onion, chopped fine
2 egg, yolks
¼ cup butter or margarine
½ cup flour
8 ounce carton half and half
5 ounce can evaporated milk
Paprika

In a skillet, sauté onions in butter. Blend in flour. Stir in milk, keeping mixture smooth; stir in half and half. Add egg yolks, salt and pepper; cook for 5 minutes. Add crabmeat and cheese to the skillet and blend well. Prepare a 1 ½ quart casserole dish, spray with cooking spray; spoon the crabmeat mixture in the casserole dish. Sprinkle the top with paprika and bake at 375° for 10-20 minutes.

EASY CRABMEAT BAKE

1 pound lump crabmeat
1 cup mayonnaise
1 tablespoon each (Worcestershire sauce, Tabasco sauce, lemon juice and dry mustard)
Lemon wedges
Parsley, chopped
Buttered cracker crumbs
2 slices bread, crust off and crumbled

Combine crabmeat, bread, mustard, Worcestershire sauce, lemon juice and Tabasco sauce and place in greased seafood shells. Top with buttered cracker crumbs and bake at 350° for 30 minutes. Serve each one with a lemon wedge and sprinkle with parsley.

CRAB SOUFFLE

2 cans crabmeat
½ cup each (mayonnaise and chopped onion)
6 slices of bread, cubed
2 eggs, beaten
1 ½ cups milk
½ can mushroom soup
½ teaspoon salt
Sharp cheddar cheese, grated
Butter

Cut 2 slices of bread into cubes; place in 8 x 8 in pan. Combine crab, onion and mayonnaise; spoon over cubes. Trim and butter remaining bread; place over crab mixture. Combine milk, eggs and salt; pour over bread. Refrigerate overnight. Spoon soup over bread and bake at 350° for 45 minutes. Top with cheese and bake for 15 minutes longer.

SOUTHERN CRAB CASSEROLE

1 can each (crabmeat, mushroom soup, Chinese noodles and fresh mushrooms)
½ cup half and half
½ teaspoon each (salt and pepper)

Mix soup and half and half. Add crab to soup mixture; add half of the noodles. Salt and pepper; mix all ingredients. Sprinkle remaining noodles over top and bake at 325° for 35-45 minutes. Serves 4.

CRAB LOVERS CRAB CASSEROLE

1 (6 ½ oz) can crabmeat, drained
½ cup onion, chopped
6 eggs, hard boiled and chopped fine
1 cup each (mayonnaise and soft bread crumbs)
¾ cup half and half
¼ teaspoon green olives, stuffed and sliced
¼ teaspoon each (salt and pepper)
2 tablespoons fresh parsley, chopped
Sliced olives for garnish

Break up the crabmeat in pieces, in a large bowl. Add mayonnaise, half and half, eggs, bread crumbs, onion, parsley, olives, salt and pepper. Stir all together. Spoon mixture into a 1 quart casserole dish. Top with buttered bread crumbs and bake at 350° for 20-25 minutes. Place olive slices on top.

SOUTHERN CRABMEAT WITH WINE SAUCE

1 pound lump crabmeat, drained and flaked
4 tablespoons each (flour and butter)
¼ cup white wine
2 egg yolks, beaten
2 cups half and half cream
½ pound fresh mushrooms, sliced and sautéed in butter
3 tablespoons parsley, chopped
1 teaspoon each (Worcestershire sauce and salt)
Bread crumbs, buttered

Melt the butter and stir in flour. Add cream and stir until thick. Remove from heat and add egg yolks, Worcestershire sauce and salt. Add wine, mushrooms, crabmeat and parsley. Pour into greased baking dish and bake at 350° for about 15 minutes. Cover with bread crumbs and bake for 25 minutes longer.

CRAB CAKES

1 (1 pound) can crabmeat
2 slices of stale bread, cut into small pieces
1 egg, beaten
1 teaspoon each (seafood seasoning, parsley and salt)
1 tablespoon each (mayonnaise, Worcestershire sauce and baking powder)

Add crabmeat to bread. Add rest ingredients; mix, fry in hot oil. Serves 8.

SOUTHERN CRAB CAKES

1 (6 oz) can crabmeat
1 egg, beaten
½ cup bread crumbs, soft
¼ cup mayonnaise
1 teaspoon onion, grated
½ teaspoon each (fresh parsley and Worcestershire sauce)
1 tablespoon vegetable oil
Dash of hot sauce
1/8 teaspoon each (pepper, mustard and seafood seasoning)

MUSTARD SAUCE
1 tablespoon Dijon mustard
2 tablespoons each (sour cream and mayonnaise)
½ teaspoon each (Worcestershire sauce and lemon juice)

In a small bowl, combine the egg, bread crumbs, Worcestershire sauce, parsley, onion, mayonnaise, seafood seasoning, pepper sauce, black pepper and mustard together. Fold in crab. Refrigerate for 30 minutes. Combine sauce ingredients in a large skillet; heat oil over medium heat. Drop crab mixture by ¼ cup into the pan; cook for 3-5 minutes on each side or until golden brown. Serve with sauce.

DEVILED CRABS

4 teaspoons butter, twice melted (8 teaspoons)
3 teaspoons each (flour and chopped onion)
1 cup milk
2 cups cooked crabmeat
1 teaspoon each (red or black pepper. Dry mustard and salt)
2 eggs, hard boiled, peeled and chopped
½ cup toasted bread crumbs

Melt 4 teaspoons butter; stir in flour and add milk. Cook until thick. Remove from heat; add crabmeat, all seasonings, and egg. Place mixture in crab shells if available, or in a greased baked dish. Sprinkle with bread crumbs and melted butter and bake at 400° for 15 minutes.

CRABMEAT CHEESECAKE

PECAN CRUST
2 cups each (all-purpose flour and ground fine pecans)
2 teaspoons salt
5 tablespoons butter, cold
3 tablespoons ice water

FILLING
1 pound lump crabmeat
1 cup onion, diced
1 tablespoon each (hot pepper sauce and butter)
1 (8 oz) package cream cheese, room temperature
2 eggs
Kosher salt and white pepper

MEUNIERE SAUCE

1 lemon, peeled and quartered
1 cup each (Worcestershire sauce, hot sauce, whipping cream and cold
butter cut, into small cubes and divided)
Kosher salt and cracked black pepper

Preparing the pecan CRUST; Preheat oven to 350°. Combine pecans, flour and salt, mix well. Transfer to a large mixing bowl and cut in butter until dough is in crumbs the size of small peas. Add ice water evenly incorporate in to mixture, which should remain fairly crumbly. Roll out dough to 1/8 inch thickness on a lightly floured surface. Press dough into a lightly greased 9 inch tart pan. Bake crust for 20 minutes or until golden.

Preparing the FILLING; Sauté onion in butter until tender. Add crabmeat and cook until heated through, remove from heat. Beat cream cheese until smooth. Mix in eggs. Fold in crabmeat mixture. Stir in hot sauce and season with salt and pepper. Spoon filling in prepared crust and bake at 300° for 30-40 minutes or until firm to the touch. Prepare MEUNIERE SAUCE, AND GARNISH; Combine lemon, Worcestershire sauce and hot sauce in saucepan, over medium heat, stirring constantly until mixture becomes thick and syrupy. Whisk in whipping cream. Reduce heat to low and blend in butter. Remove from heat and continue to stir. Add salt and pepper. Sauté mushrooms in 2 tablespoons of butter until tender and all moisture has cooked off. Stir mushrooms into meuniere sauce. Melt 1 tablespoon butter and warm crab fingers. Add salt and pepper. Slice cheesecake and top each piece with warm meuniere sauce and 3 crab fingers.

COMPANY CRAB AND SHRIMP CASSEROLE

1 pound each (cooked shrimp, crabmeat and mild cheddar cheese)
½ cup butter
1 can cream of celery soup
¾ cup flour
5 cups heavy whipping cream
¼ teaspoon pepper
3 tablespoons salt
¼ cup onion, chopped
8-10 crackers

Sauté crabmeat and onions in 3 tablespoons butter; add salt and pepper. Bring cream to a boil. Add ½ cup butter and flour. Add soup and cheese. Cook until cheese is melted and sauce is thickened. Add cooked shrimp, crab and onion. Mix together and put in a large greased casserole dish. Heat in 300° oven until bubbly and brown, about 20 minutes. Crush crackers with a little melted butter makes a nice topping.

CRAB AND SHRIMP BAKE

1 (6 ½ oz) can crabmeat, flaked
1 cup shrimp, cooked and cleaned
1 cup each (green pepper, onion and celery, chopped)
1 cup bread crumbs, buttered
1 cup mayonnaise
1 teaspoon Worcestershire sauce
½ teaspoon salt
½ teaspoon pepper

Combine all ingredients, except crumbs; place in individual sea shells, or in a casserole dish. Sprinkle with buttered crumbs and bake at 350° for 20-25 minutes.

SHRIMP AND MUSHROOMS

1 pound medium shrimp, peeled and de-veined
1 stick butter
1 cup each (diced onion and white wine)
4 cloves garlic, minced
2 cups fresh mushrooms, chopped
Flour
Creole seafood seasoning and parsley

Peel and de-vein shrimp. Sprinkle with seafood seasoning and dust with flour. Melt butter in a large sauté pan; add shrimp, parsley, garlic and mushrooms. Gradually stir in wine and cook, stirring gently, until shrimp are done, 3-5 minutes. Serve over cooked rice or buttered toast.

SHRIMP SOUFFLE

2 cups canned or cooked shrimp
8 slices dry bread, crust off, buttered and cubed
1 (3 oz) can sliced mushrooms, drained
3 eggs
2 cups milk
½ pound sharp cheddar cheese, grated
½ teaspoon each (paprika, dry mustard, salt and pepper)

Place ½ of the bread cubes in a greased baking dish. Add shrimp, mushrooms and ½ the cheese. Top with remaining bread and cheese. Beat together the eggs and seasonings; add the milk and pour over and bake at 325° for 45-50 minutes. It's best made and refrigerated overnight before cooking.

GOOD AND CRUNCHY SHRIMP CASSEROLE

3 cups shrimp, cooked
1 (8 oz) can water chestnuts, sliced
1 cup each (sliced almonds, pimentos and onions, diced)
1 (10 oz) package sharp cheddar cheese, cubed
2 cups mayonnaise
Ritz cracker crumbs, buttered

Combine all ingredients, except cracker crumbs; mix well. Pour into a large baking dish; top with the cracker crumbs and bake at 350° for 30-45 minutes.

EULA'S DEEP FRIED SHRIMP

30-35 raw shrimp, shelled and de-veined
1 ½ cups flour
2-3 eggs, beaten
2 tablespoons hot sauce
½ teaspoon salt
1 teaspoon each (black pepper and garlic powder)
Oil for frying

Place flour in bowl, add salt, pepper and garlic powder; set aside. In another bowl, whisk the eggs and hot sauce. Shell and de-vein the raw shrimp. Get oil in deep fryer hot; 360°. Dip shrimp in the egg mixture and roll in the flour mixture. (shake of any loose flour) and drop in hot oil. Cook shrimp until golden brown. Drain on paper towels.
(this same recipe can be used for fried oysters also).

SHRIMP AND CHEESE CASSEROLE

1 quart of shrimp, cooked and peeled
1 (8 oz) package cheddar cheese, grated
2 cup milk
4 tablespoons flour
8 tablespoons butter
Salt
Ritz crackers

Boil shrimp in salted water until almost done, peel and set aside. Butter casserole dish and place 1 layer of Ritz crackers. To make cheese sauce; melt butter in saucepan and stir in flour. Stir out all lumps. Add milk and grated cheese. Cook until cheese melts, stirring constantly. Combine cheese sauce and cooked shrimp. Next, pour the sauce and shrimp mixture over the Ritz crackers and bake at 350° for 15-20 minutes or until thoroughly heated.

SHRIMP CASSEROLE

2 pounds shrimp
1 cup half and half cream
½ cup each (white wine and slivered almonds)
1 (10 ¾ oz) can tomato soup
1/8 teaspoon pepper
1 teaspoon salt
1 tablespoon lemon juice
3 tablespoons salad oil
¾ cup rice, quick cooking
2 tablespoons butter
¼ cup each (onion and green pepper, minced)
½ teaspoon cayenne pepper
Paprika

Clean and cook shrimp for 5 minutes; drain and put into a casserole dish. Sprinkle shrimp with lemon juice and oil. Cook rice, sauté onion and pepper in butter and add to rice. Add the rest of the ingredients except almonds and paprika and add to shrimp in casserole. Top with almonds and paprika. Bake at 350° for 35 minutes.

SHRIMP CREOLE

2 pounds raw shrimp, cleaned
½ cup water
1 small can tomato sauce
1 medium can of tomatoes
4 stalks celery, diced
1 large onion, chopped
1 small green pepper, chopped
2 tablespoons cooking oil
1 tablespoon chili powder
½ teaspoon each (salt and pepper)
1 ½ cups quick cooking rice, cooked

Sauté onion, celery and green pepper in cooking oil. Add chili powder, tomatoes, salt, tomato sauce and water; simmer 30 minutes. Add shrimp; cook 15 minutes longer. Serve over cooked rice.

SOUTHERN SHRIMP AND GRITS

6 cup water
½ stick butter
1 ½ cups quick grits
2 teaspoon salt
1 (6 oz) roll Kraft garlic cheese, cut in chunks
1 cup cheddar cheese, grated
¼ teaspoon cayenne pepper

SHRIMP SAUCE

2-3 pounds shrimp, peeled, de-veined
3 tablespoons olive oil or bacon drippings
1 stick butter
1 bunch green onions, chopped
1 (8 oz) can mushrooms, sliced
1-2 cloves garlic, minced
2 tablespoons lemon juice
½ cup parsley, chopped
Sprinklings of each (cayenne, basil, thyme, oregano and paprika)
Salt and pepper to taste

Bring water to boil in a large saucepan; stir in grits and salt. Reduce heat and stir occasionally until thickened. Add remaining ingredients and stir until smooth. Pour into a greased casserole dish and bake at 350° for 20 minutes, while preparing shrimp sauce. SAUCE; have shrimp sauce ingredients ready. In a large skillet, sauté shrimp in oil and butter for a few minutes. Immediately add remaining ingredients. Stir well and heat on medium high for another few minutes. Do not simmer longer than 10 minutes. Serve over a scoop of cheese grits. Add a salad and French bread. Serves 8.

QUICK SHRIMP AND CORN DISH

1 (5 oz) can shrimp
1 (12 oz) can corn, whole kernel
1 (10 ½ oz) can cream of mushroom soup
½ cup milk
½ teaspoon each (paprika and pepper)

Combine soup, paprika and milk in skillet. Stir over low heat until smooth. Add shrimp, corn and pepper. Cover and cook until heated through. Good served over toast.

SHRIMP AND RICE CASSEROLE

1 pound medium-large shrimp, cooked, shelled and de-veined
1 package wild rice
1 onion, chopped
2 cups sharp cheddar cheese, shredded
1 (10 ¾ oz) can cream mushroom soup
1 green bell pepper, chopped
2 tablespoons butter
½ teaspoon each (salt and pepper)

Cook rice according to directions on package. Sauté pepper and onion in butter until soft. Combine rice, soup, shrimp, pepper, onion and 1 ½ cups cheese in a large bowl. Add salt and pepper. Mix well. Place in a greased 11 x 7 inch baking dish. Add remaining ½ cup of cheese and bake at 350° for 30 minutes or until bubbly.

SHRIMP WITH FETA CHEESE

2 ½ pounds shrimp, raw and un-peeled
4 medium ripe tomatoes
3 tablespoons parsley, chopped and divided
1 teaspoon each (salt and pepper)
1 ounce feta cheese, cut in small cubes
½ teaspoon oregano
½ cup white wine
¼ cup onion, chopped

Seed and juice tomatoes. Shell shrimp, leaving the tails on (if desired). In skillet add onion and cook 5 minutes. Stir in tomatoes, wine, oregano, 2 tablespoons parsley, salt and pepper. Cook until mixture forms a light puree, stirring constantly. Add shrimp and cook 5 minutes more. Stir in cheese. Sprinkle with remaining parsley.

SHRIMP FRITTERS

1 can shrimp
½ cup each (cheddar cheese, grated and water)
2 eggs, beaten
½ cup flour
3 tablespoons butter or margarine

Bring water and butter to a boil. Add flour; stir until all sticks together. Remove from heat; slowly add eggs, cheese and shrimp. Drop by tablespoonful into deep fat. Brown on all sides. Drain on paper towels.

COCONUT SHRIMP

1 pound medium-large shrimp, peeled and de-veined
½ cup each (bread crumbs and flour)
2 cups coconut, shredded and sweetened
1 teaspoon salt
2/3 cup beer
Oil for frying and Orange marmalade for dipping

Whisk together the flour and salt. Add the beer and whisk until smooth. (batter is better when it stands for about 10 minutes). In another bowl, combine the coconut and bread crumbs together. Put shrimp into the batter, 1 at a time. Remove shrimp and dredge in coconut mixture. Fry the shrimp in batches in a deep fryer for about 2 minutes or until golden brown. Drain on paper towels. You can buy the orange marmalade for dipping in most grocery stores.

FRANK'S LOW COUNTRY SHRIMP BOIL

1 ½ pounds large shrimp, raw, de-veined, tails on
Crab - shrimp boil mix
7-8 corn-on-cob, halved
1 package smoked sausage
1 bottle or can beer
12 medium size potatoes, cut in half
Water

Bring water to a boil in a large pot. Add sausage, potatoes and spices and cook until tender. Add corn and cook 5 minutes. Add beer and bring back to a boil; add shrimp and cook 3 minutes more. Drain pot of all liquid. Serve immediately. Serve with garlic bread and cocktail sauce.

SHRIMP SCAMPI

4 pounds jumbo shrimp, peeled
1 cup bread crumbs
4 ounces butter, melted

Split shrimp down the middle and place on baking rack. Brush with butter and sprinkle with bread crumbs. Broil 5 minutes. Place on platter and pour the sauce over the shrimp.

SAUCE
¾ cup each (Dijon mustard and white wine)
1-2 ounces butter
4 scallions
1 cup lemon juice
1 tablespoon Worcestershire sauce
1 clove garlic
½ teaspoon salt

Chop scallions, and garlic fine. Add Worcestershire sauce, salt, lemon juice and wine. Mix butter with the mustard until soft and smooth. Add to the rest of the sauce. Boil for 5 minutes, stirring constantly.

SHRIMP PIE

1 pound shrimp, cooked, shelled and cleaned
1 (4 oz) can mushrooms, drained and chopped
1 onion, minced
5 tablespoons butter
3 tablespoons flour
2 cups milk
1 tablespoon parsley, chopped
1 cup potatoes, cooked and diced
½ cup green peas, cooked
Pastry for topping
½ teaspoon each (salt and pepper)

Cook onion and mushrooms in 2 tablespoons of butter for 5 minutes; add shrimp. Prepare white sauce with 3 tablespoons butter; flour, salt, pepper and milk. Pour over shrimp mixture and add remaining ingredients except pastry. Place into casserole dish and top with the pastry, rolled to ¼ inch thick. Baked at 325° for 20 minutes.

FRIED SHRIMP BALLS

2 pounds fresh shrimp
2 eggs
5-6 cups cracker crumbs
¼ cup green onions, tops and bottoms, chopped
1 teaspoon old bay seafood seasoning
3 tablespoons salad dressing
2 teaspoons parsley flakes
½ teaspoon each (salt and pepper)

Peel and de-vein shrimp. Cut into small pieces. In a large bowl mix shrimp and all other ingredients, plus 3 cups cracker crumbs and mix well. Save the remaining 3 cups of cracker crumbs. Take a small amount of the mixture and roll into small balls. Dip balls in the remaining 3 cups of the cracker crumbs. Deep fry until golden brown.

SHRIMP WITH ARTICHOKES

2 pounds large shrimp, cooked, peeled and de-veined
1 cup artichoke hearts, drained and chopped
1 stick butter
1/3 cup each (white wine and chopped fresh basil)
¾ teaspoons each (minced garlic and salt)
¼ teaspoon black pepper
1/8 teaspoon red pepper
Juice of 1 lemon
Rice

Melt the butter and garlic in a skillet and cook, stirring often for about 1 minute. Add the wine, red pepper, black pepper, shrimp and artichoke hearts and bring to a simmer. Let liquid reduce by ½ for about 3 minutes. Add lemon juice and basil. Sprinkle with salt. Serve over hot rice.

EASY BOILED SHRIMP COCKTAIL

4-5 pounds fresh large shrimp
12 ounce box crab boil
Salt

Bring water to a boil; add salt, crab boil and shrimp. Cook until shells are pink, 3-4 minutes. Drain. When shrimp are cool enough to handle, remove shells, de-vein, wash, clean; and chill. Dip in your favorite cocktail sauce. Enjoy.

FAVORITE SHRIMP DISH

1 pound large shrimp, peeled and de-veined
2 cups ripe tomatoes, peeled and chopped
1 green pepper, chopped
Juice of 1 lemon
1 cup feta cheese, crumbled
2 tablespoons each (oregano and olive oil)
3 teaspoons Tabasco sauce
1 tablespoon capers, drained
½ tablespoon each (salt and pepper)
1 clove garlic, minced
Fresh parsley

Combine the green pepper, garlic and tomatoes together in a large skillet, sauté until the pepper is tender. Place the tomato mixture to the side of the pan and add the shrimp and cook for 3 minutes, stirring often. Add oregano, capers, Tabasco, salt and pepper. Remove skillet from heat and stir in the feta cheese. Sprinkle the lemon juice over the mixture and transfer to a serving dish. Sprinkle with parsley before serving.

SHRIMP NEWBURG WITH GREEN RICE

2 pounds shrimp, cooked and peeled
2 egg yolks, beaten
1 cup whipping cream
1 ½ cups milk, more if needed
3 tablespoons butter
3 tablespoons flour
¼ teaspoon each (salt and pepper)
1 teaspoon paprika
½ teaspoon each (mustard and red pepper)
5 tablespoons wine, divided
2 cups green rice, cooked and molded into a ring
Parsley

Melt butter in large pan. Stir in flour and cook several minutes. Add milk and stir until smooth and thick. Add seasonings and 4 tablespoons wine. Beat together the egg yolks and cream. Add cream to wine sauce. Cook 15 minutes. Add shrimp and remaining wine. Pour shrimp Newburg into center and around the green rice ring and garnish with parsley.

SPECIAL SHRIMP CREOLE

1 cup each (un-cooked rice, onion and celery chopped)
1 pound shrimp, raw. Peeled and de-veined
2 teaspoons each (sugar and chili powder)
4 tablespoons cooking oil
2 tablespoons flour
1 teaspoon each (salt and pepper)
1 (10 oz) package frozen English peas
3 cups tomatoes, sliced
2 cups water
Rice

Cook rice in boiling salt water until done. Sauté onion and celery in cooking oil until soft. Add in flour and seasonings. Add water, stirring constantly. Simmer 15 minutes, covered. Add remaining ingredients and continue cooking 5-15 minutes longer or until shrimp is done. Serve over hot rice.

GOOD SAUTEED SHRIMP

2 pounds shrimp, raw, peeled and de-veined
1 pound fresh mushrooms, sliced
3 green onions, chopped
4 tablespoons wine
½ teaspoon garlic salt
½ cup butter & Juice of 1 lemon
Parmesan cheese

Sauté onions in butter. Season with garlic salt. Add wine, lemon juice, shrimp and mushrooms. Sprinkle with parmesan cheese, simmer until shrimp is done. Can be served over rice or just in its juices along.

CLAM CASSEROLE

2 cans clams, minced
2 eggs, beaten
¼ cup each (melted butter and milk)
9 crackers, crushed
1 cup onion, minced
½ teaspoon salt

Mix all ingredients, put a 1 ½ quart casserole dish and bake at 350° for 45 minutes.

OYSTERS BAKED IN SHELLS

1 pint oysters, drained and chopped fine
½ cup each (green onion, parsley and celery, all chopped fine)
4 eggs, hard boiled, chopped fine
½ cup butter, divided
8-9 crackers, crumbled and divided
1 tablespoon each (Worcestershire sauce and hot sauce)
½ teaspoon each (red pepper and salt)

Melt ¼ cup butter in skillet; add onion and celery, cook until tender. Add oysters and juice that accumulated while chopping. Add eggs, parsley and half of the cracker crumbs. Add seasonings. Cook until oysters curl. If mixture seems too thin, cook a little longer. If mixture is too stiff, add a little more liquid. Place mixture into small oyster shells (about 10 shells). Sprinkle with remaining cracker crumbs and melted butter. Bake at 450° for 10-12 minutes. If you don't have oyster shells you may make this recipe as a casserole dish.

EULA'S DEEP FRIED OYSTERS

1 pint fresh oysters, drained
1 cup flour
1 teaspoon each (garlic powder, salt and pepper)
2 eggs, beaten
1 tablespoon hot sauce

Combine flour, salt, pepper and garlic powder together. Beat eggs, add hot sauce. Dip oysters in egg mixture and dredge in flour mixture. Heat oil to 350° - 360° in deep fryer. Drop oysters in hot oil and fry until golden brown. Drain on paper towels. (I use this same recipe for my deep fried shrimp).

OYSTER CASSEROLE

1 pint oysters
1 egg, beaten
½ stick butter
Salt and pepper to taste
Cracker crumbs

Butter casserole dish, layer with half the oysters. Dot oysters with butter. Salt and pepper oysters. Cover with cracker crumbs. Repeat layers. Pour egg over top and bake at 350° for 30 minutes.

CRAWFISH CASSEROLE

1 pound crawfish tails
1 (10 oz) package yellow rice mix
1 cup each (chopped onion and cheddar cheese, shredded)
¼ cup butter
1 (10 ¾ oz) cream of shrimp soup
8-10 crackers
1 (2.8 oz) can French onion rings
1 medium green pepper, chopped
1 (14.5 oz) can of tomatoes, diced

Cook rice according to package directions. In a medium skillet cook the onion and bell pepper in butter until tender. Stir in un-strained tomatoes and crawfish. Cook for 10 minutes, stirring occasionally. When rice is done, stir in crawfish mixture and soup. Transfer to a greased baking dish. Sprinkle with crackers and cheese. Bake at 375° for 30 minutes. Sprinkle with fried onion rings and bake 5 minutes longer or until bubbly.

FISH FAJITAS

1 ½ pound of grouper fish (or any white fish fillets)
1 package of 7 inch tortillas
1 cup salsa
1 avocado, peeled and sliced
1 lime, cut into wedges, and juice
1 tablespoon olive oil
1 teaspoon salt
½ teaspoon pepper

Cut fish into strips and season with salt and pepper. Heat oil in skillet; add the fish; cook for 4-6 minutes or until cooked all the way through; stirring often. In another skillet, place the tortillas, 1 at a time. Line a platter with a clean tea towel. Immediately transfer the hot tortillas to the platter. To assemble, divide the fish on all of the tortillas and top with salsa and avocado slices. Squeeze lime juice over the avocado and roll up the tortillas.

CRAYFISH PIE

1 (10 inch) pie shell
1 pound crayfish tails
3-4 eggs
½ tablespoon tomato sauce
4 tablespoons green onion, minced
3 tablespoons butter
½ teaspoon salt
Dash nutmeg
5 tablespoons white wine
½ - ¾ pounds mushrooms, sliced
1/8 teaspoon pepper
¼ cup each (Swiss cheese and gruyere cheese, grated)
½ cup fresh parmesan cheese, grated
1 ½ cups whipping cream

Prepare pie shell. Sauté the crayfish and green onions in butter for 2-3 minutes or until tender. Add salt, nutmeg and pepper. Add the wine and cook another minute. Cool. Sauté mushrooms in a small amount of butter and set aside. Beat the eggs in a bowl with cream, tomato sauce, salt and pepper. Gradually blend in crayfish and taste for seasoning. Add the sautéed mushrooms to the mixture. Pour the mixture into the pie shell and sprinkle the cheese over it and bake at 375° for 30 minutes or until pie puffed.

LOBSTER CASSEROLE

1 ½ cups lobster meat
1 cup milk
1 ½ cup bread crumbs
2 eggs, beaten
2 tablespoons butter, melted
½ teaspoon salt
1 tablespoon lemon juice
½ teaspoon dry mustard

Combine all ingredients together. Place in 1 ½ quart casserole dish and bake at 350° for 40 minutes. Serves 6

GOOD AND CRUNCHY FRIED FISH

2 pounds fish fillets
1 egg white, beaten stiff
1 cup of each (flour, warm water)
1 egg, yolk
1 tablespoon oil
½ teaspoon each (salt and pepper)
Oil for frying

Dry fish good; sprinkle with salt and pepper. In a bowl, put flour and drop egg yolk in center. Add warm water and 1 tablespoon of oil; stir well. Fold egg white into batter. Drop fillet in batter and fry until golden brown on both sides.

GRANNY'S FRIED CAT FISH

6 catfish fillets
1 jar yellow mustard
2-3 cups flour
1 teaspoon each (salt, pepper and garlic powder)

Spread mustard on both sides of each catfish fillet. Put in refrigerator for (4-6 hours). Mix flour and seasoning in a bowl. Keep each piece of catfish lightly covered in mustard and roll in the flour mixture. Heat oil in deep fryer to 360° and fry until a golden brown.

BAKED FISH IN SAUCE

1 pound fresh or frozen fish fillets
¼ cup sour cream
¼ cup mayonnaise
1 tablespoon butter
Juice of 1 lemon

Place fish in a buttered baking dish and bake at 350° for 10 minutes. Mix sour cream, mayonnaise and lemon juice; spoon over fish and bake for 15-20 minutes longer.

SIMPLE BAKED FISH

6 ounces fish fillets, flounder or tilapia
3 tablespoons butter
2 tablespoons green onion, sliced
1 teaspoon salt
½ teaspoon each (garlic powder and black pepper)
Zest of ½ lemon

Line a baking dish with foil. Place the fish on the foil and sprinkle with the seasonings. Mix the green onion, lemon zest and butter together. Spread the mixture on top of the fish fillets. Bake at 400° until done, approximately 10-15 minutes. Serve hot.

BAKED FLOUNDER

1 whole flounder
3-4 slices bacon
2 tablespoons flour
2-3 large potatoes
1 large onion
Salt and pepper to taste

Score flounder, salt and pepper and place in a baking pan. Fry bacon in skillet. Add oil if needed. Add flour to drippings and brown. Add water to make a medium gravy. Add salt and pepper to taste. Peel and slice potatoes and add onions. Place over fish. Pour gravy over fish, onions and potatoes. Bake at 400° for 1 hour. Baste occasionally.

OVEN FRIED FISH

1 pound fish fillets
½ cup each (fine bread crumbs and milk)
¼ stick butter, melted
½ teaspoon each (salt and pepper)

Dip fish in milk and coat with bread crumbs. Place on a greased baking pan. Add salt and pepper. Drizzle with melted butter and bake at 400° until fish flakes easily and is golden brown.

SEAFOOD CASSEROLE

2 pounds shrimp
¾ cup quick-cooking rice
¼ cup green pepper, minced
2 tablespoons each (butter and paprika)
½ cup onion, minced
1 teaspoon salt
1/8 teaspoon black pepper
½ teaspoon red pepper
1 (10 ¾ oz) can tomato soup
1 cup half and half
½ cup each (wine and slivered almonds)
¼ cup vegetable oil
Juice of 1 lemon

Cook shrimp in boiling water for 5 minutes; drain and put into a casserole dish. Sprinkle shrimp with lemon juice and oil. Cook rice. Sauté pepper and onion in butter and add to rice. Add all remaining ingredients except almonds and paprika and add to shrimp in casserole. Top with almonds and paprika and bake at 350° for 35 minutes.

THREE DIFFERENT SEAFOODS

1 pound crawfish tails
1 pound shrimp, peeled and de-veined
1 pound lump crabmeat
½ cup butter
2 onions, chopped
2 stalks celery, chopped fine
2 ½ cups chicken broth
3 tablespoons lemon juice
½ teaspoon salt
¼ cup each (flour, green onion tops, chopped and parsley, chopped)
1 tablespoon Tabasco sauce
Dash red pepper

Sauté onions and celery in butter until softened; about 10 minutes. Whisk chicken broth and flour until smooth. Add to celery mixture; bring to a boil. Reduce heat and simmer until thickened, about 30 minutes. Add crawfish and cook 15 minutes. Add lemon juice, salt, red pepper, Tabasco sauce and shrimp; cook for 5 minutes. Add crabmeat, onions, green onions and parsley and cook for 5 more minutes. Serve over rice.

STUFFED EGGPLANT WITH SEAFOOD

6 medium eggplants
4 green peppers, chopped
1 onion, chopped
½ cup celery, chopped
3 cloves garlic
1 pound each (shrimp and crabmeat)
3 tablespoons of margarine
6-8 pats of butter
½ cup parsley, chopped
¼ teaspoon each (salt and pepper)
Bread crumbs
Paprika for garnish

Boil eggplants until soft, scoop out of shell. Sauté green pepper, onion, garlic, celery and 3 tablespoons of margarine until limp. Add eggplant, salt and pepper and simmer until liquid is cooked out. Add shrimp and cook 20 minutes. Fold in crabmeat and parsley. Cook only briefly. Add enough bread crumbs to make firm and stuff the eggplant shells. Sprinkle with paprika. Dot with butter. Bake at 350° for 20-25 minutes or until brown.

HOT TUNA ON TOAST

1 (1 ½ oz) can tuna fish
2 tomatoes
2 eggs, hard boiled, chopped
1 green pepper, chopped
1 teaspoon lemon juice
1000 Island dressing
½ teaspoon each (cayenne pepper and salt)
Worcestershire sauce
Parsley

Peel and chop tomatoes, add green peppers and eggs. Drain tuna and add the remaining seasonings to the tomato mixture. Mix and steam in double boiler covered for 20 minutes. Serve on toast topped with 1000 Island dressing. Garnish with parsley.

DESSERTS

BERRY CHEESECAKE PARFAITS

1 (8 oz) package cream cheese softened
1 ½ cups cold milk
1 (3.4 oz) package jell-o vanilla instant pudding
1 ½ cups cool whip topping, thawed and divided
2 dozen vanilla wafers, chopped coarsely
1 ½ cups berries (any kind in season)

Beat cream cheese with mixer until creamy. Beat in milk. Add dry pudding mix; mix well. Whisk in 1 cup cool whip. Layer half each of wafers, berries and pudding mixture in 8 parfait dishes. Repeat layers.

DEEP FRIED CHEESECAKE

1 plain frozen cheesecake (bought)
Won ton wrappers
Powdered sugar
Chocolate syrup
Whipped topping

Slice cheesecake in 1 x 3 inch pieces. Brush wrappers with melted butter. Lay cake in center of wrappers, sprinkle chocolate on cakes. Roll in powdered sugar. Drop in deep fry at 360° only until they brown on all sides; 1-2 minutes. Remove and drain on paper towels. Drizzle chocolate syrup on top and add whipped topping.

EASY APPLE PIE CAKE

1 (18 ¼ oz) box yellow cake mix
1 (8 oz) carton sour cream
1 egg
1 stick butter
1 (20 oz) can sliced apples
1 tablespoon cinnamon
½ cup sugar

Mix cake mix and butter until crumbly. Press into a greased 9 x 13 inch baking pan, pressing up the sides a little. Bake at 350° for 10 minutes. Place sliced apples over crust while still warm. Mix cinnamon and sugar together; sprinkle over apples. Mix sour cream and egg together; spoon on top of mixture and bake at 350° for 25 minutes.

PEACHES AND CREAM CHEESECAKE

4 (8 oz) packages cream cheese, softened
1 (3 oz) package peach jell-o gelatin
1 (15 oz) can sliced peaches in juice, drained and chopped
1 (8 oz) carton cool whip topping, thawed
2 cups graham cracker crumbs
6 tablespoons butter or margarine, melted
1 cup sugar, divided

Mix graham cracker crumbs and ¼ cup sugar; press in bottom of a 13 x 9 inch pan. Refrigerate while preparing filling. Beat cream cheese and remaining sugar in a large bowl with a mixer until blended. Add dry gelatin mix, and mix well. Stir in peaches and cool whip. Spoon over crust; cover. Refrigerate for 4 hours or until firm. Always refrigerate any leftovers.

KEY LIME ICE CREAM PIE

2 cups graham cracker crumbs
¼ cup brown sugar
½ cup butter, melted
Lime slices for garnish
Key lime ice cream, softened
1 carton cool whip

Preheat oven to 350°. In a medium bowl combine cracker crumbs and brown sugar. Stir in butter, press mixture onto bottom and sides of a 10 inch spring form pan. Bake for 8-10 minutes and let cool completely. Carefully spread softened ice cream over crust. Cover and freeze for 4 hours, or until firm. Cut into wedges to serve and garnish with cool whip and lime slices.

LEMON CHEESECAKE SQUARES

1 ¼ cups flour
1 cup rolled oats
¼ teaspoon salt
½ cup seedless raspberry jam
1/3 cup brown sugar
¾ cup vegetable oil

FILLING

4 (8 oz) packages cream cheese, softened
1 ½ cups sugar
1 ¼ cups flour
4 eggs
1/3 cup lemon juice
4 teaspoons grated lemon peel

In a mixing bowl, cream oil and brown sugar. Combine flour, oats and salt; add to creamed mixture. Press dough into a greased 13 x 9 inch baking dish. Bake at 350° for 15-20 minutes or until golden brown. Spread with jam
FILLING; Beat the cream cheese, sugar and flour until fluffy. Add eggs, lemon juice and lemon peel until blended. Spoon over jam. Bake at 350° for 30-35 minutes or until center is almost set. Cool. Cover and store in refrigerator.

LAYERED STRAWBERRY CHEESECAKE BOWL

2 (8 oz) packages cream cheese, softened
1 (3.4 oz) vanilla instant jell-o pudding mix
2 cups each (pound cake, cubed and cool whip, thawed and divided)
3 cups strawberries, sliced
3 tablespoons sugar
1 ½ cups cold milk
1 square semi-sweet chocolate

Combine berries and sugar. Refrigerate until ready to use. Beat cream cheese with mixer until creamy. Add milk, pudding mix and mix well. Blend 1 ½ cups cool whip. Spoon ½ into 2 ½ quart bowl. Top with cake, berries and remaining cream cheese mixture. Refrigerate for 4 hours. Melt chocolate; drizzle over dessert. Top with remaining cool whip.

APPLE PECAN CHEESECAKE

4 (8 oz) packages cream cheese, softened
½ stick butter, melted
1 ½ plus 2 tablespoons brown sugar, divided
1 teaspoon vanilla
1 cup sour cream
4 eggs
4 cups apples, peeled and chopped
¾ cup pecans, chopped
1 teaspoon cinnamon
1 ½ cups graham cracker crumbs
1 ½ cups sugar

Mix crumbs, butter and 2 tablespoons sugar, press into bottom of a 13 x 9 inch pan, that's (lined with foil). Bake for 10 minutes. Beat the cream cheese, 1 cup sugar and vanilla with a mixer until blended well. Add sour cream; blend. Add eggs, 1 at a time, mixing on low after each until blended. Pour over crust. Mix remaining ½ sugar, apples, pecans and cinnamon; spoon over batter. Bake for 1 hour; cool. Refrigerate for 4 hours. Use foil to lift cheesecake from pan before cutting and serving.

LEMON CHEESECAKE

1 (8 oz) package cream cheese
1 cup sugar
1 (13-14 oz) can evaporated milk
½ teaspoon vanilla
1 (3 oz) package lemon gelatin
1 stick butter
About 25 graham crackers, crushed

Mix butter with graham cracker crumbs; pat into large pan. Dissolve gelatin in boiling water; refrigerate until slightly thickened. Mix well the cream cheese and sugar. Fold into gelatin. Whip evaporated milk; add vanilla. Fold whipped milk into gelatin mixture; pour into crust. Sprinkle a few crumbs over top. Refrigerate until set. Cut in squares.

MINI CHEESE CAKES

12 vanilla wafers
1 (8 oz) package cream cheese
½ cup sugar
1 teaspoon vanilla
2 eggs
Cherry pie filling and nuts or chocolate

Line 2 muffin tins with liners. Place 1 wafer in each liner, mix cream cheese, vanilla and sugar in blender on medium speed. Add eggs, mix well. Pour over wafers, filling liners ¾ full and bake at 325° for 25 minutes. Remove from oven; cool. Remove from tins and chill. Top with the pie filling, nuts or chocolate.

DIFFERENT AND GOOD LIME CHEESECAKE

1 (18 ¼ oz) box yellow cake mix
2 (8 oz) package cream cheese, softened
4 eggs
1 (14 oz) can sweetened condensed milk
1 (8 oz) container cool whip
1/3 cup lime juice
1 teaspoon vanilla
¼ cup vegetable oil
2 teaspoons grated lime zest
Lime slices for garnish

(Reserve ½ cup of the dry cake mix). In a large bowl, combine remaining cake mix, 1 egg and oil. Mix well. Press evenly in bottom and up sides of a greased 13 x 9 inch pan. In the same bowl; beat cream cheese until fluffy. Beat in condensed milk until smooth. Add remaining eggs and reserved cake mix and beat 1 minute. Stir in the zest, lime juice and vanilla. Pour into crust. Bake at 300° for 50-55 minutes or until center is firm. Cool. When ready to serve, cut into squares and garnish with lime slices.

EASY KEY LIME CHEESECAKE

1 tub (24.2 oz) ready-to-eat key lime cheesecake
1 graham cracker crust
1 carton cool whip topping

Spoon cheesecake filling into crust; smooth top with a spoon. Top with cool whip just before serving.

PUMPKIN CHEESECAKE

CRUST
1 ½ cups graham cracker crumbs
5 tablespoons butter or margarine, melted
1 tablespoon sugar

In a small bowl combine cracker crumbs and sugar; stir in the butter. Press onto the bottom and 2 inches up the sides of a greased 9 inch spring form pan. Bake at 350° for 5 minutes. Cool.

FILLING
3 (8 oz) packages cream cheese, softened
1 cup sugar
3 eggs
1 cup canned pumpkin
1 teaspoon vanilla extract
½ teaspoon ground cinnamon
¼ teaspoon each (ground nutmeg and ground allspice)
Whipped cream

In a mixing bowl, beat cream cheese, sugar and vanilla until smooth. Add eggs, pumpkin and spices; beat just until combined. Pour into crust. Bake at 350° for 1 hour or until center is almost set. Cool on wire rack for 10 minutes. Run a knife around edge of the pan to loosen; cool 1 hour longer. Refrigerate until completely cool (center will fall). Remove sides of pan just before serving. Garnish with whipped cream.

EASY CHEESE CAKE

3 (8 oz) packages cream cheese
1 cup plus 2 tablespoons sugar
5 eggs
1 ½ cups sour cream
¾ teaspoon almond extract
½ teaspoon vanilla
¼ teaspoon salt

Cream 1 cup of sugar with cream cheese; add eggs, 1 at a time. Add almond flavoring and salt. Pour into a spring form pan; Bake at 325° for 40 minutes. Cool for 20 minutes. Mix sour cream, remaining sugar and vanilla, pour over cheese cake and bake for 10 minutes longer.

CHEESECAKE POPS

3 (8 oz) packages cream cheese, softened
1 cup each (sugar and sour cream)
3 eggs, beaten
1 teaspoon vanilla extract
About 45 lollipop sticks
1 cup graham cracker crumbs
3 (10-12 oz) packages vanilla chips
3 tablespoons shortening
Coconut and chocolate, grated, assorted sprinkles and chopped nuts
for garnish

Line bottom of a 9 inch spring form pan with parchment pepper; coat paper and sides of pan with cooking spray. Beat cream cheese and sugar in a large bowl until smooth. Beat in sour cream and vanilla until blended. Add eggs; beat on low speed just until combined. Pour into prepared pan. Place pan on baking sheet and bake at 350° for 45-50 minutes or until center is almost set. Cool on wire rack for 10 minutes. Carefully run a knife around edge of the pan to loosen; cool 1 hour longer. Cover and freeze overnight. Remove from freezer and let stand for 30 minutes. Place cracker crumbs in a shallow bowl. Working quickly, scoop out 1 inch balls of cheesecake; roll each in cracker crumb and insert a lollipop stick. Place on waxed paper-lined baking sheets. Freeze for 1 hour or until firm. In a microwave, melt vanilla chips and shortening stir until smooth. Place toppings in shallow bowls. Dip cheesecake pops in vanilla chip mixture; allow excess to drip off. Roll in toppings. Place on waxed paper; let stand until set.

SIMPLE BUT GOOD CHEESECAKE

5 (8 oz) packages cream cheese, softened
1 cup sour cream
4 eggs
1 (21 oz) can cherry pie filling
3 tablespoons flour
1 tablespoon vanilla
3 tablespoons butter or margarine, melted
1 cup plus, 3 tablespoons sugar, divided
6 graham crackers, crushed

Line a 13 x 9 inch pan with foil. Mix crumbs, 3 tablespoons sugar and butter; press onto bottom of pan. Bake at 325° for 10 minutes. Beat cream cheese, sugar, flour and vanilla until blended. Add sour cream; blend. Add eggs and bake at 325° for 40 minutes or until center is almost set. Cool completely. Refrigerate 4 hours. Use foil to lift cheesecake from pan. Top with pie filling and serve.

ITALIAN CREAM CAKE

2 cups self-rising flour
5 eggs
2 cups sugar
1 stick butter or margarine, softened
1 cup buttermilk
1 (7 oz) can coconut
1 tablespoon vanilla
½ cup vegetable oil
1 teaspoon baking powder

Cream oil and butter together; add sugar and beat well. Add eggs, 1 at a time. Add flour and baking powder alternately with the buttermilk to creamed mixture. Add vanilla and coconut. Pour into 3 (9 inch) greased pans and bake at 350° for about 40 minutes.

CREAM CHEESE FROSTING

1 (8 oz) package cream cheese, softened
1 (1 pound box) powdered sugar
½ stick butter or margarine, softened
1 cup pecans, chopped
1 tablespoon vanilla

Beat cream cheese and butter until smooth. Add sugar and vanilla and beat until smooth; add nuts and beat 1 more minute. Spread on each layer, sides and top of cake.

BUTTERMILK CAKE

1 cup butter
3 cups sugar
4 eggs
¼ teaspoon baking soda
3 cups self-rising flour
1 cup buttermilk
2 teaspoons vanilla

Cream the butter and sugar together, add eggs. Combine soda and flour. Add alternately with the buttermilk. Add vanilla. In an angel food pan bake at 350° for 45-50 minutes.

PEAR PARFAIT DESSERT

2 (14 ¼ oz) cans pears, drained and sliced
17-18 squares of cinnamon graham crackers, crushed fine
½ cup powdered sugar
1 ½ cups yogurt, vanilla

In a bowl, combine yogurt and sugar. Place 3-4 slices each of pears in 5 parfait glasses; top each with 2 tablespoons of cracker crumbs and 3 tablespoons of yogurt mixture. Repeat layers. Sprinkle with remaining crumbs. Refrigerate until ready to serve.

VANILLA PUDDING DESSERT

1 (5 .1 oz) package instant vanilla pudding mix
1 (14 oz) can sweetened condensed milk
1 (12 oz) carton frozen whipped topping, thawed
3 cups fresh strawberries
4 cups vanilla wafers, crushed
2 ¾ cups cold milk

In a large bowl, whisk milk and pudding mix for 2 minutes. Let stand for 15 minutes; fold in condensed milk. Set aside 1 tablespoon whipped topping and 2 tablespoons wafer crumbs. Fold remaining whipped topping into pudding. In a 3 quart serving bowl, layer 1/3 of the strawberries, wafer crumbs and pudding mixture. Repeat layers twice. Sprinkle with reserved wafer crumbs. Top with reserved whipped topping. Refrigerate until ready to serve.

FANTASTIC BLUEBERRY DESSERT

1 can blueberry pie filling
½ cup sugar
2 eggs, beaten
1 teaspoon lemon juice
1 (8 oz) package cream cheese
Whipping cream
1 graham cracker pie crust

Combine eggs, sugar and cheese; pour in pie crust. Bake at 350° for 20 minutes; cool. Cover with blueberry pie filling mixed with lemon juice. Top with whip cream.

MERINGUES WITH WHITE CHOCOLATE MOUSSE

6 egg whites
1 1/3 cup sugar
2 drops (red food coloring)

Line a baking sheet with parchment paper; set aside. In top of double boiler, whisk together egg whites and sugar. Place over simmering water. Whisk constantly until sugar is dissolved and egg whites are warm to touch, about 3-3 ½ minutes. Pour egg mixture into a large mixing bowl, and beat at high speed until stiff peaks form, about 8-10 minutes. Sir in the food coloring. Spoon or pipe meringue into 2/3 inch bowl shapes. Bake at 225° for 20 minutes. Turn off oven and leave in oven over night. Spoon white chocolate mousse into meringue bowls. Top with fresh raspberries. Serve immediately

WHITE CHOCOLATE MOUSSE

1 (3.4 oz) box white chocolate instant pudding mix
¼ cup each (powdered sugar and milk)
1 cup heavy whipping cream
½ cup sour cream

In a large bowl, combine pudding mix, cream, sour cream, milk and powdered sugar. Beat at medium speed with an electric mixer until stiff peaks form. Cover and chill.

PINEAPPLE - MARSHMALLOW DESSERT

1 can pineapple, crushed and drained
1 container of whipped topping
1 pound marshmallows
1 cup hot milk
15 graham crackers, crushed
2/3 stick butter, melted

Mix graham cracker crumbs with melted butter. Sprinkle ½ mixture in bottom of a 9 x 9 inch baking dish. Melt marshmallows in hot milk; cool. Add pineapple and whipped topping. Pour over crumb mixture. Top with remaining crumbs. Chill.

CHOCOLATE - CARAMEL TRIFLE

1 (9 oz) box devil's food cake mix
2 (3 .9 oz) instant chocolate pudding mix
1 (7 ½-8 oz) English toffee bits or almond chips
1 (12- 14 oz) jar caramel ice cream topping
1 (12 oz) carton frozen whipped topping, thawed

Prepare and bake cake according to package directions in an 8 inch square baking pan. Cool. Prepare pudding according to package directions. Cut cake into 1 ½ inch cubes; place half of the cubes in a 3 quart trifle bowl or glass serving bowl; press down to fill in gaps. Top with half of the whipped topping, pudding, caramel topping and toffee bits; repeat layers. Cover and refrigerate until ready to serve.

DELICIOUS APPLE FRITTERS

1 cup each (flour and apples, chopped fine)
1 teaspoon baking powder
1 egg
2 tablespoons sugar
1/3 cup milk
½ teaspoon salt
Oil for frying
Powdered sugar

Beat all ingredients together until smooth; add apples. Drop by teaspoonfuls into 365° hot oil; cook until brown. Turn, brown other side. Drain on paper towels. Dust or roll in powdered sugar.

SPECIAL LEMON BARS

2 cups each (all-purpose flour and sugar)
2 sticks butter
4 eggs, beaten
½ cup powdered sugar, plus a little extra
4 tablespoons each (flour and lemon juice)

Mix together the butter, flour and powdered sugar. Pat into a 13 x 9 inch baking pan and bake at 325° for 20 minutes. Second layer; blend together the eggs, sugar 4 tablespoons flour and lemon juice. Pour over first layer. Return to oven and bake for 20-25 minutes.
Cut into bars and sprinkle with powdered sugar over top while still warm.

PEARS WITH ALMOND CREAM

1 1/3 cups all-purpose flour
½ cup vegetable oil
½ teaspoon salt

POACHED PEARS
3 large pears
2 cups white grape juice
2 teaspoons ginger
1 stick cinnamon, halved
1/8 teaspoon ground allspice
2 tablespoons cornstarch
3 tablespoons water

ALMOND CREAM

1 (8 oz) package cream cheese, softened
1 teaspoon almond extract
1 tablespoon sugar
3 tablespoons sour cream

Combine flour and salt; add oil, mix until crumbly. Add water, tossing with a fork until mixture forms a ball. On a light floured surface; roll dough to 1/8 inch thickness. Cut into 6 circles with a 4 inch cookie cutter. Place 1 inch apart on an un-greased baking sheet. Bake at 425° for 7-8 minutes or until edges begin to brown. Remove to a wire rack to cool. Peel pears and cut in half lengthwise; remove cores. In a large skillet, combine grape juice, cinnamon, ginger and allspice; add pears. Bring to a boil. Reduce heat, cover and simmer for 8-10 minutes or until pears are tender, turning once. Remove pears and set aside. Combine cornstarch and water; stir into poaching liquid. Bring to a boil; cook and stir for 2 minutes or until thickened. Remove from heat ; discard cinnamon stick. In a small mixing bowl, combine the almond cream ingredients; beat until smooth. On each dessert plate, place half on a pastry circle; drizzle with poaching liquid. Pipe almond cream over pears. Serve immediately.

PEAR SQUARES

1 ½ pounds pears, sliced
¼ cup un-sweetened apple juice
3 tablespoons all-purpose flour
½ teaspoon ground cinnamon
1/8 teaspoon ground nutmeg
3 tablespoons cold butter or margarine
½ cup whipped topping
2/3 cup graham cracker crumbs
Additional ground cinnamon

Toss pears, 1 tablespoon flour and apple juice together. Spoon into an 8 inch square baking dish coated with nonstick cooking spray. In a bowl, combine the crumbs, cinnamon, nutmeg and remaining flour. Cut in butter or margarine until mixture resembles coarse crumbs. Sprinkle over pears. Bake at 375° for 30 minutes or until pears are tender and topping is lightly browned. Serve warm or chilled. Cut into squares; top with whipped topping and cinnamon.

BERRIES WITH CUSTARD SAUCE

4 eggs, beaten
½ cup each (sugar and sour cream)
2 tablespoons cornstarch
1 ½ cups milk
1 ½ teaspoons vanilla extract
¼ teaspoon salt
Assorted fresh berries (any berries in season)

Combine sugar, cornstarch and salt in saucepan. Stir in milk until smooth. Bring to a boil over medium heat, stirring constantly. Add a small amount to eggs; return all to pan, stirring constantly. Cook and stir for 2 ½ minutes. Remove from heat; stir sour cream and vanilla. Set saucepan in ice and stir mixture for 5 minutes. Cover and refrigerate until serving. Serve over berries.

ORANGE CRÈME DESSERT

1 (8 oz) package cream cheese, softened
2 cups orange sherbet, softened
1 (14 oz) can sweetened condensed milk
½ cup orange juice
1 tub cool whip topping

Line a 9 x 5 inch loaf pan with foil. Spread sherbet onto bottom of pan to form even layer. Freeze 10 minutes. Beat cream cheese with mixer until creamy. Add milk and juice. Stir in cool whip. Pour over sherbet. Freeze 3 hours. To un-mold, invert pan on plate; remove foil.

ORANGE SOUFFLE

2 boxes instant vanilla jell-o dessert mix
1 teaspoon sugar
1 cup each (cold water and orange or pineapple juice)
1 egg, white
1 ½ teaspoons grated orange rind

Blend the dessert mix and water in an electric mixer for 2 minutes; blend in orange juice. Whip for 5 minutes; fold in orange rind. Beat egg white until foamy; gradually add sugar, beating until stiff. Fold into orange mixture; spoon into a 1 quart serving dish.

EASY CRÈME BRULEE

5 egg, yolks
3 ½ tablespoons sugar
2 cups light cream
2 tablespoons vanilla
¼ cup dark brown sugar

Heat cream in top of double boiler until warm. With an electric mixer beat egg yolks; and add sugar. Slowly add the warm cream to the egg yolk mixture. Allowing the mixture to run slowly while adding the cream; add vanilla and pour into an un-covered 1 ½ quart baking dish. Place dish in pan of hot water and bake for 40-50 minutes or until set. (do not let any water get into the mixture). Remove the baking dish and pan of water from oven and sprinkle the brown sugar over custard immediately; place custard under broiler for 1-2 minutes or until sugar melts. Chill until cold.

ALMA'S SPECIAL DESSERT

3 egg whites
1 teaspoon each (vanilla and cream of tartar)
1 (6 oz) can pineapple, crushed
1 small can coconut
16-18 soda crackers, crushed
1 cup sugar
½ cup pecans, chopped
½ pint whipping cream

Beat egg whites till foamy, add cream of tartar and sugar and beat until stiff. Fold in crackers, nuts and vanilla. Place in greased baking dish and bake at 325° for 35 minutes. Whip cream. Fold in pineapple. Spread on cooled mixture. Sprinkle coconut over top. Chill for several hours, best overnight.

KIM'S BANANA SPLIT DESSERT

2 cups graham cracker crumbs
½ cup butter, melted
4 cups milk
2 (small packages) jell-o banana instant pudding mix
1 (20 oz) can pineapple, crushed and drained
6 bananas
1 (16 oz) carton whipped cream, frozen and thawed
1 cup maraschino cherries, drained and halved
1 cup pecans, chopped

In a 3 quart baking dish, combine cracker crumbs and butter. Mix until combined good. Press onto bottom of dish. In a large bowl, whisk together pudding mix and milk for 2 minutes or until thickened. Spread over graham cracker mixture. Slice bananas over pudding. Spread pineapple on top. Carefully spread whipped cream over pineapple. Sprinkle with nuts and cherries. Cover and chill for 4-6 hours.

DORIS'S TORTILLAS DESSERT

1 tortilla per person. Fry tortillas in ¼ inch of hot oil. Drain on paper towels. Dust with powdered sugar of white sugar and cinnamon. Place on serving plate. Serve 1-2 scoops of vanilla ice cream on each tortilla. Drizzle with chocolate syrup, or hot fudge. Place 2 fresh strawberries on top.

KIM'S CHOCOLATE DESSERT

1 cup self-rising flour
½ cup butter
1 (8 oz) package cream cheese, softened
½ cup pecans, chopped fine
1 (16 oz) container whipped topping, thawed
1 cup powdered sugar
1 small package jell-o vanilla instant pudding mix
1 small package jell-o chocolate instant pudding mix
3 cups milk

In a bowl, cut butter into flour until crumbly. Stir in ½ cup pecans. Pat on bottom of a 3 quart baking dish. Bake about 15 minutes or until edges begin to brown completely. In a small mixing bowl, beat cream cheese and powdered sugar with an electric mixer on low speed until fully combined. Beat on medium speed until fluffy. Fold in ½ of the whipped topping. Spread over cooled crust. In a bowl whisk together the vanilla and pudding mix, chocolate pudding mix and milk for about 2 minutes of until thickened. Spread over cream cheese layer. Cover and chill 1 hour. Spread remaining whipped topping over pudding mixture. Sprinkle with chopped pecans. Cover and place in refrigerator. Chill for 2 hours.

GOOD CREAMY COCONUT CAKE

1 box yellow cake mix (2 layers)
3 eggs
1/3 cup vegetable oil
1 ¼ cups water
1 box jell-o vanilla instant pudding mix
3 cups milk
1 (8 oz) container whipped cream, frozen and thawed
2 large bananas
1 cup flaked coconut

Coat a 13 x 9 inch baking pan with non-stick cooking spray. Set aside. In a mixing bowl beat cake mix, eggs, oil and water with an electric mixer on low speed until combined. Beat on high speed or 2 minutes. Spread in prepared pan and bake at 350° for 30-35 minutes or until toothpick inserted in center comes out clean. In a bowl whisk together the pudding mix and milk about 2 minutes or until thickened. Let stand for 3 minutes. Spread over cake. Slice bananas on top. In a bowl fold together whipped topping and coconut. Spread over bananas. Cover and chill for 2 hours.

TIRAMISU DESSERT BOWL

1 (8 oz) package cream cheese, softened
3 cups cold milk
1 (8 oz) tub cool whipped topping
2 packages of jell-o vanilla instant pudding mix
45-50 vanilla wafers
2 squares semi-sweet baking chocolate, coarsely grated
½ cup brewed strong coffee, cooled, divided
1 cup fresh raspberries

Beat cream cheese in a bowl with an electric mixer until creamy. Beat in milk. Add dry pudding mixes; mix well. Stir in 2 cups of the whipped topping. Line bottom and sides of a 2 ½ quart bowl with half of the wafers, drizzle with half of the coffee. Layer half of the pudding mixture over wafers, and then top with half of the grated chocolate. Repeat all layers starting with the wafers and coffee. Top with remaining whipped topping and raspberries. Refrigerate at least 2 hours.

SIMPLE & EASY DESSERT

4 egg whites
1 pint of whipping cream
1 can pineapple, crushed
Almond cookies, crushed

Beat egg whites until stiff, beat whipping cream until fluffy. Fold in whites in whipped cream. Fold in pineapple. Line a small loaf pan with cling wrap, bottom and up sides also, enough left over on the sides to cover over the top Spray cling wrap in bottom of pan with cooking spray. Place pineapple mixture in pan, cover pan and put in freezer for at least 24 hours or longer. Take out of freezer 10-15 minutes before ready to serve. Slice each serving and sprinkle with crushed almond cookies on top.

GOOD PEACH PUDDING

2 cups fresh peaches, sliced
1 cup each (flour and boiling water)
¾ cup plus 1 cup sugar
½ cup milk
3 tablespoons each (butter and cornstarch)

Place peaches in a greased 9x 13 inch pan. Combine ¾ cup sugar and butter, add baking powder, flour and milk. Spread over peaches. Mix 1 cup sugar, cornstarch and salt. Sprinkle mixture over batter. Pour hot water over all and bake at 350° for 50 minutes.

STRAWBERRY PRETZEL DESSERT

1 (8 oz) package cream cheese, softened
¾ cup butter, melted
3 tablespoons sugar
2 cups coarsely crushed pretzels
2 cups boiling water
1 (8 oz) whipped topping frozen and thawed
1-2 packages strawberry jell-o gelatin
1 (10 oz) package frozen strawberries in syrup
1 cup sugar

In a 3 quart baking dish, combine butter and 3 tablespoons sugar. Stir in pretzels. Press onto bottom of dish. Bake for 8 minutes. Cool completely. In a mixing bowl beat cream cheese and 1 cup sugar with an electric mixer until combined. Fold in whipped topping. Spread over cooled crust; chill. In another bowl stir together boiling water and gelatin until gelatin dissolves. Add frozen strawberries. Gently stir until gelatin begins to thicken. Spoon over cream cheese layer. Cover and chill for 4-24 hours. Cut into squares.

FRESH FRUIT CUSTARD TART

4 eggs
½ cup sugar
2 cups milk
2 cups assorted fresh fruit (strawberries, blueberries and or peaches, sliced)
1 large carton whipped topping
1 teaspoon vanilla
1 refrigerated pie crust

Place pie crust in 9 inch plate, pressing crust firmly into bottom and up sides of plate. Flute edge. Beat eggs, sugar and vanilla in a large bowl with whisk until blended. Beat in milk until combined. Carefully pour filling into prepared crust and bake at 350° for 40 minutes or until knife inserted in center comes out clean. Cool completely. Chill until firm, about 2 hours. Arrange fruit on top. Cut pie into 8 slices, top each slice with whipped topping just before serving.

HEATH BAR DESSERT

1 (10 oz) package Lorna Doone cookies
1 stick margarine, melted

Mix crushed cookies and melted butter together. Pat into a 9 x 13 inch pan and bake at 350° for 15 minutes. Cool.

2 cups milk
1 quart vanilla ice cream, softened
2 small packages instant vanilla pudding
2 cups cool whip
4 heath bars, crushed

Mix together the milk and pudding mix. Add soft ice cream. Pour mixture into cooled crust and chill. Spread cool whip over top and sprinkle with crushed heath bars. Cut into squares.

BANANA COLADA DESSERT

1/3 cup each (brown sugar and orange juice)
6 tablespoons butter, cubed
½ cup coconut, toasted
2 pints vanilla ice cream
½ teaspoon rum extract
2 teaspoons cinnamon
4 medium bananas, sliced

In a small saucepan, combine the butter, brown sugar, cinnamon and orange juice. Cook and stir over medium heat for 4-5 minutes or until sauce is smooth. Stir in bananas; heat through. Remove from heat; stir in rum extract. Serve warm over vanilla ice cream. Sprinkle with coconut.

EASY BLUEBERRY DESSERT

1 can blueberry pie filling
1 small box instant vanilla pudding mix
1 (8 oz) carton whipped cream
1 graham cracker pie crust, baked

Mix pudding according to directions on package. Refrigerate until set. Beat into pudding 1 ½ cups of the whipped topping until blended. Fold in pie filling; put remainder of whipped topping on top of pie and garnish with fresh blueberries.

DELICIOUS LEMON DESSERT

CRUST
2 cups vanilla wafers, crushed
1 ¼ cups butter or margarine, melted

Pour butter over cookie crumbs and mix well. Press in bottom of a baking dish and bake at 400° for about 10 minutes.

FIRST LAYER
3 (3 oz) packages cream cheese, softened
2 cups powdered sugar
1 stick butter, softened

Cream all ingredients together until fluffy. Spread over cookie crumbs.

SECOND LAYER
2 cans lemon pie filling
1 (9 oz) container of whipped topping

Spread pie filling over cream cheese mixture. Top with whipped topping. Garnish with fresh fruit to match the filling. Chill before serving. Toasted coconut is also good to sprinkle on top.

GOOD CHERRY DESSERT

1 (8 oz) package cream cheese
1 can cherry pie filling
¾ cup sugar
1 teaspoon vanilla
1 large container whipped topping
1 graham cracker crust

Cream the cream cheese and sugar, add vanilla. Add whipped topping to the cream cheese mixture. Spread ½ of mixture over crust. Top with pie filling. Spread other ½ of mixture over top of pie filling. Chill several hours before serving.

STRAWBERRIES IN THE SNOW

1 angle food cake
¾ cup milk
1 (8 oz) carton frozen whipped topping, thawed
1 (8 oz) package cream cheese, softened

Tear cake into chunks and place in a 9 x 13 inch baking dish. Combine the cream cheese and milk, mixing until smooth; fold in whipped topping. Spread mixture over cake chunks. Chill.

GLAZE
1 cup water
2 tablespoons cornstarch
1 teaspoon lemon juice
1 cup sugar
A Few drops of red food coloring
2 pints strawberries, cut in halves

Combine the lemon juice, sugar, water and cornstarch in a saucepan. Bring to a boil; cook until thickened. Remove from heat. Add food coloring and mix well. Add strawberries into glaze. Let stand until cool. Pour glaze over cake. Chill.

BOURBON STRAWBERRIES

1 ½ quarts strawberries, fresh and stemmed
2 cups sugar
¼ cup butter
½ cup each (heavy cream and bourbon)
Whipping cream

In a heavy skillet or pot, placed over medium heat until pot is hot. In hot pot add sugar. Stir with wooden spoon. When sugar starts to melt, stir until sugar turns a golden colored syrup. Remove from heat and add butter. After butter melts add the cream a little at a time. Stir in the bourbon (not from the bottle, but in another container). Cool sauce down and pour into glass container. Cover and refrigerate. The sauce will caramelize when cooled. When ready to serve place strawberries in individual stemmed glasses or dessert dishes. Pour caramel sauce over strawberries, top with whipped cream and a strawberry on top.

COCONUT POUND CAKE

3 cups flour
3 sticks butter
6 eggs
1 can coconut
3 cups sugar
1 can evaporated milk
1 teaspoon each (baking soda and vanilla)
¼ teaspoon salt

Cream sugar and butter together. Add eggs, 1 at a time.. Mix together the dry ingredients. Stir vanilla in the milk. Add dry ingredients alternately with milk. Stir in coconut. Pour into greased bundt pan and bake at 350° for 1 hour and 15 minutes. Cool for 10-15 minutes before removing from pan.

ORANGE SLICE CAKE

3 ½ - 4 cups flour
½ cup buttermilk
4 eggs
1 teaspoon soda
1 tablespoons grated orange rind
2 cups sugar
1 cup each (butter or margarine and chopped pecans)
1 pound orange slice candy, chopped
½ teaspoon salt

Mix 3 ½ cups flour with salt. Combine candy, nuts and remaining flour and mix well. Cream butter with sugar. Add eggs, 1 at a time, beating well after each addition. Combine buttermilk and soda; and alternately with flour and salt mixture to creamed mixture and blend well. Add candy mixture; mix well. Pour into greased tube or bundt pan and bake at 350° for 1 hour and 45 minutes. Placing a pan of water under the rack will keep the cake moist.

GOOD KENTUCKY POUND CAKE

2 ½ cups self-rising flour
4 eggs, separated
½ cup vegetable oil
2 cups sugar
1 cup each (chopped walnuts and crushed pineapple, drained)
1 teaspoon vanilla
2 tablespoons hot water
2 teaspoons cinnamon

Mix together the sugar, egg yolks, oil and vanilla. Add flour, pineapple, cinnamon and water, mix well. Set aside. Beat egg whites until stiff. Stir in nuts into whites. Fold into batter. Pour into a greased and floured tube or bundt pan and bake at 350° for 1 hour and 10 minutes. Cool in pan for 10-15 minutes before removing from pan.

PINEAPPLE POUND CAKE

½ cup shortening
2 sticks margarine
2 ¾ cups sugar
6 large eggs
3 cups plain flour
1 teaspoon each (baking powder and vanilla flavoring)
¼ cup milk
¾ cup pineapple, crushed, drained

GLAZE
¼ cup margarine
1 ½ cups powdered sugar
1 cup pineapple, crushed, drained

Cream shortening, margarine and sugar, eggs, flour, and baking powder alternately with milk. Add vanilla. Stir in pineapple and juice. Blend well. Pour into a greased and floured tube or bundt pan and bake at 325° for 1 ½ hours or until done. Mix all glaze ingredients and pour over cake while hot.

BUTTER CREAM POUND CAKE

3 cups plus 2 tablespoons flour
5 large eggs
½ cup shortening
1 stick margarine
½ pound butter
1 cup milk
1 teaspoon each (baking powder and butter flavoring)
2 teaspoons vanilla flavoring
3 cups sugar

Cream butter, margarine, shortening and sugar until creamy. Add eggs 1 at a time, beating after each addition. Add flour and baking powder, add to mixture alternately with milk and flavorings, beating at low speed. Pour into a 10 inch tube or bundt pan and bake at 325o for 1 hour; reduce heat to 300° and bake 30 minutes longer. Cool in pan for 20 minutes. Remove from pan.

BUTTER FROSTING
1 cup light brown sugar
1 stick butter
½ cup milk
1 teaspoon butter flavoring
Powdered sugar

Combine brown sugar, butter and milk; boil for 4 minutes; cool. Add enough powdered sugar to get a good spreading consistency also, add flavoring and beat until smooth. Spread over cake.

FRESH PEACH POUND CAKE

3 cups self-rising flour
1 cup fresh peaches, mashed
2 ¼ cups sugar
¾ cup milk
3 sticks butter or margarine, melted
6 eggs
1 teaspoon each (lemon and vanilla extract)

Combine butter, eggs, sugar, flour, lemon and vanilla extract in mixing bowl. Beat for 2 minutes. Add peaches. Pour into a greased and floured bundt pan. Place in cold oven and bake at 300° for 1 hour and 10 minutes or until cake is done; cool.

SWEET POTATO CAKE

2 cups each (flour and sugar)
1 ¼ cups vegetable oil
4 eggs
1 cup pecans, chopped
3 cups sweet potatoes, raw and grated
2 teaspoons baking soda
¼ teaspoon salt
2 teaspoons each (cinnamon and baking powder)

Line two 8 inch cake pans with wax paper and grease inside of pan. Combine the eggs, oil and sugar in a large bowl and beat well. Add the dry ingredients to the oil mixture. Stir in nuts and sweet potatoes. Divide mixture into prepared cake pans and bake at 350° for 35-40 minutes. Remove from pans and let cool before frosting.

FROSTING
1 pound box powdered sugar
1 (8 oz) package cream cheese
1 stick butter
2 teaspoons vanilla

Combine cream cheese, sugar, butter and vanilla. Beat with electric mixer until smooth. Frost cake and store in the refrigerator.

EASY CREAM CHEESE POUND CAKE

3 cups flour
1 ½ cups butter or margarine, softened
1 (8 oz) package cream cheese, softened
3 cups sugar
1 teaspoon each (vanilla and almond extract)
1/8 teaspoon salt
4 eggs

Cream butter, eggs, cream and sugar together in a mixing bowl and mix until light and fluffy. Add salt, vanilla and almond extracts; mix well. Add flour alternately with the eggs mixing well after each addition. Spoon into a greased and floured tube or bundt pan and bake at 300° for approximately 1 ½ hours. Cool in pan before transferring to cake plate.

PINEAPPLE CAKE

2 cups all-purpose flour
1 (20 oz) can crushed pineapple, with juice
2 cups each (sugar and powdered sugar)
2 eggs
1 cup pecans, chopped
1 (8 oz) package cream cheese, softened
1 teaspoon each (baking soda and pure vanilla extract)
¼ cup butter, softened

In a large bowl, combine un-drained pineapple, sugar, pecans, flour, eggs and baking soda; mix well. Spread in a greased 13 x 9 inch baking pan and bake at 350° for 30-35 minutes or until toothpick inserted in center comes out clean. Cool completely. In mixing bowl beat cream cheese, butter and vanilla with an electric mixer until combined. Beat in powdered sugar. Spread on top of cake. Keep in refrigerator.

SOUR CREAM POUND CAKE

3 cups flour
¼ teaspoon baking powder
1 (8 oz) carton sour cream
3 cups sugar
2 sticks butter or margarine, softened
6 eggs
1 ½ teaspoons almond extract

Combine flour and baking powder together. In another bowl, cream, butter and sugar mix well; add sour cream and almond extract; mix well. Add eggs and mix well. Add flour mixture ½ at a time, and mix well after each addition. Pour into a greased and floured tube or bundt pan and bake at 325° for 1 ½ hours. Cool for 10 minutes.

SEVEN - UP - POUND CAKE

3 cups flour
¾ cup 7 - up
3 cups sugar
5 eggs
1 ½ cups butter, softened
2 tablespoons lemon extract

Cream sugar and butter, add eggs and flour. Add lemon extract and 7-up. Pour mixture into a greased bundt pan and bake at 325° for 1 ¼ hours.

BLUEBERRY AND LEMON POUND CAKE

2 ¾ cups all-purpose flour
¼ teaspoon each (baking soda and salt)
1 ½ teaspoons baking powder
1 ¾ cups sugar
1 cup butter, softened
4 eggs
2 tablespoons lemon juice
2 teaspoons each (lemon peel and vanilla extract)
1 cup buttermilk
1 ¼ cups fresh or frozen blueberries
1 tablespoon flour
Lemon glaze

Grease a 10 inch fluted tube pan; set aside. In a medium bowl combine 2 ¾ cups flour, baking powder, soda and salt; set aside. In a large mixing bowl, beat sugar and butter with an electric mixer until fluffy, add eggs, lemon juice, lemon peel and vanilla. Beat until combined. Add flour mixture and buttermilk, beating until just combined after each addition. In a small bowl toss blueberries with 1 tablespoon flour. Fold into batter. Spread in prepared pan and bake at 350° for 45-50 minutes. Cool in pan 15 minutes. Remove from pan and cool completely.

GLAZE; In a bowl combine 1 ½ cups powdered sugar, 2 tablespoons lemon juice and 1 tablespoon light corn syrup. Drizzle glaze over cake.

CHOCOLATE CREAM CHEESE POUND CAKE

2 ¼ cups self-rising flour
¾ cup cocoa
6 eggs
2 sticks butter, softened
1 (8 oz) package cream cheese, softened
1 ¾ cups sugar
1 teaspoon each (vanilla and baking powder)

Grease and flour a 10 inch bundt pan . With an electric mixer, cream together, cream cheese, butter and sugar. Add eggs, 1 at a time, beating after each addition. Add vanilla. In another bowl, stir together the flour, baking powder and cocoa. Add ½ of the flour mixture to the creamed mixture, beat well. Add the remaining ½ of the flour mixture and continue to beat for 2 minutes. Bake at 325° for 1 ½ hours. (do not open oven door). Keep door closed for a least 1 hour.

ORANGE POUND CAKE

3 cups each (flour and sugar)
2/3 cup shortening
5 eggs
1 1/3 cups milk
1 teaspoon salt
2 sticks butter

Cream shortening, sugar and butter together. Add eggs, 1 at a time, beating after each one. Beat for 3 minutes on high speed. Mix flour and salt add flour and milk, alternately in 1/3 to creamed mixture, beating well after each addition. Beat on high speed 3-4 minutes. Pour in greased bundt pan and bake at 300° for 2 hours. Keep oven closed while baking.

FILLING
Juice of 2-3 oranges, grated, rind of 1 orange, 1 ½ box powdered sugar. Combine ingredients, mix well. Spread over warm cake.

ICING
2 egg whites
1 small box powdered sugar
½ teaspoon cream of tartar
1 tablespoon light corn syrup
5 tablespoons cold water
1 teaspoon lemon flavoring

CHERRY POUND CAKE

3 ¾ cups flour
Large jar maraschino cherries
6 eggs
1 stick butter
1 cup vegetable oil
¾ cup milk
2 teaspoons butternut flavoring
2 ½ cups sugar

Chop cherries and set aside. Cream and butter, oil and sugar together. Add eggs, beat well. Add flour alternately with milk. Add vanilla and fold in cherries. Bake at 325° for 2 hours. (do not pre-heat oven).

DELICIOUS PEACH CAKE

1 box yellow cake mix
4 eggs
1/3 cup oil
2 cans peach pie filling
¼ teaspoon almond extract

Preheat oven to 350°. Grease a bunt pan; spread 1 can of peach pie filling into the bottom of the pan. Mix cake mix, eggs, oil and extract until smooth. Fold the second can of peach pie filling into the mixture, and pour over peaches in the pan. Bake for 45-50 minutes.

FRIED ICE CREAM BALLS

4 egg whites
2 cups cornflakes, crushed
1 quart vanilla ice cream
Cinnamon
Whipped cream
Maraschino cherries
Chocolate syrup

Whisk egg whites and set aside. Roll ice cream in medium size balls, dip in egg whites and roll in crushed cornflakes. Place in freezer for a least 2 hours. To get the extra crispy, dip and roll them twice before freezing. Remove from freezer and drop in hot oil in deep fryer and fry for 1 minute. Sprinkle with cinnamon and garnish with whipped cream, chocolate syrup and cherries.

PINA COLADA CAKE

1 (15 oz) can cream of coconut
1 (18.25 oz) box yellow cake mix
1 (3.4 oz) box vanilla instant pudding mix
½ cup vegetable oil
½ cup plus 2 tablespoons rum
4 large eggs
1 cup un-sweetened grated coconut frozen, thawed
1 (8 oz) can crushed pineapple, in juice, drained

COCONUT WHIPPED CREAM

1 cup heavy whipped cream
1 (8.5 oz) can cream of coconut

Grease a bundt pan with vegetable spray and set aside. Stir the cream of coconut, and pour ½ cup into a liquid measuring cup and keep the remaining 1 cup for the syrup. Combine the cake mix, pudding mix, eggs, oil, ½ cup cream of coconut and ½ cup of rum in a mixing bowl. Blend with an electric mixer for about 3 minutes. The batter will look thick and smooth. Fold in the crushed pineapple until it is well blended. Pour the batter into the prepared bundt pan, smoothing it out with a spatula. Bake at 350° for 50-55 minutes. Remove the pan from oven and cool for 20 minutes. Place coconut in an aluminum pie pan and toast it in the oven until lightly browned 4-5 minutes. Remove the pan and set aside. Then invert cake onto a serving plate. Prepare the rum syrup. Place the reserved 1 cup cream of coconut and the remaining 2 tablespoons rum in a small mixing bowl. Stir until well combined. While cake is still warm, poke holes in the top with a fork or toothpicks. Spoon the rum syrup over the top; allowing it to seep into the holes and drizzle down the sides and in the center of the cake. Cool cake completely. For the coconut whipped cream, place the heavy cream and cream of coconut in a mixing bowl. Beat with an electric mixer on high speed until stiff peaks form, 2-3 minutes. Garnish each slice with coconut whipped cream and toasted coconut.

KIM'S PEANUT BUTTER CAKE

CAKE
1 ¾ cups self-rising flour
2 cups sugar
2 sticks butter or margarine, melted
1 cup peanut butter
3 eggs
1 cup milk
1 teaspoon vanilla extract

Combine flour and sugar in a mixing bowl. Add eggs, butter, peanut butter, vanilla and milk; beat well. Pour into 3 greased cake pans and bake at 350° for 45 minutes or until layers are done. Spread the hot frosting over layers.

FROSTING
1 cup peanut butter
2 cups powdered sugar
¼ cup milk
½ stick butter or margarine

Combine powdered sugar, milk, butter and peanut butter in a saucepan. Cook until smooth. Spread on cake.

ALL TIME FAVORITE 1 2 3 4 CAKE

1 cup milk
1 teaspoon vanilla extract
2 sticks butter, softened
2 cups sugar
3 cups self-rising flour
4 eggs

Grease and flour 3 (9 inch) cake pans. With an electric mixer, cream butter until fluffy. Add sugar and continue to mix for 2 minutes. Add eggs 1 at a time, beating after each addition. Add flour and milk to creamed mixture, beginning and ending with flour. Add vanilla and continue to beat until mixed. Divide batter among the 3 pans. Bake at 350° for 25-35 minutes or until done. Cool in pans 5-10 minutes. Spread your favorite frosting on each layer, sides and top.

SOUTHERN COLA CAKE

1 package white cake mix
4 tablespoons un-sweetened cocoa powder
1 stick butter or margarine, melted
2 large eggs
½ cup buttermilk
1 cup cola (Coke or Pepsi)
1 ½ cups miniature marshmallows
1 teaspoon vanilla extract
Vegetable oil

FROSTING
4 cups powdered sugar
4 tablespoons un-sweetened cocoa powder
½ cup cola
1 cup pecans, chopped
1 stick butter or margarine

Grease a 13 x 9 inch baking pan with vegetable oil; set aside. Combine cake mix, melted butter, cocoa powder, cola, eggs, buttermilk and vanilla in a large mixing bowl. Blend with an electric mixer on low speed for 1 minute. Increase the speed to medium and beat 2 minutes more. Fold in the marshmallows. Pour the batter into the prepared pan, smoothing it out with a spatula. Bake at 350° for 40-45 minutes. Remove from oven. Cool 15 minutes. Prepare the frosting; place the butter in a medium saucepan over low heat, stir in the cocoa powder and cola. Let the mixture come to a boil; stirring constantly and remove it from the heat. Stir in the powdered sugar until the frosting is thickened and smooth. Fold in pecans. Pour the frosting over the top of the cake, spreading it out with a rubber spatula to reach the edges of the cake. Cool for 20 minutes before serving.

BLACK FOREST CAKE

1 box chocolate cake mix
1 (21 oz) can cherry pie filling
1 (8 oz) package cream cheese, softened
1 (8 oz) carton frozen whipped topping, thawed
1 egg
2 tablespoons sugar
½ cup water

Beat cake mix, water and egg for 3 minutes. Pour into a greased 9 inch spring form pan; bake at 350° for 25 minutes; cool. Beat cream cheese and sugar together; add whipped topping. Spread pie filling over cake; top with cream cheese. Cover and refrigerate.

PEANUT BUTTER AND CHOCOLATE CAKE

2 ¼ cups flour
1/3 cup baking cocoa
1 ½ cups sugar
1 ½ teaspoons each (vanilla extract and baking soda)
½ teaspoon salt
1 ½ cups water
½ cup vegetable oil
1 ½ teaspoons white vinegar

BATTER
4 ounces cream cheese, softened
½ cup sugar, divided
¼ cup peanut butter, creamy
1 egg
½ cup each (chopped pecans and semi-sweet chocolate chips)
1/8 teaspoon salt

In a large bowl, combine flour, cocoa, baking soda, sugar and salt. Stir in water, vinegar, oil and vanilla; mix well. Pour into a greased 13 x 9 inch baking pan. In another bowl, beat cream cheese, 1/3 cup sugar, peanut butter, egg and salt until smooth. Stir in chocolate chips. Drop by tablespoonful over cake batter, cut through batter, take knife to swirl the peanut butter mixture. Sprinkle with pecans and remaining sugar. Bake at 350° for 30-35 minutes or until a toothpick inserted in the center comes out clean. Cool before cutting.

PEAR CAKE

3 cups flour
2 cups each (sugar and canned pears)
3 eggs
1 ¼ cup oil
1 teaspoon each (cinnamon, soda, salt and vanilla)
1 cup walnuts

Beat oil, sugar and eggs by hand. In mixing bowl add flour, soda, cinnamon and salt. Add to oil mixture and stir in vanilla, pears and walnuts. Bake in a greased bundt pan at 350° for 1 hour and 20 minutes.

MISSISSIPPI MUD CAKE

1 ½ cups self-rising flour
½ cup milk
2 cups sugar
1 cup each (vegetable oil and chopped pecans)
4 eggs
2 teaspoons baking powder
1 (10 oz) package miniature marshmallows
1 tablespoon vanilla extract
1/8 teaspoon salt
½ cup cocoa

Combine cocoa, oil, eggs, sugar, flour, milk, vanilla and salt in a mixing bowl; beat until smooth. Add pecans; spoon into greased 10 x 14 inch sheet cake pan. Bake at 300° for 45-50 minutes or until cake is done. Sprinkle with marshmallows

FROSTING
1 (1 pound) box powdered sugar
½ cup each (melted butter and chopped pecans)
1/3 cup each (milk and cocoa)
1 teaspoon vanilla extract

Combine sugar, cocoa, milk and vanilla in a mixing bowl; mix well. Add pecans. Spread over marshmallows on cake.

CHOCOLATE MOCHA CAKE

1 cup flour
¾ cup sugar
½ cup each (sugar, milk and light brown sugar)
3 tablespoons each (butter, cocoa and chocolate syrup)
2 teaspoons each (baking soda and vanilla extract)

Grease a 9 inch square baking pan. Mix together ¾ cup sugar, flour and soda. Mix the chocolate syrup and butter in a saucepan and add to flour mixture. Add milk and vanilla, mixing well. Pour mixture into a greased pan. Mix the ½ cup sugar, cocoa and brown sugar. Sprinkle over batter. Bake at 350° for 30-35 minutes. (cake will have chocolate syrup base on bottom). Cut cake in to serving pieces and spoon extra cocoa mixture over cake. Cake is better served warm.

MILKY WAY CAKE

3 cups flour
1 cup pecans, chopped
1 ¼ cups buttermilk
4 eggs, separated
8 mini milky way candy bars
½ cup butter or margarine, softened
1 ½ cups sugar
1 teaspoon vanilla extract
½ teaspoon baking powder

Combine ½ cup butter and candy bars in heavy saucepan; cook over low heat until candy bars are melted, stirring constantly. Cool. Cream sugar and butter together until light and fluffy; add egg yolks, beating well after each yolk; add vanilla. Combine buttermilk and baking powder, add to creamed mixture. Add flour. Stir in candy bar mixture and pecans. Fold in stiffly beaten egg whites. Pour batter into greased 10 inch tube or bundt pan. Bake at 325° for 1 hour and 40 minutes or until done. Let cool in pan for 1 hour. Remove from pan and finish cooling on wire rack. Frost with milk chocolate frosting.

MOLTEN CHOCOLATE CAKES

1 (8 oz) bar bittersweet chocolate baking bar, broken into pieces
3 large eggs, separated
¼ cup white sugar
1 ½ sticks butter, divided
1 tablespoon flour
1 teaspoon vanilla
Powdered sugar

Butter 6 (6 oz) ramekins or custard cups with 2 tablespoons butter. Stir ¾ cup butter and chocolate in heavy duty saucepan over low heat until chocolate is melted and mixture is smooth. Remove from heat. Beat egg whites, egg yolks, sugar and vanilla in a large mixing bowl until thick and pale yellow, about 7 minutes. Fold 1/3 of the chocolate mixture into egg mixture. Fold remaining chocolate mixture and flour until well blended. Divide batter evenly among prepared ramekins. Place on baking sheet. Bake at 350° for 12-13 minutes or until sides are set and 1 inch center move slightly when shaken. Remove from oven to wire rack. To serve; run a thin knife around top edge of cakes to loosen slightly carefully invert on to serving plates. Lift ramekins off of cakes, sprinkle with powdered sugar. Serve at once.

CHOCOLATE CAKE WITH FUDGE SAUCE

2 cups each (flour and brown sugar)
3 eggs
½ cup cooking oil
1 cup milk
1 teaspoon each (vanilla and baking powder)
½ teaspoon salt
2 ounces un-sweetened chocolate, melted

Cream together the brown sugar, milk, oil and vanilla. Add melted chocolate, add eggs; beat for 2 minutes. Add flour, baking powder and salt, add to cream mixture. Beat 2 more minutes. Pour into a 13 x 9 inch greased pan. Bake at 350° for 40-50 minutes.

FUDGE SAUCE

1 (4 oz) bar German chocolate
1 stick butter
3 cups powdered sugar
1 2/3 cups evaporated milk
1 ¼ teaspoons vanilla
½ ounce un-sweetened chocolate

Melt chocolate and butter in saucepan over low heat. Stir in powdered sugar, alternating with the evaporated milk, blending well. Bring to a boil, stirring constantly. Cook and stir until mixture is thick and creamy, about 8 minutes. Stir in vanilla, serve warm over chocolate cake.

MATTHEW'S HEATH BAR CAKE

2 cups flour
6 heath candy bars, crushed
2 cups brown sugar
½ cup each (butter and chopped pecans)
1 egg
1 cup milk
1 teaspoon each (vanilla and soda)

Combine flour and sugar; cut in butter, reserve 1 cup of flour mixture. Add egg; mix well. Dissolve soda in milk; add vanilla to mixture and mix well. Pour into greased 9 x 13 inch pan. Sprinkle reserved cup of mixture over top; sprinkle with pecans and candy. Bake at 350° for 30-40 minutes.

AMBROSIA CAKE

CAKE
1 (18 .25 oz) box white cake mix with pudding
1/3 cup vegetable oil
3 eggs
1 ¼ cups water
1 (6 oz) package un-sweetened frozen coconut, thawed (for garnish)
Marshmallow frosting

FILLING
1 (8 oz) can pineapple in juice, crushed and drained
1 cup each (orange juice and sugar)

Combine pineapple, sugar and orange juice in saucepan. Cook over medium heat, stirring constantly, until mixture is thickened, (about 20 minutes). Pour the filling in a bowl and cover with plastic wrap Refrigerate the filling to cool completely; about 1 hour. (stir before using it). Grease three 9 inch round cake pans with vegetable oil. Combine the cake mix, water, eggs and oil in a large bowl. Blend with an electric mixer for about 3 minutes. The batter should be well mixed and thickened. Fold in coconut until it is well mixed. Divide the batter among the 3 greased cake pans, smoothing it out with a spatula. Bake at 350° for 15-20 minutes. (don't over bake). Remove pans from oven and cool for 10 minutes. Then invert them onto a cake or serving plate, so the cakes are right side up. Cool completely (about 30 minutes). Prepare the marshmallow frosting. Place 1 cake layer; right side up on cake plate. Spread the top with half of the filling, spreading the filling with a spatula up to 1 inch from the edge of the cake. Place second layer right side up, on top of the filling. Spread second layer with the remaining half of the filling. Spread it like the first layer. Add third layer and spread frosting on the top and sides of the cake. Garnish with the coconut, pressing it around the sides and top of the cake.

GOOD CHESS CAKE

1 box each (butter cake mix and powdered sugar)
1 stick butter
2 eggs
1 teaspoon vanilla
1 (8 oz) package cream cheese
1 cup pecans, chopped

Mix cake mix and butter together and place in baking dish. Mix 1 box powdered sugar, eggs, vanilla and cream cheese. Pour over cake mixture and bake at 350o for 35 minutes. Sprinkle with powdered sugar and pecans.

BANANA PUDDING CAKE

CAKE
1 (18.25 oz) box yellow cake mix
1 stick butter, melted
1 cup milk
3 large eggs
1 teaspoon pure vanilla extract

PUDDING
1 (5.1 oz) box vanilla instant pudding mix
3 cups milk
½ stick butter, cut up
3 large bananas, sliced
2 teaspoons pure vanilla extract

TOPPING
1 (12 oz) carton whipped topping, frozen and thawed
½ cup vanilla wafer cookies, crushed
1 cup heavy whipping cream
¼ cup powdered sugar

Grease lightly a 13 x 9 inch baking pan, set aside. Place cake mix, egg, milk and vanilla in a mixing bowl. Blend with an electric mixer about 3 minutes. Pour batter into prepared pan, smoothing it out with a spatula. Place in oven and bake at 350° for 30-35 minutes or until golden brown. Remove from oven and let cool.

PREPARE PUDDING
Place the pudding mix and milk in a saucepan. Add butter and vanilla and cook over low heat, stirring until the butter melts, 3-4 minutes. Cool about 5 minutes. Fold in banana slices.

PREPARE WHIPPING CREAM

Place a mixing bowl and electric beaters in the freezer for 5 minutes while you assemble the ingredients. Pour the whipped cream into the chill bowl and beat with the electric mixer until cream has thickened, about 1 ½ minutes. Add sugar, beat cream and sugar on high speed until stiff peaks form (1-2 minutes more). Spoon the pudding and banana mixture on top of the cooled cake, spreading the mixture out to the edges of the cake with a spatula. Cover the pudding with whipped topping, spread it out to the edges of cake. Scatter the crushed vanilla wafer cookies over the top.

FIVE FLAVOR CAKE

3 cups self-rising flour
1 cup each (milk and softened butter)
½ cup vegetable oil
5 eggs
3 cups sugar
1 teaspoons each (vanilla, almond, rum, pure lemon and coconut extracts)
Almond frosting

Grease and flour two 9 x 5 inch loaf pans; set aside. In a large mixing bowl beat butter and shortening with an electric mixer on medium speed until combined. Add sugar, beat about 10 minutes or until light and fluffy. Add all 5 extracts. Beat until combined. Add eggs, 1 at a time, beating well after each addition. Alternately add flour and milk, beating until just combined after each addition. Spread batter in prepared pans. Bake at 325° for 55-60 minutes or until toothpick inserted in center comes out clean. Cool cakes in pan for 10 minutes. Remove from pans. Cool completely.

FROSTING; In a small bowl beat ¼ cup vegetable oil and ¼ cup softened butter until combined. Add 3 cups powdered sugar and 1 teaspoon almond extract. Beat until combined. Gradually beat in 2-3 tablespoons milk to make desired consistency. Spread tops and sides of cake with almond frosting.

VANILLA WAFER CAKE

1 (12 oz) box vanilla wafers, crushed
2 sticks butter, melted
1 can coconut
1 cup pecans, chopped
½ cup milk
4 eggs
2 cups sugar
1 teaspoon vanilla

Beat eggs, add sugar, vanilla, milk and wafer crumbs. Add butter, beating well. Combine coconut and nuts; mix into batter. Pour into tube or bundt pan; bake at 350o for 30-40 minutes or until done. Cool

ICING;
1 cup brown sugar
2 cups powdered sugar
¾ can evaporated milk
1 stick butter or margarine

Combine milk, butter, sugar; bring to a boil, cool; add powdered sugar, cool. Ice cake.

ALMA'S WHITE FRUITCAKE

1 ¾ cups self-rising flour
1 cup sugar
1 ½ cups each (softened butter and whole candied cherries, cut up)
5 eggs
4 cups pecan halves
2 cups candied pineapple, cut up
½ teaspoon each (salt and baking powder)
1 tablespoon each (vanilla and lemon extract)

Grease and flour two 8 x 4 inch loaf pans. In a large bowl, combine all ingredients except pecans and fruit; beat on low speed until moistened. Beat 2 minutes at medium speed. Stir in pecans and fruit. Spoon and spread into greased and floured pans. Bake at 300° for 1-1 ¾ hours or until toothpick inserted in center comes out clean. Cool 15 minutes. Remove from pans. Cool 1 hour or until completely cooled. Wrap tight in foil and store in refrigerator.

GOOD LEMON SOUFFLE CAKE

2/3 cup sweetened condensed milk
1 cup vanilla wafers, crushed
2 tablespoons each (brown sugar and grated lemon rind)
3 tablespoons butter
3 eggs, separated
¼ cup lemon juice

Mix cookie crumbs, butter and sugar until crumbly. Press onto bottom and sides of a 9 inch plate, do not spread mixture on rim. Beat egg yolks until thick and light colored; stir in lemon rind, lemon juice and milk. Fold in stiffly beaten egg whites. Pour into a prepared pie plate and bake at 400o for 20 minutes or until cake is done.

KIM'S SOUR CREAM COCONUT CAKE

1 box yellow cake mix
1 1/3 cups water
1/3 cup vegetable oil
3 eggs
1 (16 oz) package flaked coconut
1 (16 oz) carton sour cream
1 (16 oz) carton whipped topping, frozen and thawed
1 cup sugar

Coat two 9 inch round baking pans with cooking spray; set aside. In a mixing bowl beat cake mix, eggs, water and oil with an electric mixer on low speed until combined. Beat on high speed for 2 minutes. Spread in prepared pans. Bake at 350° for 30-35 minutes or until toothpick inserted in center comes out clean. Cool in pans for 10 minutes. Remove from pans and cool completely. In a large bowl, fold together the whipped topping, coconut, sour cream and sugar. Split cake layers horizontally. Place 1 layer on serving platter. Spread with 1 ½ cups of topping mixture. Repeat layers 3 times. Spread remaining topping mixture on sides of cake. Store in refrigerator.

SPECIAL COCONUT CAKE

1 box butter cake mix, baked and cooled
¼ cup coconut milk (optional)
2 cups sugar
1 (16 oz) carton sour cream
1 (12 oz) package coconut
1 (9 oz) container cool whip

Split cake layers. Sprinkle layers with coconut milk, if desired. Mix sugar, sour cream, and coconut. (save ½ cup for frosting). Chill. Spread remaining portion between layers. Combine cool whip with reserved 1 cup of frosting mixture. Pile frosting on top and sides of cake and sprinkle with reserved 1 cup of frosting mixture. Pile frosting on top and sides of cake and sprinkle with reserved ½ cup coconut. Cover with cake saver and refrigerate for 3 days.

MULTI - LAYER COCONUT CAKE

4 cups all-purpose flour
1 teaspoon baking soda
½ teaspoon each (baking powder and salt)
6 egg whites
2 cups buttermilk
1 cup butter, softened
3 cups sugar
2 teaspoons vanilla extract

FILLING

½ cup each (sugar and butter)
1 teaspoon orange extract
2 tablespoons grated orange peel
4 eggs, beaten
1 cup orange juice
2 tablespoons cornstarch

FROSTING

1 cup sugar
½ cup water
2 cups flaked coconut
¼ teaspoon each (salt and vanilla)
1/8 teaspoon cream of tartar
2 egg whites

Cream butter and sugar until fluffy. Add vanilla. Combine flour, baking powder, soda and salt; add to cream mixture. Add buttermilk. In another mixing bowl, beat egg whites until stiff; fold into batter. Pour into 3 greased 9 inch round cake pans. Bake at 350° for 25-30 minutes or until done. Cool for 10 minutes before removing from pans. Cool completely. In a saucepan, combine cornstarch and sugar, stir in orange juice until smooth. Bring to a boil; cook and stir for 2 minutes or until thickened. Remove from heat, stir ½ cup into eggs; return all to pan, stirring constantly. Bring to a boil; cook and stir for 2 minutes. Remove from heat. Stir in butter, orange peel and orange extract. Cover and refrigerate. In another saucepan, combine water, salt, egg whites and cream of tartar. Beat 1 minute. Continue beating on low heat for 5 minutes. Pour into a large mixing bowl; add vanilla. Beat until frosting forms stiff peaks, about 6-7 minutes. Split each cake layer in half horizontally. Place 1 layer on cake plate; spread with ½ cup of the filling. Repeat 4 times. Top with remaining cake layer. Spreading frosting over top and sides. Sprinkle with coconut. Store in refrigerator.

UP - SIDE DOWN APPLE CAKE

1 (18.25 oz) box spice cake mix
1 stick butter, melted
1 cup buttermilk
½ cup dark corn syrup
2 large eggs
1 teaspoon ground cinnamon

TOPPING
1 cup light brown sugar
4 medium apples, peeled, cored and sliced (about 3 cups)
1/3 cup butter
1 teaspoon cinnamon

Prepare the topping; Place butter in a 10 inch iron skillet and heat the skillet over low heat to melt the butter. Remove skillet from heat, add brown sugar and cinnamon and stir with a fork. Spread the mixture out evenly in the bottom of skillet. Arrange the apple slices over the bottom of the skillet. Place the cake mix, buttermilk, melted butter, eggs, corn syrup and cinnamon in a large mixing bowl. Blend with an electric mixer on low speed for 1 minute. Increase speed to medium and beat for 2 more minutes. Pour batter on top of the apples in skillet. Smooth out with a spatula. Place skillet in oven and bake at 350° for 45-50 minutes. Remove skillet from oven. Carefully invert the skillet onto a serving plate. The cake is best served warm with ice cream or whipped cream.

PINEAPPLE AND COCONUT CAKE

1 box butter cake mix
1 (8 oz) container cool whip
1 can pineapple, crushed, drained
1 (8 oz) container sour cream
2 cups powdered sugar
3 cups coconut
1 tablespoon vanilla

Make cake according to direction on box (2 layers). Bake at 325° for 25-30 minutes. Remove from oven and slice the layers in half. While cake is cooling, mix small container of cool whip with small container of sour cream. Add 2 cups powdered sugar, 3 cups coconut, 1 can crushed pineapple, drained and 1 tablespoon vanilla. Spread between each layer on top and sides.

KENTUCKY RAISIN CAKE

1 (18.25 oz) box yellow cake mix, with pudding mix
1 cup each (buttermilk and golden raisins)
½ cup Kentucky bourbon
4 large eggs
1 teaspoon vanilla extract
1 stick butter, melted
1 tablespoon grated orange zest

BUTTERED GLAZE
½ cup light brown sugar
¼ cup each (Kentucky bourbon and water)
½ stick butter

Grease a bundt pan with cooking spray and set aside. Place raisins, orange zest and bourbon in a small sauce pan and heat to warm over low heat (do not boil) until raisins are plump. Place the cake mix, melted butter, buttermilk, eggs, raisin mix and vanilla in a large mixing bowl. Blend with an electric mixer until it is well distributed. Pour the batter into the prepared bundt pan. Bake at 350° for 45-50 minutes. Invert on serving plate. Prepare glaze. Place brown sugar, butter, bourbon and water in a small saucepan. Bring the glaze to a boil and boil about 3 minutes, stirring constantly. Polk holes in the top of cake with a fork or toothpicks. Spoon the hot glaze over the top of cake, allowing it to seep into the holes and drizzle down the sides and into the center of cake. Cool completely before slicing.

EASY DUMP CAKE

1 (18.25 oz) box yellow cake mix
1 (20 oz) can crushed pineapple
1 (21 oz) can cherry pie filling
1 cup pecans, chopped
½ cup coconut
¾ cup butter, melted

Dump pie filling and pineapple into the bottom of a greased baking pan. Smooth out with a spoon. Sprinkle cake mix evenly over the pie filling and pineapple. Pour butter over all and sprinkle with coconut and pecans. Bake at 350° for 1 hour. Serve from the pan ,when ready to serve.

GRANNY'S HUMMINGBIRD CAKE

3 cups self-rising flour
1 ½ cups vegetable oil
2 cups sugar
3 eggs, beaten
1 (8 oz) can crushed pineapple, drained
2 cups bananas, chopped
1 cup nuts, chopped
1 teaspoon each (cinnamon, baking powder and salt)
1 ½ teaspoon vanilla

Combine all dry ingredients together; add oil and eggs, stir until well mixed. Add pineapple, nuts, bananas and vanilla. Spoon batter in to a greased baking dish or pan and bake at 350° for 40-50 minutes.

ICING
1 (1 pound) box powdered sugar
1 (8 oz) package cream cheese, softened
1 cup nuts, chopped
1 teaspoon vanilla
½ cup butter or margarine, softened

Combine butter, cream cheese, sugar and vanilla. Mix until smooth. Spread on top of cake and sprinkle chopped nuts on top.

DELICIOUS BUTTER CAKE

1 box butter cake mix
4 eggs
½ cup butter, softened
1 can mandarin oranges, save juice

FROSTING
1 small box instant vanilla pudding
1 large container cool whip
1 small can crushed pineapple, drained

In a bowl, mix the cake mix, eggs and butter, beat 2 minutes with electric mixer. Add oranges and juice, mix well. Pour batter in 3 greased cake pans and bake at 350° for 25-30 minutes. Cool completely, before frosting. Store in refrigerator.
FROSTING; Beat all ingredients, except cool whip. Fold in cool whip and frost cake.

COCONUT CHIFFON PIE

1 cup sugar
1 envelope un-flavored gelatin
1 ½ cups milk
2 eggs, separated
3 tablespoons flour
1 ½ cups grated coconut
2 tablespoons powdered sugar
1 teaspoon vanilla
1 small carton cool whip
½ cup cold water
1 9 inch pie shell, baked

Beat sugar, flour and egg yolks until lemon colored. Add milk; cook in top of double boiler until thickened. Dissolve gelatin in water, fold into custard with 1 cup coconut. Beat egg whites until stiff, add powdered sugar and vanilla. Fold into custard, pour into pie shell; chill. Spoon whip cream over chilled custard. Sprinkle with remaining coconut.

EAST PEAR PIE

4 cups fresh pears, sliced
1 cup each (sugar and flour)
½ cup brown sugar
½ cup butter
3 tablespoons quick cooking tapioca
2 teaspoons ground ginger
1 9 inch pie shell, un-baked

Blend pears, ginger, sugar and tapioca; let stand for 20 minutes. Place in pie shell. Cut butter into flour, add sugar. Sprinkle over pie filling,. Bake at 425° for 15 minutes. Reduce heat to 375° and bake 30 minutes longer.

CHOCOLATE MOUSSE CAKE

CRUST
2 cups chocolate wafer crumbs
4 tablespoons butter, softened

A day ahead, mix chocolate wafer crumbs and butter. Press into bottom of a spring form pan. Refrigerate while making filling

FILLING
1 ½ sticks butter, cut into small pieces
2 ¼ packages semi-sweet chocolate pieces
2 cups whipping cream, divided
5 large eggs, separated
2 teaspoons instant coffee
1/3 cup orange-flavor liqueur

In a heavy 4 quart saucepan over low heat, heat butter and chocolate pieces until melted and mixture is smooth, stirring frequently. Remove pan from heat. Stir in ¼ cup whipping cream. In a medium bowl with wire whisk, beat egg yolk mixture into melted chocolate mixture, slowly beat in orange liqueur. In a large bowl with mixer beat remaining heavy cream until stiff peaks form. Fold in whipping cream, ½ at a time, into chocolate mixture. In a small bowl with mixer at high speed, beat egg whites until they stand in stiff peaks. Fold in beaten whites, ½ at a time, into chocolate mixture until blended. Pour mixture over crust in spring form pan. Cover and refrigerate overnight.

GLAZE

1 ½ cups semi-sweet chocolate pieces
2 tablespoons powdered sugar
3 tablespoons each (orange-flavor liqueur and milk)
1 teaspoon instant coffee

Next day prepare glaze. In a 2 quart saucepan over low heat; combine chocolate, sugar, liqueur, milk and coffee; until chocolate melts and mixture is smooth. Stirring constantly. Remove from heat and let stand at room temperature to cool slightly, until its of a good spreading consistency. Remove side of spring form pan from cake. Place cake, still on pan bottom, or wire rack over wax paper. Spread glaze over top and down sides of cake. Refrigerate cake until ready to serve. You may top with extra whipping cream if you desire.

PUNCH BOWL CAKE

1 (18 ¼ oz) box yellow cake mix
1 ½ cups water
2 (3.4 oz) boxes banana instant pudding mix
2 (21 oz) cans cherry pie filling
4 ripe bananas, sliced ½ inch thick
4 cups milk
½ cup vegetable oil
1 (20 oz) pineapple, crushed and drained
1 (12 oz) container whipped topping frozen, thawed
1 cup pecans, chopped and toasted
3 large eggs

Grease a 13 x 9 inch baking pan and set aside. Place cake mix, oil, water and eggs in a mixing bowl. Mix with an electric mixer for about 3 minutes. Pour the batter into the prepared baking pan. Bake at 350° for 30-35 minutes or until cake is golden brown. Remove pan from oven and cool completely; about 40 minutes. Place the pudding mix and milk in a bowl and blend according to package directions. Set aside. Remove the cooled cake from the pan and crumble it in to 1 inch pieces with your hands. Place ½ of the crumbles in the bottom of a large glass punch bowl. Top with 1 can cherry pie filling, ½ of the crushed pineapple and ½ of the pudding. Add ½ of the banana slices, ½ of the whipped topping and ½ of the pecans. Repeat layers, beginning with remaining cake crumbles and ending with the pecans. Cover the bowl with plastic wrap and place in the refrigerator. Chill at least 1 hour before ready to serve. Serve cake with a big spoon.

PASTEL JELL-O CAKE

1 package (layer yellow cake mix
1 Package (4 serving size) lime flavor jell-o gelatin
1 package (4 serving size) lemon flavor jell-o gelatin
2 tubs (8 oz) cool whipped topping, thawed
Jelly beans for garnish

Prepare cake mix as directed on package. Divide batter between 2 bowls. Add lime gelatin to 1 bowl and lemon gelatin the other bowl. Pour into separate greased and floured 9 inch round pans. Bake at 350° for 25-30 minutes or until toothpick inserted in center comes out clean. Cool 15 minutes, remove from pans. Place lime cake layer on serving plate; spread with ½ tub of the whipped topping. Top with lemon cake layer. Frost cake with remaining whipped topping.

CRANBERRY CAKE WITH CREAM SAUCE

2 cups flour
1 cup sugar
1 egg
3 tablespoons butter, softened
2 teaspoons baking powder
1 teaspoon ground nutmeg
1 cup milk
2 tablespoons orange or lemon peel, grated
2 cups cranberries

CREAM SAUCE
11/3 cup sugar
1 cup whipping cream
2/3 cup butter

In mixing bowl, cream butter and sugar; beat in egg. Combine the flour, baking powder and nutmeg; add to the creamed mixture alternately with milk. Stir in cranberries and orange peel. Pour into a greased 11 x 7 inch baking dish. Bake at 350° for 35-40 minutes or until toothpick inserted in center comes out clean. In a saucepan, combine sauce ingredients. Cook and stir over medium heat until heated through. Cut warm cake into squares; serve with cream sauce.

SOUTHERN PORK AND BEAN CAKE

2 cups self-rising flour
1 cup vegetable oil
2 cups sugar
1 (8 oz) can pineapple
½ cup walnuts, chopped
1 (16 oz) can pork and beans
2 tablespoons cinnamon
1/8 teaspoon salt

Drain pineapple and beans and mix together. Add sugar, oil, flour and cinnamon, stir well. Add walnuts, stir well. Pour into a greased 12 x 8 inch baking pan or dish and bake at 350° for 35-45 minutes. A bundt pan is recommended to use.

SOCK - IT - TO - ME - CAKE

1 (18 ¼ oz) box butter cake mix
1 cup sour cream
¼ cup each (sugar and water)
4 eggs
½ cup cooking oil

Combine sour cream, oil, sugar, eggs and water in a mixing bowl and beat just until moistened. Beat at high speed for 2 minutes. Pour 2/3 of the batter into a greased and floured bundt pan. Sprinkle with filling. Spread remaining batter over filling and bake at 375° for 40-45 minutes or until cake is done. Cool in pan 20 minutes. Drizzle glaze over cake.

FILLING
2 tablespoons brown sugar
1 teaspoon cinnamon
1 cup pecans, chopped

Combine all ingredients together and mix well.

GLAZE
1 cup powdered sugar
2 tablespoons milk

Combine the 2 ingredients in a bowl and mix until smooth.

GOOD BUTTER PECAN CAKE

1 (18 ¼ oz) box butter pecan cake mix
4 eggs
1 (16 oz) can coconut pecan icing
1 cup each (vegetable oil and water)
Sugar
Pecans, chopped

In a greased bundt pan, sprinkle with sugar and pecans. Combine the cake mix, eggs, oil and icing in mixing bowl and mix well. Pour into bundt pan and bake at 350° for approximately 50 minutes or until cake is done. Cook 10 minutes in pan.

SPICE CAKE WITH MERINGUE

1 ¼ cups flour
1 egg yolk
1 cup brown sugar
1 tablespoon shortening
2/3 cup sour milk
½ teaspoon each (vanilla, cloves, cinnamon, soda and baking powder)
¼ teaspoon salt

Cream shortening with sugar and egg yolk. Mix together dry ingredients and add alternately with milk and vanilla to creamed mixture, beating good after each addition. Pour in to greased 8 x 8 inch pan.

MERINGUE
½ cup light brown sugar
1 egg white
½ cup pecans, chopped

Slowly combine sugar to egg white, beating until smooth. Spread mixture over cake batter and sprinkle with nuts. Bake at 350° for 45 minutes.

MERINGUE CAKE WITH BERRIES

1 cup each (flour and sugar)
2 eggs, separated
2 teaspoons baking soda
¼ teaspoon salt
7 tablespoons milk
4 tablespoons cooking oil
1 teaspoon vanilla
Berries of choice

Cream oil and ½ cup sugar, mix well. Add egg yolks. Add together flour, salt and soda to mixture. Combine milk and vanilla and add to mixture. Pour into a greased baking pan. Beat whites until foamy. Add remaining sugar, 2 tablespoons at a time, until mixture peaks. Pile on batter and bake at 350° for 50-60 minutes. Remove from oven and let stand 10 minutes, loosen edges and cut into squares and top with crushed berries of choice. We like raspberries.

SUGAR CRUSTED LIME CAKE

CAKE
1 cup self-rising flour
¾ cup sugar
2 egg whites, room temperature
1/3 cup milk
¼ cup vegetable oil
1 tablespoon grated lime peel
½ teaspoon baking powder
1 teaspoon salt

TOPPING
¼ cup sugar and 1 tablespoon of lime juice

Spray a 9 inch round cake pan with nonstick cooking spray; set aside. Combine egg whites and ½ teaspoon baking powder; beat until stiff peaks form. Set aside. In another bowl combine all remaining cake ingredients; beat at low speed until moistened. Beat 2 minutes at medium speed. Gently fold stiffly beaten egg whites into batter. Pour into sprayed pan. Bake at 350° for 30-35 minutes or until toothpick inserted in center comes out clean. In a small bowl, combine topping ingredients; mix well. Spread over hot cake. Cool for 45 minutes or until completely cooled before serving.

GOOD PECAN CAKE

1 (18 ¼ oz) box yellow cake mix
1 egg
1/2 cup butter, melted

Mix ingredients well. Reserve 2/3 cup of batter. Pour remainder into a greased 9 x 13 inch baking dish and bake at 325° for 15-20 minutes or until brown.

FILLING
½ cup dark brown sugar
1 ½ cups karo syrup
3 eggs
2/3 cup reserved batter
1-2 cups pecans, chopped
1 teaspoon vanilla

Combine all ingredients together; pour over top of above crust and bake at 325° for 1 hour.

UP - SIDE DOWN BANANA FOSTER CAKE

TOPPING
1 cup light brown sugar
3 cups bananas, sliced on the diagonal (1/3 inch thick)
1/3 cup butter
2 tablespoons rum
½ teaspoon ground cinnamon

CAKE
1 (18 ¼ oz) box butter cake mix
1 stick butter, melted
1 ½ cups milk
2 large eggs
4 teaspoons fresh lemon juice

Prepare the topping; place butter in a 10 inch skillet and heat skillet to melt butter. Remove skillet from heat and with a fork stir in the brown sugar, rum and cinnamon. Using fork spread the mixture out evenly in the bottom of the skillet. Arrange banana slices over the bottom of the skillet to cover it well. Place cake mix, melted butter, milk, lemon juice, and eggs in a mixing bowl. Blend with an electric mixer on low speed for 1 minute. Increase mixer speed to medium and beat for 2 more minutes. Pour the batter on top of the banana in skillet. Smooth out with a spatula. Place skillet in oven and bake at 350° for 34-50 minutes. Remove from oven and run a long sharp knife around the edge. Carefully invert the cake onto a serving plate. Cake is best sliced and served warm with ice cram or whipped cream.

CHRISTMAS FRUIT CAKE

1 ½ cups self-rising flour
3 eggs, separated
1 ½ cups sugar
3 cups dates
1 ¾ cups brazil nuts, chopped
2 ¼ cups English walnuts, chopped
1 bottle of each (red and green maraschino cherries)
1 teaspoon baking powder
¼ teaspoon salt

Combine dates and nuts; cover with sugar, cherries and juice. Mix flour, baking powder and salt. Add beaten egg whites. Bake at 350° for 1 hour and 15 minutes. Make 2 loaves.

PEACHES AND CREAM CAKE

1 (29 oz) can peach halves, in heavy syrup, drain and save syrup
1 (18.25 oz) box yellow cake mix (plain)
4 large eggs
1 teaspoon pure vanilla
1 stick butter
Vegetable oil
Sweetened cream

SWEETENED CREAM
1 cup whipping cream
¼ cup powdered sugar

Grease 2 (9 inch) round cake pans with vegetable oil; set aside. Place about 8 of the peach halves in a food processor and process until smooth. Should be 1 ½ cups. Reserve ½ cup syrup and the remaining peach halves. Combine the cake mix, peach puree, melted butter, eggs and vanilla in a large mixing howl. Blend with an electric mixer on low speed for 1 minute. Increase the speed to medium and beat 2-3 minutes longer. The batter should be well blended. Divide the batter between the 2 prepared pans. Place the pans in the oven side by side and bake at 350° for 25-35 minutes or until golden brown and springs back when lightly touched with your fingers. Remove pans from oven. Cool for 10 minutes. While layers are still warm, poke holes in the top of them with a toothpick or fork. Pour the reserved peach syrup over the layers, about ¼ cup over each, so that the cake soaks up all the juice. Cool layers completely.

PREPARED SWEETENED CREAM
Place a large mixing bowl and electric beaters in the freezer for about 5 minutes. Pour the whipping cream into chilled bowl and beat with an electric mixer on high speed until cream has thickened, 1 ½ minutes. Add sugar. Beat the cream and sugar on high speed until stiff peaks form, 1-2 minutes. Frost cake.

CAKE
Cut the remaining peach halve into ½ inch thick slices. Place 1 cake layer right side up, second layer right side up on top of first layer and frost the top and sides of cake. Arrange peach slices on top of cake.

STRAWBERRY CAKE WITH CREAM CHEESE FROSTING

1 (18.25 oz) box white cake mix
1 (3 oz) package strawberry gelatin
1 cup fresh strawberries, with juice and mashed
4 large eggs
1 cup frozen un-sweetened coconut, thawed and grated, divided
½ cup pecans, chopped, divided
1 cup vegetable oil
½ cup milk
Flour for dusting
1 (8 oz) package cream cheese, softened
¼ cup sugar
½ stick butter
Cream cheese frosting

Grease 3 (9 inch) cake pans with vegetable oil, and dust with flour; set aside. Combine the cake mix, strawberry gelatin, strawberries and juice, milk, oil and eggs in a large mixing bowl and blend with an electric mixer on low speed for 1 minute. Increase the mixer speed to medium and beat for 2 minutes longer, scraping down the sides if needed. The strawberries should be well blended into the batter. Fold in the coconut and pecans. Divide the batter among the 3 prepared pans and place them in the oven. Place 2 pans on center of lowest rack and the third in center on highest rack. Bake at 350° for 25-30 minutes or until they are light brown and start to pull away from the sides. Remove pans from rack and cool for 10 minutes. Run a knife around the edge of each layer and invert each onto a rack, then invert again onto another rack so the cakes are right side up. Allow cakes to cool completely, about 30 minutes or more.

FROSTING

Combine the cream cheese and butter in a bowl with an electric mixer on low speed, mix for about 30 seconds. Add sugar and drained strawberries. Blend the frosting on low until the sugar has been incorporated. Raise the speed to medium and mix the frosting another minute or until the frosting lightens and is well combined. Fold in the coconut and pecans. To assemble, place 1 cake layer, right side up, on serving plate. Spoon the top with frosting. Add another cake layer right side up, and frost the top. Repeat this process with the third layer and frost the top and sides of cake.

ITALIAN CREAM CAKE

2 cups each (self-rising flour and sugar)
5 eggs
1 stick butter or margarine, softened
1 cup buttermilk
1 (7 oz) can coconut
1 tablespoon vanilla
½ cup vegetable oil
1 teaspoon baking powder

Cream oil and butter together; add sugar and beat well. Add eggs, 1 at a time. Add flour and baking powder alternately with the buttermilk to creamed mixture. Add vanilla and coconut. Pour into 3 (9 inch) greased baking pans and bake at 350° for about 40 minutes.

CREAM CHEESE FROSTING

1 (8 oz) package cream cheese, softened
1 (1 pound) box powdered sugar
½ stick butter or margarine, softened
1 cup pecans, chopped
1 tablespoon vanilla

Beat cream cheese and butter until smooth. Add sugar and vanilla and beat until smooth; add nuts and beat 1 more minute. Spread on each layer, sides and top of cake.

WHIPPED CREAM CAKE

2 cups flour
½ cup cold water
3 egg whites, stiffly beaten
1 cup heavy cream
3 teaspoons baking powder
1 teaspoon vanilla
¼ teaspoon salt
1 ½ cups sugar

Mix whipped cream and egg whites; add water. Slow add the dry ingredients. Add vanilla and bake at 350o° for 25 minutes in a greased 9 x 13 inch baking pan or dish.

PISTACHIO CAKE

1 (18 ¼ oz) box white cake mix
1 (3.4 oz) package instant pistachio pudding mix
1 cup each (chopped walnuts, lemon or lime soda and vegetable oil)
3 eggs

FROSTING
1 ½ cups cold milk
1 (3.4 oz) instant pistachio pudding mix
1 (8 oz) carton frozen whipped topping, thawed
½ cup pistachio nuts, whole red shell pistachio nuts toasted

Combine the cake mix, pudding mix, soda, oil and eggs in a mixing bowl. Beat for 2 minutes; stir in walnuts. Pour into a greased 13 x 9 inch baking pan and bake at 350° for 45-50 minutes or until done. Cool.

FROSTING

In a mixing bowl, beat milk and pudding mix for 2 minutes. Fold in whipped topping. Spread over cake. Sprinkle with pistachios. Refrigerate for 30 minutes before cutting. Garnish with whole pistachios.

CHOCOLATE CARAMEL CAKE

1 cup sugar
1 Stick butter
4 eggs, beaten
1 can chocolate syrup
½ teaspoon each (baking soda and vanilla)
1 cup self-rising flour

Cream sugar, butter and vanilla together. Add rest of the ingredients and mix for 2 minutes. Pour into an 8 x 10 inch greased baking pan and bake at 350° for 40 minutes. Leave cake in pan and pour topping over hot cake.

TOPPING

1 cup brown sugar
1 stick butter
½ cup evaporated milk

Combine all ingredients in a heavy saucepan and cook over medium heat for about 2 ½ minutes. Pour over hot cake.

EULA'S GOOD RUM CAKE

1 box yellow cake mix
1 small box vanilla instant pudding mix (optional)
4 eggs
½ cup each (vegetable oil, light or dark rum and water)
1 cup pecan pieces

Grease and flour a bundt pan and line with pecan pieces. Combine all rest ingredients. Mix well. Pour cake batter over pecans. Bake at 350° for 30-40 minutes or until cake is done. Cool 10 minutes before removing from pan. Turn onto cake plate. Punch holes in the cake with a fork.

GLAZE

1 stick butter
1 cup sugar
¼ cup water
½ cup rum

Combine all ingredients in a heavy saucepan; except rum. Boil for 5 minutes, stirring constantly. Remove from heat and stir in rum. Drizzle the glaze over the cake where you made the holes and down the middle and sides. Let glaze soak in for a few hours before serving. (This glaze recipe makes plenty for 2 cakes and I usually make 2 cakes at a time). But to half the recipe won't work. Just don't use all of the glaze on 1 cake, it will make the cake too soggy. They freeze good and taste fresh when thawed out.

EASY BLUEBERRY CAKE

1 box white cake mix
1 (16 oz) carton whipped cream or cool whip
1 (21 oz) can blueberry pie mix
1 (8 oz) package cream cheese, softened
½ cup each (white sugar and powdered sugar)

Mix cake mix according to direction on box. (2 layers). Bake at 350° for 30-40 minutes; cool. Slice each layer horizontally into halves. Combine cream cheese, sugar, and powdered sugar; mix well. Add whipped topping. Spread each layer with cream cheese mixture and pie filling. Stack layers together. Spread remaining cream cheese mixture on top of cake. Chill until ready to serve.

DELICIOUS CHOCOLATE CAKE

2 cups each (flour and sugar)
1 stick butter
2 eggs
½ cup each (vegetable oil and water)
1 cup buttermilk
½ cup cocoa
1 teaspoon each (salt, baking soda and vanilla)

Cream together, the butter, sugar and oil; add eggs, 1 at a time. Combine dry ingredients; add to creamed mixture a little at a time, alternating with buttermilk. Beat in vanilla and ½ cup water. Pour into 2 greased cake pans and bake at 325° for 45-50 minutes or until done. Prepare the icing 5 minutes before the cake is done.

ICING
1 box powdered sugar
½ cup cocoa
1 stick butter
¼ cup milk

Place sugar into a mixing bowl and set aside. Melt butter in a small saucepan; add the milk and cocoa and bring to a boil, stirring constantly. Pour over sugar and beat well. Make holes in the cake with a fork so the icing will soak in. Pour icing over entire cake.

GOOD FRESH PEAR CAKE

3 cups each (flour, pears peeled, cored and diced)
1 ½ teaspoons each (baking powder and salt)
1 teaspoon each (allspice, cloves, cinnamon and vanilla extract)
3 eggs
2 cups sugar
1 ½ cups vegetable oil

Grease and flour a bundt pan. Combine flour, baking powder, sugar, cinnamon, allspice, cloves and salt together in a large bowl. Add oil, eggs, vanilla and pears; mix well. Pour mixture into prepared pan and bake at 300° for 1 hour and 15 minutes or until done.

MATTHEW'S FAVORITE TURTLE CAKE

CAKE
1 (18.25 oz) box of German chocolate cake mix
1 (14 oz) package caramel candy
1 cup nuts, pecans chopped
1 (14 oz) can sweetened condensed milk
1 (6 oz) package semi-sweet chocolate chips
2 tablespoons butter

FROSTING
1/3 cup milk
½ stick butter
3 tablespoons cocoa
1 tablespoon light corn syrup
1 teaspoon vanilla extract
2 cups powdered sugar
1/8 teaspoon salt

Prepare cake according to directions on box. Pour ½ batter in a greased 13 x 9 inch baking pan. Bake at 350° for 15 minutes. Remove from oven and cool. Melt caramel candy with butter in saucepan. When melted, remove from heat and stir in condensed milk until smooth. Let mixture cool. Add chocolate chips and nuts. Spread mixture over cooled cake. Pour remaining batter over mixture and return to oven for 25-30 minutes longer. While cake is baking, prepare the frosting. FROSTING; Mix together butter, milk, cocoa, corn syrup and salt in a saucepan over medium heat. Bring ingredients to a full boil and boil for 3 minutes, stirring often. Remove from heat. With an electric mixer beat the powdered sugar and vanilla into the cocoa mixture; beat until smooth. Pour icing over warm cake.

PEAR PRESERVE CAKE

3 ¼ cups flour
1 cup each (buttermilk, pear preserves, chopped pecans and shortening)
1 teaspoon each(vanilla, allspice, cloves, cinnamon and soda)
1 ½ cups sugar
4 eggs

Cream shortening and sugar. Add eggs and beat well. Add vanilla. Mix cinnamon, allspice, cloves and flour. Dissolve soda in buttermilk and add alternately with dry ingredients. Fold in preserves and pecans. Pour into a greased bundt pan and bake at 325° for 1 hour and 45 minutes.

CAKE WITH PEAR FILLING

2 cups flour
1 teaspoon each (baking powder and soda)
½ cup each (softened butter and sugar)
3 eggs
½ teaspoon vanilla
¾ - 1 cup orange juice

FILLING
½ cup each (brown sugar, ripe pears, peeled and sliced almonds)
4 ½ teaspoons butter, melted
½ teaspoon ground cinnamon
2 tablespoons flour

GLAZE
½ cup powdered sugar
2 ¼ teaspoons orange juice

Cream butter and sugar together. Add eggs, beat in vanilla. Combine flour, baking powder and soda; add to creamed mixture. Add orange juice. Pour half of the batter into a greased 10 inch bundt pan. Combine the filling ingredients; sprinkle over batter. Top with remaining batter. Smooth top with a spatula and bake at 350° for 35-45 minutes or until a toothpick inserted in the center comes out clean. Cool for 10 minutes before removing from pan. Combine glaze ingredients and drizzle over cake.

GRAHAM CRACKER CAKE

1 pound graham crackers, crumbled
2 sticks butter
2 cups sugar
5 eggs
1 cup nuts, chopped
1 box coconut
2/3 cup milk
2 teaspoons baking powder

Cream butter and sugar; add eggs, crackers, and baking powder alternately with milk to creamed mixture; add coconut and nuts. Pour into three 9 inch pans. Bake at 350° for 25-30 minutes. FILLING; 1 stick butter, 1 cup milk, 1 ½ cups sugar, 1 can coconut and 1 can crushed pineapple. Combine all ingredients in a saucepan; cook until thick. Spread over cake layers.

CHIFFON CAKE

2 cups all-purpose flour
1 ½ cups sugar
¾ cup water
½ cup oil
3 teaspoons baking powder
¼ teaspoon salt
7 eggs, separated
½ teaspoon each (vanilla and cream of tartar)
4 teaspoons grated lemon peel

In a large bowl, combine, baking powder, sugar and salt; mix well. Add water, oil, egg yolks and vanilla; beat at low speed until moistened. Beat at high speed for about 5 minutes or until very smooth. Fold in lemon peel. In another large bowl combine the egg whites and cream of tartar; beat 3 minutes or until stiff peaks form. Add egg yolk mixture to egg whites; folding gently to combine. Pour into an un-greased 10 inch tube pan.. Bake at 325° for 1 3/4 hours or until top springs back when lightly touched. Immediately invert cake onto funnel or coke bottle; let hang 1 hour or until completely cooled. To remove cake from pan, run edge of knife around outer edge of pan and tube.

BUTTERSCOTCH APPLE CAKE

2 ½ cups flour
3 eggs
1 ¼ cups vegetable oil
1 teaspoon each (vanilla, cinnamon, baking soda and salt)
2 cups sugar
1 (11 oz) package butterscotch chips
1 cup pecans, chopped
4 medium tart apples, peeled and chopped
2 teaspoons baking powder

In a mixing bowl, beat the eggs, oil and vanilla. Combine flour, sugar, baking powder, salt, soda and cinnamon; add to egg mixture and mix well. Stir in apples and pecans. Pour into an un-greased 13 x 9 inch baking dish. Sprinkle with butterscotch chips and bake at 325° for 40-45 minutes or until cake is done. Cool.

BANANA SPLIT CAKE

2 (8 oz) packages cream cheese, softened
¾ cup each (melted butter and maraschino cherries, drained)
3 cups graham cracker crumbs
½ cup each (softened butter and chopped pecan)
1 1/3 cups Splenda sweetener
3-4 ripe bananas
1 (20 oz) can crushed pineapple in it's own juice, drained
1 (16 oz) carton frozen whipped topping, thawed
2 cups fresh strawberries, hulled and sliced
½ cup pecans, chopped

CRUST; In a large bowl combine cracker crumbs and ¾ cup melted butter. Press crumb mixture into bottom of a 13 x 9 inch baking pan. In a large bowl, beat cream cheese and ½ cup softened butter with electric mixer on low speed until combined. Add Splenda. Beat about 5 minutes or until smooth and creamy. Spread over crust in bottom. Slice bananas; arrange slices evenly over cream cheese layer. Sprinkle drained pineapple evenly over fruit. Arrange cherries and strawberries on top of dessert topping. Sprinkle with nuts. Chill several hours or until firm.

GOOD BANANA DESSERT

1 large box ice cream sandwiches
1 jar maraschino cherries
1 large carton cool whip
6 bananas
1 bottle butterscotch topping for ice cream
1 jar chocolate topping for ice cream
1 bag toffee bites

Line a baking dish with foil, layer with ice cream sandwiches. Add layer of sliced bananas next, then a layer of cherries, next drizzle chocolate syrup, next sprinkle toffee bites, next drizzle butterscotch topping. Repeat layers, top with whipped cream and freeze until ready to serve.

CHUNKY APPLE CAKE WITH SAUCE

6 cups tart apples, peeled and chopped
½ cup butter, softened
2 cups each (flour and sugar)
½ teaspoon each (vanilla extract, salt and baking soda)
2 eggs
1 ½ teaspoons ground cinnamon
1 teaspoon ground nutmeg

BUTTERSCOTCH SAUCE;
½ cup each (brown sugar and heavy whipping cream)
¼ cup butter, cubed

In a mixing bowl, cream butter, sugar and vanilla; add eggs. Combine flour, cinnamon, nutmeg, salt and soda; add to creamed mixture and mix well. (batter will be stiff). Stir in apples until well blended. Spread into a greased 13 x 9 inch baking dish and bake at 350° for 40-45 minutes or until top is lightly browned and springs back when lightly touched. Cool for 30 minutes before serving. SAUCE; In a saucepan, combine brown sugar and butter. Cook until butter is melted. Add cream. Bring to a slow boil, stirring constantly. Remove from heat. Serve with cake.

FRANK'S FRESH APPLE CAKE

3 cups self-rising flour
3 eggs
2 cups sugar
1 ½ cups vegetable oil
2-3 cups apples, peeled and chopped
1 cup each (chopped pecans and brown sugar)
1/3 cup lemon juice
1 teaspoon each (vanilla extract and cinnamon)

Combine flour, oil and sugar in mixing bowl. Beat in eggs. Add vanilla.
Add flour mixture and apples to sugar mixture, mixing well. Add
pecans. Pour into greased tube or bundt pan and bake at 350° for 1 ¼
hours. Cool in pan for 10 minutes. Place on cake plate. Mix brown
sugar with lemon juice in bowl and drizzle over warm cake.

COCONUT ORANGE CAKE

2 ½ cups cake flour
2 ½ teaspoons baking powder
1 cup orange juice
1/3 cup each (butter and shortening)
1 ½ cups sugar
2 teaspoons grated orange rind
1 teaspoon salt
3 eggs

Combine butter, shortening, orange rind and sugar; cream together. Add
eggs. Mix flour with salt and baking powder. Add to creamed mixture
with orange juice, beginning and ending with flour. Place batter into 2
greased 9 inch round cake pans and bake at 350° for 25 minutes. Fill
layers with orange filling.

ORANGE FILLING

1 cup orange juice
2/3 cup sugar
3 tablespoons each (flour and butter)
3 egg yolks

Mix sugar and flour in a saucepan; add orange juice and egg yolks. Bring to a boil, stirring constantly; cook for 1 minutes; add butter, stir well. Cool before using. Fill layers of cake with filling. Frost with seven minute frosting.

SEVEN - MINUTE FROSTING

1 ½ cups sugar
3 egg whites
1 tablespoon light corn syrup
5 tablespoons water
1 (3 ½ oz) can coconut
1 teaspoon vanilla
¼ teaspoon cream of tartar

Combine egg whites, corn syrup, water, sugar and cream of tartar in double boiler. Beat 1 minute to blend; place over boiling water and beat until peaks form, about 7 minutes. Remove from water; add vanilla and continue beating until thick enough to spread. Frost top and sides of cake. Sprinkle top and sides with coconut.

GOOD PINEAPPLE CAKE

1 (16 oz) can crushed pineapple in syrup
2 cups Bisquick
¾ cup sour cream
1 cup each (flour and sugar)
1 teaspoon baking powder
1 stick butter
2 teaspoons vanilla
2 eggs
2 tablespoons rum

Drain pineapple and reserve syrup. Stir Bisquick, flour and baking powder together and set aside. Beat sour cream, butter, sugar and vanilla together for 2 minutes. Add eggs and beat 1 more minute. Add flour mixture and beat 1 minute longer. Mix in drained pineapple and rum. Pour into a greased bundt pan and bake 350° for 45 minutes or until cake is done. Remove from oven and spoon about ½ the glaze over cake. Let stand 10 minutes and turn onto serving plate. Spoon on remaining glaze. Cool before cutting.

PRIZE PINEAPPLE CAKE

1 (18 ¼ oz) box yellow cake mix
1 cup sour cream
1 (8 oz) package cream cheese, softened
1 (3 oz) box vanilla instant pudding
1 ½ cups cold water
3 eggs
¼ cup powdered sugar
1 (20 oz) can crushed pineapple, drained, save the juice
1 (12 oz) container whipped topping
1/3 cup vegetable oil
1 (3 oz) box French vanilla instant pudding mix

Mix the cake mix, water, vanilla pudding mix, oil and eggs in a mixing bowl; mix well. Pour into 3 greased 9 inch cake pans and bake at 350° for 20-25 minutes or until done. Cool 5 minutes. Beat cream cheese and sour cream in a mixing bowl until smooth and creamy. Add powdered sugar, whipped topping and French vanilla pudding. Add drained pineapple. Drizzle each layer with 1/3 of reserved pineapple juice. Spread pineapple mixture between layers and over top and sides of cake. Cover and chill for 2 days before serving.

MEGAN'S ORANGE DREAMSICLE CAKE

1 (18 .25 oz) box yellow cake mix
3 large eggs
¾ cup each (fresh orange juice and mayonnaise)
2 tablespoons grated orange zest
1 small carton whipped topping

GLAZE
½ cup powdered sugar
4-5 tablespoons fresh orange juice

Spray a 10 inch tube or bundt pan with vegetable spray. Combine the cake mix, mayonnaise, whipped topping, eggs, orange juice and orange zest in a mixing bowl. Blend with an electric mixer for about 3 minutes. Pour the batter into the prepared baking pan. Bake at 350° for 40-45 minutes. Remove from oven and cool in pan for 15 minutes. Place cake on cake plate and cool completely, about 30 minutes more. Prepare glaze. Combine the powdered sugar and orange juice in a small bowl and mix with a spoon until smooth. Spoon the glaze over top of cooled cake and let it drizzle in to the center and down the sides. Let set for 20 minutes for the glaze to set. Serve.

MANDARIN ORANGE CAKE

1 (18 ¼ oz) box butter cake mix
4 eggs
½ cup vegetable oil
1 (11 oz) can mandarin oranges, un-drained

Mix all ingredients and mix 2 minutes. Bake at 350o for 30 minutes in a greased 9 x 13 inch baking pan.

ICING

1 (6 oz) box vanilla instant pudding
1 (20 oz) can crushed pineapple, drained
1 (8 oz) carton cool whip

Mix pudding and pineapple, refrigerate. When cake is cooled, add cool whip to pudding and pineapple mixture. Frost cake and then refrigerate.

TIRAMISU CAKE

1 (18.25 oz) box white cake mix
3 large eggs
1 1/3 cups water
2 tablespoons vegetable oil
1 teaspoon pure vanilla extract

SYRUP
¾ cup hot water
2 tablespoons instant coffee powder
3 tablespoons sugar
1/4 cup Kahlua or coffee flavored liqueur

TOPPING
1 (16 oz) package cream cheese, softened
¼ cup powdered sugar
2 cups vanilla yogurt
1 teaspoon un-sweetened cocoa powder

Spray a 13 x 9 inch baking pan with vegetable oil. Set aside. Combine the cake mix, water, eggs, oil and vanilla in a mixing bowl. Beat with an electric mixer for about 3 minutes. Pour batter into the prepared baking pan, smoothing out with a spatula. Place pan in oven and bake at 350° for 30-35 minutes. Remove pan from oven. Prepare the syrup. Place the hot water, coffee powder and sugar in a small bowl and stir to combine until the coffee and sugar is dissolved. Stir in the coffee liqueur. Poke holes in the cake with a fork and spoon the syrup over the cake so that the syrup can seep down into the holes. Set cake aside. Prepare the topping. Place yogurt, cream cheese and powdered sugar in a mixing bowl and blend with an electric mixer for about 3 minutes. Mixture should be well combined and thick. Spread the topping over the syrup-soaked cake, 1 hour before serving. Dust the cocoa powder over the topping so that it covers the top of the cake. Slice the cake into squares and serve.

OLD FASHION MOLASSES CAKE

1 cup each (molasses and sugar)
¾ cup sour milk
2 eggs, beaten
2 teaspoons each (ground cinnamon, ginger and cloves)
1 teaspoon each (allspice and soda)
1 ½ cups flour
½ teaspoon salt
½ cup margarine

Mix molasses with sugar, eggs and margarine and mix well. Add dry ingredients alternately with sour milk. Pour into greased 8 x 12 inch baking pan. Bake at 350° for about 35 minutes or until done.

FROSTING

1 egg white
3 tablespoons water
¾ cup sugar
1 tablespoon white corn syrup
1 teaspoon vanilla
¼ teaspoon salt

Combine all ingredients except vanilla; place over boiling water. Beat until mixture stands in stiff peaks. Fold in vanilla. Frost cake.

BETTER THAN SEX CAKE

1 box yellow cake mix
1 (20 oz) can crushed pineapple
1 ½ cups sugar
1 cup coconut, toasted
1 ½ cups heavy cream
1 box vanilla instant pudding

Prepare cake as directed on package. Pour into a greased 13 x 9 inch pan. Bake at 350° for 30-35 minutes. Combine pineapple and 1 cup sugar in saucepan and bring to a boil; stirring constantly. Remove from heat and cool slightly. When cake is done, remove from oven and pierce holes in cake with a fork. Pour pineapple mixture over hot cake. Prepare pudding according to directions on package. Spread over cake and refrigerate until thoroughly chilled. Before ready to serve, beat cream and remaining sugar together until stiff. Cover top of cake with whipped cream and sprinkle with toasted coconut.

FRUIT COCKTAIL CAKE

2 cups all-purpose flour
1 ¼ cups sugar
½ cup vegetable oil
2 large eggs
2 teaspoons baking soda
1 (15 .25 oz) can fruit cocktail, un-drained
½ teaspoon salt
1 (2 .25 oz) bag walnuts, chopped
½ cup coconut, un-sweetened, flaked

In a large bowl, beat sugar, oil and eggs at medium speed with an electric mixer until fluffy. In a medium bowl, combine flour, soda and salt. Add to sugar mixture, beating well. (the batter will be thick). Stir in fruit cocktail. Pour into a greased 13 x 9 inch baking dish. Sprinkle evenly with coconut. Bake at 350° for 40-50 minutes or until a toothpick inserted in center comes out clean. Pour coconut frosting over hot cake. Sprinkle with walnuts. Cool completely before cutting in squares to serve.

COCONUT FROSTING

½ cup each (evaporated milk, butter and sweetened flaked coconut)
¾ cup sugar
1 teaspoon vanilla extract

Combine the sugar, milk and butter in a saucepan and bring to a boil over medium heat boil for 2 minutes, stirring occasionally. Stir in coconut and vanilla. Frost cake.

MULTI - BERRY CAKE

1 pound cake, frozen and cut into layers
1 box jell-o instant vanilla pudding
1 ½ cups cool whip, thawed
2 ½ cups mixed raspberries, strawberries, blackberries and blueberries
2 cups cold milk

Beat pudding and milk with whisk for 2 minutes. Stir in 1 cup cool whip. Combine berries; reserve ½ cup. Brush cake layer with juice; stack on plate, filling each layer with ½ each of remaining berries and pudding mixture. Top with remaining cool whip and reserved berries.

PEANUT BUTTER SHEET CAKE

2 cups each (self-rising flour and sugar)
1 teaspoon each (baking soda, vanilla extract and salt)
1 cup water
¾ cup butter or margarine
½ cup each (chunky peanut butter and buttermilk)
¼ cup vegetable oil
2 eggs

GLAZE
2/3 cup sugar
1/3 cup each (evaporated milk, chunky peanut butter and miniature marshmallows)
½ teaspoon vanilla extract
1 tablespoon butter or margarine

In a mixing bowl, combine flour, sugar, soda and salt; set aside. In a saucepan bring water and butter to a boil; stir in peanut butter and oil until blended. Add to dry ingredients; mix well. Combine eggs, butter, buttermilk and vanilla; add to peanut butter mixture. Mix well. Pour into a greased 15 x 10 inch baking pan and bake at 250° for 15-20 minutes or until done. Combine sugar milk and butter in saucepan. Bring to a boil, stirring constantly; cook and stir for 2 minutes. Remove from heat; stir in peanut butter, marshmallows and vanilla, stir until marshmallows are melted. Spoon over warm cake and spread over the top. Cool completely.

OLD FASHION LANE CAKE

3 ½ cups all-purpose flour
1 ½ cups butter or margarine, softened and divided
4 cups sugar
1 cup each (coconut, milk, red wine, chopped raisins and chopped nuts)
8 eggs, separated
2 teaspoons each (vanilla divided and baking soda)

Cream 2 cups sugar and 1 cup butter together until fluffy. Add soda to flour. Add flour mixture to the creamed butter mixture, add milk, 1 teaspoon vanilla and wine. Fold in stiffly beaten egg whites. Spoon batter into 3 (9 inch) greased cake pans and bake at 350° for 20-30 minutes or until done. Beat egg yolks, add remaining sugar and butter; cook until thick, stirring constantly. Add raisins, nuts and coconut. Add remaining 1 teaspoon vanilla. Spread filling thickly between layers of cake, on top and sides.

ORANGE COBBLER

½ cup each (biscuit mix and water)
3 tablespoons milk
1/8 teaspoon nutmeg
2 tablespoons each (sugar and orange juice)
1 tablespoon cornstarch
2 teaspoons butter or margarine
¼ cup orange marmalade
½ cup water
Vanilla ice cream

Combine sugar and cornstarch. Stir in water, marmalade and orange juice. Cook and sir over medium heat until thickened. Stir in the butter until melted. Pour into a greased 1 quart baking dish. In a bowl, combine biscuit mix and nutmeg; stir in milk just until moistened. Drop by tablespoonful over orange mixture. Bake un-covered at 400° for 20-25 minutes or until top is golden brown. Best served warm with ice cream.

GOOD PEACH COBBLER

½ cup biscuit mix
2 teaspoons sugar
2 tablespoons milk
1 (8 ½ oz) can sliced peaches, un-drained
1 tablespoon each (cold water and vegetable oil)
1 ½ teaspoon cornstarch
Vanilla ice cream

In a saucepan combine cornstarch and water until smooth; stir in peaches. Bring to a boil; cook and stir for 1 minute or until thickened. Pour into 2 greased 8 ounce custard cups. In a small bowl, combine biscuit and sugar; stir in milk and oil just until moistened. Drop by teaspoonful over hot peach mixture. Bake un-covered at 400° for 18-25 minutes or until topping is golden brown. Serve with ice cream.

PEACH COBBLER IN SKILLET

Put skillet on stove with ½ stick butter; and 2 cups peaches, ¼ cup bourbon, ¼ cup sugar, heat through. Combine 1 cup flour, 2 teaspoons baking powder, 2 tablespoons cornstarch, ½ teaspoon salt. Pour over peaches. Transfer to a baking dish. Pour 1 cup cream on top and sprinkle with sugar and bake until top is golden brown.

PEACH COBBLER

1 can sliced peaches
1 cup sugar
1 cup milk
1 cup self-rising flour
1 stick butter
1 egg, slightly beaten
1 teaspoon vanilla

Mix all ingredients together and put in a large baking dish. Bake at 350° until brown on top. Serve with ice cream or whipped cream.

CHESS SQUARES

1 box yellow cake mix
1 egg, beaten
1 stick butter
1 box powdered sugar
1 (8 oz) package cream cheese, softened

Mix cake mix and butter. Press into a 9 x 13 inch greased pan. Mix sugar, cream cheese and beaten egg, spread on top of cake. Bake at 350° for 50 minutes or until golden brown. Cool, cut into squares.

FROZEN BANANA SPLIT

Ice cream sandwiches
6 bananas, sliced
Chocolate fudge sauce
Whipping cream
Toffee bits
Butterscotch topping
Small jar maraschino cherries

In a 9 x 13 inch dish lined with foil; layer, ice cream sandwiches, sliced bananas, maraschino cherries, chocolate fudge sauce and butterscotch topping. Layer more ice cream sandwiches, top with whipped cream and sprinkle with toffee bits. Freeze.

APPLE AND WALNUT COBBLER

4 cups cooking apples, peeled and sliced
1 cup each (chopped walnuts, sugar and flour)
1 teaspoon each (cinnamon and baking powder)
¼ teaspoon salt
1 egg, beaten
½ cup evaporated milk
1/3 cup butter, melted
Sweet whipping cream or vanilla ice cream

Grease a 2 quart baking dish; set aside. In a large bowl stir together ½ cup sugar and cinnamon until well combined. Add apple slices and ½ cup of the walnuts; toss lightly to coat. Transfer apple mixture to prepared baking dish. In a large bowl stir together, flour, 1 cup sugar, baking powder and salt. In a small bowl stir together egg mixture in pan. Sprinkle with remaining walnuts. Bake for 40-45 minutes or until top is golden brown. Cool slightly before serving. Top with whipped cream or ice cream.

BLUEBERRY COBBLER

1 quart blueberries
1 teaspoon salt
2 ½ cups sugar, plus 2 tablespoons
3 tablespoons each (lemon juice and butter)
4 teaspoons baking powder
½ cup shortening
2/3 cup milk
1 egg, beaten

Combine 1 1/2 cups sugar, ½ cup flour, 1 teaspoon salt, berries and lemon juice. Pour into a greased 13 x 9 inch baking dish; dot with butter. Bake at 400° for 15 minutes or until mixture is hot and bubbly. Combine remaining ingredients, drop by tablespoonful onto blueberry mixture. Bake for 30 minutes longer or until top is browned.

LEMON RICE PUDDING BRULEE

½ cup long grain rice, un-cooked
1 1/3 cups lemonade
1/3 cups plus 3 tablespoons sugar, divided
1 tablespoon all-purpose flour
½ teaspoon salt
2 cups milk
2 eggs, beaten
¼ cup dried cranberries
3 tablespoons brown sugar
1/3 cup toasted pecans, chopped
1 teaspoon grated lemon peel

In a saucepan, bring lemonade and rice to a boil. Reduce heat; cover and simmer for 20 minutes. Remove from heat; stir in lemon peel. Cover and let stand for 5 minutes. Cool to room temperature. In a large saucepan, combine 1/3 cup sugar, flour and salt. Stir in milk until smooth. Cook and stir until thickened and bubbly. Reduce heat; cook and stir 2 minutes longer. Remove from heat and stir in cranberries and cooled rice. Divide among 6 (8 oz) ramekins. Place on baking sheet. Combine brown sugar and remaining sugar; sprinkle over pudding. Bring 3-4 inches from the heat for 3-5 minutes or until sugar is melted and bubbly. Sprinkle with pecans. Serve warm.

CARAMEL APPLE BREAD PUDDING

½ cup each (peeled and chopped apples, brown sugar and egg substitute)
½ cup each (caramel ice cream topping and whipped topping)
6 cups of day old bread cubes
1 cup each (milk and un-sweetened applesauce)
½ teaspoon each (vanilla and cinnamon)

Combine applesauce, milk, brown sugar, egg substitute, vanilla and cinnamon together. Fold in bread cubes and apples. Pour into an 8 inch square baking dish, coated with cooking spray. Bake un-covered at 325° for 35-40 minutes or until done. Serve warm with whipped topping and caramel topping. Refrigerate any left over.

BANANA FOSTER BREAD PUDDING

1 (12 oz) loaf stale French bread, cut in small pieces
4 cups half and half
2 ½ cups sugar
1 cup milk
3-4 bananas, sliced
4 eggs
8-9 tablespoons butter, melted
2 tablespoons vanilla extract

Combine all ingredients together. Pour into a buttered 9 x 13 inch baking dish and bake at 350° for 1 hour and 15 minutes, or until golden brown. Serve warm with banana foster sauce.

BANANA FOSTER SAUCE

2 cups dark brown sugar
2-3 bananas, cut in small pieces
2 ounces of banana liqueur
2 ounces of dark rum
½ cup butter

Melt butter and brown sugar to make a paste. Stir in the liqueurs until smooth. Add bananas and simmer for about 2 minutes. Serve over pudding.

RAISIN PUDDING

1 cup each (raisins and white sugar)
2 cups each (brown sugar, flour and sour milk)
4 cups hot water
2 tablespoons butter
2 teaspoons soda
1 teaspoon each (nutmeg and cinnamon)
Whipped cream

Combine water, brown sugar in 9 x 13 inch pan; bring to a boil. Remove from heat. Cream butter and sugar; add dry ingredients with sour milk. Fold in raisins. Drop by teaspoonful into syrup and bake at 375° for 30 minutes or until firm to touch. Serve warm with whipped cream.

BREAD PUDDING WITH SAUCE

5 cups white or wheat bread, cubed
2 ½ cups warm milk
1 cup each (chopped nuts and raisins)
2 eggs, beaten
½ cup sugar
1 teaspoon each (cinnamon, nutmeg and vanilla)

Grease a 2 quart casserole dish. Combine bread cubes and milk. Place in greased dish. In another bowl, combine sugar, cinnamon, nutmeg, eggs and vanilla, mix well. Stir in raisins and nuts. Add mixture to soaked up bread cubes; blend well. Bake at 350° for about 1 hour.

BRANDY SAUCE
2 cups powdered sugar
½ cup butter, softened
2 tablespoons brandy
1 tablespoon hot water

In a small bowl, combine all sauce ingredients. Beat with electric mixer on high speed until well blended. Cover, refrigerate until ready to serve. Serve over warm pudding.

RICE PUDDING

½ cup rice, un-cooked
3 cups boiling water
1 (14 oz) can sweetened condensed milk
½ cup raisins
1 tablespoon vanilla
½ stick butter
½ teaspoon salt

Combine rice, salt and boiling water in top of double boiler. Cook over boiling water until rice is tender, about 30 minutes. Stir in condensed milk, raisins and butter. Cook, stirring often until slightly thickened about 20 minutes. Remove from heat and stir in vanilla. Serve warm or cold.

DELICIOUS SOUR CREAM CHERRY PIE

CRUST
1 ½ cups flour
½ cup vegetable oil
3-5 tablespoons cold water
1 teaspoon grated orange peel
¾ teaspoon salt
2 tablespoons toasted almonds, ground

Mix flour, salt and orange peel. Add shortening. Sprinkle with water, 1 tablespoon at a time, mixing until dough begins to stick together. Shape into a ball. Roll out 1/8 of an inch thick on floured surface. Place into a 9 inch pie pan. Trim and flute edges. Press almonds into bottom of pie plate.

FILLING
1 (21 oz) can cherry pie filling
1/3 cup sugar
3 eggs
1 tablespoon lemon juice
1 teaspoon vanilla extract
½ teaspoon almond extract
¾ cup sour cream
1 teaspoon grated orange peel

In a bowl, mix together the cherry pie filling, peel and juice; spoon over nuts in crust. Beat eggs, sugar, almond extract and vanilla extract until thick and lemon in color, about 10 minutes. Add sour cream. Pour cream mixture over cherries and bake at 350° for 45 minutes or until crust is brown. Chill and serve.

LEMONADE ICE CREAM PIE

½ gallon vanilla ice cream, softened
1 can frozen lemonade concentrate, thawed
1 carton frozen whipped topping, thawed
Lemon slices
2 ready to fill graham cracker pie crusts

Place crust in freezer. Put soft ice cream, lemonade and ¾ of the whipped cream into a large bowl and stir until blended. Spread ½ in each crust. Top with remaining whipped topping. Freeze until topping is firm. Cover with air tight foil. Freeze 4 hours or until hard. Serve with lemon slices on top.

EULA'S FAVORITE PEANUT BUTTER PIE

2 cup powdered sugar
½ cup peanut butter, crunchy
1 pie shell, baked and cooled

Mix peanut butter and powdered sugar together. Spread all (except 3 tablespoonful) on the bottom of cooled pie crust. Save the rest for topping.

FILLING

2 cups milk, scalded
2/3 cup sugar
¼ cup cornstarch
3 egg yolks, beaten
2 tablespoons butter
¼ teaspoon salt

Mix cornstarch, sugar and salt. Add scalded milk. Place over medium heat. Cook, stirring constantly. Add egg yolks and butter. Continue stirring until thickened. Stir in vanilla and set aside. Pour over peanut butter mixture.

MERINGUE

3 egg whites
1/8 teaspoon cream of tartar
3 tablespoons sugar

Beat egg whites, sugar and cream of tartar until fluffy. Spread over filling. Dot meringue with the remaining peanut butter mixture. Place in 300° oven just long enough to brown the meringue.

FRENCH SILK PIE

1 stick butter, softened
3 eggs
¾ cup sugar
1 teaspoon vanilla
4 tablespoons cocoa
1 9 inch pie shell, baked

Mix sugar, cocoa, and vanilla. Beat 5 minutes. Add eggs, 1 at a time, beating 1 minute after each addition. Pour into pie shell and chill at least 2 hours or overnight before serving. Serve with whipped cream.

SOUTHERN PECAN PIE

3 eggs, beaten
½ cup sugar
¼ cup butter or margarine, melted
1 cup each (dark corn syrup and pecans)
1 teaspoon vanilla
¼ teaspoon salt
1 pie shell, un-baked

Mix the eggs, syrup, sugar, butter, salt and vanilla together. Spread nuts in bottom of pie shell. Pour filling in shell and bake at 400° for 25-30 minutes.

SWEET POTATO PIE

3 medium sweet potatoes, cooked and mashed
1 stick butter, melted
¾ cup sugar
3 eggs
1 cup evaporated milk
1 tablespoon flour
1 teaspoon vanilla
2 teaspoons lemon juice
½ teaspoon salt
2 9 inch pie shells, un-baked

Beat eggs and milk. Mix together the sugar and butter, add to mashed potatoes. Beat flour and flavorings into potatoes. Add milk and egg mixture. Pour into two 9 inch pie shells. Bake at 350° for 35 minutes.

STRAWBERRY PIE

1 quart strawberries
1 cup sugar
1 ½ cups water
1 box strawberry jell-o gelatin
2 ½ tablespoons cornstarch
1 pie shell, baked

Boil sugar, water and cornstarch until thick and clear. Add jell-o and let cool. Add berries and put into baked pie shell. Chill until ready to serve. Serve with whipped cream or ice cream.

JUDY'S BUTTERSCOTCH PIE

1 cup brown sugar
4 tablespoons flour
1 ½ cups milk
3 eggs, separated
1 teaspoon vanilla
1/8 teaspoon salt
Meringue on top
1 pie shell, baked

In a saucepan, mix flour, sugar and salt. Add milk, stir constantly, after it thickens some, add egg yolks and continue cooking until thick. Pour in baked pie shell. Beat 3 egg whites with an electric mixer until soft peaks, add 3 tablespoons of sugar and continue beating until stiff peaks. Place on top of pie, making sure to cover all top and sides. Brown in oven.

GRANNY'S APPLE BUTTER PIE

1 ¼ cups apple butter
¾ cup canned pumpkin
4 eggs, beaten
¾ cup evaporated milk
1 large carton whipped topping
½ cup brown sugar, dark or light
½ teaspoon salt
1 teaspoon each (nutmeg and cinnamon)
¼ teaspoon ginger
1 9 inch pie shell, un-baked

Mix pumpkin, sugar, spices and apple butter in a bowl. Add eggs. Add milk and mix well. Pour into an un-baked pie shell and bake at 350° for approximately 45-60 minutes or until pie has set. Cover top with whipping topping. My family loves it.

COCONUT CHIFFON PIE

1 cup sugar
1 envelope un-flavored gelatin
1 ½ cups milk
2 eggs, separated
3 tablespoons flour
1 ½ cups grated coconut
2 tablespoons powdered sugar
1 teaspoon vanilla
1 small carton cool whip
½ cup cold water
1 9 inch pie shell, baked

Beat sugar, flour and egg yolks until lemon colored. Add milk; cook in top of double boiler until thickened. Dissolve gelatin in water, fold into custard with 1 cup coconut. Beat egg whites until stiff, add powdered sugar and vanilla. Fold into custard, pour into pie shell; chill. Spoon whip cream over chilled custard. Sprinkle with remaining coconut.

EASY PEAR PIE

4 cups fresh pears, sliced
1 cup each (sugar and flour)
½ cup brown sugar
½ cup butter
3 tablespoons quick cooking tapioca
2 teaspoons ground ginger
1 9 inch pie shell, un-baked

Blend pears, ginger, sugar and tapioca; let stand for 20 minutes. Place in pie shell. Cut butter into flour, add sugar. Sprinkle over pie filling,. Bake at 425° for 15 minutes. Reduce heat to 375° and bake 30 minutes longer.

GOOD MULTIPLE LAYER PIE

¾ cup sugar, divide
2 eggs, separated
1 (6 oz) package semi-sweet chocolate chips
1 cup whipping cream
¼ cup water
½ teaspoon vinegar
1 teaspoon vanilla, divided
¼ teaspoon salt
1 9 inch pie crust, baked and cooled

Separate eggs and set aside. Combine egg whites, salt, ½ teaspoon vanilla and vinegar in a mixing bowl. Beat until soft peaks form. Add ½ cup sugar and beat until stiff peaks form. Spread meringue over bottom and up sides of cooled baked pie crust. Bake at 325° for 15-20 minutes or until light brown. Cool. Melt chocolate chips in top of a double boiler. Blend in egg yolks and water; stirring until smooth. Spread 4 tablespoons of this mixture over cooled meringue. Chill remaining chocolate mixture until it begins to thicken. In a mixing bowl, beat whipping cream until soft peaks form. Spread ½ of the whipped cream over chocolate layer. Fold chilled chocolate mixture into remaining whipped cream. Spread this over whipped cream layer in pie. Refrigerate until ready to serve.

OLD FASHION CUSTARD PIE

½ cup sugar
4 eggs, beaten
2 ½ cups milk, scalded
1/8 teaspoon almond extract
¼ teaspoon salt
½ teaspoon each (vanilla and nutmeg)
1 pie shell, un-baked, chilled
2 tablespoons cornstarch

Blend all ingredients except the milk and nutmeg. Stir in the milk, pour into a chilled pie shell. Sprinkle with nutmeg. Bake at 400° for 25-30 minutes or until knife inserted in center of custard comes out clean. Cool 15-20 minutes. Refrigerate.

DELICIOUS FRENCH PIE

½ cup nuts, chopped
1 small bottle maraschino cherries, chopped
½ pint heavy cream
½ box vanilla wafers, crushed
2 eggs, beaten
1 cup powdered sugar
½ cup butter

Cream together butter and powdered sugar. Add eggs and stir well. Cover bottom of 8 x 10 inch pan or dish with ½ of the crushed wafers. Pour egg mixture into shell. Combine whipped cream, cherries and nuts and spread over egg mixture. Cover with wafer crumbs. Chill for 24 hours. Serve with whipped cream.

CHESS PIE

1 ½ cups sugar
1 stick butter, melted and cooled
1 tablespoon vinegar
3 eggs
1 teaspoon vanilla
1 tablespoon cornmeal
1 pie shell, un-baked

Beat eggs until well blended. Add other ingredients. Pour into an un-baked pie shell and bake at 350° for 40 minutes or until set.

PINEAPPLE WHIP CREAM PIE

2 ½ cans pineapple, crushed
2 tablespoons cornstarch
1 cup sugar
¼ teaspoon salt
Juice of ½ lemon
Whipping cream
1 9 inch pie shell, un-baked

Combine and cook pineapple, sugar, salt, lemon juice and cornstarch until thickened. Pour into pie shell and bake at 375° for 30 minutes. Cool. Top with whip cream before serving.

CHOCOLATE MOUSSE PIE

CRUST
1 ¼ cups Oreo cookie crumbs
¼ pound butter, melted

Combine both ingredients and press into the bottom of a 10 inch pie pan. Set aside.

FILLING
1 (7 oz) jar marshmallow crème
1 (1 oz) square un-sweetened chocolate
2 cups heavy cream for whipping, divided
2 tablespoons sugar
1 teaspoon vanilla
2 tablespoons cream
½ ounce semi-sweet chocolate for garnish

Melt chocolate in a microwave bowl or sauce pan over low heat. Remove from heat. In a mixing bowl, combine marshmallow crème, vanilla and melted chocolate. Mix well. Add 2 tablespoons cream, blend until smooth. Beat 1 cup of cream until stiff peaks form; fold into chocolate mixture. Spread in crust. Whip remaining topping. Cover and refrigerate for 2 ½ hours.

EARLE'S FROZEN STRAWBERRY MARGARITA PIE

1 (14 oz) can sweetened condensed milk
½ cup frozen strawberries with syrup, thawed
2 cups heavy cream
6 tablespoons margarita (Jose Cuervo Margaritas) Tequila already in it
¼ cup lime juice
1 graham cracker pie crust

Beat condensed milk, lime juice and margarita in a large bowl with an electric mixer at medium speed for 2 plus minutes or until smooth. Reduce speed; add in strawberries with syrup mix for 1 minute. Fold whipping cream into strawberry mixture. Mix well. Pour into graham cracker crust. Freeze overnight. Take out of refrigerator 30 minutes before serving. Garnish with additional whipped cream around edges and strawberries and lime slices.

CHOCOLATE MARSHMALLOW PIE

20-22 marshmallows
16 graham crackers, crushed
½ cup nuts
3 eggs, separated
½ cup each (chocolate syrup and butter)
1 carton whipped topping, thawed

Press ½ of the crumbs in to a pie pan. Melt marshmallows and butter in syrup. Add beaten yolks; cool. Add stiffly beaten egg whites and nuts. Pour into pie shell. Cover with rest of crumbs. Chill for 12 hours. Serve with the whipped topping.

RITZ CRACKER PIE

20 Ritz crackers, crushed
3 egg whites, stiffly beaten
1 cup each (pecan and sugar)
½ teaspoon each (vanilla and baking powder)

Beat egg whites until foamy; sprinkle with baking powder and continue beating until stiff. Add sugar; beat until sugar dissolves. Add crackers, vanilla and pecans; mix well. Pour into a 9 inch buttered pie pan and bake at 350° for 30 minutes; cool. Serve with whip cream or plain.

LEMON PIE

1 (16 oz) can frozen lemonade
1 (14 oz) can eagle brand milk
1 (9 oz) carton cool whip
1 graham cracker crust

Mix all ingredients and pour in crust. Chill for several before serving.

TURTLE PIE

1 (14 oz) can sweetened condensed milk, divided
12 caramels
2 (1 oz) squares chocolate, un-sweetened
2 eggs
¼ cup butter or margarine
½ cup pecans, chopped
1 teaspoon vanilla extract
¼ teaspoon salt
2 tablespoons water
1 9 inch pie crust, baked

Melt caramels with 1/3 cup milk in heavy saucepan over medium heat. Spread this mixture evenly on the bottom of the pie crust. In medium saucepan melt chocolate with butter. In a large mixing bowl, beat eggs with remaining milk, water, vanilla and salt. Add chocolate mixture and mix well. Pour into pie crust; top with pecans and bake at 325° for 35 minutes or until center is set. Cool and chill. Top with whipped cream.

GRAHAM CRACKER PIE

20 graham crackers, crushed
2 cups milk, scalded
½ teaspoon cinnamon
¾ cup plus 2 tablespoons sugar
½ stick butter
2 tablespoons cornstarch
¼ teaspoon salt
3 eggs, separated
1 teaspoon vanilla

Mix graham crackers, softened butter, ¼ cup sugar and cinnamon, pat into a 9 inch pie plate, keep ¼ cup for topping. Combine milk, ¼ cup sugar, cornstarch, egg yolks, salt and vanilla. Cook until thickened. Pour into cooled pie crust. Beat egg whites until stiff; adding 6 tablespoons sugar. Spread over filling. Sprinkle reserved graham cracker mixture over meringue. Bake at 425° for 5 minutes or until meringue browns.

LEMON CHESS PIE

1 ½ cups sugar
2 tablespoons cornmeal
1 tablespoon flour
½ cup butter, melted
4 teaspoons grated lemon rind
¼ cup each (milk and lemon juice)
4 eggs
1 9 inch pie crust, un-baked

Combine flour, sugar, cornmeal and eggs. Mix thoroughly. Add lemon rind, milk, lemon juice and butter. Mix well. Pour into an un -baked pie crust. Bake at 425° for 10 minutes. Reduce heat to 325o and bake 40-50 minutes.

STRAWBERRIES AND CREAM PIE

1 (8 oz) package cream cheese, softened
1/3 cup sugar
2 pints fresh strawberries
1 cup whipping cream, whipped
½ teaspoon almond extract
½ cup semi-sweet chocolate chips
1 tablespoon shortening
1 9 inch pie shell, baked

In a large bowl, beat cream cheese until fluffy. Gradually add sugar and almond extract, blending well. Fold in whipped cream. Spoon into cooled baked pie shell. Arrange strawberries, pointed side up, over filling. Refrigerate. In a small saucepan, melt the chocolate chips and shortening over low heat, stirring constantly until smooth. Drizzle over strawberries and filling. Refrigerate for 1 hour or until set.

BLUEBERRY PIE

1 pint fresh blueberries
2/3 cup sugar
3 eggs
1 (8 oz) package cream cheese, softened
1 teaspoon vanilla---1 pie shell un-baked

Cream sugar and cream cheese; add eggs to mixture, beating well. Add vanilla. Pour mixture into a 9 inch pie shell. Sprinkle blueberries over the top and bake at 350° for 25 minutes. Cool and chill several hours before serving.

BANANA SPLIT PIE

CRUST
2 cups graham cracker crumbs
1 stick butter
2 tablespoons sugar

Combine all ingredients and press into baking pan and bake at 400° for 8-10 minutes.

FIRST LAYER
1 stick butter or margarine, softened
2 cups powdered sugar
1 (3 oz) package cream cheese, softened

Cream all ingredients together until light and fluffy. Spread over crust.

SECOND LAYER
1 can crushed pineapple, drained
1 large container whipped topping
4 bananas, sliced
Garnish; Fresh whole strawberries and pecan halves.

CREAM DE - MENTHE PIE

18 cream filled chocolate cookies, crushed
1/3 stick butter, melted
½ pint heavy cream, whipped
2 tablespoons crème de-menthe
28 large marshmallows
1 ½ cups milk

Combine the marshmallows and milk in a double boiler; cook until dissolved; cool. Add crème de-menthe; cool. Combine cookies and butter; mix well. Press into an 8 inch pie pan. Fold whipped cream into marshmallow mixture. Pour into pie shell. Sprinkle with additional cookie crumbs; chill at least 5-6 hours before serving.

KENTUCKY DERBY PIE

4 eggs, beaten
2 sticks margarine
2 cups sugar
1 cup each (nuts and chocolate chips)
2 teaspoons vanilla
2 tablespoons flour
2 pie crust, un-baked

Mix eggs, margarine and vanilla. Melt chips and add to mixture. Add flour and vanilla, then nuts. Pour into 2 un-baked pie crusts and bake at 350° for 30 minutes.

TOFFEE DREAM PIE

5 toffee bars
1 cup heavy cream, whipped
½ pound marshmallows
1/3 cup milk
2 tablespoons slivered almonds, toasted
1 9 inch gram cracker or baked pie crust

Cook marshmallows in milk until melted, stirring occasionally. Remove from heat; stir in toffee bars until partially melted. Chill until thickened. Fold whipped cream into toffee mixture. Pour into pie shell. Garnish with almonds.

CHOCOLATE MOUSSE

1 (8 oz) package semi-sweet chocolate, cut into pieces
¼ cup each (butter and sugar)
1 cup whipping cream, whipped
1 (8 oz) carton of frozen fat-free egg product, thawed
1 teaspoon vanilla

Melt butter and chocolate, stirring constantly. Remove from heat and stir in vanilla. Beat egg product until foamy; beat in sugar. With wire whisk add the chocolate mixture. Blend well. Fold in whipped cream. Refrigerate for a least 1 hour. Serve with additional whipped cream.

PUMPKIN MOUSSE PIE

1 (15 oz) can pumpkin
1 ½ cups graham cracker crumbs
¼ cup brown sugar
1 (7 oz) jar marshmallow crème
6 tablespoons butter, melted
1 (12 oz) container cool whip, frozen and thawed
2 teaspoons pumpkin pie spice
1/3 cup brown sugar

In a bowl stir together the graham cracker crumbs and 1/3 cup brown sugar. Stir in butter until mixed well. Press mixture into bottom and sides of a deep dish 9 inch pie plate. Bake at 350° for 8-10 minutes or until lightly browned. Cool. For the filling; Mix together the marshmallow crème, pumpkin, ¼ cup brown sugar and pumpkin pie spice. Fold in ½ of the cool whip. Spoon mixture into cooled graham cracker crust. Cover and freeze 5-24 hours or until good firm. When ready to serve let pie stand at room temperature for 10-15 minutes. Spread with remaining cool whip. Slice and enjoy.

APPLE SOUR CREAM PIE

1/3 cup brown sugar
2/3 cup white sugar
1 egg, beaten
1 cup sour cream
4 cups tart apples, peeled, cored and sliced thin
½ cup light raisins
1 9 inch pie shell, un-cooked and enough for a lattice top

Combine sugars, egg and sour cream, stir in sliced apples and raisins. Turn into the pie crust, add lattice on top, seal edges and flute. Bake at 400° for 50 minutes or until done. Covering edges with foil during last 15 minutes of baking time, so crust won't burn.

DERBY PIE

1 cup each (sugar and pecan pieces)
½ cup flour
2 eggs, slightly beaten
¼ tablespoon butter, melted
1 (6 oz) package semi-sweet chocolate chips
1 teaspoon vanilla
1 pie shell, un-baked

Mix all ingredients together and place in frozen pie shell and bake at 350° for 1 hour.

TURTLE CAKE

1 box German chocolate cake mix
¾ cup butter
¾ cup evaporated milk
1 package caramels
½ cup evaporated milk
1 cup pecans
1 (12 oz) package chocolate chips

Pour ½ mixture of cake mix, butter and ¾ cup evaporated milk into a 9 x 13 inch greased baking pan. Bake at 350° for 6 minutes. Melt caramels with ½ cup evaporate milk in double boiler; spoon over cake while hot. Sprinkle with chocolate chips and pecans, top with rest of cake mix. Bake at 350° for 30 minutes.

MARGARITA PIE

2 cups miniature pretzel twists
2 tablespoons each (sugar and butter)
1 (6 oz) can frozen limeade concentrate
1 tablespoon orange flavored liqueur
1 quart vanilla ice cream, lightly softened
3 tablespoons tequila
1 teaspoon grated lime peel

In blender, blend pretzels until crumbs form. Add sugar; and mix. Add butter, mix well. Add 2 tablespoons of the limeade; process until well mixed. Place mixture in a 9 inch pie pan, sprayed with cooking spray. Press mixture firmly in bottom and up sides of pan and bake at 375° for 5-7 minutes or until set. Cool baked shell in freezer for 10-15 minutes. With an electric mixer, combine remaining limeade, ice cream, lime peel, tequila and liqueur; mix just until blended; spoon into baked shell. Freeze 2 hours.

DELICIOUS EGGNOG PIE

1 1/8 teaspoons un-flavored gelatin
¼ cup cold water
¾ cups sugar
2/3 cup milk
3 egg yolks, beaten
1 teaspoon vanilla
2 tablespoons cornstarch
1 ½ cups whipping cream, whipped
1/8 teaspoon ground nutmeg
1 pie shell, baked

Soften gelatin cold water; set aside. In a saucepan, combine sugar and cornstarch. Stir in milk until smooth. Bring to a boil; cook and stir for 2 minutes or until thickened. Remove from heat. Stir a small amount of hot mixture into the egg yolks. Return all to the pan; bring to a boil, stirring constantly. Remove from heat; stir in gelatin and vanilla. Cool to room temperature stirring occasionally. Fold in the whipped cream. Pour into pie shell. Sprinkle with nutmeg. Refrigerate until set (about 2 hours).

FRENCH SILK CHOCOLATE PIE

1 (3 oz) package un-sweetened chocolate, cut into pieces
1 cup each (butter, softened and sugar)
4 eggs
½ teaspoon vanilla
½ cup sweetened whipped cream
Chocolate curls
1 pie shell, baked and cooled

Melt chocolate in a small saucepan over low heat; cool. In a small bowl, beat butter until fluffy. Gradually add sugar, beating until light and fluffy. Add cooled chocolate and vanilla, blend well. Add eggs, 1 at a time, beating for 2 minutes after each addition. Beat until mixture is smooth and fluffy. Pour into a cooled baked pie shell. Refrigerate at least 2 hours before serving. Top with whipped cream and chocolate curls.

PECAN PUMPKIN PIE

1 large can pumpkin pie mix
1 cup sugar
1 (4 oz) can evaporated milk
2 tablespoons ground cinnamon
½ teaspoon salt
1 (18 ¼ oz) box yellow cake mix
3 eggs
1 cup butter or margarine, melted
1 ½ cups pecans, chopped

CARAMEL SAUCE
1 cup butter or margarine
2 cups brown sugar
1 cup whipping cream

TOPPING
2 cups of whipping cream
3 tablespoons powdered sugar
1 ½ teaspoons vanilla extract

Line 2 (9 inch) pie plates with wax paper. Coat the paper with cooking spray. Set aside. In a mixing bowl, combine pumpkin, sugar and milk. Beat in eggs, cinnamon and salt. Pour into prepared pans. Sprinkle with dry cake mix. Drizzle with butter. Sprinkle with pecans; press down lightly. Bake at 350° for 50-60 minutes or until golden brown. Cool for 2 hours. Carefully run a knife around edge of pan to loosen. Invert pie onto a serving plate. Remove wax paper; chill. In a heavy saucepan over low heat, melt butter. Add brown sugar and cream; cook and stir until sugar is dissolved. For topping; In a mixing bowl, beat cream until foamy. Beat in powdered sugar and vanilla until soft peaks form. Cut the pie into slices. Drizzle with caramel sauce and dollop with topping.

FRESH PEACH PIE

8-10 ripe peach halves
2 eggs
1 cup sugar
1 tablespoon butter, melted
½ teaspoon almond flavoring
1 9 inch pie shell, un-baked

Place peach halve cavity side up in pie shell. Beat eggs with sugar, butter and flavoring, pour over peaches and bake at 325° for 25 minutes and peaches are tender.

SOUR CREAM APPLE PIE

FILLING
2 cups Rome apples, peeled and sliced
1 (9 inch) pie shell, un-baked
¾ cup sugar
4 tablespoons flour
1 egg, beaten
1 cup sour cream
½ teaspoon vanilla
1/8 teaspoon salt

TOPING
1/3 cup each (sugar and flour)
¼ cup butter
1 teaspoon cinnamon

Arrange peeled and sliced apples into an un-baked pie shell. Mix remaining filling ingredients together and pour over apples. Bake at 350° for 1 hour. While pie is baking, blend topping ingredients together. Crumble this mixture over top of baked pie. Bake 15 minutes longer. Serve warm.

ORANGE AND LEMON PIE

2 lemons (grated rind and juice)
1 orange (grated rind and juice)
½ cup boiling water
1 cup sugar
2 eggs, separated
5 teaspoons flour
1 tablespoon butter
1 pie shell, baked

Place grated rinds of orange and lemons in a saucepan; add boiling water, sugar, lemon juice, orange juice and well beaten egg yolks. Bring to a boiling point. Mix butter and flour to a medium paste; add to hot mixture. Cook until spoon is coated; cool. Pour into pie shell. Beat egg whites until stiff; spread over pie filling. Brown in oven for about 4-5 minutes.

EASY LEMON PIE

1 cup sugar
1 ½ cups water
1/3 cup lemon juice
¼ cup cornstarch
3 eggs, separated
1 tablespoon margarine
1/3 cup sugar
1 small box lemon jell-o (dissolved in 2/3 cup boiling water)
3 egg whites
1 grated lemon peel
1 pie crust, baked

Combine 1 cup sugar and cornstarch. Add water mix until blended. Add egg yolks, stirring constantly. Bring to a boil. Stir in lemon peel, juice and margarine. Add jell-o and water to the lemon mix and blend well. Spoon into a baked pie crust. Beat egg whites at high speed until foamy, add sugar. Beat until very stiff. Spread evenly over pie filling, making sure to seal edge of crust. Bake at 350° for 8-10 minutes or until golden brown.

SPECIAL COFFEE PIE

1 chocolate crumb pie crust (9 inch)
¼ cup each (hot fudge ice cream topping, warm milk and cold milk)
3 cups coffee ice cream, softened
1 (5.9 oz) box instant chocolate pudding mix
½ cup cold brewed coffee
1 ¾ cups whipped topping
1 cup marshmallow cream
¼ cup miniature semi-sweet chocolate chips

Spread ice cream topping into pie crust. In a large bowl; beat ice cream, pudding mix, coffee and milk until blended; spoon into crust. Combine the whipped topping and marshmallow crème in another bowl; spread over top. Sprinkle with chocolate chips. Cover and freeze until firm.

LEMON PIE WITH BERRIES

1 (14 oz) can sweetened condensed milk
½ cup lemon juice
1 cup each (fresh strawberries and blueberries)
¼ cup each (water and slivered almonds, toasted)
1 (8 oz) container whipped topping, frozen and thawed
2 eggs, beaten
1 (9 inch) graham cracker crumb pie shell

In a bowl whisk together milk, lemon juice and eggs. Spread in pie shell. Bake at 350° for 20-25 minutes or until center is almost set. In a saucepan combine the berries and water. Bring to a boil; reduce heat simmer un-covered, about 5 minutes or until berries soften. Remove from heat. Cool completely. Spoon berry mixture over pie. Cover and chill for 2 hours. When ready to serve, spread whipped topping over pie. Sprinkle with almonds.

RAISIN MERINGUE PIE

1 cup brown sugar
2 tablespoons self-rising flour
1 (8 oz) cup sour cream
3 eggs, separated
½ teaspoon each (ground nutmeg, cinnamon and allspice)
¼ teaspoon salt
1 cup raisins, chopped
6 tablespoons sugar
¼ teaspoon cream of tartar
1 pie shell, baked

In a saucepan, combine the brown sugar and flour. Stir in sour cream, egg yolks, spices and salt until smooth. Bring mixture to a boil. Remove from heat. Stir in raisins; cover and set aside. In mixing bowl, beat egg whites and cream of tartar until foamy, about 1 minute. Gradually add in sugar, beat until glossy peaks form and sugar is dissolved, about 3 minutes. Pour hot raisin filling into pie shell. Spread meringue evenly over filling; seal edges to crust and bake at 350° for 12-15 minutes or until golden brown. Cool 1 hour. Refrigerate for at least 2 hours before serving.

DELICIOUS LIME PIE

MERINGUE SHELL
4 egg whites, reserve yolks
1 cup sugar
½ teaspoon cream of tartar

Butter a 9 inch pie plate. In a mixing bowl, beat egg whites and cream of tartar until foamy. Beat in sugar about 1 minute. Place into pie plate; pushing up round sides. Bake for 1 hour. Turn off oven, but leave pie in oven with door closed for 1 hour. Remove from oven and let cool.

FILLING
4 egg yolks
1/3 cup lime juice
½ cup sugar
¼ teaspoon salt
1 tablespoon grated lime peel
1 cup whipping cream, chilled
Whipping cream and lime peel for garnish

Beat egg yolks until lemon colored. Stir in sugar, salt and lime juice. Cook over medium heat, stirring constantly, until mixture thickens, about 4-5 minutes. Cool. In a bowl that has been chilled, beat cream until stiff. Fold in filling mixture and grated peel. Pile into meringue shell and chill for 5 hours. Garnish with whipped cream and lime peel twists.

PINEAPPLE SOUR CREAM PIE

1 large box instant vanilla pudding mix
2 small cans crushed pineapple (1 drained and 1 un-drained)
1 (8 oz) carton sour cream
1 tablespoon sugar
1 (8 oz) carton cool whip
1 pie shell, baked and cooled

Combine all ingredients and mix with a fork, do not use an electric mixer. Pour into pie crust and refrigerate 2-3 hours before serving.

EGGNOG PUMPKIN PIE

1 ¼ cups self-rising flour
3-4 tablespoons cold water
3 tablespoons each (butter, cubed and vegetable oil)
¼ teaspoon salt

FILLING
2 eggs
½ cup sugar
1 cup each (eggnog and pumpkin)
1 teaspoon cinnamon
½ teaspoon each (salt, nutmeg and ginger)
¼ teaspoon cloves

TOPPING
½ cup each (chopped pecans and brown sugar)
2 tablespoons butter, softened

Combine flour and salt in a food processor and pulse to blend. Add oil and butter; cover and pulse until mixture resembles crumbs. While still processing, gradually add the water until dough forms a ball. Wrap in plastic wrap. Refrigerate for 1-1 ½ hours or until easy to handle. Roll out pastry to fit a 9 inch pie plate. Transfer pastry to pie plate. Trim pastry to ½ inch beyond edge of plate; flute edges. In another bowl, whisk the pumpkin, eggnog, eggs, sugar, cinnamon, salt, ginger and cloves until well blended. Pour into crust. In a small bowl, beat brown sugar and butter until crumbly, about 2 minutes. Stir in pecans; sprinkle over filling and bake at 350° for 50-60 minutes or until a knife inserted in the center comes out clean. Cool. Refrigerate leftovers.

CHOCOLATE ALMOND PIE

4 (1 ½ oz) Hershey chocolate bars with almonds
½ cup milk
18-20 large marshmallows
1 cup heavy cream
1 teaspoon vanilla extract
1 (8 inch) graham cracker crust

Melt candy bars and marshmallows together in a double boiler. Remove from heat and cool. Whip cream until stiff and fold into cooled mixture. Add vanilla. Pour in pie crust and chill. Top with whipped cream.

CANDY
COOKIES & BARS

MARTHA WASHINGTON CANDY

½ pound butter, melted
1 can condensed milk
2 cups pecans, chopped
½ cup cherries, drained and chopped
2 boxes powdered sugar
2 cups coconut
1 teaspoon vanilla
1 tablespoon paraffin, melted
1 (6 oz) package semi-sweet chocolate chips

Mix butter, sugar and milk well. Add rest of the ingredients (except chocolate chips and paraffin). Chill well several hours or overnight. Form into balls. Combine chocolate chips and paraffin in top of double boiler; place over hot water, stirring until chocolate is melted. Using a toothpick, dip each ball into chocolate mixture. Place on waxed paper. Remove toothpick.

TUMBLEWEEDS

1 (12 oz) package butterscotch chips
2 tablespoons peanut butter
1 (12 oz) can peanuts
1 (4 oz) can shoestring potatoes

Melt chips and peanut butter in double boiler. Combine peanuts and shoestring potatoes to butterscotch mixture. Drop by teaspoonful onto waxed paper. Cool.

CRUNCHY BUTTERSCOTCH CANDY

1 (6 oz) package butterscotch morsels
1 (3 oz) can show mein noodles
¾ - 1 cup dry roasted peanuts

Melt morsels over hot water; add other ingredients. Drop by tablespoonful on wax paper. Let set for 20 minutes.

BOURBON BALLS

½ cup butter, softened
3 tablespoons Eagle Brand sweetened condensed milk
1/3 cup bourbon
7 ½ cups powdered sugar
½ cup pecans, chopped fine
1 (6 oz) package semi-sweet chocolate chips
1 tablespoon melted paraffin
Pecan halves

Combine butter condensed milk and bourbon in a large mixing bowl; add sugar, and knead until mixture is well blended and does not stick to hands.. Knead in chopped pecans. Shape into 1 inch balls. Combine chocolate chips and paraffin in top of a double boiler; place over hot water, stirring until chocolate is melted. Using a toothpick, dip each ball of candy into chocolate mixture. Place on waxed paper. Remove toothpick, and gently press a pecan half on each ball. Makes about 6 dozens.

CREAMY CARAMELS

½ cup finely chopped nuts
2 cups sugar
¾ cup light corn syrup
½ cup butter or margarine
2 cups half and half

Butter square pan 8 x 8 inches. Spread nuts in pan. Heat sugar, corn syrup, butter and 1 cup of half and half to boiling in 3 quart saucepan over medium heat, stirring constantly. Stir in remaining half and half. Cook over medium heat, stirring frequently, to 245° on candy thermometer or until small amount of mixture dropped into very cold water forms a firm ball. Immediately spread over nuts in pan. Cool; cut into about 1 inch squares. Makes about 3 dozen.

SOUTHERN RUM BALLS

1 (12 oz) box vanilla wafers, crushed
1 cup each (chopped pecans and powdered sugar)
3 tablespoons each (cocoa and light Karo syrup)
½ cup rum

Combine all ingredients except powdered sugar, roll in small balls, then roll in powdered sugar. Makes about 60 balls. Keep covered in tins or jars.

DIVINITY

2 ½ cups sugar
½ cup white Karo syrup
1/8 teaspoon salt
2/3 cup water
2 egg whites
1 ½ cups chopped pecans
1 tablespoon vanilla

Combine sugar, karo, salt and water. Cook until a small amount forms a soft ball when dropped in cold water or candy thermometer registers 238°. Take out ½ cup of this mixture and cook the remainder until it forms a hard ball when dropped in cold water or registers 260° on a candy thermometer. Pour the ½ cup of syrup slowly over the stiffly beaten egg whites, beat constantly. Continue beating, add remaining syrup in small amounts, beating well. Add vanilla and nuts. Continue beating until mixture holds its shape when dropped from a spoon. Drop from a teaspoon onto a greased cookie sheets or waxed paper. Swirl each piece with a spoon to form a peak. Pitted dates are good stuffed with a small amount of divinity.

PARTY MINTS

1 (8 oz) package cream cheese, softened
2 (16 oz) boxes powdered sugar
1 teaspoon peppermint flavoring
Food coloring (your choice)

Gradually add cream cheese to sugar. Add food coloring and peppermint. The mixture will be very stiff. Form into balls and place on waxed paper. Flatten each ball with bottom of a glass. Dust with sugar if desired.

MERINGUE PUFFS

2 large egg whites, room temperature
1/3 cup white sugar
¼ cup powdered sugar
¼ teaspoon white vinegar

Line a baking pan with foil. Beat egg whites and vinegar until they turn white and hold soft peaks. Still beating, add the white sugar, keep beating, gradually adding the powdered sugar. Drop by teaspoonful of sticky meringue onto the baking sheet, scraping the meringue off the teaspoon with another spoon. Bake at 175° for 2 hours or until you can easily detach the meringue puffs from the foil.

DELICIOUS CANDY

1 stick butter
1 pound pecans
1 package white almond bark
1 (12 oz) package semi-sweet chocolate chips

Preheat oven to 300°. Melt butter and add pecans. Place in oven and toast pecans. Watch very carefully. It usually takes about 15 minutes. Stir frequently. It is easy to burn nuts. Dip toasted nuts from butter onto a dish to cool while you are melting you almond bark and chocolate chips. Melt almond bark in microwave. Start with about 90 seconds and stir. Microwave at short intervals until fully melted. Stir in chocolate chips. Most chips will melt but you will have to microwave a short time to finish melting them. Mixture should be very smooth.
Stir chocolate mixture into cooled toasted pecans. Drop with a teaspoon onto a piece of wax paper or foil.

EULA'S POTATO CANDY

½ cup mashed potatoes
2 boxes powdered sugar
Peanut butter, smooth or crunchy

Mix the potato and sugar until smooth and no lumps. Roll out flat and spread with a thin layer of peanut butter. Roll up like a jelly roll and wrap in wax paper or plastic wrap and chill in the refrigerator until firm. Slice into 1 inch piece when chilled and store in a covered container.

GOOD COCONUT CANDY

1 cup butter, melted
1 teaspoon vanilla
1 (16 oz) boxes powdered sugar
1 (15 oz) can Eagle Brand milk
2 cans flaked coconut
2 cups nuts, chopped

Combine the above ingredients and mix well. Shape into balls and store in the refrigerator until set.
COATING; 1 (12 oz) bag semi-sweet chocolate chips and ½ block paraffin. Melt the paraffin and chocolate chips in a double boiler and dip balls to coat. Set on wax paper to cool.

PEANUT BRITTLE

3 cups white sugar
1 cup white corn syrup
1 cup water
3 ½ cups raw Spanish peanuts
2 tablespoons butter
1 teaspoon vanilla
¼ teaspoon salt
1 tablespoon baking soda

Bring sugar, corn syrup and water to 260o or hard boil. Add peanuts. Reheat to 300° (this is a must). Add butter, vanilla, salt and soda; stir well. Pour into buttered shallow pan.

TRADITIONAL CANDIED PECANS

3 tablespoons butter, plus enough to coat pan
½ cup sugar
1 ½ cups pecan halves
1 teaspoon vanilla

Line baking sheet with foil. Butter foil. In heavy 10 inch skillet, melt 3 tablespoons butter over medium heat; stir in ½ cup sugar. Add 1 ½ cups pecan halves. Cook over medium - low heat; stirring constantly, 4-5 minutes or until sugar melts and turns rich golden brown. Remove skillet from heat, add vanilla and stir. Spread pecan mixture onto prepared baking sheet. Cool completely. Break pecan mixture into small pieces. Makes about 1 ½ cups.

CANDIED WALNUTS

1 cup brown sugar
½ cup each (white sugar and sour cream)
1 teaspoon vanilla extract
3-4 cups shelled walnuts (pecans may also be used)

Stir together sugars and sour cream in a 2 quart saucepan over medium heat until sugar is dissolved. Without stirring, bring to a boil until mixture reaches the soft-ball state 235°-240°. Remove from heat. Quickly stir in vanilla and nuts. Mix well. Spoon mixture onto a 10 x 15 inch baking sheet, lined with waxed paper. Let cool 2-3 hours. Remove nuts from waxed paper and place in serving dish.

HOMEMADE MARSHMALLOWS

2 teaspoons butter
3 envelopes un-flavored gelatin
1 cup cold water, divided
2 cups sugar
1 cup light corn syrup
1/8 teaspoon salt
1 teaspoon vanilla extract
Optional toppings (melted chocolate, crushed candies, chopped nuts, sprinkles, etc.)

Line a 13 x 9 inch pan with foil and grease the foil with butter; set aside. In a large metal bowl, sprinkle gelatin over ½ cup water; set aside. In a large heavy saucepan, combine the sugar, corn syrup, salt and remaining water. Bring to a boil, stirring occasionally. Cook, without stirring until a candy thermometer reads 240° (soft ball). Remove from heat and gradually add to gelatin. Beat on high speed until mixture is thick and volume is doubled, about 15 minutes. Beat in vanilla. Spread into prepared pan. Cover and let stand at room temperature for 6 hours or overnight. Using foil, lift marshmallows out of pan. With a knife or pizza cutter coated with cooking spray, cut into 1 inch squares. Dip or drizzle marshmallows with toppings if desired; coat with garnishes as desired. Roll other marshmallows in the garnishes of your choice. Store in an airtight container in a cool dry place.

WHITE FUDGE

1 teaspoon plus ¼ cup butter divided
2 ½ cups powdered sugar
2/3 cup milk
12 (1 oz each) white baking chocolate, chopped
¼ teaspoon almond extract
¾ cup sliced almonds, toasted
¼ cup each (chopped dried apricots, dried cherries and dried cranberries)

Line a 9 inch square pan with foil and grease the foil with butter; set aside. In a heavy saucepan, combine the powdered sugar, milk and remaining butter. Cook and stir over medium heat until combined. Bring to a boil; boil for 5 minutes without stirring. Reduce heat to low; stir in white chocolate and extract. Cook and stir until chocolate is melted. Remove from heat. Fold in almonds, apricots, cherries and cranberries. Immediately spread into prepared pan. Refrigerate for 2 hours or until set. Using foil, lift fudge out of pan. Discard foil, cut fudge into 1 inch squares. Store in refrigerator. Makes about 2 pounds.

LEMON BARS

CRUST
2 cups all-purpose flour
1 cup powdered sugar
2 sticks butter, softened

FILLING
3 eggs, beaten
1 cup sugar
2 teaspoons each (lemon juice and flour)
½ teaspoon vanilla

Prepare crust; combine crust ingredients and pat into bottom of an 8 inch baking pan. Bake at 350° for 15-20 minutes. Cool. Combine filling ingredients and pour over cooled crust and bake at 350° for 25 minutes. Cool.

LEMON CREAM CHEESE FROSTING
1 (3 oz) package cream cheese, softened
1 teaspoon lemon juice
1 ½ cups powdered sugar
½ teaspoon grated lemon rind

Combine all ingredients and beat until smooth. Spread on cooled filling. Cut into bars.

ORANGE COCONUT BALLS

3 cups vanilla wafers, crushed fine
2 cups flaked coconut
1 cup pecans, chopped fine
1 (6 oz) can orange juice, concentrate thawed

Combine all ingredients and shape into bite-size balls. Roll in crushed vanilla wafer crumbs. Refrigerate in an air tight container.

CREAM CHEESE COOKIES

1 (8 oz) package cream cheese
1 ¾ cups all-purpose flour
1 tablespoon sugar
1 cup pecans, chopped fine
½ cup butter, softened
1 teaspoon vanilla extract
¼ teaspoon salt
Powdered sugar

Cream the butter and cream cheese together. Beat in vanilla. Combine the flour sugar and salt; add to creamed mixture. Stir in pecans. Shape tablespoonful into 2 inch logs. Place 2 inches apart on an un-greased baking sheet. Bake at 375° for 12-14 minutes or until lightly browned. Roll warm cookies in powdered sugar; cool. Makes 2 dozen.

NO - BAKE OAT COOKIES

¼ cup quick cooking oats
1 cup flaked coconut
1 teaspoon vanilla extract
½ cup milk
¼ cup butter or margarine
2 cups sugar
3 tablespoons cocoa

Combine oats and coconut; set aside. In a saucepan, combine milk and butter. Stir in sugar and cocoa; mix well. Bring to a boil. Add oat mixture, stirring constantly. Cook for 1 minute. Remove from heat; stir in vanilla. Drop by tablespoonful 1 inch apart onto waxed paper; cool. Makes about 3 dozen.

CHOCOLATE CAKE MIX COOKIES

1 box German chocolate cake mix, with pudding mix included
1 (6 ox) package semi-sweet chocolate chips
½ cup each (rolled oats, raisins and oil)
2 eggs, beaten

Combine all ingredients; blend well. Drop dough by teaspoonful 2 inches apart onto an un-greased cookie sheet. Bake at 350° for 8-10 minutes or until set. Cool 1 minute; remove from cookie sheet.

PECAN BLONDIES WITH BUTTER FROSTING

BARS
1 cup sugar
½ cup each (brown sugar, softened butter and chopped pecans)
1 teaspoon vanilla
2 eggs
1 ½ cups all-purpose flour
1 teaspoon baking powder
½ teaspoon salt

FROSTING
2 tablespoons butter (do not use margarine)
2 cups powdered sugar
¼ teaspoon vanilla
2-4 tablespoons milk

GARNISH; 36 pecan halves

Grease 13 x 9 inch pan. In a large bowl, combine white and brown sugars and ½ cup butter; beat until light and fluffy. Add 1 teaspoon vanilla and eggs; blend well. Add flour, baking powder and salt; mix well. Stir in ½ cup pecans. Spread in bottom of greased pan. Bake at 350° for 25-30 minutes or until toothpick inserted in center comes out clean. Cool 1 hour or until completely cooled. Heat 2 tablespoons butter in medium saucepan over medium heat until light golden brown. Remove from heat. Stir in powdered sugar, ¼ teaspoon vanilla and enough milk for desired spreading consistency; blend until smooth. Spread over cooled bars. Arrange pecan halves over frosting. Cut into bars.

SNICKER BAR COOKIES

1 cup each (white and brown sugar, softened butter and peanut butter)
2 teaspoons vanilla extract
2 eggs, beaten
3 cups all-purpose flour
1 teaspoon each (baking powder and baking soda)
1 (16 oz) package snicker candy bars (small)

Combine the sugars and butter in a bowl, beat until fluffy. Beat in peanut butter, vanilla and eggs. In another bowl, combine flour, baking powder and soda; add to batter; mix well. Cut candy bars into 1/3; wrap dough around each piece; arrange on greased baking sheet and baking at 350° for 12-18 minutes. Makes about 30 cookies.

FRUITCAKE COOKIES

8 ounces candied green cherries, chopped
8 ounces candied red cherries, chopped
8 ounces candied pineapple, chopped
1 pound golden raisins
10 tablespoons butter, melted
1 cup brown sugar
1 cup sherry or wine
3 eggs
3 cups all-purpose flour
1 teaspoon ground cloves
2 teaspoons cinnamon
1 teaspoon baking soda
1 tablespoon buttermilk
1 teaspoon vanilla extract
8 ounces almonds, chopped
8 ounces pecans, chopped
Dash of nutmeg
Dash of allspice

In a large bowl soak the fruits in the sherry for 6 or more hours. In a separate bowl beat the eggs, butter and sugar. Combine the flour with the spices and add to the brown sugar mixture. Dissolve the baking soda in the buttermilk. Add to the batter along with the vanilla, nuts and soaked fruit. Chill for 15 minutes. Preheat the oven to 325°. Drop the batter by rounded teaspoonful onto a baking sheet. Bake for 15-20 minutes. Store in an air tight container. Cookies will stay fresh for 3 weeks.

KIM'S FAVORITE COOKIES

2 cups white sugar
2 sticks butter, softened
1 (15 oz) container ricotta cheese
2 large eggs
4 cups all-purpose flour
2 tablespoons baking powder
2 teaspoons vanilla extract
1 teaspoon salt

FROSTING

1 ½ cups powdered sugar
3 tablespoons milk
Sprinkles for decorating

Preheat the oven to 350°. For the cookies, in a large bowl with a mixer on low speed, beat the sugar and butter until fluffy. Beat in ricotta, vanilla and eggs at medium speed until well combined. Reduce the speed to low. Add the flour, baking powder and salt; beat until soft dough forms. Drop the dough by tablespoonful about 2 inches apart onto an un-greased baking sheet. Bake 15 minutes, or until the cookies are light golden. (cookies will be soft). Remove the cookies to a wire rack to cool. For the frosting, stir the powdered sugar and milk in a small bowl until smooth. Spread the icing on the cookies; decorate with the sprinkles. Set the cookies aside for the icing to firm.

POTATO CHIP COOKIES

1 cup light brown sugar
1 cup white sugar
2 sticks butter, softened
2 eggs, beaten
1 cup potato chips, crushed fine
½ cup nuts, chopped (any kind) optional
2 cups all-purpose flour
2 teaspoons vanilla extract
1 teaspoon baking soda
Powdered sugar

Preheat oven to 350°. In a large bowl beat the sugars and butter until fluffy. Beat in the eggs. In a separate bowl sift the flour with the baking soda; add to the creamed butter mixture. Stir in the vanilla, potato chips and nuts. Drop by teaspoonful 3 inches apart on un-greased baking sheets. Bake for 10-12 minutes. When cool, sprinkle with the powdered sugar.

VANILLA - MAPLE CHIP COOKIES

3 cups all-purpose flour
2 teaspoons baking soda
2 cups each (vanilla or white chips and brown sugar)
½ cup each (chopped pecans and butter softened)
1 cup vegetable oil
2 eggs
1 teaspoon each (vanilla and maple flavoring)

FROSTING
¼ cup butter or margarine, softened
4 cups powdered sugar
4-5 tablespoons milk
3 ½ cups pecan halves
1 teaspoon maple flavoring

Cream the oil, brown sugar and butter together. Add eggs, beating well. Beat in vanilla and maple flavoring. Combine the flour and baking soda; add to cream mixture. Stir in vanilla chips and pecans. Drop by rounded tablespoonful 2 inches apart onto an un-greased baking sheet. Bake at 350° for 8-10 minutes or until golden brown. Cool for 2 minutes. In a mixing bowl, cream butter and powdered sugar. Beat in maple flavoring and enough milk to achieve spreading consistency. Frost cooled cookies. Top each with a pecan half. Makes about 7 dozen.

GOOD APPLE - OATMEAL - COOKIES

1 ½ cups flour
½ cup each (apples chopped and white sugar)
3 cups old-fashion oats
1 teaspoon each (vanilla and baking soda)
2 teaspoons ground cinnamon
2 eggs
1 cup each (brown sugar and softened butter)

In a mixing bowl, cream butter and sugars. Beat in eggs and vanilla. Combine the flour, cinnamon and soda; add to creamed mixture and mix well. Fold in oats and apples. Drop by rounded tablespoonful 2 inch apart onto un-greased baking sheets. Bake at 350° for 10-12 minutes. Let stand for 1 minute. Makes about 4 dozen.

ITALIAN CHRISTMAS COOKIES

1 cup butter (not margarine) softened
2 cups sugar
3 eggs
1 carton (15 oz) ricotta cheese
2 teaspoon vanilla extract
4 cups all-purpose flour
1 teaspoon each (salt and baking soda)

FROSTING
½ cup butter (not margarine) softened
3-4 cups powdered sugar
½ teaspoon vanilla extract
3-4 tablespoons milk
Colored sprinkles

In a mixing bowl cream butter and sugar. Add the eggs, 1 at a time, beating well after each addition. Beat in ricotta and vanilla. Combine flour, salt and baking soda; gradually add to creamed mixture. Drop by rounded teaspoonful 2 inches apart onto a greased baking sheet. Bake at 350° for 10-12 minutes or until lightly browned. Remove to wire racks to cool. In a mixing bowl cream butter, sugar and vanilla. Add enough milk until frosting reaches spreading consistency. Frost cooled cookies and immediately decorate with sprinkles. Store in refrigerator. Makes about 8 dozen.

PECAN CHRISTMAS COOKIES

1 cup butter or margarine, softened
1 teaspoon vanilla extract
½ cup powdered sugar
2 ½ cups all-purpose flour
¼ teaspoon salt
¾ cup pecans, chopped fine
Additional powdered sugar

In a mixing bowl, cream the butter, sugar and vanilla; mix well. Combine the flour and salt; add to creamed mixture. Stir in pecans. Chill. Roll dough into 1 inch balls and place on an un-greased baking sheet. Bake at 350° for 10-12 minutes. Roll in powdered sugar while warm. Cool and roll in sugar again. Makes about 4 dozen.

GLAZED FRESH APPLE COOKIES

2 cups all-purpose flour
1 teaspoon baking soda
½ cup vegetable oil
1 1/3 cups brown sugar
½ teaspoon each (salt and ground cloves)
1 teaspoon cinnamon
¼ teaspoon nutmeg
1 egg
1 cup each (chopped nuts, un-peeled chopped apples and chopped raisins)
¼ cup apple juice

Mix flour with soda. Mix oil, sugar, salt, cinnamon, cloves, nutmeg and egg until well blended. Stir in half of flour mixture, then nuts, apple and raisins. Blend in apple juice, then remaining flour mixture. Drop tablespoonful of dough 2 inches apart onto a greased cookie sheet. Bake at 400° for 11-15 minutes or until done. While cookies are still hot spread thinly with glaze. Makes about 3 ½ dozen.

GLAZE
1 ½ cups powdered sugar
1 tablespoon butter, softened
¼ teaspoon vanilla extract
1/8 teaspoon salt
2 ½ tablespoons light cream

Mix all ingredients and spread on hot cookies

ALMOND BARK COOKIES

1 package almond bark coating
2 cups each (Rice Krispies, corn flakes and chopped walnuts)
3 cups miniature marshmallows
1 cup coconut

Melt almond bark in double boiler. When melted, mix all ingredients together and drop tablespoonful on wax paper. (you can also freeze them).

BUTTERSCOTCH CASHEW BARS

2 ½ cups all-purpose flour
¾ cup plus 2 tablespoons brown sugar
1 cup plus 2 tablespoons butter, softened
¾ teaspoon salt

TOPPING
1 (10-11 oz) package butterscotch chips
½ cup plus 2 tablespoons light corn syrup
1 ½ cups salted cashew halves
3 tablespoons butter

Cream butter and brown sugar together. Combine flour and salt; add to creamed mixture just until combined. Press into a greased 15 x 10 inch baking dish and bake at 350° for 10-12 minutes or until lightly browned. Combine butterscotch chips, corn syrup, butter and water in saucepan. Cook and stir until chips and butter are melted. Spread over crust. Sprinkle with cashews; press down lightly. Bake at 350o for 11-13 minutes or until topping is bubbly and lightly browned; cool. Cut into bars. Makes 3 ½ dozen.

ORANGE COOKIES

1 ½ cups brown sugar
¾ cup butter
2 eggs, beaten
1 teaspoon vanilla
2 ½ cups flour
½ teaspoon each (soda and salt)
½ cup buttermilk
1 ½ teaspoons orange rind
1 cup pecans, chopped

GLAZE
½ cup orange juice
1 cup white syrup

Cream sugar and butter. Add eggs and vanilla. Add flour, soda and salt together. Add to cream mixture alternately with buttermilk. Add orange rind and pecans. Mix together thoroughly. Drop on greased cookie sheet and bake at 350° for 12 minutes. Glaze.

MELT - IN - YOUR - MOUTH COOKIES

COOKIES
2 sticks butter, softened
¾ cup white sugar
1 teaspoon almond extract
2 cups all-purpose flour
½ teaspoon baking powder

GLAZE
1 ½ cups powdered sugar
1 teaspoon almond extract
4-5 teaspoons water
Red food coloring
Sliced almonds

For the cookies; Combine the butter, sugar, almond extract, flour and baking powder in a large bowl. With an electric mixer, beat at medium speed, scraping the bowl often until creamy. Drop the dough by rounded teaspoonful 2 inches apart onto an un-greased baking sheet. Flatten the balls to ¼ inch thickness with the bottom of a buttered glass dipped into sugar. Bake at 400° for 7-9 minutes, or until edges are lightly browned. Cool for 1 minute on the baking sheet. Remove and cool completely and glaze.

OATMEAL RAISIN COOKIES

¾ cup each (sugar and all-purpose flour)
¼ cup brown sugar
½ cup each (soft butter, chopped nuts and raisins)
½ teaspoon each (vanilla, cinnamon and baking soda)
1 egg
¾ cup all-purpose flour
¼ teaspoon salt
1 ½ cups quick-cooking rolled oats

Grease cookie sheets. In a large bowl, combine sugar, brown sugar and butter; beat until light and fluffy. Add vanilla and egg; blend well. Add flour, baking soda, cinnamon and salt; mix well. Stir in oats, raisins and nuts. Drop dough by rounded teaspoonful 2 inches apart onto a greased cookie sheets. Bake at 375° for 7-10 minutes or until edges are light golden brown. Cool 1 minute; remove from cookie sheets.

PECAN PIE BARS

2 cups flour
1 ½ cups powdered sugar
1 cup each (butter, almond brickle chips and chopped pecans)
1 (14 oz) can sweetened condensed milk
1 egg, beaten
1 teaspoon vanilla extract

Combine flour and powdered sugar in bowl, cut in butter until crumbly. Press in a 9 x 13 inch greased baking pan and bake at 350° for 15 minutes. Beat condensed milk, egg and vanilla in a small bowl. Stir in almond brickle chips and pecans. Spread over baked crust. Bake for 25 minutes longer or until golden brown, cool. Cut into bars.

BUTTERY MELT - AWAY COOKIES

1 cup butter, softened
½ cup powdered sugar
2 ¼ cups cake flour
¼ teaspoon salt
1 teaspoon vanilla extract
½ cup powdered sugar, plus enough to sprinkle on top

Cream butter and powdered sugar in mixing bowl. Add flour, salt and vanilla; mix well. Chill for 1 hour. Drop by tablespoonful 3 inches apart onto a cookie sheet lined with foil. Bake at 350° for 10 minutes or until set (but not brown). Remove from pan. Sprinkle powdered sugar over top. Makes about 3 dozen.

LEMON COOKIES

1 box lemon cake mix
1 stick butter, softened
1 (8 oz) package cream cheese, softened
1 egg

Mix all ingredients, blending well. Drop by teaspoonful onto a lightly greased cookie sheet and bake at 375° for 10-12 minutes.

HEATH BARS

1 cup brown sugar
1 cup butter
6 ounces chocolate chips
Soda crackers
Pecans, chopped

Line cookie pan (sides) with foil. Grease foil with a little butter and place soda crackers side by side on foil. Heat together brown sugar and butter. Stir well until butter is complete dissolved into sugar. Pour over crackers and bake at 400° for 5 minutes. Remove from oven and sprinkle chocolate chips over the entire pan. Let stand until melted. Spread like frosting. Sprinkle with chopped nuts.

ENGLISH TOFFEE BARS

1 cup each (butter and brown sugar)
1 ½ cups pecans, chopped
1 (12 oz) package milk chocolate chips
Graham crackers

Line a 10 x 15 inch jelly roll pan with foil. Butter and line with graham crackers. In sauce pan bring butter and brown sugar to a boil (2 minutes). Pour over crackers and bake at 350° for 8 minutes. Remove from oven and sprinkle pecans and chocolate chips over top. Allow chips to melt, then spread smooth with a frosting knife. Refrigerate. Cut into squares. Makes about 24 bars.

PEANUT CARAMEL BARS

1 (14 oz) package caramels
¼ cup water
¾ cup peanut butter, divided
4 cups Cherrios
½ cup butter or margarine, softened
1 cup each (salted peanuts and milk chocolate chips)

Combine caramels, water ½ cup peanut butter, place in microwave on high for 1 minute. Stir, cook 1-2 minutes longer or until melted. Add cereal and peanuts, coat well. Spread into a greased 13 x 9 inch pan; set aside. In another microwave bowl, heat chips, butter and remaining peanut butter on high for 45-60 seconds or until smooth. Spread over mixture. Refrigerate before cutting. Makes about 3 dozen.

DELICIOUS ORANGE BARS

2 ¼ cups flour, divided
½ cup powdered sugar
2 cups white sugar
1 cup butter, softened
4 large eggs
1 teaspoon baking powder

Combine 2 cups flour and powder sugar. Cut in butter blend until mixture is crumbly. Press evenly into bottom of a 13 x 9 inch baking pan. Bake 20 minutes, or until lightly browned; in a bowl whisk together the sugar and eggs; mix well. Combine ¼ cup flour and baking powder, add to sugar mixture, stirring to combine. Pour onto hot baked crust, and bake at 350° for 25 minutes or until set. Sprinkle with powdered sugar.

CHOCOLATE CHERRY BARS

1 box Devil's good cake mix, with pudding added
1 (21 oz) can cherry pie filling
2 eggs, beaten
1 teaspoon almond extract

FROSTING
1 cup sugar
1/3 cup milk
1 (6 oz) package semi-sweet chocolate chips
5 tablespoons butter

Grease and flour a 15 x 10 inch baking pan. In a large bowl, combine all bar ingredients; stir until well blended. Spread in pan. Bake at 350° for 25-30 minutes or until a toothpick inserted in the middle comes out clean. In a small saucepan, combine sugar, milk and butter; mix well. Bring to a boil. Boil 1 minute, stirring constantly. Remove from heat; stir in chocolate chips until smooth. Pour and spread over warm bars. Cool 1 ½ hours or until completely cooled. Cut into bars.

ENGLISH TOFFEE

½ cup each (semi-sweet chocolate chips and vanilla or white chips)
1 cup each (milk chocolate chips, chopped walnuts and slivered almonds)
2 cups butter plus ½ teaspoon
2 cups sugar
1 ½ teaspoons vegetable oil

Butter a 15 x 10 inch baking dish with ½ teaspoon butter. In a heavy saucepan over medium heat bring sugar and remaining butter to a boil, stirring constantly. Cover and cook for 2-3 minutes. Un-cover; add almonds. Cook and stir with a spoon until a candy thermometer reads 300° (hard crack stage) and mixture is golden brown. Pour into prepared pan (do not scrape sides of pan). Cook for 1-2 minutes. Spread chocolate over top. Sprinkle with walnuts; press down with the back of a spoon. Chill for 10 minutes. In a saucepan, melt semi-sweet chips, stir until smooth. Drizzle over walnuts. Cover and refrigerate for 1-2 hours. Break into pieces. Make about 2 ½ pounds.

VANILLA FUDGE ICE CREAM BARS

42 Oreo cookies
½ stick butter
½ gallon vanilla ice cream
1 cup cashews
1 (8-9 oz) carton cool whip
Jar fudge topping

Crush cookies, save ½ cup of crumbs. Mix remaining crumbs with melted butter. Spread evenly in bottom of a 9 x 13 inch pan. Soften ice cream and spread over crust. Place in freezer until firm. Spread fudge topping on ice cream. Sprinkle with cashews. Spread cool whip on top. Sprinkle with remaining cookie crumbs. Cover with foil and freeze. Makes 12-15.

TOFFEE BARS

1 cup each (butter and brown sugar)
1 egg yolk
2 cups flour
10 (1 oz) Hershey bars---Plus chocolate ice cream topping.
½ cup chopped nuts

Melt butter; add sugar and egg. Add flour and pour into a 9 x 13 inch greased pan and bake at 350° for 20 minutes. Place candy bars over toffee mixture to melt; spread chocolate evenly over top. Sprinkle nuts over chocolate. Let cool and cut into bars.

GOOD PUMPKIN BARS

1 (15 oz) can pumpkin
1 cup vegetable oil
2 ½ cups powdered sugar
1 (3 oz) package cream cheese, softened
1 cup nuts, pecans or walnuts, chopped
½ cup butter, softened
4 eggs, beaten
2 cups self-rising flour
½ teaspoon cinnamon
2 cups sugar
2 teaspoons baking powder

In a large bowl, mix together the sugar, baking powder, flour and cinnamon; set aside. In another bowl stir together the eggs, pumpkin and oil until mixed good. Stir pumpkin mixture into flour mixture until combined, stir in nuts. Spread into an un-greased 15 x 10 inch baking dish. Bake about 25-30 minutes or until done. Cool completely. For the frosting; beat the cream cheese and butter for 30-35 seconds with an electric mixer. Gradually beat in powdered sugar until smooth. Spread over cooled pumpkin bars.

CREAM CHEESE PASTRY AND FILLING

PASTRY
2 (3 oz) packages of cream cheese
2 sticks butter, softened
2 cups flour

Beat cream cheese with butter until well blended. Add flour ½ at a time. Work dough until smooth. Shape into 1 inch balls. In a small muffin tin, place a ball in each cup and press down in middle with thumb.

FILLING
1 stick butter, softened
1 cup walnuts, chopped
1 cup sugar
2 eggs, separated
¼ teaspoon salt
1 teaspoon vanilla
1 cup dried cranberries

Cream together the sugar, salt, vanilla and butter. Add beaten yolks, add nuts and cranberries, fold in beaten whites, add to mixture, fill cups and bake at 350°-15 minutes.

DELICIOUS MINT BROWNIES

FILLING
1 (8 oz) package cream cheese, softened
¼ cup sugar
1 egg
1 teaspoon mint extract
4 drops green food color

BROWNIES
1 cup butter or margarine
4 ounces un-sweetened chocolate, cut into pieces
2 cups sugar
2 teaspoons vanilla
4 eggs
1 cup all-purpose flour

FROSTING
2 tablespoons each (butter, corn syrup and water)
2 ounces un-sweetened chocolate, cut into pieces
1 teaspoon vanilla
1 cup powdered sugar

FILLING;
Grease and flour a 13 x 9 inch pan. In a small bowl, combine cream cheese and ¼ cup sugar; beat until smooth. Add 1 egg, mint extract and food color; mix well. Set aside. BROWNIES; In large saucepan, melt 1 cup butter and 4 ounces chocolate over low heat stirring constantly. Remove from heat; cool 15 minutes or until slightly cooled. Stir 2 cups sugar and 2 teaspoons vanilla into chocolate mixture. Add 4 eggs one at a time, beating well after each addition. Stir in flour; mix well. Spread in greased and floured pan. Pour filling over brownie mixture. Swirl filling into brownie mixture. Bake at 350° for 45-50 minutes or until set. Cool 1 hour or until completely cooled.

FROSTING

In medium saucepan, combine 2 tablespoons butter, corn syrup and water; bring to a rolling boil. Remove from heat. Add 2 ounces of chocolate; stir until melted. Stir in 1 teaspoon vanilla and powdered sugar; beat until smooth. Frost cooled brownies. Cut into bars. Store in refrigerator.

RASPBERRY ALMOND BARS

1 cup all-purpose flour
½ cup each (butter, sugar, seedless raspberry jam)
1 (10-12 oz) vanilla or white chips, divided
2 eggs
¼ cup almonds, sliced
½ teaspoon salt
1 teaspoon almond extract

In a saucepan, melt butter. Remove from heat; add 1 cup chips (do not stir). In a small mixing bowl, beat eggs until foamy; gradually add sugar. Stir in chip mixture and almond extract. Combine flour and salt; add egg mixture just until combined. Spread half of the batter into a greased 9 inch baking dish and bake at 325o for 15-20 minutes or until golden brown. In a small saucepan over low heat; melt jam; Spread over warm crust. Stir remaining chips into the remaining batter; drop by teaspoonful over the jam layer. Sprinkle with almonds and bake at 325° for 30-35 minutes longer or until a toothpick inserted in the center comes out clean. Cool. Cut into bars.

MAPLE NUT BARS

1 (2 pound) package of powdered sugar
1 (3 oz) package vanilla pudding mix (cook kind)
2 teaspoons maple flavoring
½ cup evaporated milk
1 cup peanut butter
2 ½ cups cocktail peanuts
2 cups butter or margarine
1 (12 oz) package semi-sweet chocolate chips
1 (11.5 oz) package milk chocolate chips

Line a 15 x 10 inch baking pan with foil. Spray with nonstick cooking spray. In a saucepan, melt chocolate chips and 1 cup butter over low heat, stirring often. Remove saucepan from heat, add peanut butter; mix well. Spread ½ of mixture in prepared foil. Freeze 10 minutes or until set. Place pan in refrigerator. Stir peanuts into remaining chocolate mixture. Set aside. Melt remaining 1 cup butter in a large saucepan over low heat. Stir in the evaporated milk. Stir in pudding mix. Cool until mixture is slightly thickened, stirring constantly. (do not boil). Remove saucepan from heat. Add powdered sugar and maple flavoring, mix well. Cool 10 minutes. Spread pudding mixture over chilled chocolate layer. Refrigerate 30 minutes. Stir in reserved chocolate peanut mixture. Drop by teaspoonful onto the chilled pudding layer; spread to cover. Refrigerate at least 3-4 hours or until firm. Cut into bars.

GOOD CREAM BARS

CRUST
2 cups graham crackers, crushed
1 cup flaked coconut
½ cup each (chopped nuts and melted butter)
5 tablespoons sugar
¼ cup cocoa
1 teaspoon vanilla

Mix cocoa with sugar; stir in remaining ingredients. Press into an ungreased 9 x 13 inch pan. Chill

FILLING
4 squares of semi-sweet chocolate
3 tablespoons milk
2 cups powdered sugar
1 tablespoon vanilla
¼ cup plus 1 tablespoon butter, melted
1 box instant vanilla pudding mix

Mix pudding mix, milk, powdered sugar and ¼ cup melted butter; spread on crust. Chill. Melt chocolate with remaining butter; spread over sugar mixture; chill. Cut into bars.

PECAN BARS

CRUST
1 cup flour
½ cup butter
¼ cup powdered sugar

FILLING
2 eggs
2 tablespoons flour
¾ cup Karo syrup
1/3 cup brown sugar
½ teaspoon each (cinnamon, nutmeg, vanilla and salt)
1 cup pecans

Mix crust ingredients and press into a 13 x 9 inch greased pan and bake at 350° for 15 minutes. Beat eggs, in remaining filling ingredients and bake for 25-30 minutes longer. Cool before cutting.

APPLE BROWNIES

2 sticks butter, melted
2 cups sugar
2 eggs
1 cup chopped nuts
6 medium apples, peeled and sliced thin
2 cups all-purpose flour
1 teaspoon each (baking soda and baking powder)
½ teaspoon salt
2 teaspoons cinnamon
Powdered sugar

In a bowl combine the butter, sugar and eggs and mix well. Stir in the nuts and apples. Combine the flour, baking powder, soda, salt and cinnamon. Add to the butter mixture in 3 parts, mixing well after each addition. Pour into a 13 x 9 inch greased and floured pan. Bake and serve alone, with ice cream or whipped cream.

CINNAMON TOFFEE BARS

BARS
1 cup each (brown sugar, chopped nuts and butter softened)
1 egg, separated
2 cups all-purpose flour
1 teaspoon cinnamon

GLAZE
½ cup semi-sweet chocolate chips
2 teaspoons shortening

In a large bowl, combine brown sugar and butter; beat until light and fluffy. Add egg yolk; blend well. Add flour and cinnamon; mix well. Press dough in an un-greased 15 x 10 inch baking pan. In a small bowl, slightly beat egg white; brush over dough. Sprinkle with nuts; press lightly into dough. Bake at 350° for 15-20 minutes or until light golden brown. Cool 30 minutes or until completely cooled.

EGGNOG TRUFFLES

8 ounce white chocolate, divided
4 ounces cream cheese, softened
¼ cup powdered sugar
¼ teaspoon each (nutmeg and rum extract)

Melt the white chocolate as directed on package. Beat cream cheese, powdered sugar, nutmeg and extract in a large bowl with an electric mixer on medium speed until well blended and smooth. Add melted chocolate; beat until well mixed; cover. Refrigerate 4 hours or until firm. Shape into 24 (about ¾ inch) balls. Place on wax paper-lined tray. Refrigerate until ready to dip. Coat only 12 truffles at a time. Melt 4 ounces of the remaining chocolate in small microwavable bowl on medium 1 ½ minutes, stirring after 1 minute. Using fork to dip 1 truffle at a time into the chocolate. Place on wax paper-lined tray. Sprinkle truffles with nutmeg. Repeat with remaining 4 ounces of chocolate and remaining truffles. Refrigerate 1 hour or until chocolate is set. Store truffles in refrigerator. Makes 2 dozen.

EGGNOG COOKIES

2 ¼ cups flour
1 teaspoon each (baking powder and vanilla)
½ teaspoon each (ground cinnamon and ground nutmeg)
1 ¼ cups white sugar
¾ cup butter, softened
½ cup eggnog
2 large egg yolks

Preheat oven to 300°. In a bowl, combine all the dry ingredients together, except sugar. In a large bowl; cream together the sugar and butter until it resembles a grainy paste. Add eggnog, vanilla and egg yolks and beat at medium speed until smooth. Add the flour mixture and beat at low speed until blended. Do not over-mix. Drop by teaspoonful onto an un-greased baking sheet, 1 inch apart. Sprinkle light with additional nutmeg. Bake for 23-25 minutes or until bottoms turn light brown. Transfer from pans immediately to cool.

CARAMEL APPLE BARS

CRUST
½ cup each (butter, and chopped pecans)
¼ cup vegetable oil
1 cup each (brown sugar and quick-cooking oats)
1 ¾ cups all-purpose flour
1 teaspoon each (salt and soda)

FILLING
4 ½ cups apples, peeled and chopped
3 tablespoons each (all-purpose flour and butter)
1 (14 oz) package caramels, un-wrapped

Prepare crust; cream butter, oil and brown sugar until fluffy. Add flour, oats, salt and soda, mix well. Stir in pecans. Set aside 2 cups. Press remaining oat mixture into the bottom of an un-greased 13 x 9 inch baking pan.

Prepare filling; Toss apples with flour and spoon over the crust. Melt caramels and butter over low heat and drizzle over apples. Top with the reserved oat mixture. Bake at 400° for 25-30 minutes or until lightly browned. Cool before cutting into bars.

CHESS BARS

½ cup butter
2 tablespoons each (sugar and all-purpose flour)
2 eggs
1 ½ cups brown sugar
1 teaspoon baking powder
1 tablespoon grated lemon rind
1 cup pecans, chopped

Cream butter and 2 tablespoons sugar until light and fluffy. Add 1 cup flour, mix well. Pat dough into the bottom of a 9 inch cake pan and bake at 350° for 10 minutes while you make the filling. Beat eggs well; add brown sugar, flour, baking powder and lemon rind and blend well. Stir in pecans and pour over partially baked pastry layer. Bake at 350° for 25 minutes. When lightly cooled cut into small bars.

CHOCOLATE CARAMEL BARS

1 box chocolate cake mix, pudding included
1 cup evaporated milk
½ cup butter or margarine, melted
35-40 vanilla caramels
1 (12 oz) package miniature semi-sweet chocolate pieces

Grease a 13 x 9 inch baking pan. In a large bowl, combine cake mix, butter and 2/3 cup of milk, mix well. Spread half of batter (about 2 cups) in the greased pan. Bake at 350° for 25 minutes. In a small saucepan, heat caramels with remaining 1/3 cup milk over low heat until melted, stirring constantly. Remove pan from oven; sprinkle with 1 cup of the chocolate pieces. Drizzle with caramel mixture. Drop remaining batter by heaping teaspoonful over caramel mixture. Sprinkle with remaining 2/3 cup of the chocolate pieces. Return to oven; bake at 350° for additional 20-25 minutes or until center is set. Cool 1 hour or until completely cooled. Cut into bars.

DELICIOUS LEMON BARS

BASE
2 cups flour
½ cup powdered sugar
1 cup butter or margarine, softened

FILLING
4 eggs, beaten
2 cups sugar
¼ cup each (flour and lemon juice)
1 teaspoon baking powder

FROSTING
1 cup powdered sugar
2-4 tablespoons lemon juice

In a large bowl, combine flour, powdered sugar and butter; beat at low speed until crumbly. Press mixture evenly in bottom of an un-greased 13 x 9 inch baking pan. Bake at 350° for 20-30 minutes or until light golden brown. In a large bowl, combine all filling ingredients except lemon juice; blend well. Stir in ¼ cup lemon juice. Remove pan from oven. Pour filling over warm base. Bake an additional 25-30 minutes or until light golden brown. Cool 1 hour or until completely cooled. In a small bowl, combine 1 cup powdered sugar and enough lemon juice or desired spreading consistency; blend until smooth. Frost cooled bars. Cut into bars. Sprinkle with powdered sugar and garnish with lemon peel.

BREADS
ROLLS & BREAKFAST

SOURDOUGH STARTER

2 tablespoons yeast
4 cups flour
1 ½ cups warm water
½ cup instant potatoes
2 tablespoons sugar
1 ½ cups milk

Mix ingredients together in a non-mental container large enough to allow the mixture to double. Let mixture stand slightly covered for 2 days before using. Replenish starter with this recipe.

SOURDOUGH BREAD

2 ½ cups sourdough starter
2 quarts warm water
¾ cup yeast
1 ¼ cup sugar
2 ½ tablespoons salt
1 cup instant potato flakes
8 cups flour

Blend all ingredients together. Slowly add more flour until dough has an elastic, non-sticky texture. Shape into desired size loaves and let rise until double. Bake at 350° for 45 minutes.

TOMATO BREAD

4 ½ cups tomato juice
2 tablespoons butter
1 tablespoon each (basil and oregano)
½ cup sugar
4 teaspoon salt
½ cup each (oil and ketchup)
3 tablespoons yeast

Heat tomato juice, sugar, butter, basil, oregano and salt, then add oil, ketchup and yeast. Add flour to get the right consistency. Knead well. Let rise in warm place for 20 minutes. Punch down and let rise for 20 minutes more. Put in pans and let rise until double. Bake at 350° for 1 hour.

POPOVERS

1 ¼ cups each (milk and flour)
3 eggs
½ teaspoon salt

Preheat oven to 450°. Grease popover cups. Pour milk into medium size mixing bowl. Add flour and salt. With wire whisk beat until well blended. Add the eggs, 1 at a time. Beat just until completely blended after each addition. Pour batter into popover cups, filling ¾ full. Do not scrap bowl. Bake at 450° for 20 minutes. Reduce heat to 350° and continue baking 15-20 minutes or until golden brown. Serve immediately.

ANGEL BISCUITS

2 ½ cups flour
1 teaspoon each (salt and baking powder)
1 cup buttermilk
¼ cup warm water
1/8 cup sugar
½ cup shortening
1 package dry yeast

Dissolve yeast in warm water. Mix dry ingredients. Add shortening, stir in buttermilk and yeast. Refrigerate or roll out on a floured board and cut with a biscuit cutter. Place biscuits on greased cookie sheet. Bake at 400° for 10-12 minutes.

DINNER ROLLS

3 ½ cups flour
¼ cup sugar
1 egg
¼ cup shortening
1 package dry yeast
1 cup scalded milk
¼ cup warm water

Melt shortening into scalded milk. Mix yeast with warm water. Mix flour and sugar; add milk and shortening to flour mixture. Add egg, yeast and water. Put into warm bowl, greased with butter. Cover and chill for 2 hours or until it rises. Take dough out and roll out. Put some butter on top. Pull apart and roll in little balls on greased baking sheet. Let rise 1 hour more. Bake at 400° for 12-15 minutes.

CHEESE BREAD

½ cup margarine, melted
½ bottle Italian dressing
1 loaf French bread
Grated mozzarella cheese

Combine margarine and dressing. Cut bread in half the long way. Pour dressing mixture over bread; top with grated mozzarella cheese. Bake at 350° for about 12-15 minutes. Slice into serving size portions.

WHEAT BREAD

1 package dry yeast
½ cup each (warm water, shortening and wheat bran)
½ cup sugar
1 tablespoon salt
2 teaspoons sugar
2 cups water
3 tablespoons molasses
Flour

Mix warm water and 2 teaspoons sugar in cup. Add yeast and let rise in cup until comes to the top. In another pan, put 2 cups water, molasses, ½ cup sugar, salt, wheat bran and solid shortening. Add yeast and mix. Add flour until it kneads good. Let rise until double in size. Grease bread pans. Knead dough into 2 loaves and then grease the loaves with shortening. Put in pans and let rise until double in size. Bake at 350° for 45 minutes.

QUICK DELICIOUS ROLLS

2 cups self-rising flour
1 cup milk
1 teaspoon sugar
4 tablespoons mayonnaise

Mix all ingredients in a mixing bowl, about 2 minutes. Fill muffin tins 2/3 full and bake at 450° for 10 minutes or until golden brown.

MASHED POTATO ROLLS

1 package dry yeast
½ cup warm water
1 cup mashed potatoes
2 eggs
½ cup sugar
1 cup milk, scalded
2/3 cup shortening
1 teaspoon salt
5-6 cups flour

Mix yeast in warm water. In large bowl place potatoes, sugar, eggs, salt, shortening and milk. Add yeast and flour to make a stiff dough. Place in greased bowl and cover. Let stand 2 hours. Punch down and knead slightly. Shape into rolls and let rise 1 ½ hours or until double in bulk. Bake at 400° for 8 minutes.

YEAST ROLLS

2-3 cups all-purpose flour
1 package yeast
1 egg
1 cup boiling water
1/3 cup sugar
¼ cup each (shortening and margarine)
1 teaspoon salt

In a mixing bowl, pour the boiling water over the margarine and shortening. When the shortening and margarine have melted, add sugar. When liquid has cooled to lukewarm, add yeast and stir until dissolved. Add egg and salt to liquid. Sift flour into liquid, about ¾ cup at a time. Add enough flour to make a soft dough. Let rise or put into refrigerator until ready to use. Make rolls. Let rise. Bake at 350° for 10-15 minutes.

BEER ROLLS

2 cups Bisquick
3 tablespoons sugar
¾ cup warm beer (any kind)

Combine dry ingredients together. Add beer, mix until almost smooth. Grease muffin tins and fill 2/3 full. Let rise until dough is at top of muffin tin. Bake at 350° for 20-30 minutes or until brown.

RAISIN BREAD

3 cups flour
2 eggs, beaten
1 cup pecans, chopped
2 cups each (white raisins, water and sugar)
½ teaspoon salt
1 teaspoon vanilla
2 teaspoons baking soda

Mix raisins, water and soda in saucepan. Bring to a boil. Cool overnight in refrigerator. Combine with remaining ingredients. Grease 2 loaf pans. Filling slightly over half full. Bake at 350° for 1 hour. Best served hot.

ZUCCHINI BREAD

3 cups all-purpose flour
2 cups each (raw zucchini, peeled, grated, drained and sugar)
1 cup cooking oil
3 eggs
1 teaspoon each (vanilla extract, salt and baking soda)
3 ½ teaspoons cinnamon
¼ teaspoon baking powder
½ cup pecans, chopped

Beat eggs until foamy. Add oil, sugar and vanilla. Mix well; stir in grated zucchini. Add flour, salt, soda, cinnamon and baking powder. Add to egg mixture and blend well. Fold in nuts. Pour into 2 greased 9 x 5 inch loaf pans and bake at 325° for 1 hour.

PUMPKIN BREAD

3 ½ cups flour
1 (16 oz) can pumpkin
½ teaspoon baking powder
1 ½ teaspoon each (salt, ground allspice and cinnamon)
½ cups pecans, chopped
4 eggs
1 cup oil
3 cups sugar

Combine pumpkin, oil and eggs. Add dry ingredients plus nuts, blend thoroughly. Pour into 2 greased 9 x 5 inch loaf pans and bake at 300° for 1 hour.

PEAR BREAD

3 cups flour
3 eggs
1 ½ cups each (vanilla extract, salt, cinnamon and nutmeg)
1 ½ teaspoons baking soda
1 ½ cups each (sugar and corn oil)
½ teaspoon ground cloves
3 cups fresh pears, peeled and chopped fine

Combine sugar, corn oil, eggs and vanilla in a mixing bowl and beat until well blended. Mix flour, soda, salt, cinnamon, nutmeg and cloves together. Add to sugar mixture gradually, beating well after each addition. Add pears and stir until well mixed. Pour batter into 2 greased and floured loaf pans. Bake at 350° for 45-55 minutes or until loaves test done; do not over bake. Cool in pans 15 minutes. Turn onto racks to cool.

APPLE - WALNUT BREAD

3 cups all-purpose flour
2 cups sugar
1 cup vegetable oil
3 eggs
3 cups apples, chopped
1 cup walnuts, chopped
2 teaspoons vanilla extract
1 teaspoon each (salt, cinnamon and soda)

Combine sugar, oil, eggs and vanilla in bowl; mix well. Add dry ingredients; mix well. Stir in apples and walnuts. Pour into 2 greased and floured 5 x 9 inch loaf pans. Sprinkle with a small amount of additional sugar. Bake at 350° for 1 hour or until loaves test done. Remove from pans and cool on wire racks.

BANANA BREAD

3 ½ cups flour
4 eggs
2 cups bananas, mashed---nuts optional
1 1/3 cups sugar
4 teaspoons baking powder
½ teaspoon each (salt and soda)
2/3 cup margarine

Mix all together and bake in greased loaf pans at 350° for about 1 hour.

FRANK'S HOT WATER CORN BREAD

3 cups corn meal
1 teaspoon salt
½ cup onion, chopped
Boiling water

Mix corn meal, onion and salt. Add enough boiling water to get the consistency of mush. Drop by tablespoonful in hot grease and brown on both sides.

MEXICAN CORN BREAD

1 ½ cups corn meal
2 eggs
1 cup sour cream
1 cup cream-style corn
2/3 cup oil
3 teaspoons baking powder
1 tablespoon salt
2 green jalapeno peppers (seeds removed and chopped)
2 tablespoons green pepper, chopped
1 cup cheddar cheese, grated

Mix all ingredients, except cheese. Pour half of the mixture into hot, well greased pan. Sprinkle half of the cheese over batter. Add remaining corn meal mixture and top with the rest of the cheese. Bake at 350° for 1 hour.

SPOON BREAD

1 cup white corn meal
3 eggs, separated
1 cup buttermilk
3 tablespoons butter, melted
1 ½ cups boiling water
1 teaspoon salt
½ teaspoon baking soda
¼ teaspoon baking powder
½ teaspoon sugar

Combine meal, salt and sugar; scald with boiling water. Add butter, well beaten egg yolks, buttermilk, baking powder and soda; fold in stiffly beaten egg whites. Pour in a greased baking dish and bake at 350° for 40-45 minutes. Serve immediately.

SOUR CREAM CORN BREAD

1 cup self-rising corn meal mix
1 cup each (sour cream and cream-style corn)
2 eggs
½ cup margarine or vegetable oil

Combine all ingredients and mix well. Pour into a hot, well greased skillet and bake at 325° for about 30 minutes or until firm and light-medium brown.

JALAPENO CORN BREAD

1 ¼ cups plain corn meal
½ cup plain flour
1 tablespoon each (sugar and baking powder)
3 egg whites, beaten
1 whole egg, beaten
1 cup milk
1 (8 oz) can cream style corn
1 (4 oz) package sharp cheddar cheese
1 (4 oz) can green chilies, with juice and chopped
¼ cup onion, chopped
1 small fresh jalapeno pepper, minced
¾ cup salad oil
½ teaspoon salt

Grease a 9 x 13 inch baking pan. In a small bowl, mix corn meal, flour, sugar, baking powder and salt. In a large bowl, beat the remaining ingredients; then add the corn meal mixture to the milk mixture until barely moistened. Place the baking pan in the preheated oven at 450° for a couple of minutes to get hot; then pour in the corn bread batter. Bake for 30 minutes or until done. Cut in squares. Serve hot.

CORN FRITTERS

1 cup flour
1 teaspoon baking powder, plus ½ teaspoon salt
1 tablespoon of vegetable oil
1 2/3 cups fresh cut corn or canned
1 egg
5 tablespoons each (milk and sugar)

Mix dry ingredients together; add egg to milk and oil; mix with dry ingredients; stir in corn. Drop by tablespoonful in hot oil and fry until golden brown.

HOMEMADE BISCUITS

2 cups self-rising flour
2 tablespoons sugar
1 cup buttermilk
½ cup margarine
½ tablespoon baking powder

Mix all ingredients and roll into biscuits. Brush with butter on top. Bake at 400° until golden brown.

GRANDMA'S CORN BREAD

2 cups white cornmeal
¼ cup vegetable shortening
2 tablespoons all-purpose flour
2 teaspoons baking powder
1 egg
2 cups buttermilk
1 teaspoon salt
1 teaspoon baking soda

Melt shortening in a 9 inch baking pan in the oven, brushing sides of pan with melted shortening. Sift together dry ingredients; combine egg and buttermilk and stir into the dry ingredients along with melted shortening. Pour batter into hot pan. Bake at 450° for 20-25 minutes or until browned.

HUSH PUPPIES

1 ½ cups self-rising corn meal
1 medium onion, chopped
1 egg, well beaten
1 tablespoon sugar
Milk
Dash black pepper

Mix all ingredients except milk. Add enough milk to form balls. Drop from teaspoonful into hot fat. Cook until well browned and cooked throughout.

HASH BROWN BRUNCH BREAKFAST

1 (24 oz) package hash browns, thawed
2 pounds sausage or ham, cooked
½ cup butter or margarine, melted
2 cups cheddar cheese, shredded
8 eggs
2 cups mozzarella cheese
1 cup milk
½ teaspoon salt

Spread hash browns in a 13 x 9 inch pan or baking dish. Pour melted butter over them. Pat down, and bake at 425° for 25 minutes. Sprinkle cooked sausage over hash browns. Add shredded cheese. Beat eggs, milk and salt together. Pour over everything and bake at 350° for 40 minutes more.

OVERNIGHT BREAKFAST CASSEROLE

1 ½ pounds sausage, cooked
1 small can mushrooms
2 ½ cups milk
8 slices bread, cubed
2 cups cheddar cheese, grated
6 eggs
½ teaspoon salt
1 teaspoon dry mustard

Layer bread, sausage, cheese and mushrooms in a 9 x 13 inch pan. Combine eggs, mustard, salt and milk, pour over layers. Refrigerate overnight. Bake at 300° for 1 ½ hours.

SCRAMBLED EGGS LOADED

10 slices bacon, cooked crisp and crumbled
½ cup cheddar cheese, shredded
8 eggs
1 ¼ cups milk
1 teaspoon each (salt, dried onion and butter.

Beat eggs, milk, salt and onion until blended. Melt butter in skillet. Pour on egg mixture and reduce heat to low. Turn and cook all portions evenly. When eggs are cooked, transfer to serving bowl. Sprinkle with cheese and bacon. Serve immediately.

SPINACH AND CHEESE QUICHE

6 large eggs
½ cup milk
¾ cup Swiss cheese, shredded
1 (10 oz) box frozen spinach, thawed, squeezed and chopped
½ teaspoon salt
¼ teaspoon pepper
1 pie crust, un-baked

Whisk eggs, milk, salt and pepper together. Layer spinach, and ½ the cheese over crust. Pour on egg mixture. Bake at 375° for 10 minutes. Sprinkle with remaining cheese and bake 15-20 minutes more or until top is golden brown.

GRITS AND SAUSAGE CASSEROLE

1 pound pork sausage
4 cups water
1 cup quick-cooking grits
4 eggs, beaten
½ cup milk
1 ½ cups cheddar cheese, shredded and divided
1 stick margarine
1 teaspoon salt

Place water in saucepan and bring to a boil. Add grits, stirring constantly. Stir in salt. Simmer 5 minutes. Remove from heat. Add margarine to hot mixture, stirring until melted. Brown sausage in skillet, stirring until crumbly; drain. Whisk eggs and milk together in a bowl. Add sausage and egg mixture to grits; mix well. Stir in 1 cup cheese. Spoon into a 9 x 13 inch baking dish. Sprinkle remaining ½ cup cheese over top. Bake at 350° for 40 minutes or until set and bubbly.

QUICHE LORRAINE

1 cup ham chopped or 8 slices bacon, cooked crisp and crumbled
1 cup Swiss cheese, shredded
1 cup half and half or light cream
1/8 teaspoon each (nutmeg and black pepper)
½ teaspoon salt
6 eggs
1 pie crust, un-baked

Beat eggs. Brush pie shell with small amount of beaten eggs. Prick bottom and sides with fork. Bake shell at 425° for about 5 minutes, until golden brown. Cool. Sprinkle ham or bacon and cheese in to pie plate. Beat cream and seasonings with eggs. Pour into pie plate. Bake in pre-heated oven at 375° for about 35-40 minutes or until knife inserted halfway between center and outside edge comes out clean. Let stand 10 minutes before serving.

BACON QUICHE

12 slices bacon, cooked crisp and crumbled
1 cup Bisquick
4 eggs
1 cup Swiss cheese, shredded
2 cups milk
1/3 cup onions, chopped
¼ teaspoon each (salt and pepper)

Lightly grease a 10 inch pie plate. Sprinkle bacon, cheese and onions into pie plate. Beat milk, eggs, Bisquick and seasonings until smooth, about 1 minute. Pour into pie plate. Bake at 400° for 35 minutes or until top is golden brown and when knife inserted halfway between center and edge comes out clean. Let stand 10 minutes.

FRUIT AND CEREAL BREAKFAST

1 cup each (raisins, grape-nuts and wheat germ)
½ cup each (sunflower seeds and banana chips)
¼ cup almonds
2 cups oats
Fruit (Kiwi, blueberries or strawberries, also honey and yogurt)

Using ½ of the above mixture, except fruit, honey and yogurt. Drizzle with honey, add 2/3 cup yogurt, top with fruit and drizzle again with honey.

SAUCES
GRAVIES & BUTTER

WHISKEY SAUCE

1 (5.33 oz) can evaporated milk
3 tablespoons whiskey
1 egg, beaten
1 ½ cups light brown sugar
4 tablespoons margarine

Combine all ingredients except the whiskey in top of double boiler. Cook, stirring well until thick. Add whiskey just before serving. Serve warm. Good served over bread pudding and pound cake.

WINE SAUCE

1 (10 oz) jar currant jelly
1 tablespoon each (orange rind, grated and orange juice)
½ cup red wine

Melt current jelly. Add orange juice, orange rind and red wine.

WHITE WINE SAUCE

2 tablespoons each (flour and butter)
2 cups milk
½ teaspoon white pepper
1 (2 oz) can mushrooms, drained and sliced
¼ cup dry white wine
¼ teaspoon salt

Melt butter in saucepan. Stir in flour until smooth. Add milk. Cook, stirring until thick. Remove from heat and add salt, white pepper, mushrooms and wine.

HARD SAUCE

1 cup powdered sugar
1 egg white
½ stick butter
Bourbon or brandy to taste

Beat butter and sugar together. Beat in egg white and brandy or bourbon. Refrigerate.

JEZEBEL SAUCE

½ cup pineapple preserves
1 cup water
½ cup white sugar
½ cup light brown sugar
1 (10-12 oz) bag cranberries
3 tablespoons horseradish
1 tablespoon Dijon mustard

Bring white sugar, brown sugar and water to a boil. Add cranberries and reduce heat and cook for 10 minutes or until skins pop and thicken. Remove from heat. Add pineapple preserves, horseradish and mustard; cool. Can be stored in refrigerator for 2 weeks. This is good on beef, pork or seafood.

BAR - B - Q - SAUCE

2 cups catsup
1 small can coca-cola
2 teaspoons vinegar
1 package dry onion soup
1 teaspoon each (garlic powder and mustard)
1 bay leaf
1 tablespoon Worcestershire sauce
½ teaspoon salt
1/8 teaspoon pepper

Mix all ingredients together and simmer on low heat for 1 hour, stirring occasionally. This sauce is good for chicken, beef or pork. It's good thick and delicious.

WHITE BAR - B - Q - SAUCE

1 pint mayonnaise
4 tablespoons sugar
1 tablespoon salt
6 tablespoons each (vinegar and lemon juice)
2 tablespoons pepper

Mix all ingredients together in saucepan. Mix until smooth, about 2 minutes. Can be used as basting sauce for meat, especially meat cooked on the grill.

REMOULADE SAUCE

1 cup mayonnaise
1 egg, hard boiled and chopped fine
2 teaspoons capers
1 teaspoon each (tarragon leaves, chopped, minced garlic and dry mustard)

Place mayonnaise in mixing bowl with the chopped egg. Stir in mustard, capers, tarragon leaves and garlic. This is god served with beef.

TARTAR SAUCE

1 cup mayonnaise
3 tablespoons sweet pickle relish
1 teaspoon each (pickle juice and onion, grated)
1 tablespoon each (chopped parsley and chopped capers)
2 tablespoons stuffed olives, chopped

Mix all ingredients well and chill. Good with seafood.

BLENDER HOLLANDAISE SAUCE

3 egg yolks
1-2 tablespoons lemon juice
¼ teaspoon each (cayenne pepper and salt)
½ cup butter, melted

Blend egg yolks, lemon juice, salt and pepper together. Add melted butter. Let sauce stand at room temperature for 1 hour before serving.

VINAIGRETTE SAUCE

2 tablespoons vinegar
3 tablespoons butter
1 teaspoon each (paprika, chopped parsley, grated onion and salt)

Combine all ingredients together and bring to a boil. Makes ½ cup.

HORSERADISH SAUCE

1/2 cup each (mayonnaise and sour cream)
2 tablespoons horseradish sauce
1 tablespoon onion, grated
½ teaspoon salt
1 teaspoon Tabasco sauce
Paprika

Mix all ingredients together and sprinkle with paprika.

PIZZA SAUCE

2-3 tablespoons cooking oil
¾ cup onion, chopped
1 (8 oz) can tomato sauce
½ cup water
2 (6 oz) cans tomato paste
1 ½ teaspoons oregano
¾ teaspoon pepper
1/8 teaspoon garlic salt
1 ½ teaspoon salt

Sauté onions in oil until clear. Add rest ingredients and simmer for 15-20 minutes.

HOLLANDAISE SAUCE

1 stick butter
2 teaspoons lemon juice
½ teaspoon each (paprika and salt)
2/3 cup mayonnaise

Melt butter and remove from heat. Add mayonnaise and whip with wire whisk until well blended. Add more mayonnaise for a thicker sauce. Add lemon juice; (2 more teaspoons for a more tart sauce). Add salt and paprika; blend well. Serve warm.

EASY COCKTAIL SAUCE

2 cups catsup
2 teaspoons Tabasco sauce
7 tablespoons each (lemon juice and horseradish sauce)

Mix all ingredients together, and refrigerate. Makes 2 cups.

BEARNAISE SAUCE

4 egg yolks
3 sticks butter or margarine, melted
Juice of 1 lemon
½ teaspoon each (dried tarragon and salt)
1/8 teaspoon pepper
1 tablespoon each (chopped fine green pepper and tarragon vinegar)
2 tablespoons each (capers and green onion)
½ cup parsley, chopped

Beat egg yolks and lemon juice in top of double boiler. Cook over low heat. Never allow to boil. Add melted butter, stirring constantly with a wooden spoon. Add salt, pepper and dried tarragon. Stir in green onion, capers, parsley and vinegar. Keep warm in double boiler. Beat with wire whisk just before serving to re-blend all ingredients. Delicious with steaks.

SAUCE FOR VENISON

1 cup each (brown sugar and vegetable oil)
½ cup each (vinegar, catsup and Worcestershire sauce)
Juice of 2 lemons
1 clove garlic
1 teaspoon each (chili powder, salt, red pepper, black pepper and soy sauce)

Mix all ingredients together. Bring to a boil and simmer for 5 minutes.

SOUTHERN TOMATO SAUCE

1 (16 oz) can tomatoes
1 cup sugar
¼ teaspoon salt
1 small onion, chopped
1 green pepper, chopped
1 tablespoon cornstarch

Cook tomatoes, onions and peppers until they are tender. Add sugar and cornstarch. Cook until thick. This is good on black-eyed peas, lima beans or beef.

CREOLE SAUCE

½ cup each (sherry wine, chopped parsley and chopped green onion)
¼ cup each (flour and bacon drippings)
2 cups onion, chopped
2 cloves garlic, minced
1 cup green pepper, chopped
1 teaspoon thyme
½ teaspoon each (salt and pepper)
2 bay leaves
1 teaspoon Tabasco sauce
1 cup celery with leaves, chopped
1 (16 oz) can tomatoes
1 (6 oz) can tomato paste
1 (8 oz) can tomato sauce
1 tablespoon lemon juice

In a dutch oven make a brown roux using the flour and bacon drippings. Add onions, green pepper, garlic, celery, thyme, bay leaves, salt and pepper. Sauté onions until soft. Add tomatoes, tomato paste and tomato sauce. Cover and simmer over low heat for about 2 hours, stirring occasionally. Add remaining ingredients. Stir, remove from heat, let stand several hours before pouring over fish.

GOOD WHITE SAUCE

Stir in 2 tablespoons melted butter and 2 tablespoons flour in a saucepan or skillet until mixture is smooth. Cook over low heat for several minutes. Remove pan from heat and add ¾-1 cup milk all at once, beating constantly with a wire whisk. Return sauce to medium heat and cook until thickened stirring constantly. Add salt and pepper to taste. Serve warm or hot.

CREAMY CHEESE SAUCE

1 cup each (milk and chopped cheddar cheese)
4 tablespoons margarine
2 tablespoons flour
¼ teaspoon salt

Melt margarine in saucepan, add flour and mix with a fork until smooth. Add milk and continue to cook, stirring constantly until thickened. Stir in salt and cheese, continue cooking until cheese melts.

RAISIN AND LEMON SAUCE

1 cup each (seedless raisins and hot water)
4 tablespoons lemon juice
1 tablespoon each (butter and cornstarch)
¼ teaspoon each (ginger and salt)
½ cup white sugar
¼ cup brown sugar
Rind of 1 lemon, grated

Combine sugars, salt, ginger and cornstarch together. Add hot water and cook until thickened and clear. Add remaining ingredients and serve warm over ginger-bread or any plain cake. Also, good on baked ham.

ITALIAN SAUCE FOR MEATS

1 (6 oz) can tomato paste
3 tablespoons red wine
½ cup whipping cream
½ teaspoon each (Italian seasoning, lemon pepper seasoning and salt)
½ teaspoon each (oregano and minced garlic)
2 tablespoons each (butter and chopped onion)
8 ounces fresh mushrooms, sliced lengthwise

Sauté onions in butter until transparent, add mushrooms and sauté. Add spices and tomato paste and blend. Add the wine and simmer 4-5 minutes. Before serving add ½ cup whipping cream. Serve immediately. Also, good on hamburgers.

ZAPATA SAUCE

1 (16 oz) can tomatoes diced or 2 cups fresh chopped
1 tablespoon each (tomato paste and oil)
¼ teaspoon salt
½ cup onion, chopped
¼ cup green pepper, chopped
2 tablespoons green chilies, chopped

Sauté onion, green pepper and chilies in oil until soft. Add other ingredients and simmer 5 minutes.

Would you like to see your manuscript become a book?

If you are interested in becoming a PublishAmerica author, please submit your manuscript for possible publication to us at:

acquisitions@publishamerica.com

You may also mail in your manuscript to:

**PublishAmerica
PO Box 151
Frederick, MD 21705**

www.publishamerica.com

CPSIA information can be obtained at www.ICGtesting.com
Printed in the USA
LVOW041952240912

300122LV00004B/1/P